ULTIMATE

SPIDER-MAN

POWER AND RESPONSIBILITY

STORY
BILL JEMAS &
BRIAN MICHAEL BENDIS

SCRIPT
BRIAN MICHAEL BENDIS

PENCILS
MARK BAGLEY

INKS
ART THIBERT &
DAN PANOSIAN

COLORS
STEVE BUCCELLATO,
MARIE JAVINS &
COLORGRAPHIX, & JC

LETTERS
RICHARD STARKINGS
& COMICRAFT

ORIGINAL SERIES EDITOR
RALPH MACCHIO

ULTIMATE SPIDER-MAN®: POWER AND RESPONSI-BILITY. Contains material originally published in magazine form as ULTIMATE SPIDER-MAN #1-7. Third printing, April 2002. ISBN 0-7851-0786-X. Published by MARVEL COMICS, a division of MARVEL ENTERTAINMENT GROUP, INC. OFFICE OF PUBLICATION: 10 EAST 40th STREET, NEW YORK, NY 10016. Copyright © 2000, 2001 and 2002 Marvel Characters, Inc. All rights reserved. Price $14.95 in the U.S. and $23.95 in Canada (GST# R127032852). No similarity between any of the names, characters, persons, and/or institutions in this publication with those of any living or dead person or institutions is intended, and any such similarity which may exist is purely coincidental. This publication may not be sold except by authorized dealers and is sold subject to the conditions that it shall not be sold or distributed with any part of its cover or markings removed, nor in a mutilated condition. SPIDER-MAN (including prominent characters featured in this publication and the distinctive likenesses thereof) is a trademark of MARVEL CHARACTERS, INC. Printed in Canada. STAN LEE, Chairman Emeritus.

10 9 8 7 6 5 4 3

AND

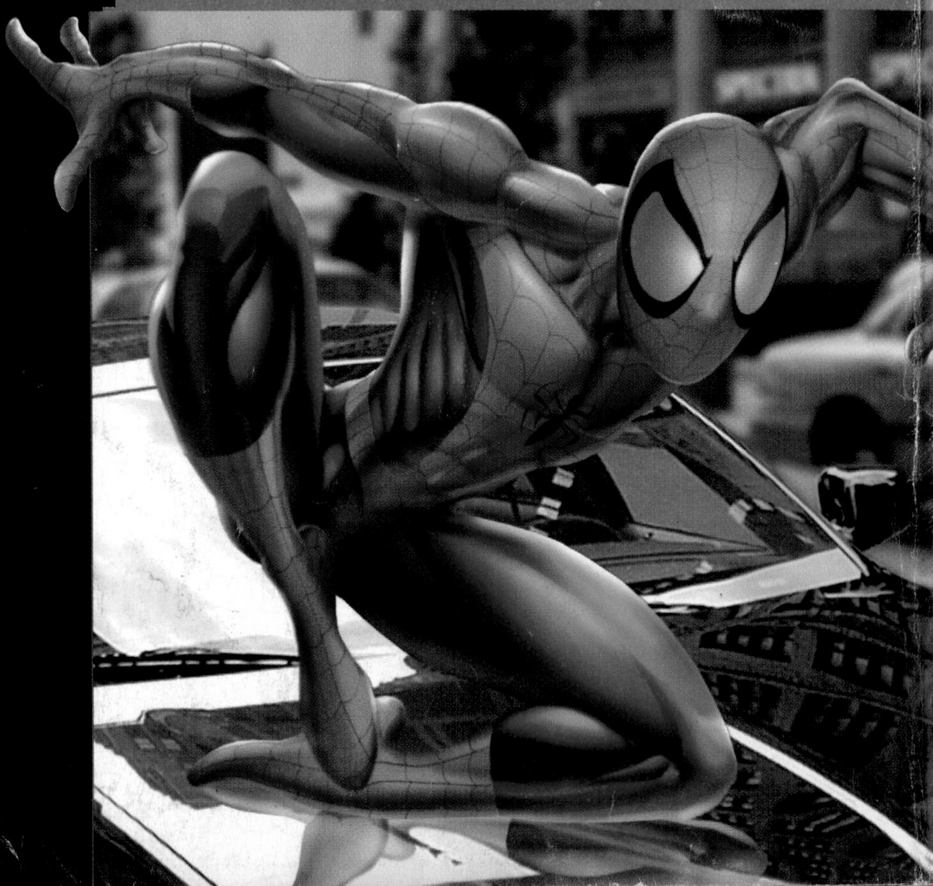

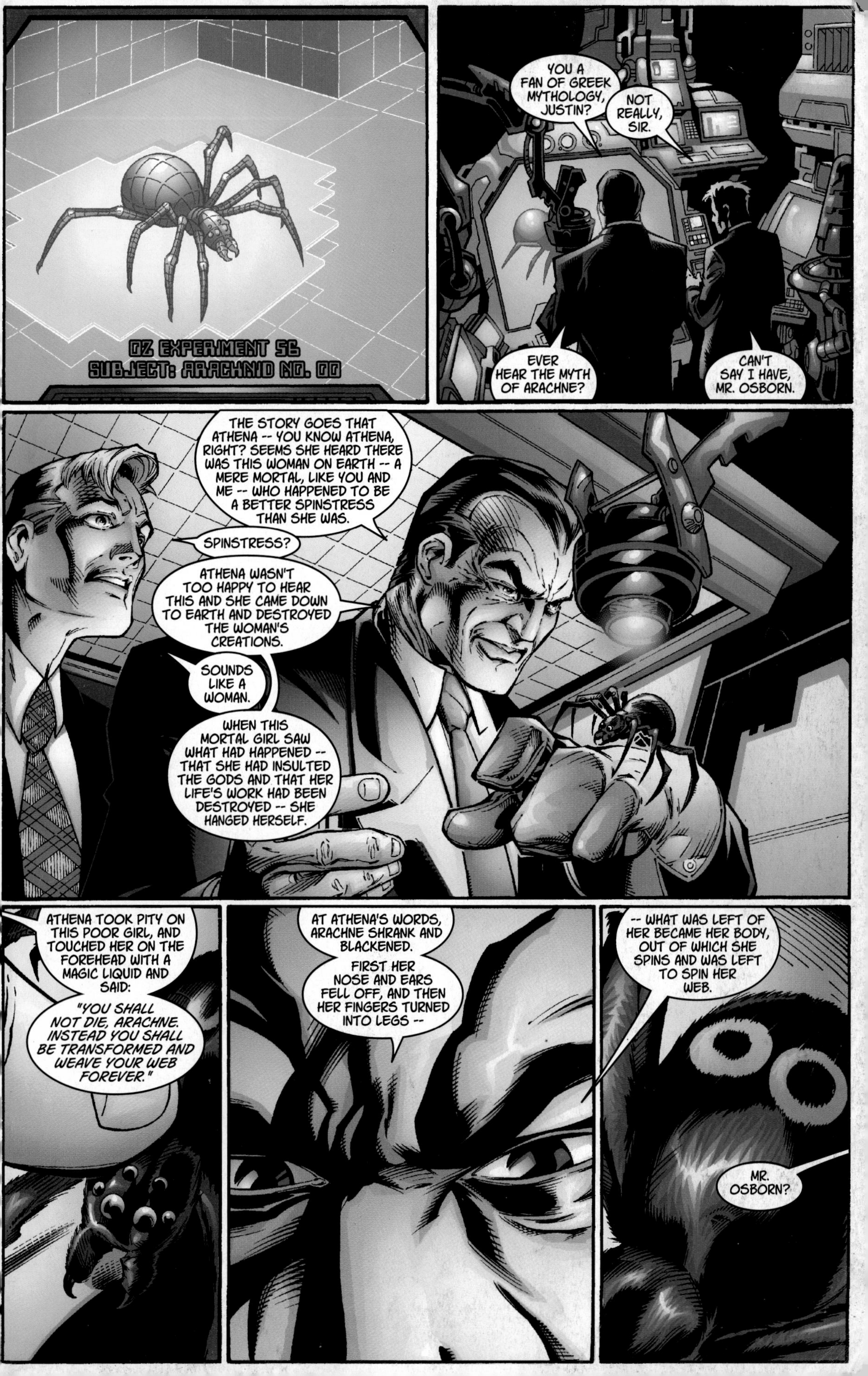

OZ EXPERIMENT 56
SUBJECT: ARACHNID NO. 00
YOU A FAN OF GREEK MYTHOLOGY, JUSTIN?
NOT REALLY, SIR.
EVER HEAR THE MYTH OF ARACHNE?
CAN'T SAY I HAVE, MR. OSBORN.
THE STORY GOES THAT ATHENA -- YOU KNOW ATHENA, RIGHT? SEEMS SHE HEARD THERE WAS THIS WOMAN ON EARTH -- A MERE MORTAL, LIKE YOU AND ME -- WHO HAPPENED TO BE A BETTER SPINSTRESS THAN SHE WAS.
SPINSTRESS?
ATHENA WASN'T TOO HAPPY TO HEAR THIS AND SHE CAME DOWN TO EARTH AND DESTROYED THE WOMAN'S CREATIONS.
SOUNDS LIKE A WOMAN.
WHEN THIS MORTAL GIRL SAW WHAT HAD HAPPENED -- THAT SHE HAD INSULTED THE GODS AND THAT HER LIFE'S WORK HAD BEEN DESTROYED -- SHE HANGED HERSELF.
ATHENA TOOK PITY ON THIS POOR GIRL, AND TOUCHED HER ON THE FOREHEAD WITH A MAGIC LIQUID AND SAID:
"YOU SHALL NOT DIE, ARACHNE. INSTEAD YOU SHALL BE TRANSFORMED AND WEAVE YOUR WEB FOREVER."
AT ATHENA'S WORDS, ARACHNE SHRANK AND BLACKENED.
FIRST HER NOSE AND EARS FELL OFF, AND THEN HER FINGERS TURNED INTO LEGS --
-- WHAT WAS LEFT OF HER BECAME HER BODY, OUT OF WHICH SHE SPINS AND WAS LEFT TO SPIN HER WEB.
MR. OSBORN?

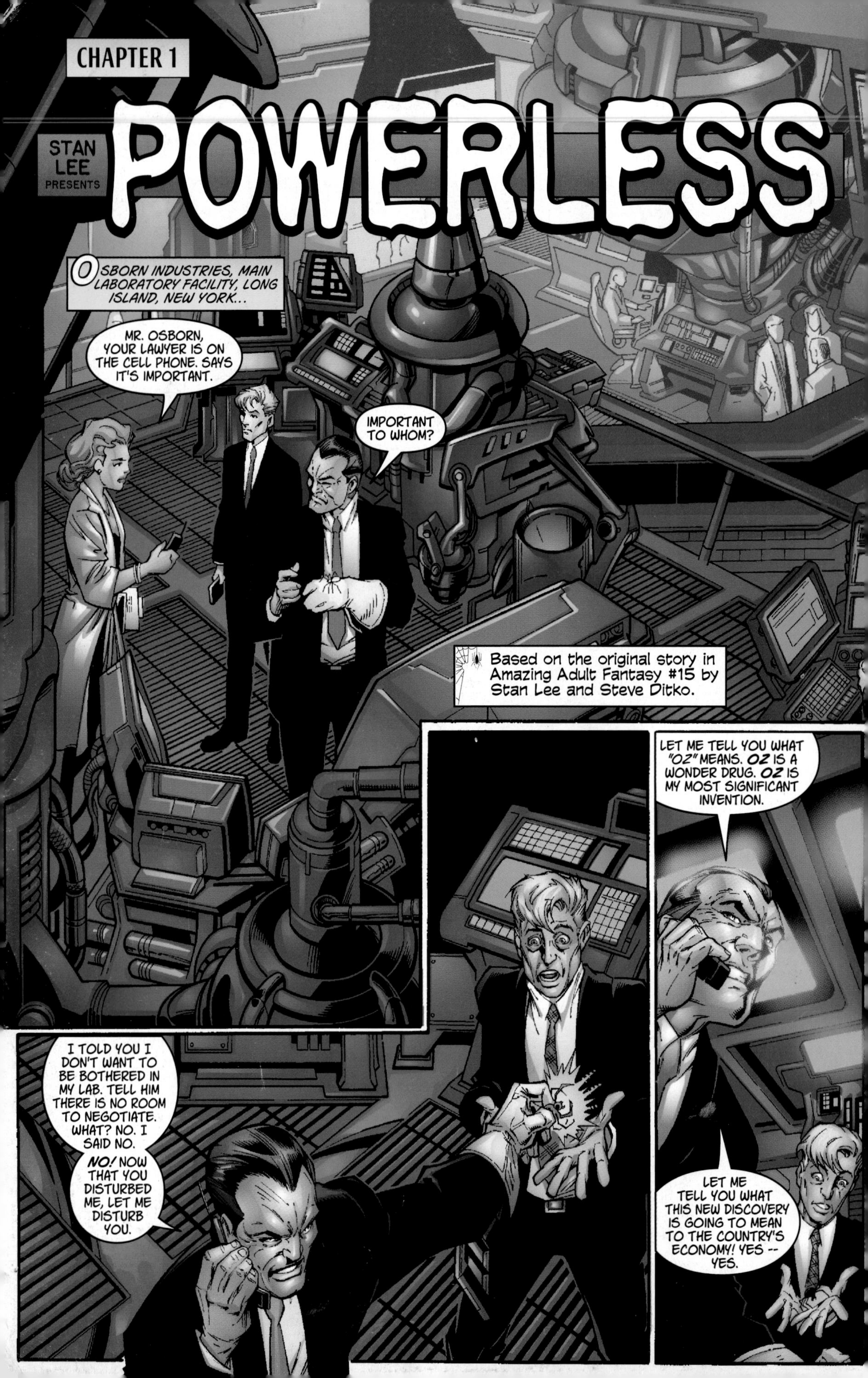
CHAPTER 1
STAN LEE PRESENTS
POWERLESS
OSBORN INDUSTRIES, MAIN LABORATORY FACILITY, LONG ISLAND, NEW YORK...
MR. OSBORN, YOUR LAWYER IS ON THE CELL PHONE. SAYS IT'S IMPORTANT.
IMPORTANT TO WHOM?
Based on the original story in Amazing Adult Fantasy #15 by Stan Lee and Steve Ditko.
I TOLD YOU I DON'T WANT TO BE BOTHERED IN MY LAB. TELL HIM THERE IS NO ROOM TO NEGOTIATE. WHAT? NO. I SAID NO.
NO! NOW THAT YOU DISTURBED ME, LET ME DISTURB YOU.
LET ME TELL YOU WHAT "OZ" MEANS. OZ IS A WONDER DRUG. OZ IS MY MOST SIGNIFICANT INVENTION.
LET ME TELL YOU WHAT THIS NEW DISCOVERY IS GOING TO MEAN TO THE COUNTRY'S ECONOMY! YES -- YES.

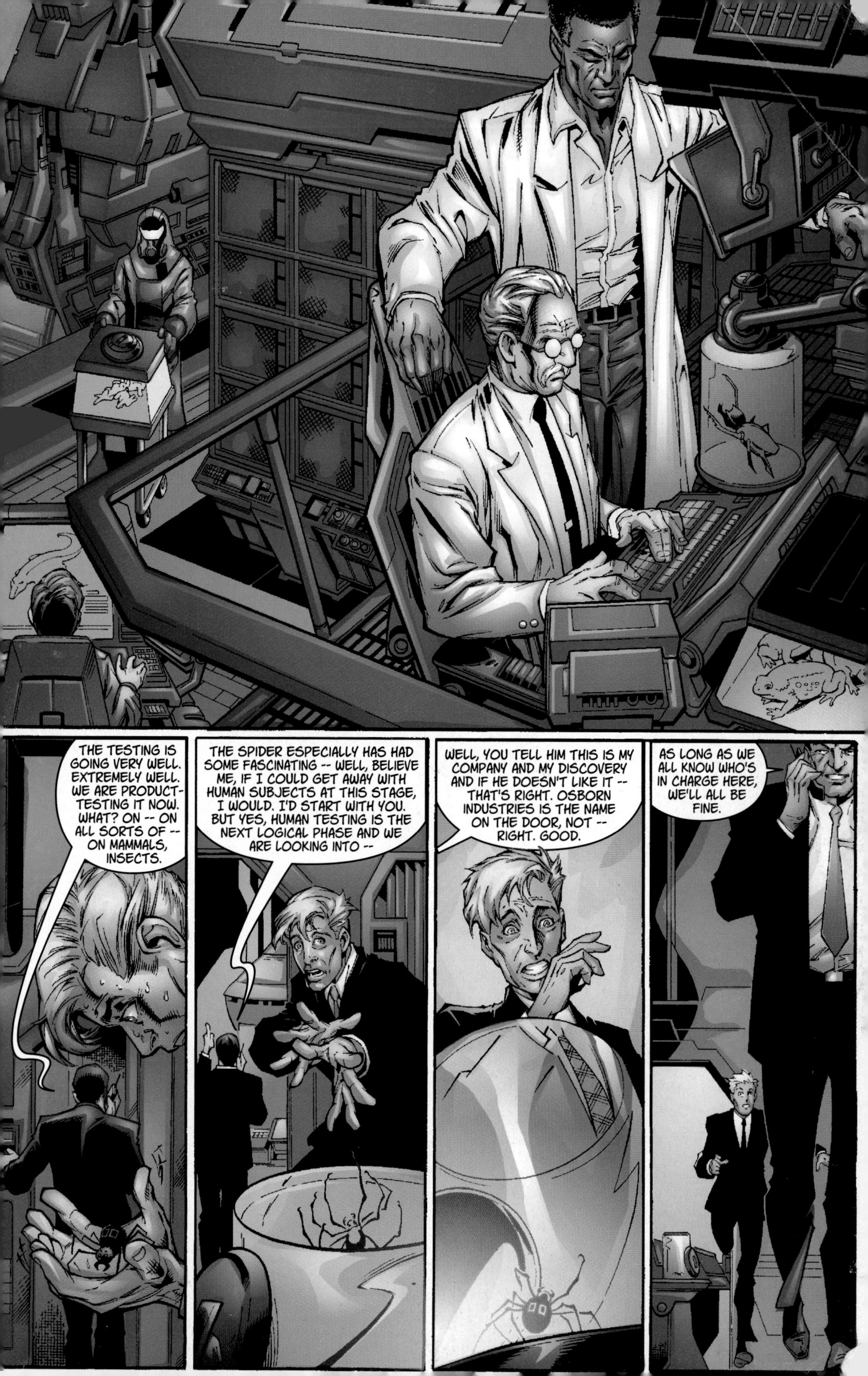
THE TESTING IS GOING VERY WELL. EXTREMELY WELL. WE ARE PRODUCT-TESTING IT NOW. WHAT? ON -- ON ALL SORTS OF -- ON MAMMALS, INSECTS.
THE SPIDER ESPECIALLY HAS HAD SOME FASCINATING -- WELL, BELIEVE ME, IF I COULD GET AWAY WITH HUMAN SUBJECTS AT THIS STAGE, I WOULD. I'D START WITH YOU. BUT YES, HUMAN TESTING IS THE NEXT LOGICAL PHASE AND WE ARE LOOKING INTO --
WELL, YOU TELL HIM THIS IS MY COMPANY AND MY DISCOVERY AND IF HE DOESN'T LIKE IT -- THAT'S RIGHT. OSBORN INDUSTRIES IS THE NAME ON THE DOOR, NOT -- RIGHT. GOOD.
AS LONG AS WE ALL KNOW WHO'S IN CHARGE HERE, WE'LL ALL BE FINE.

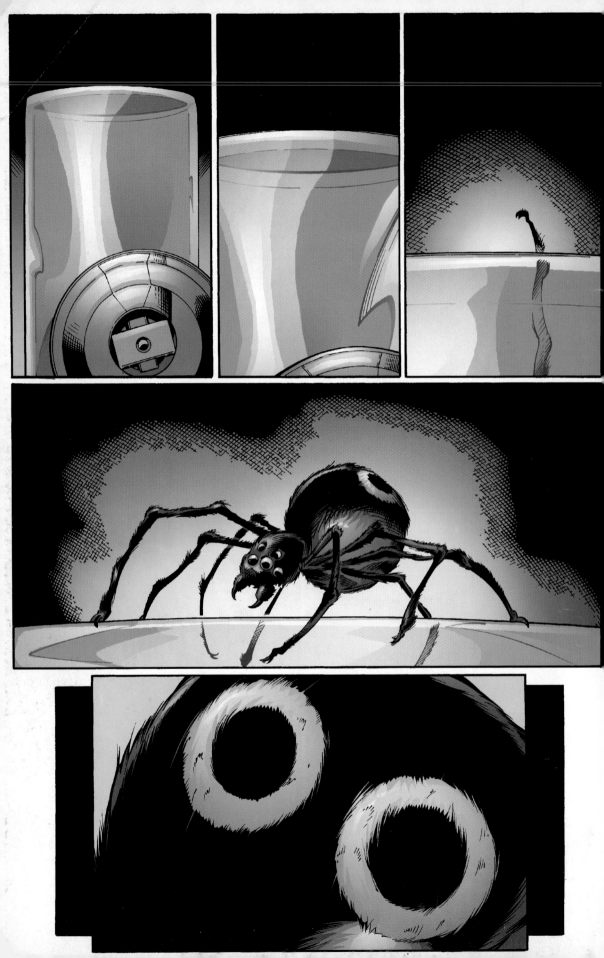

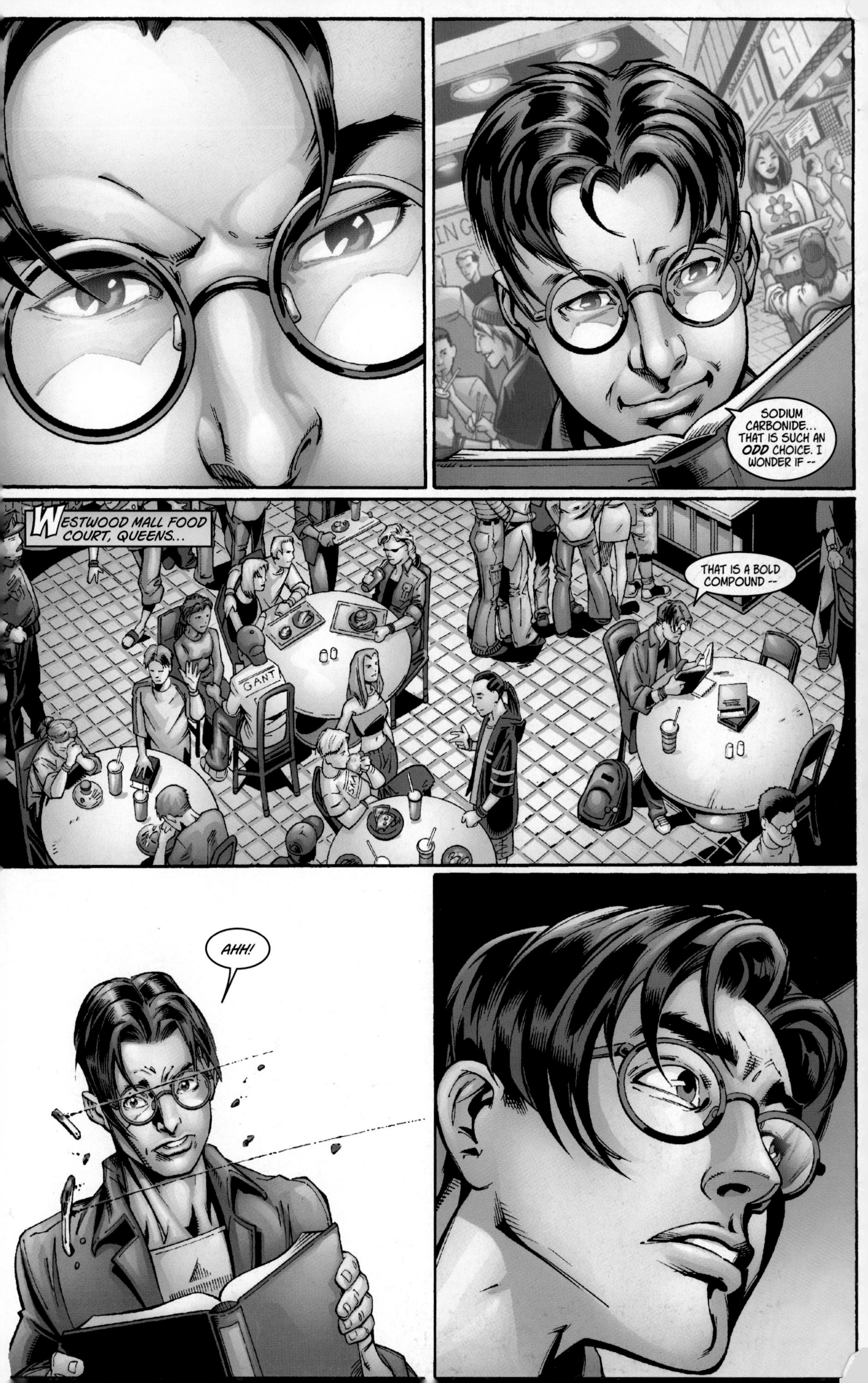
SODIUM CARBONIDE... THAT IS SUCH AN ODD CHOICE. I WONDER IF --
WESTWOOD MALL FOOD COURT, QUEENS...
THAT IS A BOLD COMPOUND --
GANT
AHH!

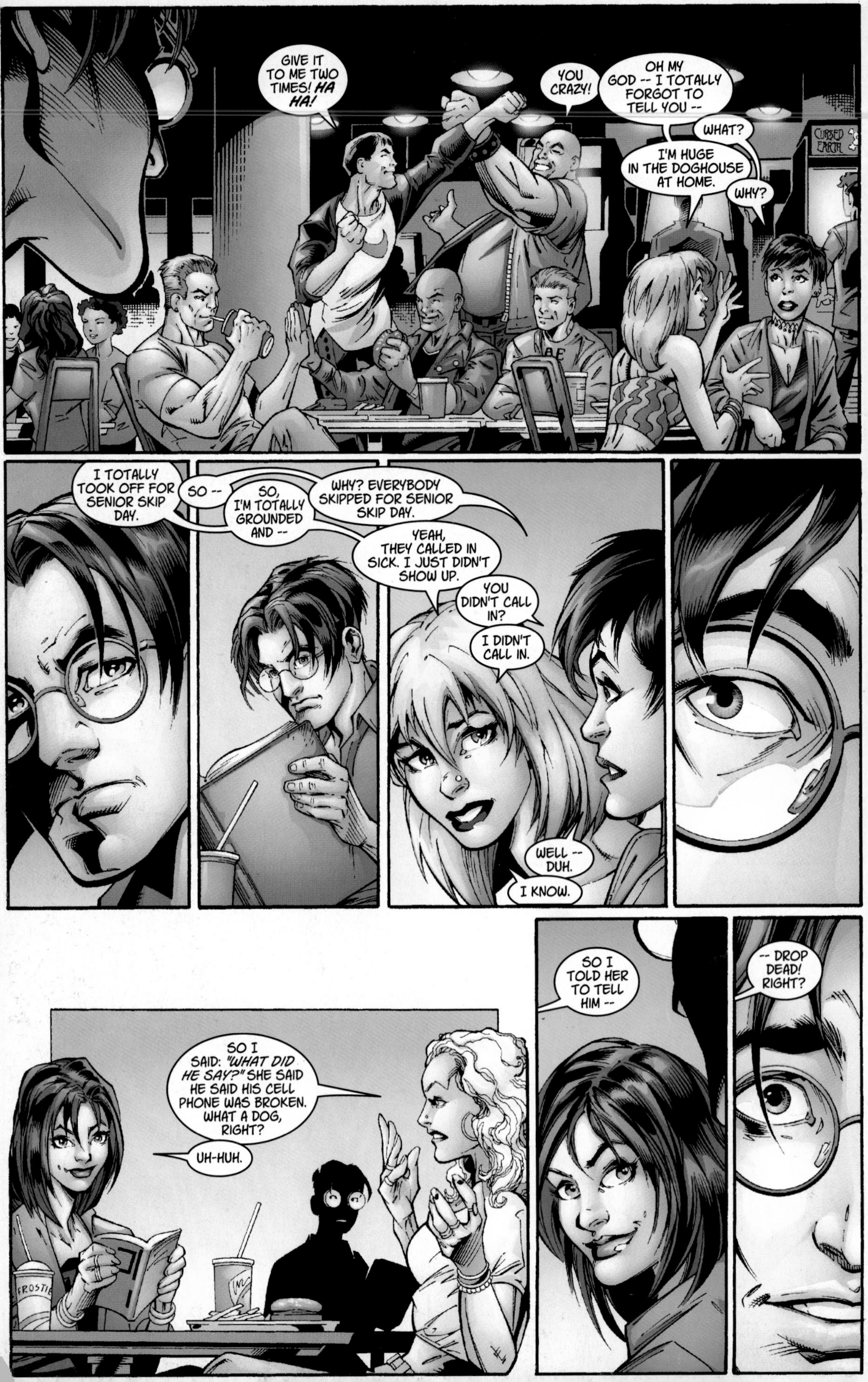
GIVE IT TO ME TWO TIMES! HA HA!
YOU CRAZY!
OH MY GOD -- I TOTALLY FORGOT TO TELL YOU --
WHAT?
I'M HUGE IN THE DOGHOUSE AT HOME.
WHY?
CURSED EARTH
I TOTALLY TOOK OFF FOR SENIOR SKIP DAY.
SO --
SO, I'M TOTALLY GROUNDED AND --
WHY? EVERYBODY SKIPPED FOR SENIOR SKIP DAY.
YEAH, THEY CALLED IN SICK. I JUST DIDN'T SHOW UP.
YOU DIDN'T CALL IN?
I DIDN'T CALL IN.
WELL -- DUH.
I KNOW.
SO I SAID: "WHAT DID HE SAY?" SHE SAID HE SAID HIS CELL PHONE WAS BROKEN. WHAT A DOG, RIGHT?
UH-HUH.
FROSTIE
SO I TOLD HER TO TELL HIM --
-- DROP DEAD! RIGHT?

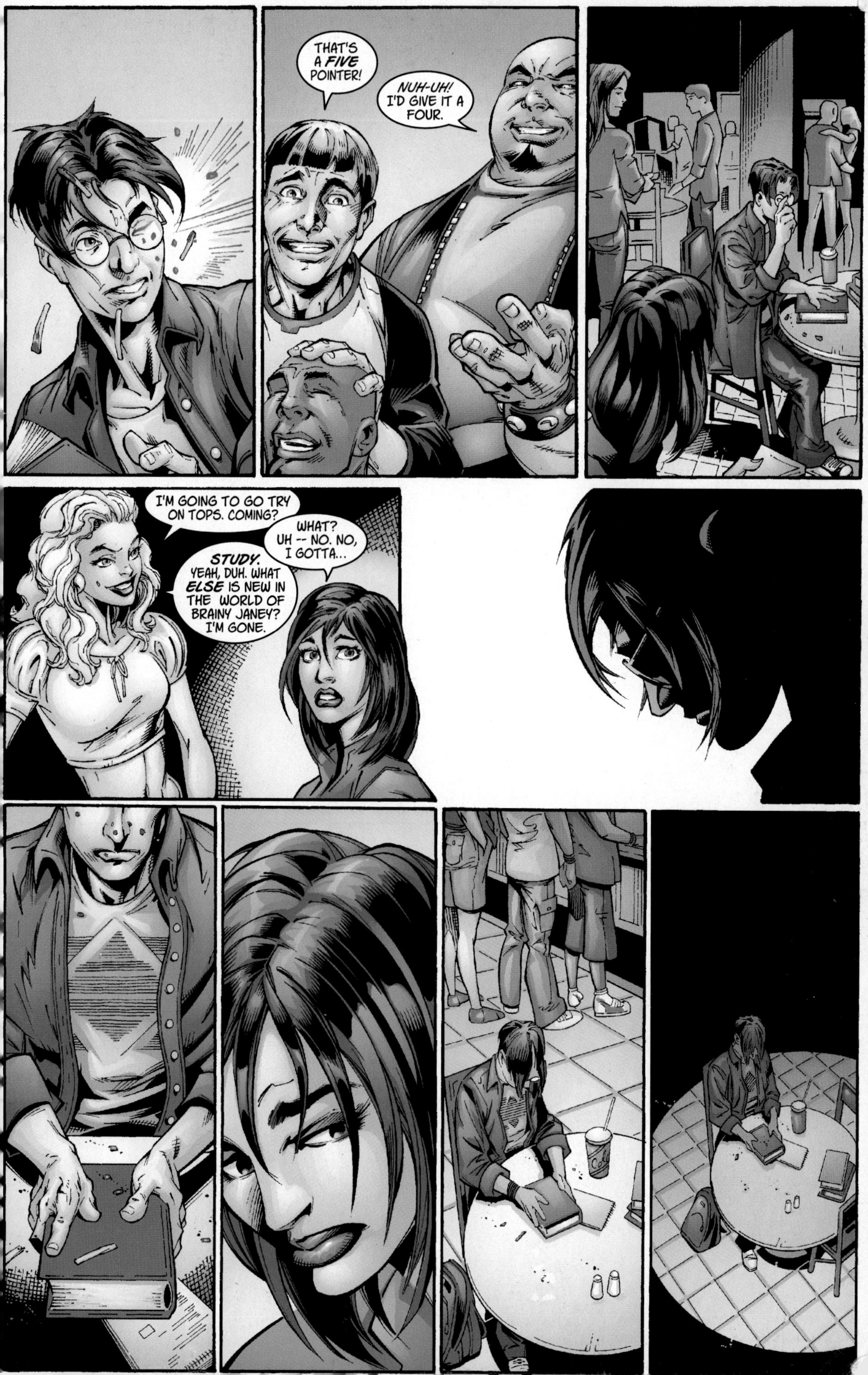
THAT'S A *FIVE* POINTER!
NUH-UH! I'D GIVE IT A FOUR.
I'M GOING TO GO TRY ON TOPS. COMING?
WHAT? UH -- NO. NO, I GOTTA...
STUDY. YEAH, DUH. WHAT *ELSE* IS NEW IN THE WORLD OF BRAINY JANEY? I'M GONE.

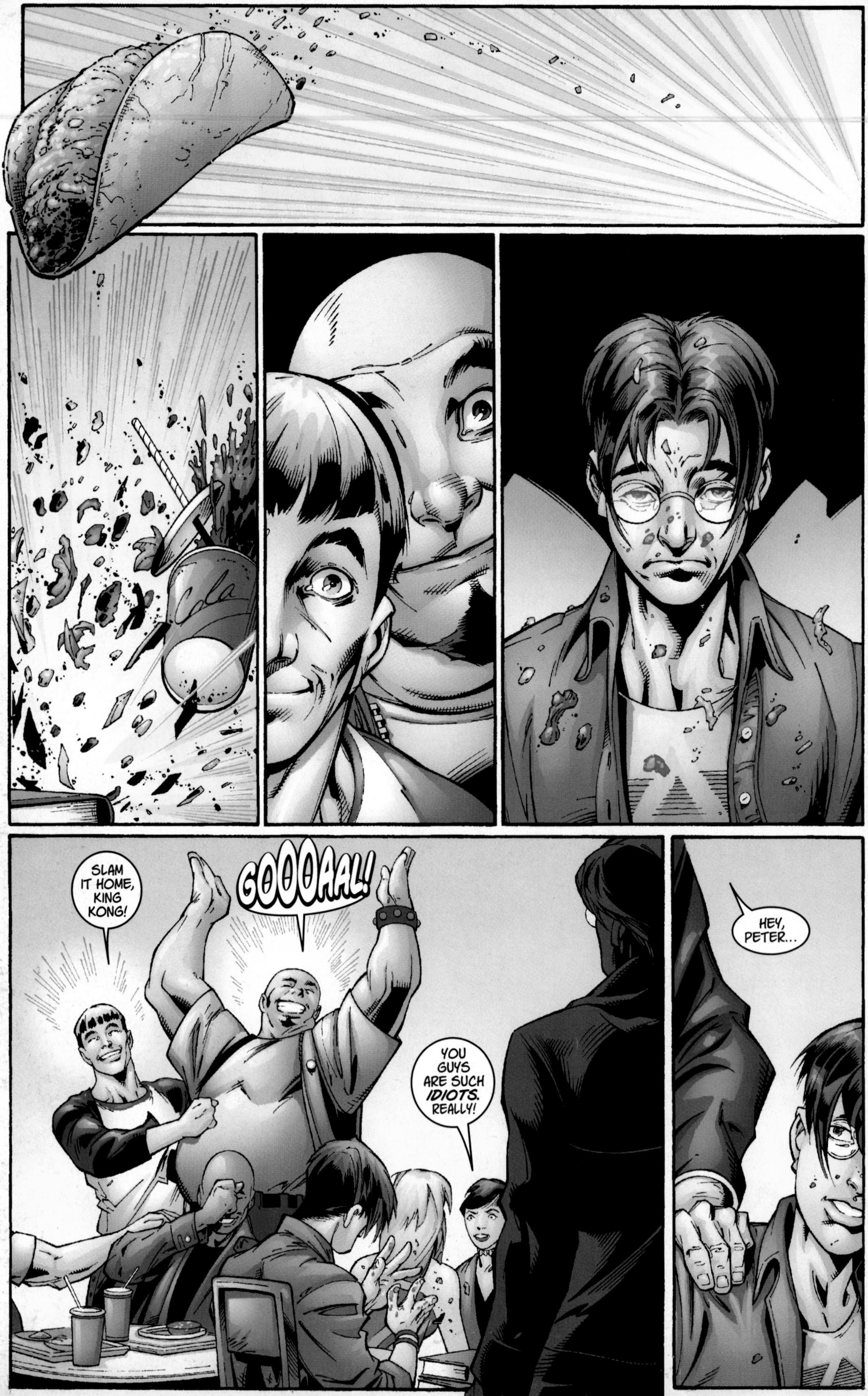
SLAM IT HOME, KING KONG!
GOOOAAL!
YOU GUYS ARE SUCH IDIOTS. REALLY!
HEY, PETER...

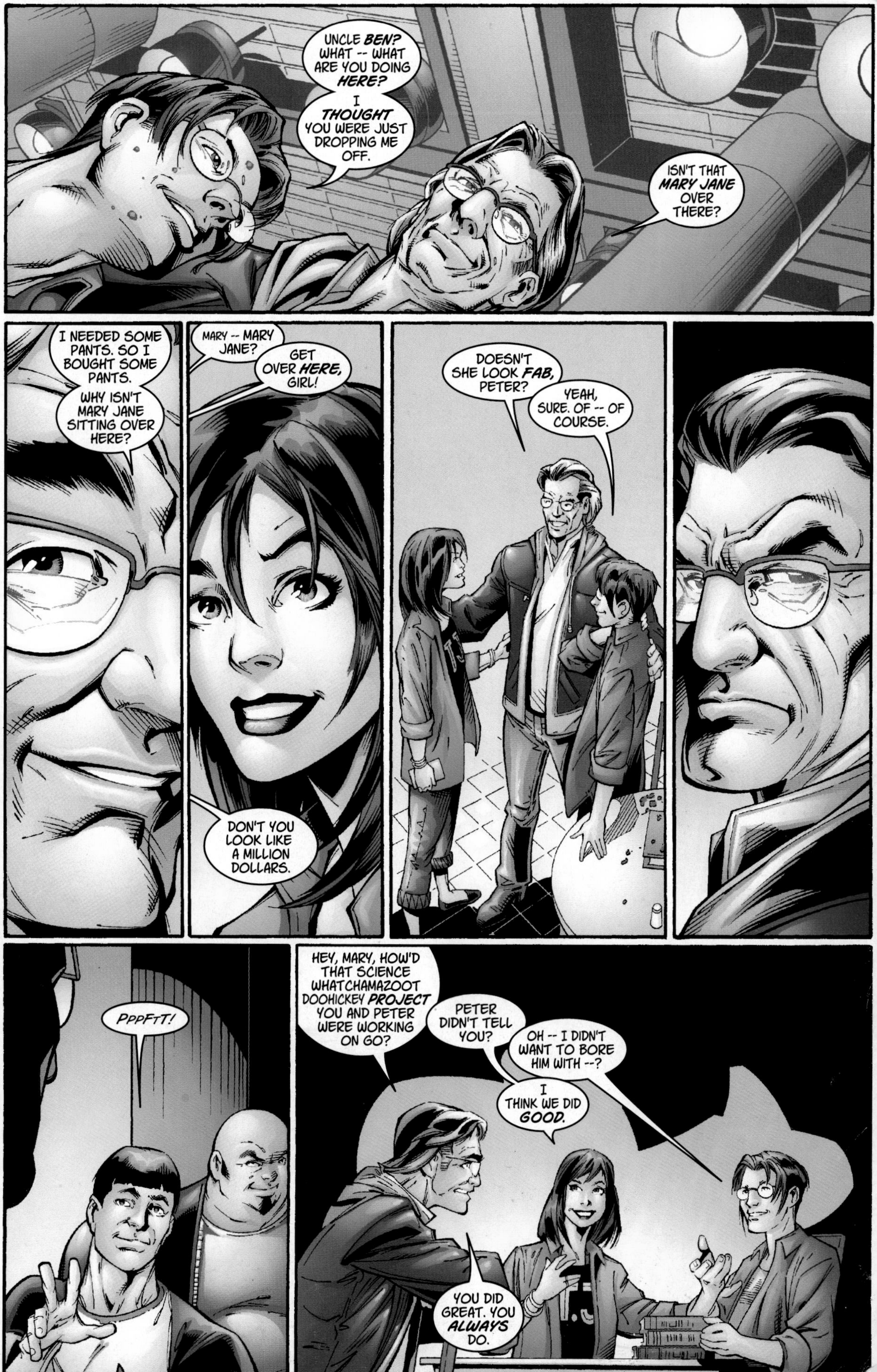
UNCLE BEN? WHAT -- WHAT ARE YOU DOING HERE?
I THOUGHT YOU WERE JUST DROPPING ME OFF.
ISN'T THAT MARY JANE OVER THERE?
I NEEDED SOME PANTS. SO I BOUGHT SOME PANTS.
WHY ISN'T MARY JANE SITTING OVER HERE?
MARY -- MARY JANE?
GET OVER HERE, GIRL!
DON'T YOU LOOK LIKE A MILLION DOLLARS.
DOESN'T SHE LOOK FAB, PETER?
YEAH, SURE. OF -- OF COURSE.
PPPFTT!
HEY, MARY, HOW'D THAT SCIENCE WHATCHAMAZOOT DOOHICKEY PROJECT YOU AND PETER WERE WORKING ON GO?
PETER DIDN'T TELL YOU?
OH -- I DIDN'T WANT TO BORE HIM WITH --?
I THINK WE DID GOOD.
YOU DID GREAT. YOU ALWAYS DO.

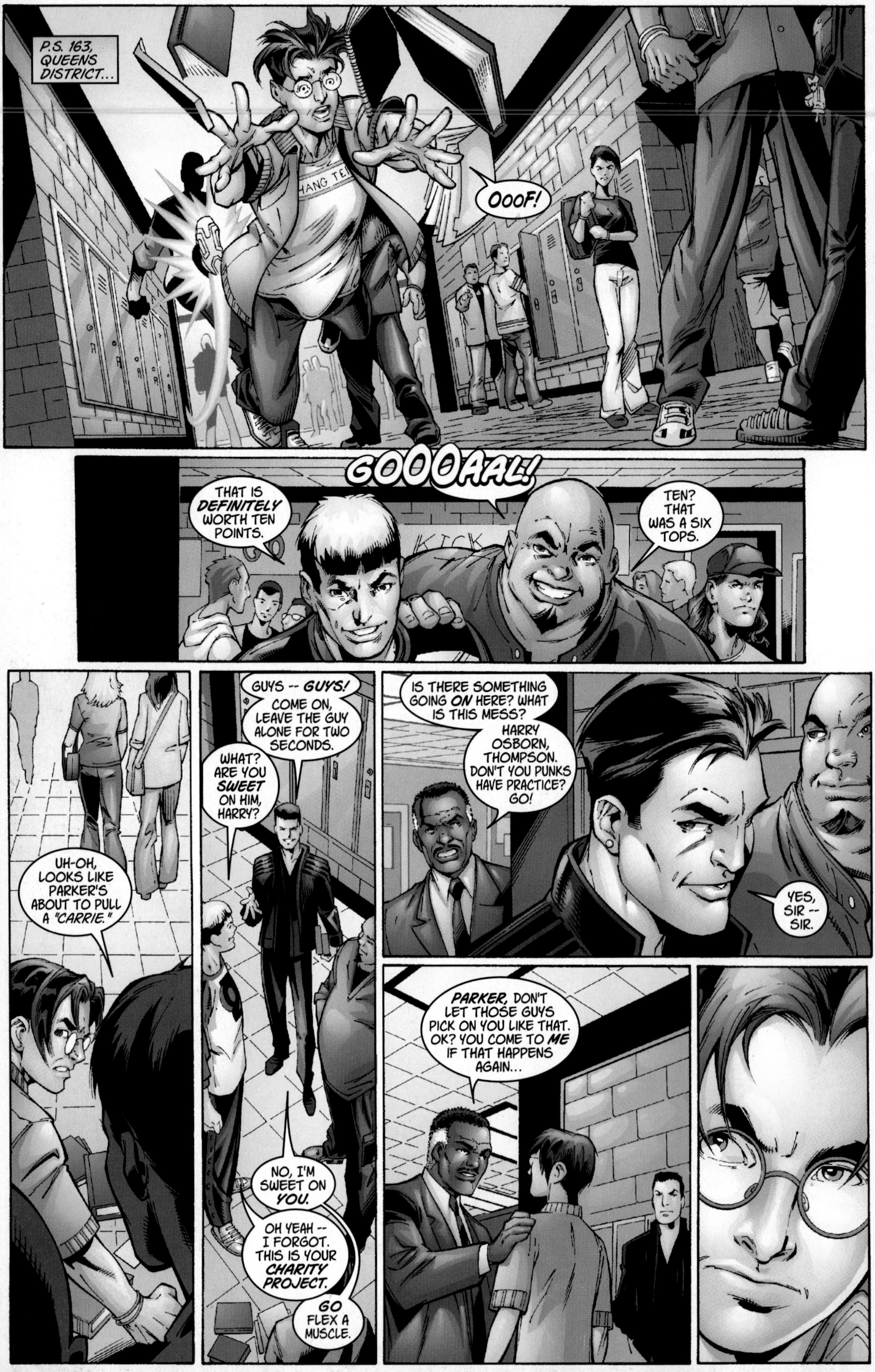
P.S. 163, QUEENS DISTRICT...
HANG TEN
OOOF!
GOOOAAL!
THAT IS DEFINITELY WORTH TEN POINTS.
TEN? THAT WAS A SIX TOPS.
KICK
UH-OH, LOOKS LIKE PARKER'S ABOUT TO PULL A "CARRIE."
GUYS -- GUYS! COME ON, LEAVE THE GUY ALONE FOR TWO SECONDS.
WHAT? ARE YOU SWEET ON HIM, HARRY?
NO, I'M SWEET ON YOU.
OH YEAH -- I FORGOT. THIS IS YOUR CHARITY PROJECT.
GO FLEX A MUSCLE.
IS THERE SOMETHING GOING ON HERE? WHAT IS THIS MESS?
HARRY OSBORN, THOMPSON. DON'T YOU PUNKS HAVE PRACTICE? GO!
YES, SIR -- SIR.
PARKER, DON'T LET THOSE GUYS PICK ON YOU LIKE THAT. OK? YOU COME TO ME IF THAT HAPPENS AGAIN...

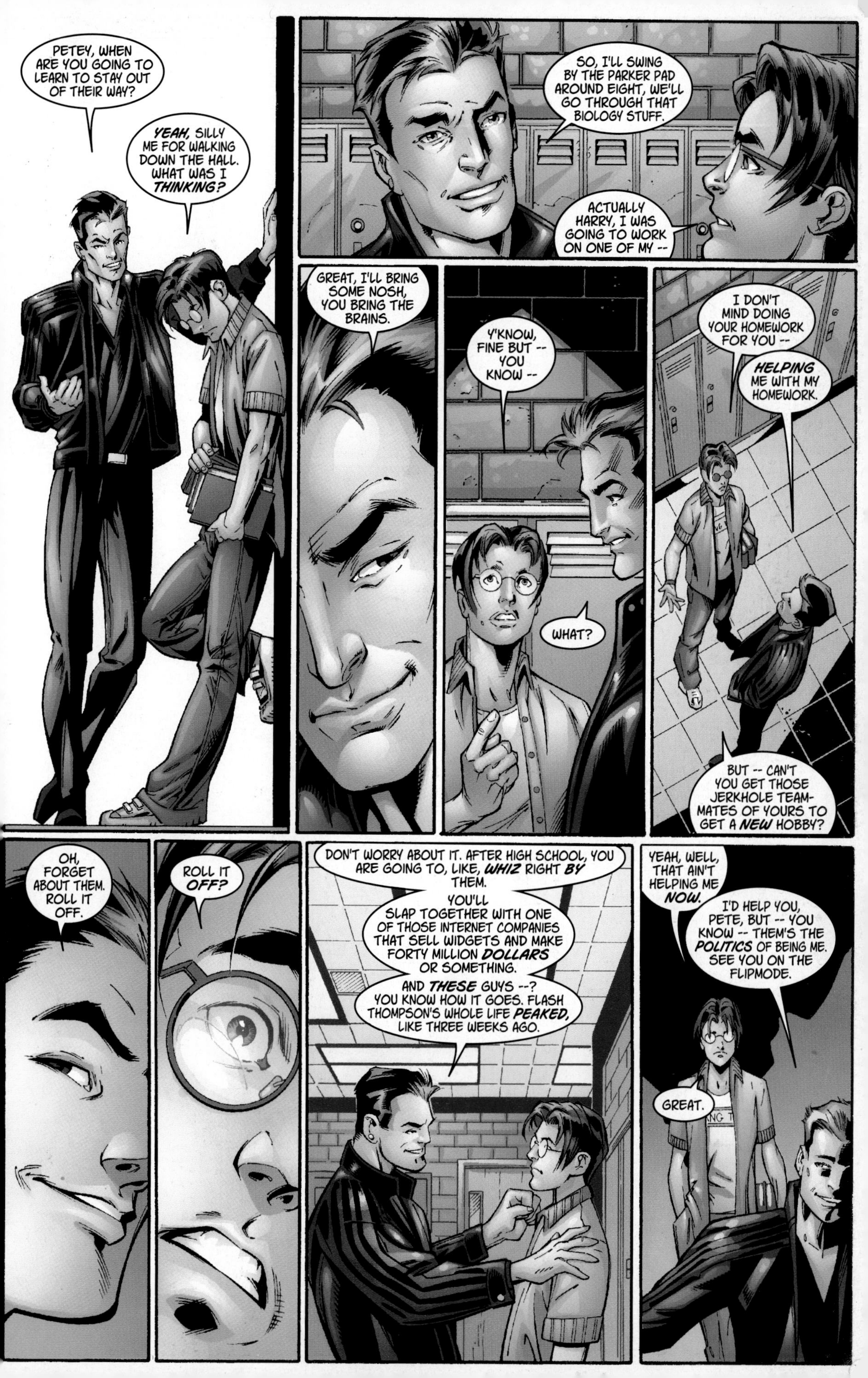
PETEY, WHEN ARE YOU GOING TO LEARN TO STAY OUT OF THEIR WAY?
YEAH, SILLY ME FOR WALKING DOWN THE HALL. WHAT WAS I THINKING?
SO, I'LL SWING BY THE PARKER PAD AROUND EIGHT, WE'LL GO THROUGH THAT BIOLOGY STUFF.
ACTUALLY HARRY, I WAS GOING TO WORK ON ONE OF MY --
GREAT, I'LL BRING SOME NOSH, YOU BRING THE BRAINS.
Y'KNOW, FINE BUT -- YOU KNOW --
WHAT?
I DON'T MIND DOING YOUR HOMEWORK FOR YOU --
HELPING ME WITH MY HOMEWORK.
BUT -- CAN'T YOU GET THOSE JERKHOLE TEAM-MATES OF YOURS TO GET A NEW HOBBY?
OH, FORGET ABOUT THEM. ROLL IT OFF.
ROLL IT OFF?
DON'T WORRY ABOUT IT. AFTER HIGH SCHOOL, YOU ARE GOING TO, LIKE, WHIZ RIGHT BY THEM.
YOU'LL SLAP TOGETHER WITH ONE OF THOSE INTERNET COMPANIES THAT SELL WIDGETS AND MAKE FORTY MILLION DOLLARS OR SOMETHING.
AND THESE GUYS --? YOU KNOW HOW IT GOES. FLASH THOMPSON'S WHOLE LIFE PEAKED, LIKE THREE WEEKS AGO.
YEAH, WELL, THAT AIN'T HELPING ME NOW.
I'D HELP YOU, PETE, BUT -- YOU KNOW -- THEM'S THE POLITICS OF BEING ME. SEE YOU ON THE FLIPMODE.
GREAT.

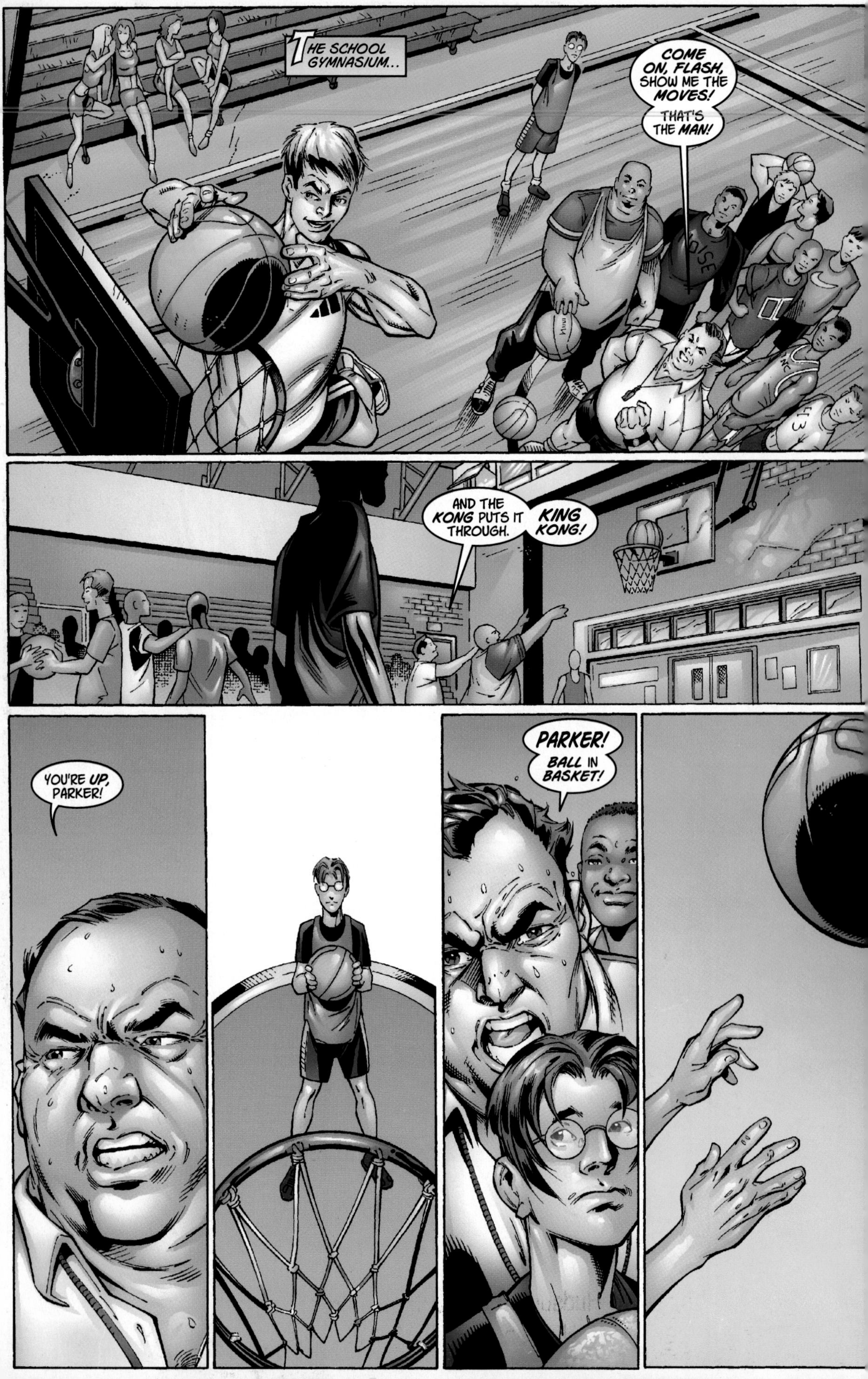

THE SCHOOL GYMNASIUM...
COME ON, FLASH, SHOW ME THE MOVES!
THAT'S THE MAN!
AND THE KONG PUTS IT THROUGH.
KING KONG!
YOU'RE UP, PARKER!
PARKER! BALL IN BASKET!

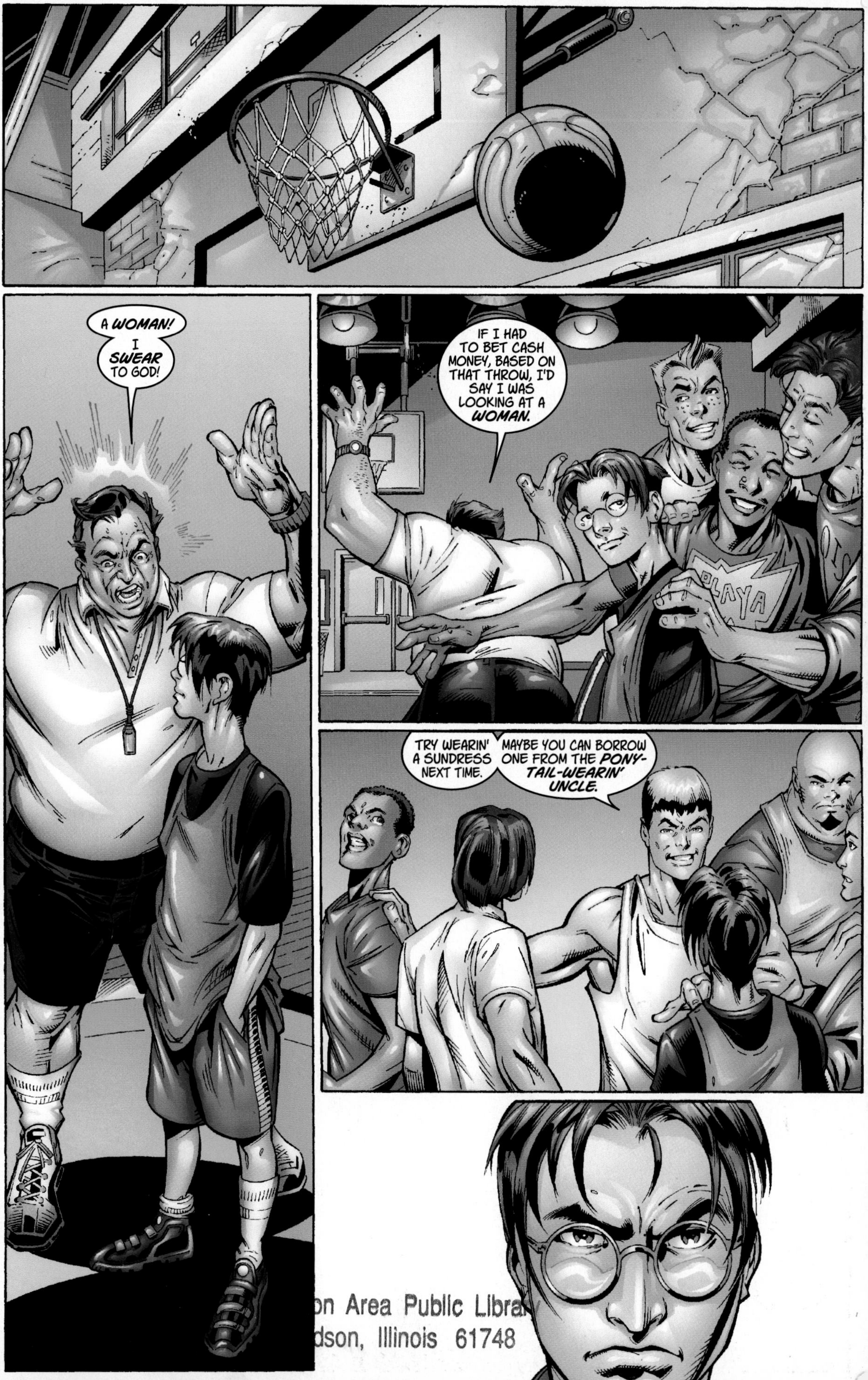
A *WOMAN!* I *SWEAR* TO GOD!
IF I HAD TO BET CASH MONEY, BASED ON THAT THROW, I'D SAY I WAS LOOKING AT A *WOMAN*.
PLAYA
TRY WEARIN' A SUNDRESS NEXT TIME.
MAYBE YOU CAN BORROW ONE FROM THE *PONY-TAIL-WEARIN' UNCLE*.

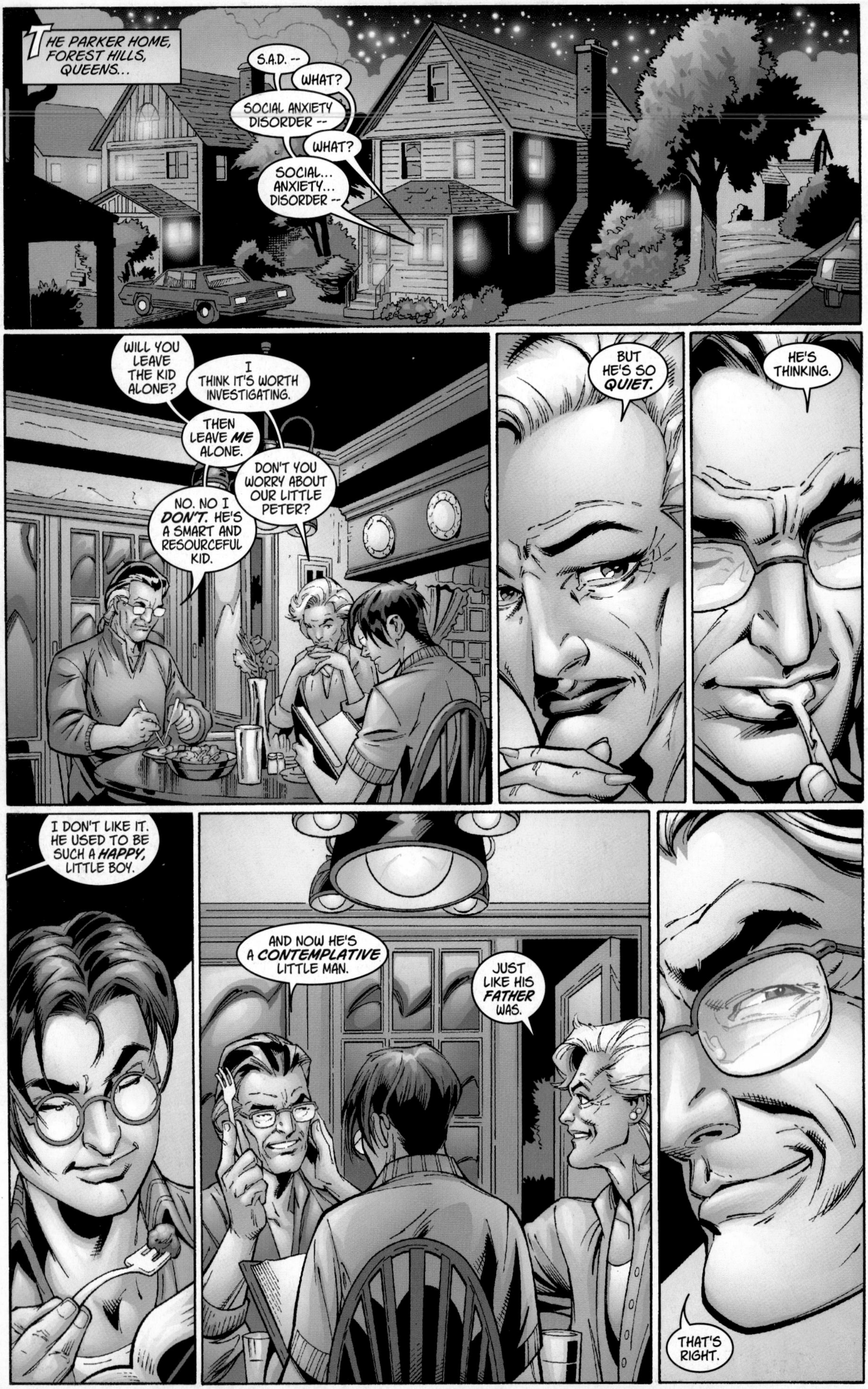
THE PARKER HOME, FOREST HILLS, QUEENS...
S.A.D. --
WHAT?
SOCIAL ANXIETY DISORDER --
WHAT?
SOCIAL... ANXIETY... DISORDER --
WILL YOU LEAVE THE KID ALONE?
I THINK IT'S WORTH INVESTIGATING.
THEN LEAVE ME ALONE.
DON'T YOU WORRY ABOUT OUR LITTLE PETER?
NO. NO I DON'T. HE'S A SMART AND RESOURCEFUL KID.
BUT HE'S SO QUIET.
HE'S THINKING.
I DON'T LIKE IT. HE USED TO BE SUCH A HAPPY, LITTLE BOY.
AND NOW HE'S A CONTEMPLATIVE LITTLE MAN.
JUST LIKE HIS FATHER WAS.
THAT'S RIGHT.

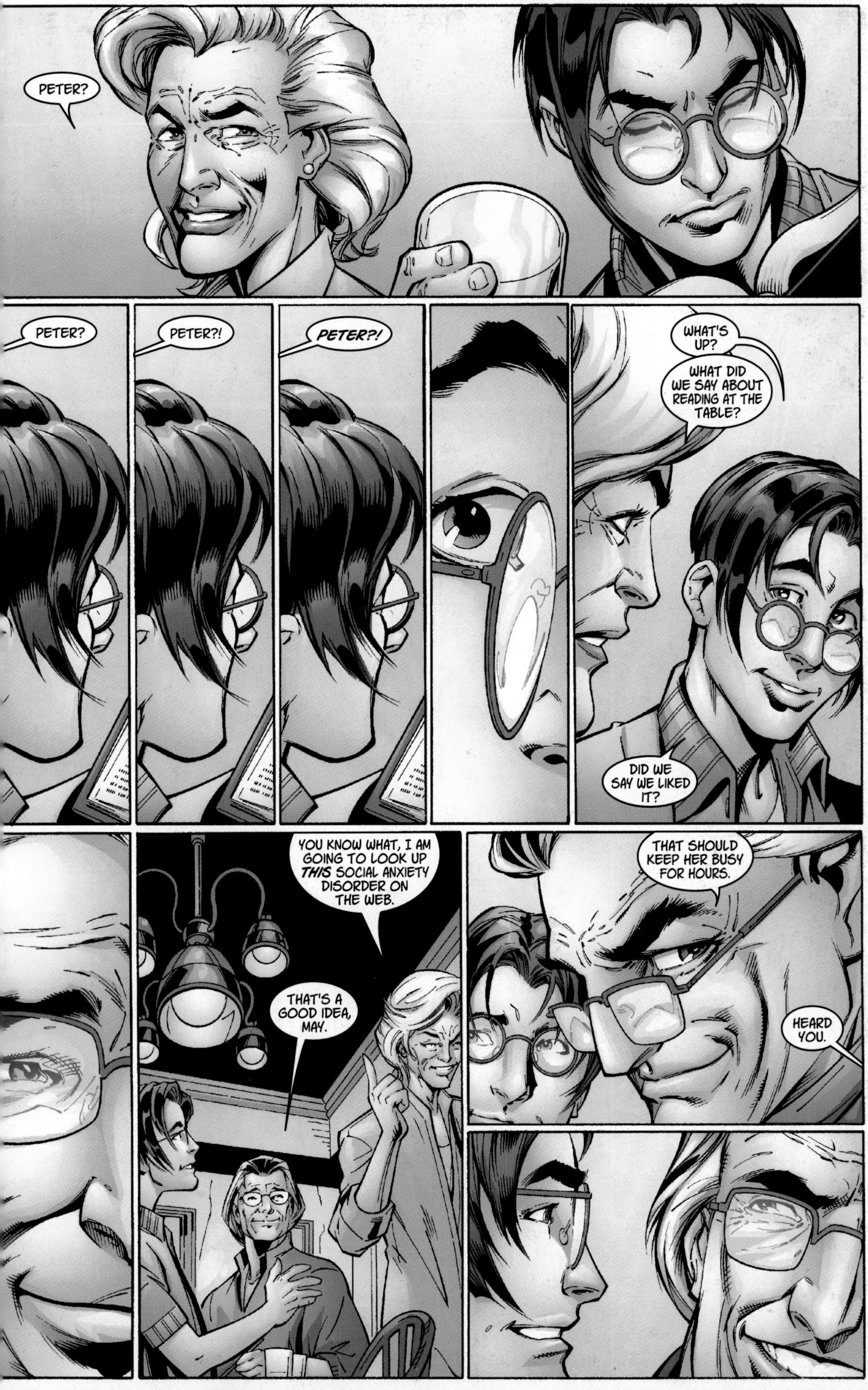
PETER?
PETER?
PETER?!
PETER?!
WHAT'S UP?
WHAT DID WE SAY ABOUT READING AT THE TABLE?
DID WE SAY WE LIKED IT?
YOU KNOW WHAT, I AM GOING TO LOOK UP THIS SOCIAL ANXIETY DISORDER ON THE WEB.
THAT'S A GOOD IDEA, MAY.
THAT SHOULD KEEP HER BUSY FOR HOURS.
HEARD YOU.

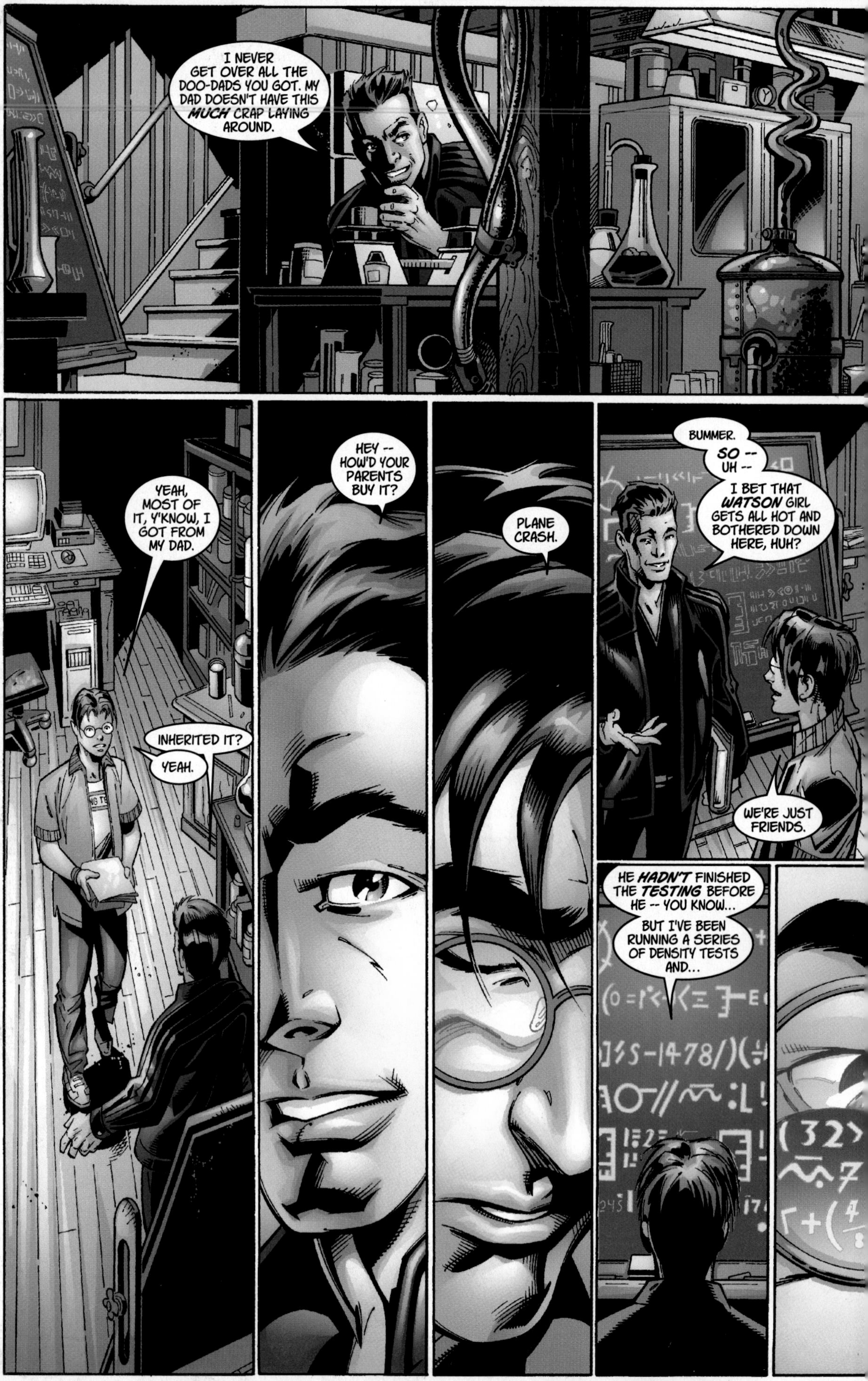
I NEVER GET OVER ALL THE DOO-DADS YOU GOT. MY DAD DOESN'T HAVE THIS *MUCH* CRAP LAYING AROUND.
YEAH, MOST OF IT, Y'KNOW, I GOT FROM MY DAD.
INHERITED IT?
YEAH.
HEY -- HOW'D YOUR PARENTS BUY IT?
PLANE CRASH.
BUMMER.
SO -- UH --
I BET THAT *WATSON* GIRL GETS ALL HOT AND BOTHERED DOWN HERE, HUH?
WE'RE JUST FRIENDS.
HE *HADN'T* FINISHED THE *TESTING* BEFORE HE -- YOU KNOW...
BUT I'VE BEEN RUNNING A SERIES OF DENSITY TESTS AND...

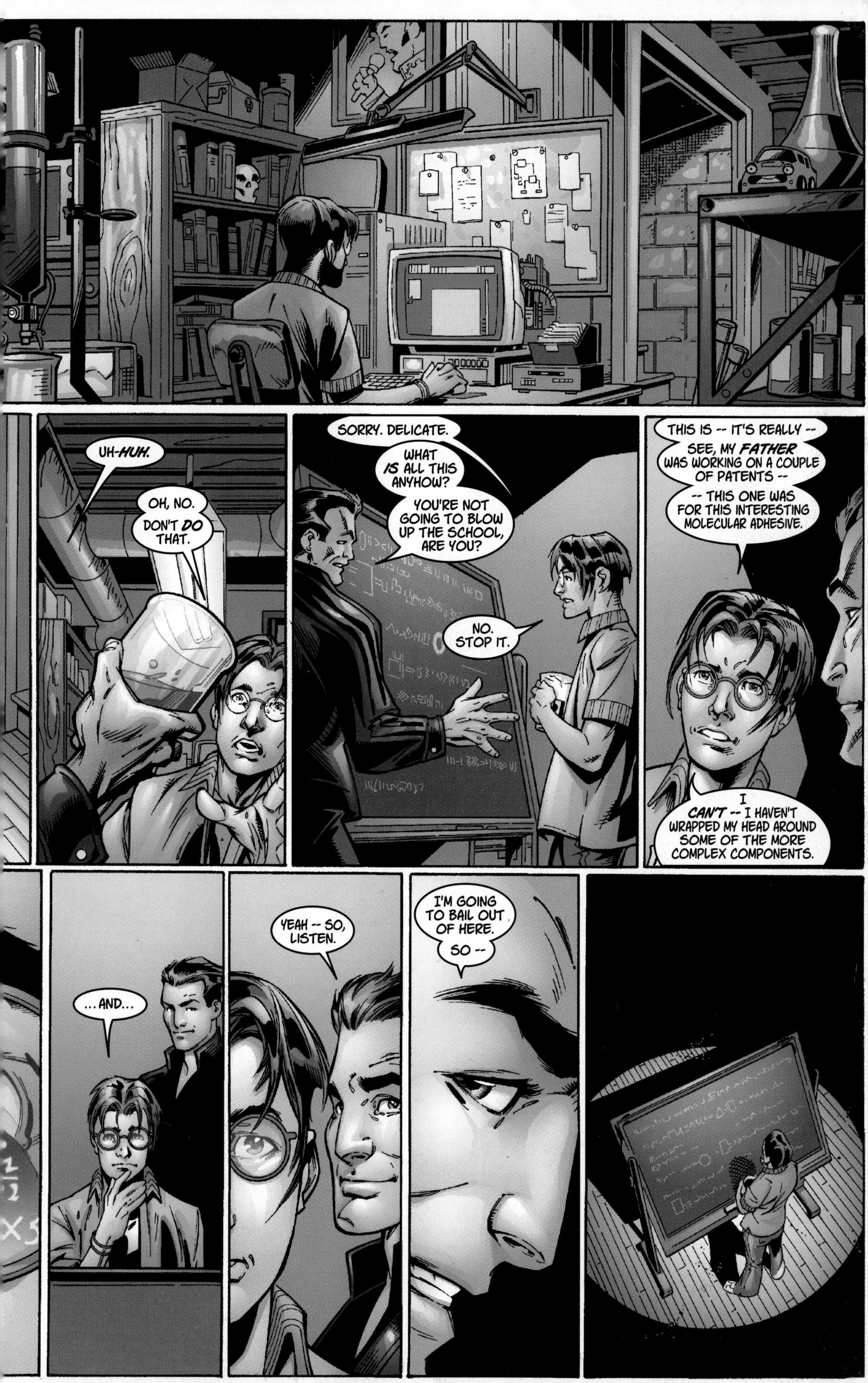
UH-HUH.
OH, NO.
DON'T DO THAT.
SORRY. DELICATE.
WHAT IS ALL THIS ANYHOW?
YOU'RE NOT GOING TO BLOW UP THE SCHOOL, ARE YOU?
NO. STOP IT.
THIS IS -- IT'S REALLY --
SEE, MY FATHER WAS WORKING ON A COUPLE OF PATENTS --
-- THIS ONE WAS FOR THIS INTERESTING MOLECULAR ADHESIVE.
I CAN'T -- I HAVEN'T WRAPPED MY HEAD AROUND SOME OF THE MORE COMPLEX COMPONENTS.
...AND...
YEAH -- SO, LISTEN.
I'M GOING TO BAIL OUT OF HERE.
SO --

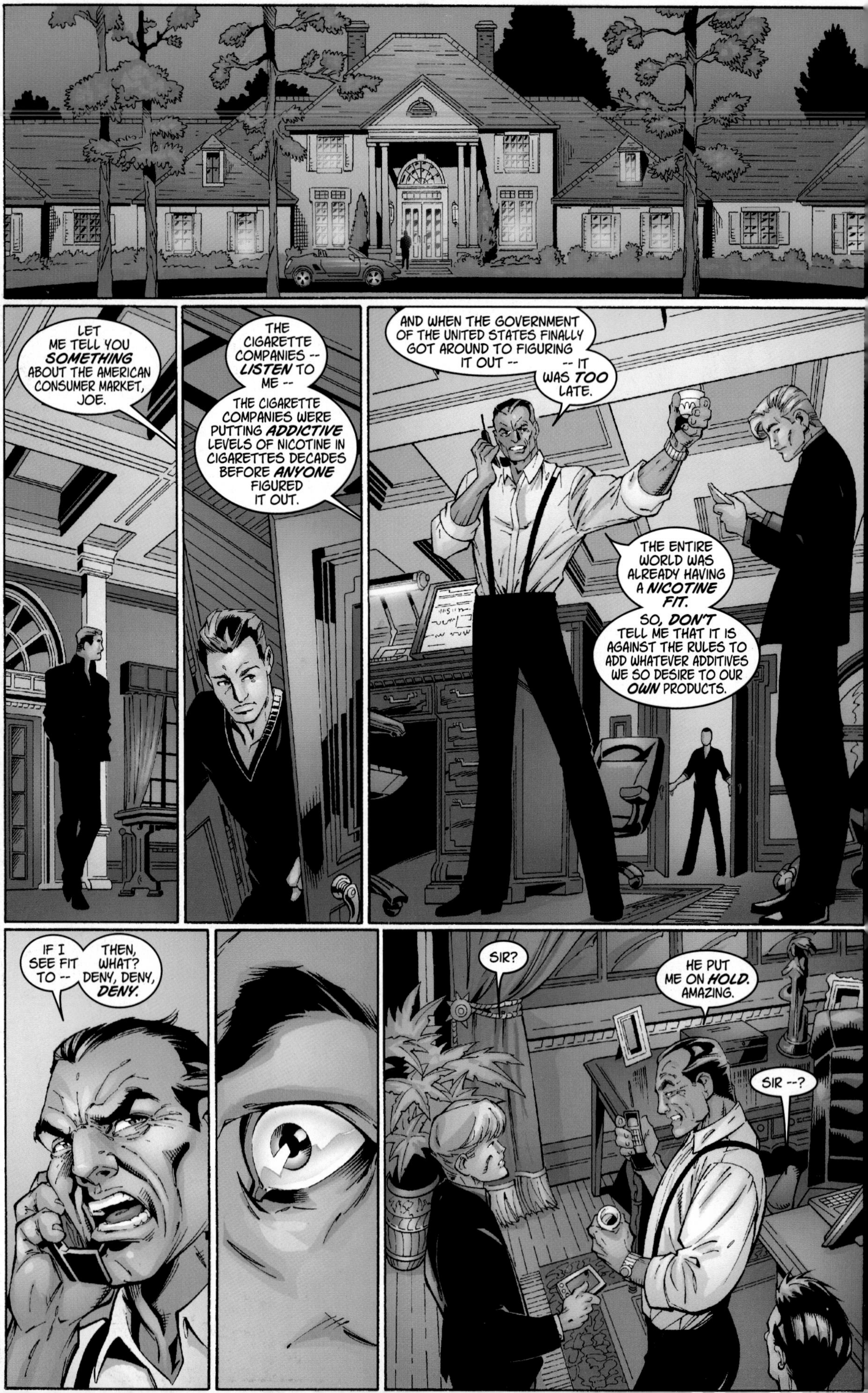

LET ME TELL YOU SOMETHING ABOUT THE AMERICAN CONSUMER MARKET, JOE.
THE CIGARETTE COMPANIES -- LISTEN TO ME --
THE CIGARETTE COMPANIES WERE PUTTING ADDICTIVE LEVELS OF NICOTINE IN CIGARETTES DECADES BEFORE ANYONE FIGURED IT OUT.
AND WHEN THE GOVERNMENT OF THE UNITED STATES FINALLY GOT AROUND TO FIGURING IT OUT --
-- IT WAS TOO LATE.
THE ENTIRE WORLD WAS ALREADY HAVING A NICOTINE FIT.
SO, DON'T TELL ME THAT IT IS AGAINST THE RULES TO ADD WHATEVER ADDITIVES WE SO DESIRE TO OUR OWN PRODUCTS.
IF I SEE FIT TO --
THEN, WHAT? DENY, DENY, DENY.
SIR?
HE PUT ME ON HOLD. AMAZING.
SIR --?

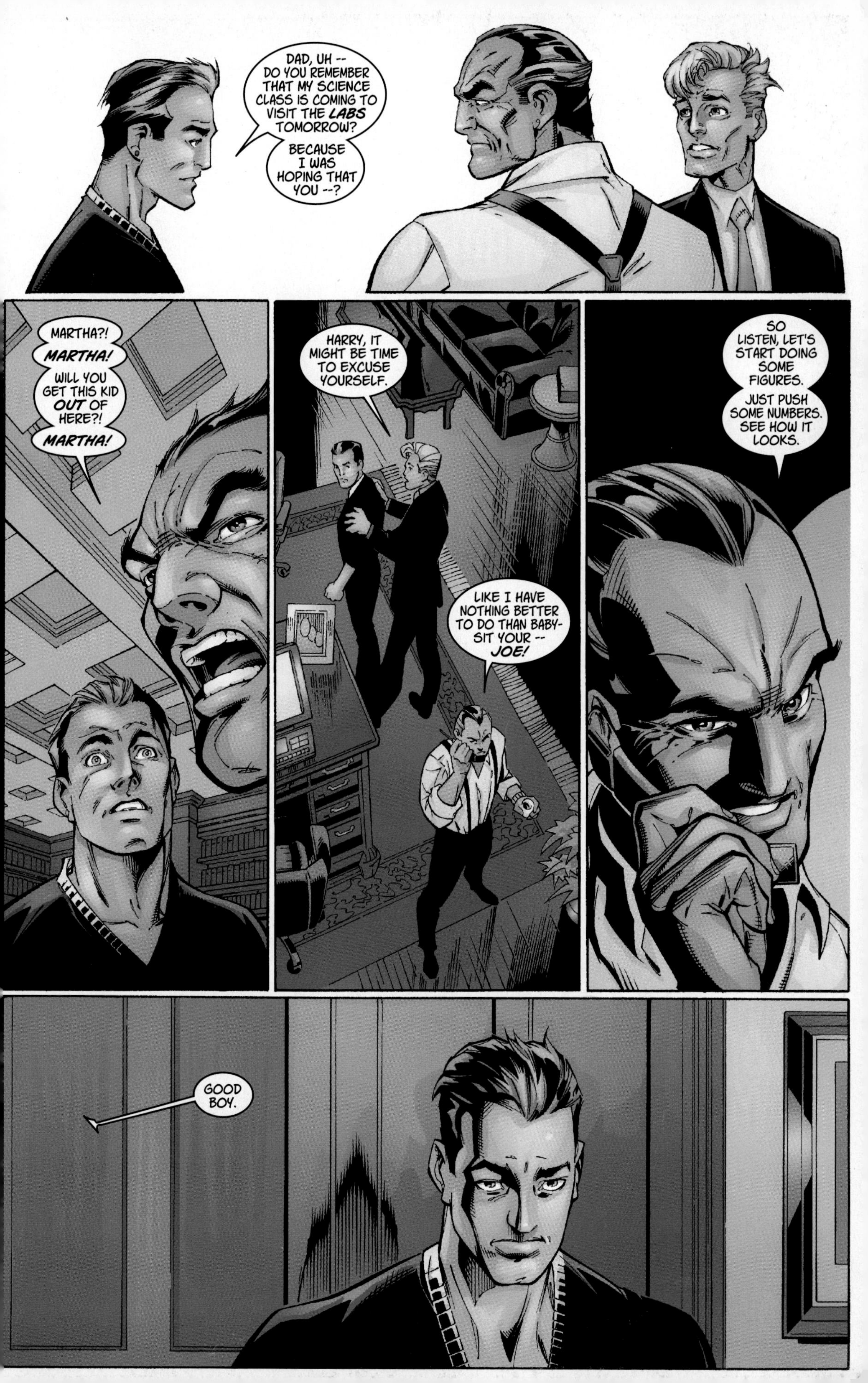
DAD, UH -- DO YOU REMEMBER THAT MY SCIENCE CLASS IS COMING TO VISIT THE LABS TOMORROW?
BECAUSE I WAS HOPING THAT YOU --?
MARTHA?!
MARTHA!
WILL YOU GET THIS KID OUT OF HERE?!
MARTHA!
HARRY, IT MIGHT BE TIME TO EXCUSE YOURSELF.
LIKE I HAVE NOTHING BETTER TO DO THAN BABY-SIT YOUR -- JOE!
SO LISTEN, LET'S START DOING SOME FIGURES.
JUST PUSH SOME NUMBERS. SEE HOW IT LOOKS.
GOOD BOY.

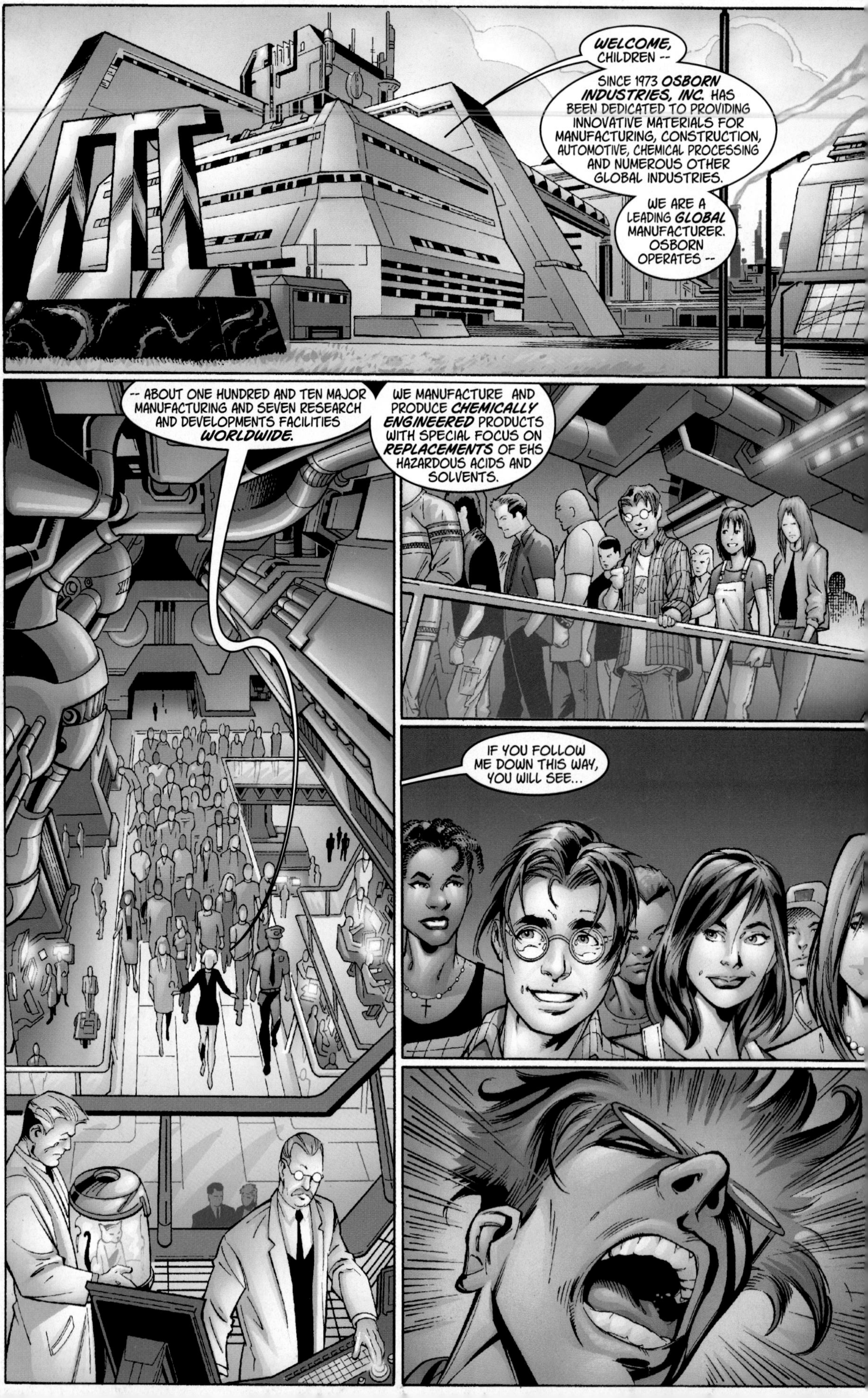
WELCOME, CHILDREN --
SINCE 1973 OSBORN INDUSTRIES, INC. HAS BEEN DEDICATED TO PROVIDING INNOVATIVE MATERIALS FOR MANUFACTURING, CONSTRUCTION, AUTOMOTIVE, CHEMICAL PROCESSING AND NUMEROUS OTHER GLOBAL INDUSTRIES.
WE ARE A LEADING GLOBAL MANUFACTURER. OSBORN OPERATES --
-- ABOUT ONE HUNDRED AND TEN MAJOR MANUFACTURING AND SEVEN RESEARCH AND DEVELOPMENTS FACILITIES WORLDWIDE.
WE MANUFACTURE AND PRODUCE CHEMICALLY ENGINEERED PRODUCTS WITH SPECIAL FOCUS ON REPLACEMENTS OF EHS HAZARDOUS ACIDS AND SOLVENTS.
IF YOU FOLLOW ME DOWN THIS WAY, YOU WILL SEE...

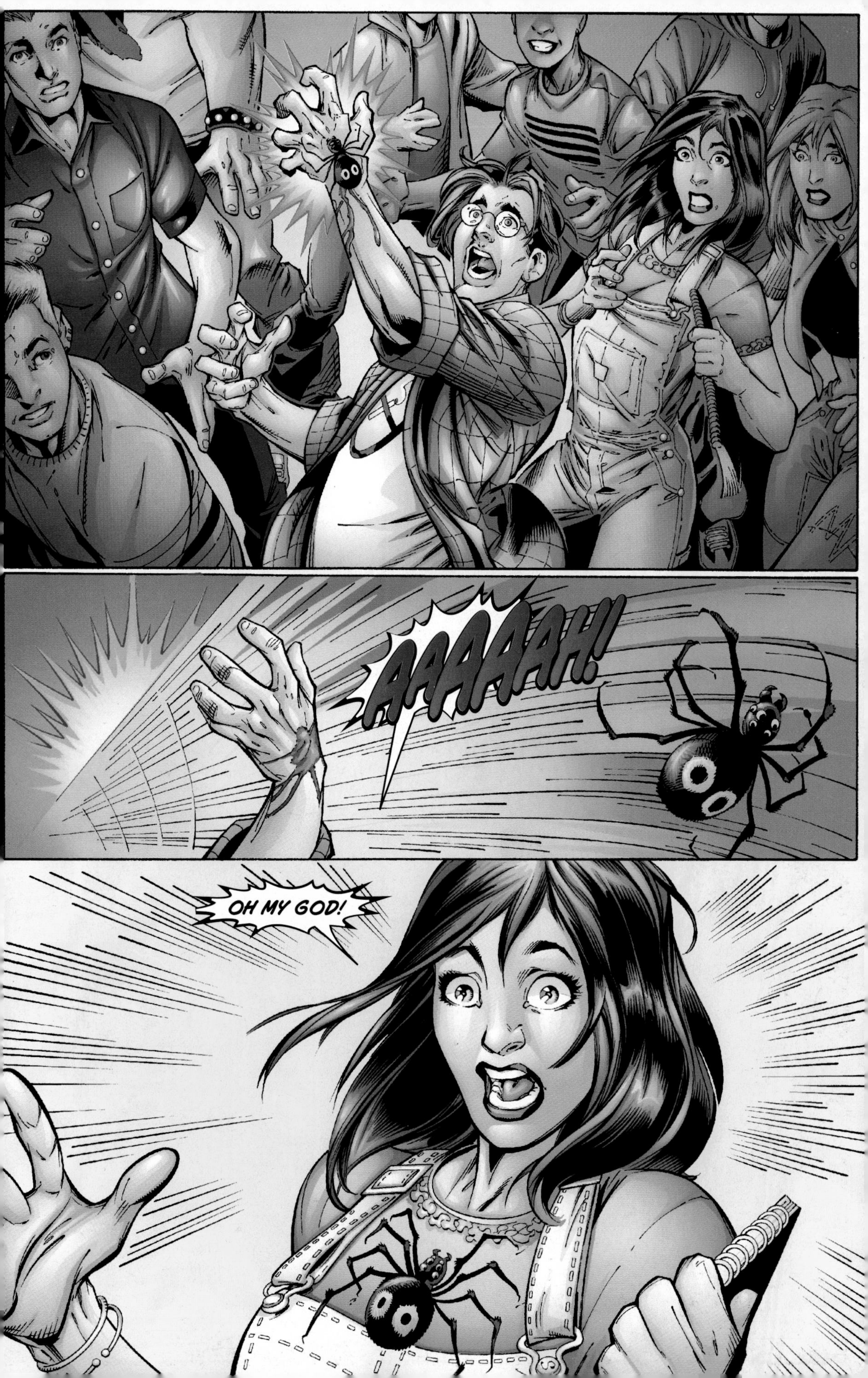
AAAAAH!
OH MY GOD!

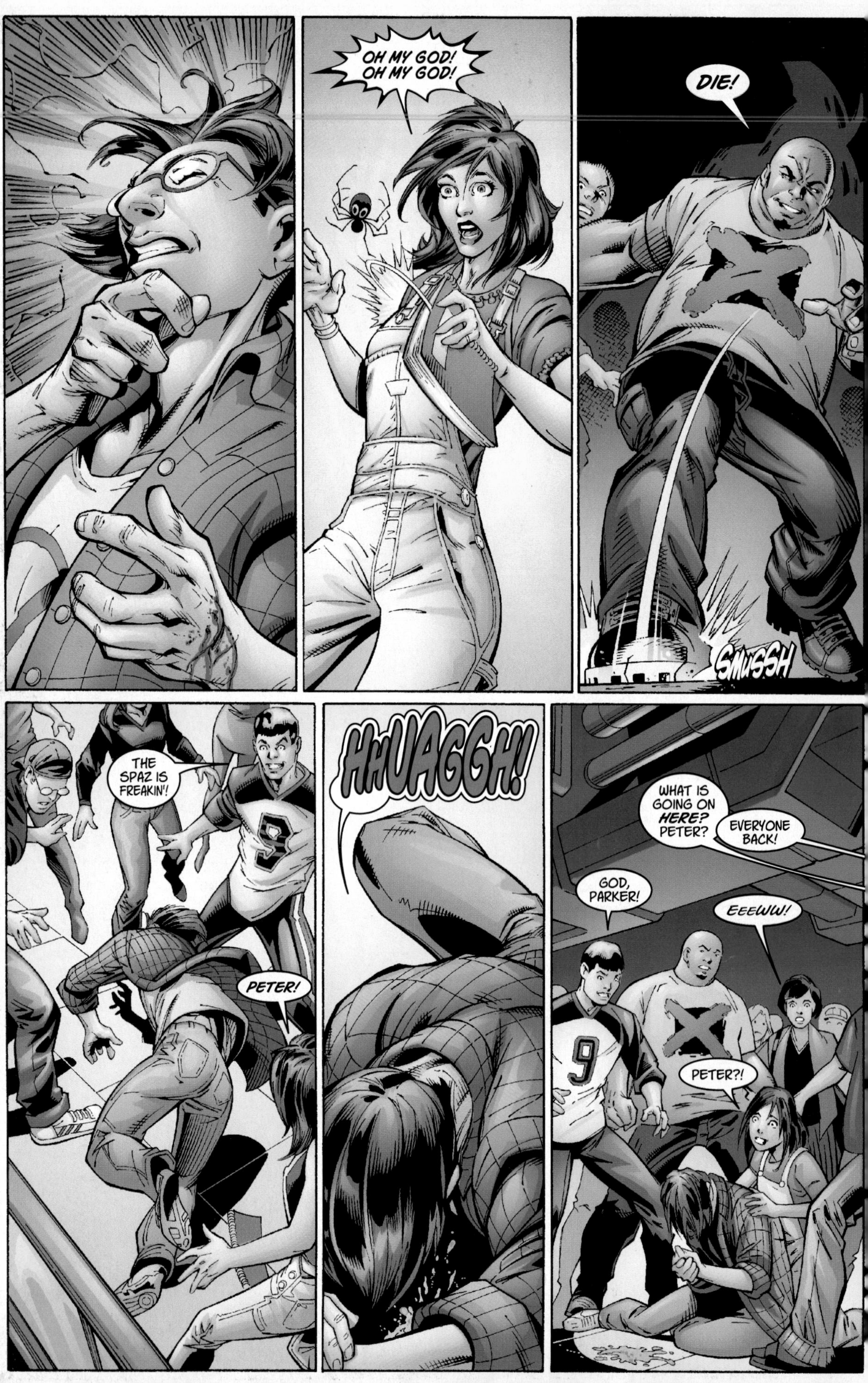
OH MY GOD! OH MY GOD!
DIE!
SMUSSH
THE SPAZ IS FREAKIN'!
PETER!
HHUAGGH!
WHAT IS GOING ON HERE? PETER?
EVERYONE BACK!
GOD, PARKER!
EEEWW!
PETER?!

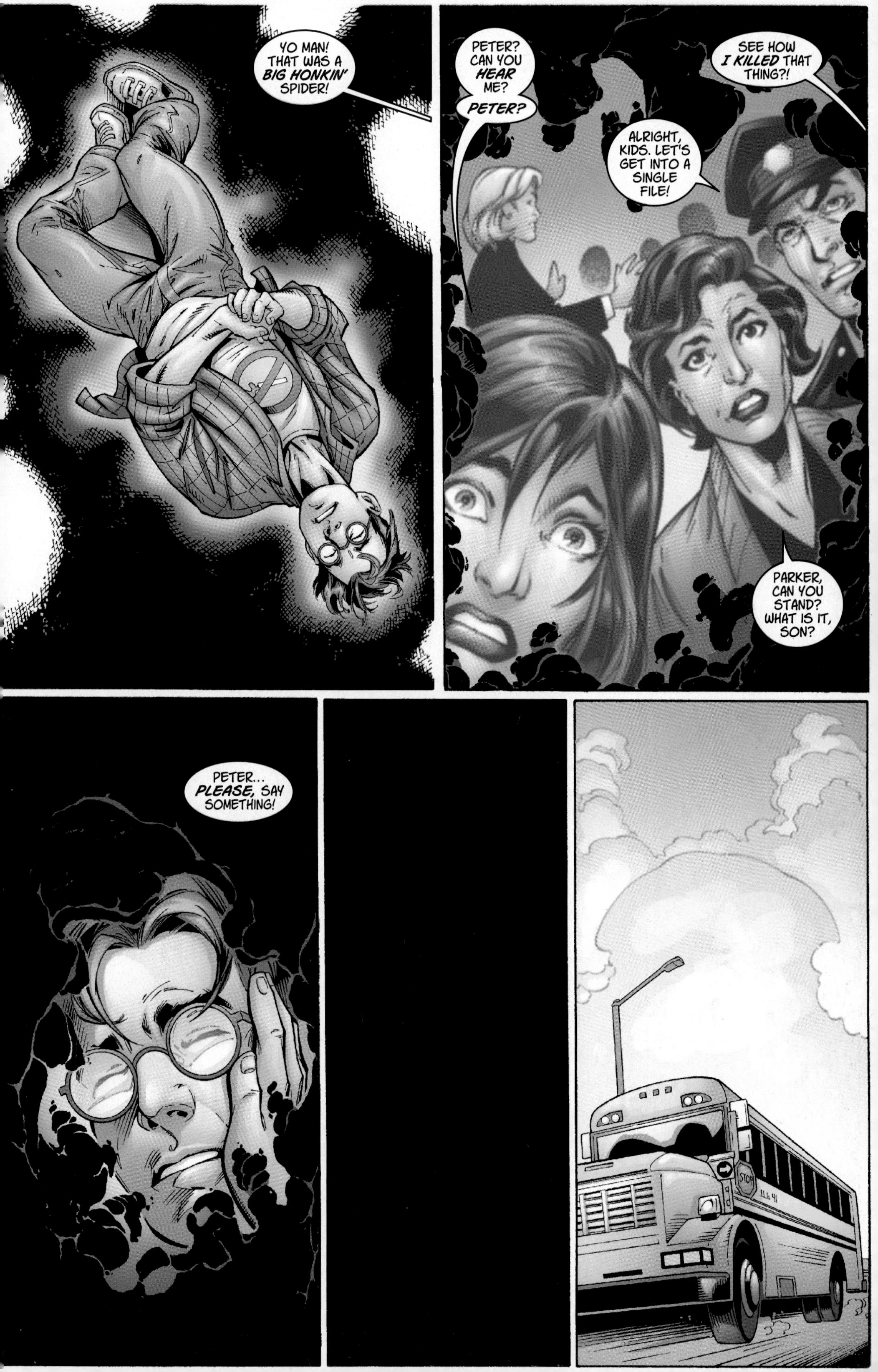
YO MAN! THAT WAS A BIG HONKIN' SPIDER!
PETER? CAN YOU HEAR ME?
PETER?
SEE HOW I KILLED THAT THING?!
ALRIGHT, KIDS. LET'S GET INTO A SINGLE FILE!
PARKER, CAN YOU STAND? WHAT IS IT, SON?
PETER... PLEASE, SAY SOMETHING!
STOP

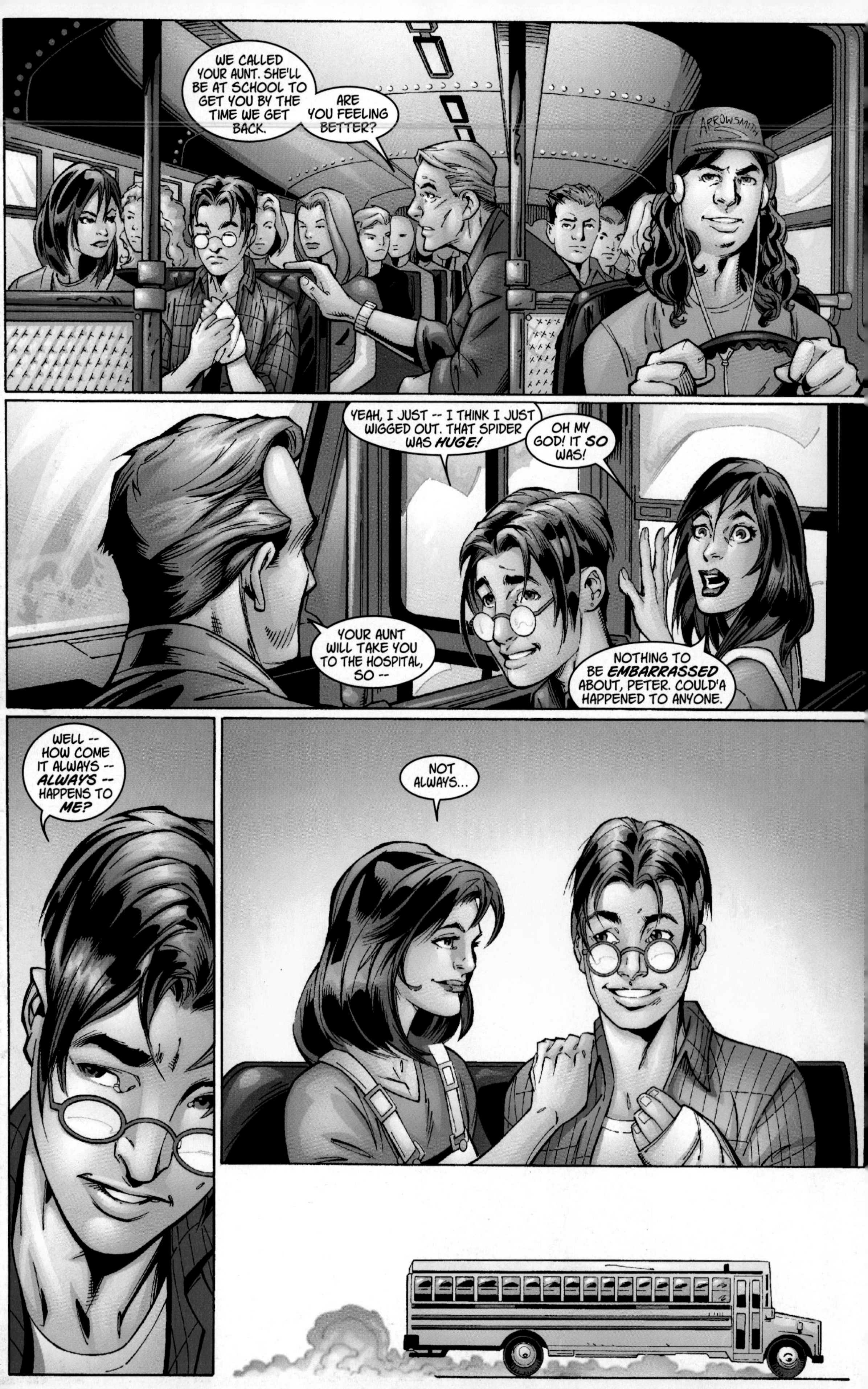

WE CALLED YOUR AUNT. SHE'LL BE AT SCHOOL TO GET YOU BY THE TIME WE GET BACK.
ARE YOU FEELING BETTER?
ARROWSMITH
YEAH, I JUST -- I THINK I JUST WIGGED OUT. THAT SPIDER WAS HUGE!
OH MY GOD! IT SO WAS!
YOUR AUNT WILL TAKE YOU TO THE HOSPITAL, SO --
NOTHING TO BE EMBARRASSED ABOUT, PETER. COULD'A HAPPENED TO ANYONE.
WELL -- HOW COME IT ALWAYS -- ALWAYS -- HAPPENS TO ME?
NOT ALWAYS...

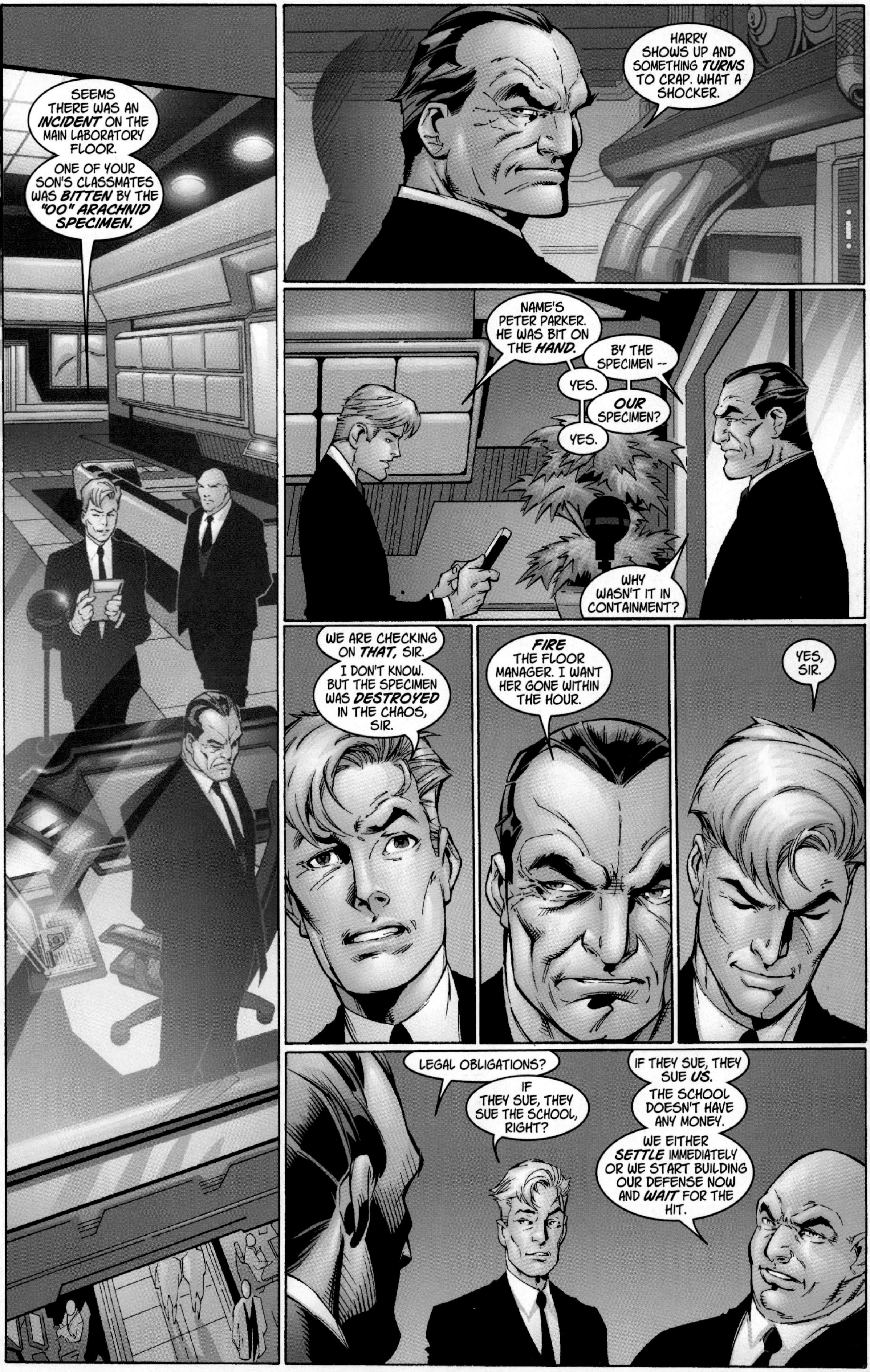
SEEMS THERE WAS AN INCIDENT ON THE MAIN LABORATORY FLOOR.
ONE OF YOUR SON'S CLASSMATES WAS BITTEN BY THE "OO" ARACHNID SPECIMEN.
HARRY SHOWS UP AND SOMETHING TURNS TO CRAP. WHAT A SHOCKER.
NAME'S PETER PARKER. HE WAS BIT ON THE HAND.
BY THE SPECIMEN --
YES.
OUR SPECIMEN?
YES.
WHY WASN'T IT IN CONTAINMENT?
WE ARE CHECKING ON THAT, SIR.
I DON'T KNOW. BUT THE SPECIMEN WAS DESTROYED IN THE CHAOS, SIR.
FIRE THE FLOOR MANAGER. I WANT HER GONE WITHIN THE HOUR.
YES, SIR.
LEGAL OBLIGATIONS?
IF THEY SUE, THEY SUE THE SCHOOL, RIGHT?
IF THEY SUE, THEY SUE US.
THE SCHOOL DOESN'T HAVE ANY MONEY.
WE EITHER SETTLE IMMEDIATELY OR WE START BUILDING OUR DEFENSE NOW AND WAIT FOR THE HIT.

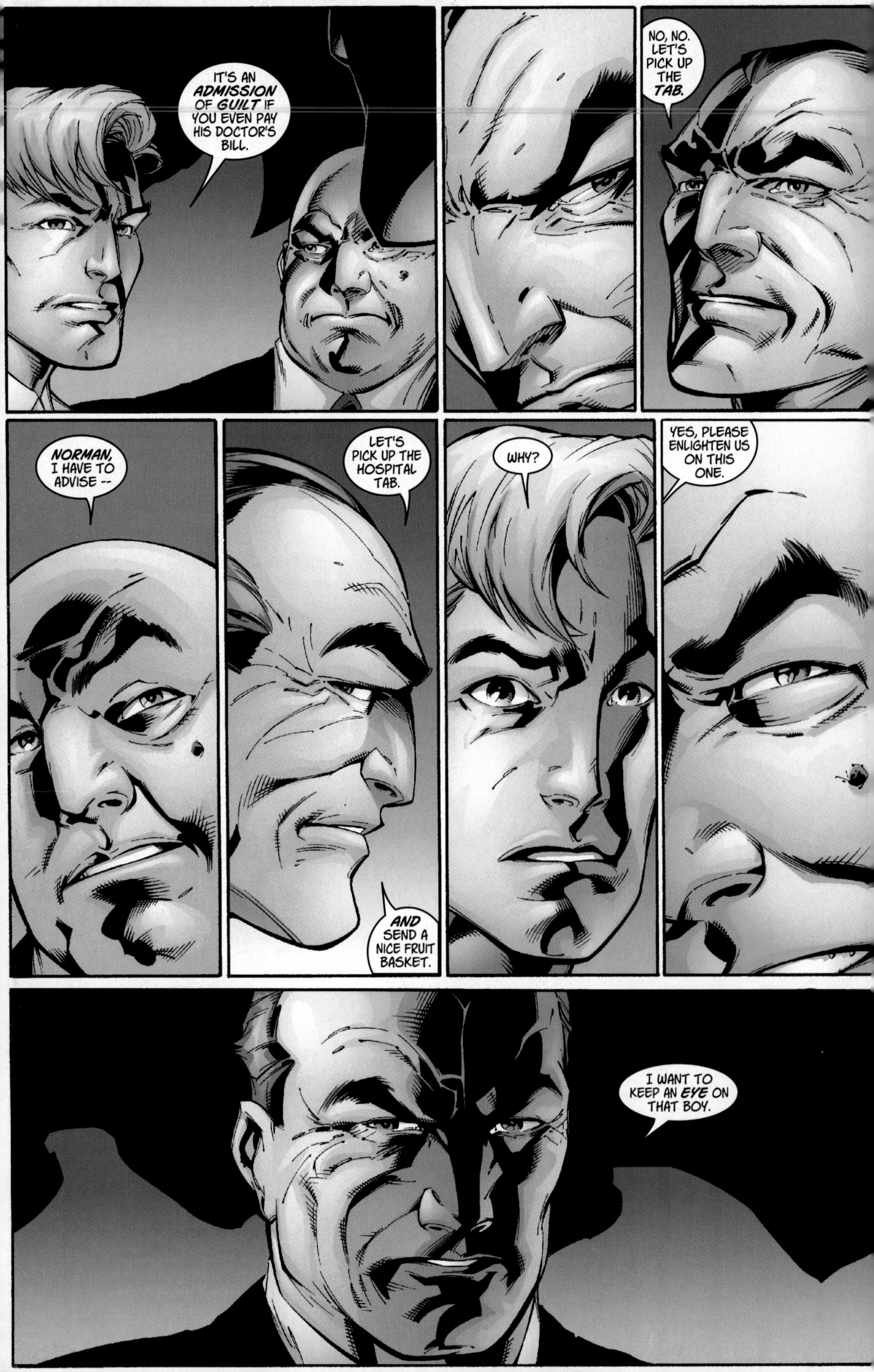
IT'S AN ADMISSION OF GUILT IF YOU EVEN PAY HIS DOCTOR'S BILL.
NO, NO. LET'S PICK UP THE TAB.
NORMAN, I HAVE TO ADVISE --
LET'S PICK UP THE HOSPITAL TAB.
AND SEND A NICE FRUIT BASKET.
WHY?
YES, PLEASE ENLIGHTEN US ON THIS ONE.
I WANT TO KEEP AN EYE ON THAT BOY.

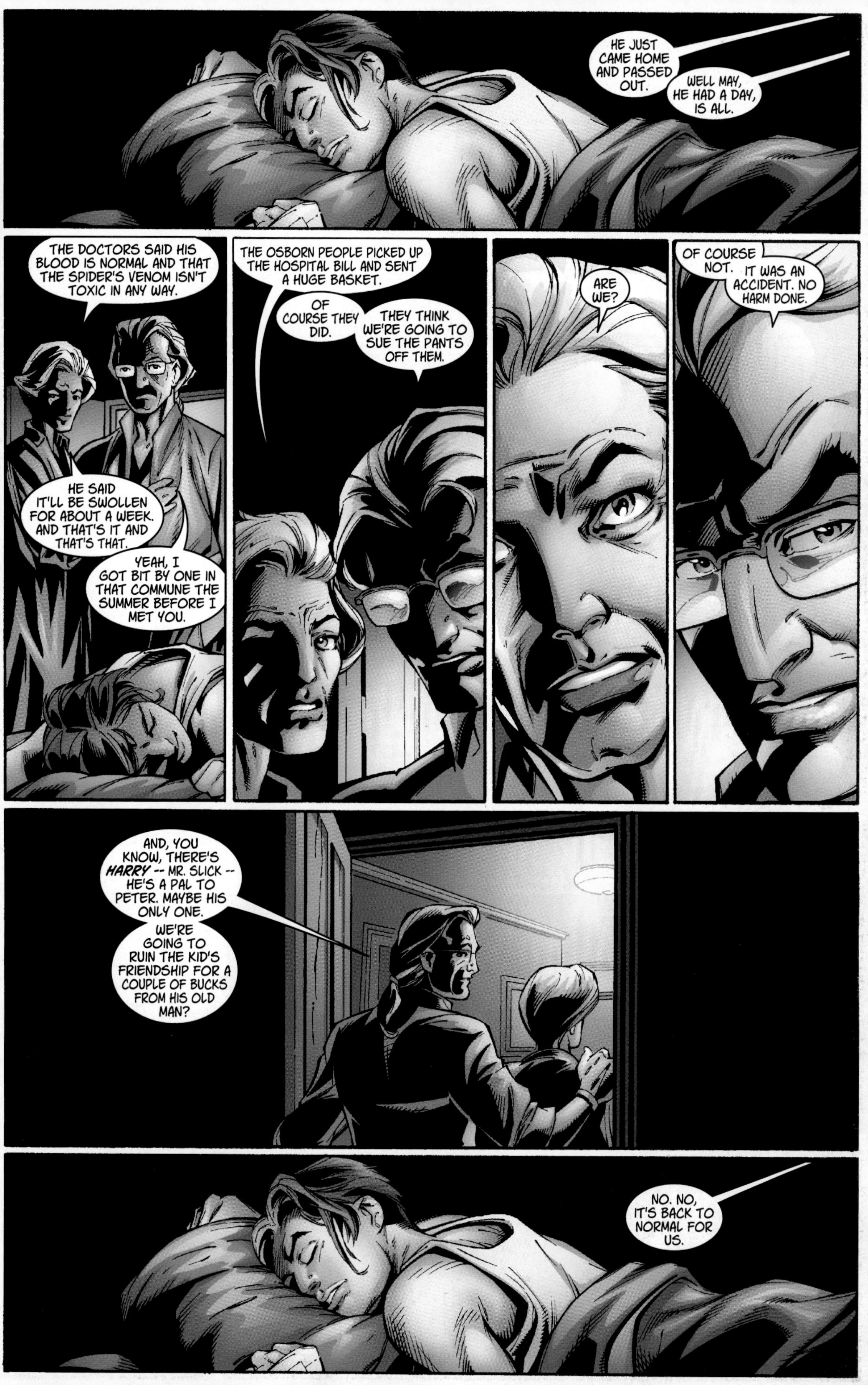
HE JUST CAME HOME AND PASSED OUT.
WELL MAY, HE HAD A DAY, IS ALL.
THE DOCTORS SAID HIS BLOOD IS NORMAL AND THAT THE SPIDER'S VENOM ISN'T TOXIC IN ANY WAY.
HE SAID IT'LL BE SWOLLEN FOR ABOUT A WEEK. AND THAT'S IT AND THAT'S THAT.
YEAH, I GOT BIT BY ONE IN THAT COMMUNE THE SUMMER BEFORE I MET YOU.
THE OSBORN PEOPLE PICKED UP THE HOSPITAL BILL AND SENT A HUGE BASKET.
OF COURSE THEY DID.
THEY THINK WE'RE GOING TO SUE THE PANTS OFF THEM.
ARE WE?
OF COURSE NOT.
IT WAS AN ACCIDENT. NO HARM DONE.
AND, YOU KNOW, THERE'S HARRY -- MR. SLICK -- HE'S A PAL TO PETER. MAYBE HIS ONLY ONE.
WE'RE GOING TO RUIN THE KID'S FRIENDSHIP FOR A COUPLE OF BUCKS FROM HIS OLD MAN?
NO. NO, IT'S BACK TO NORMAL FOR US.

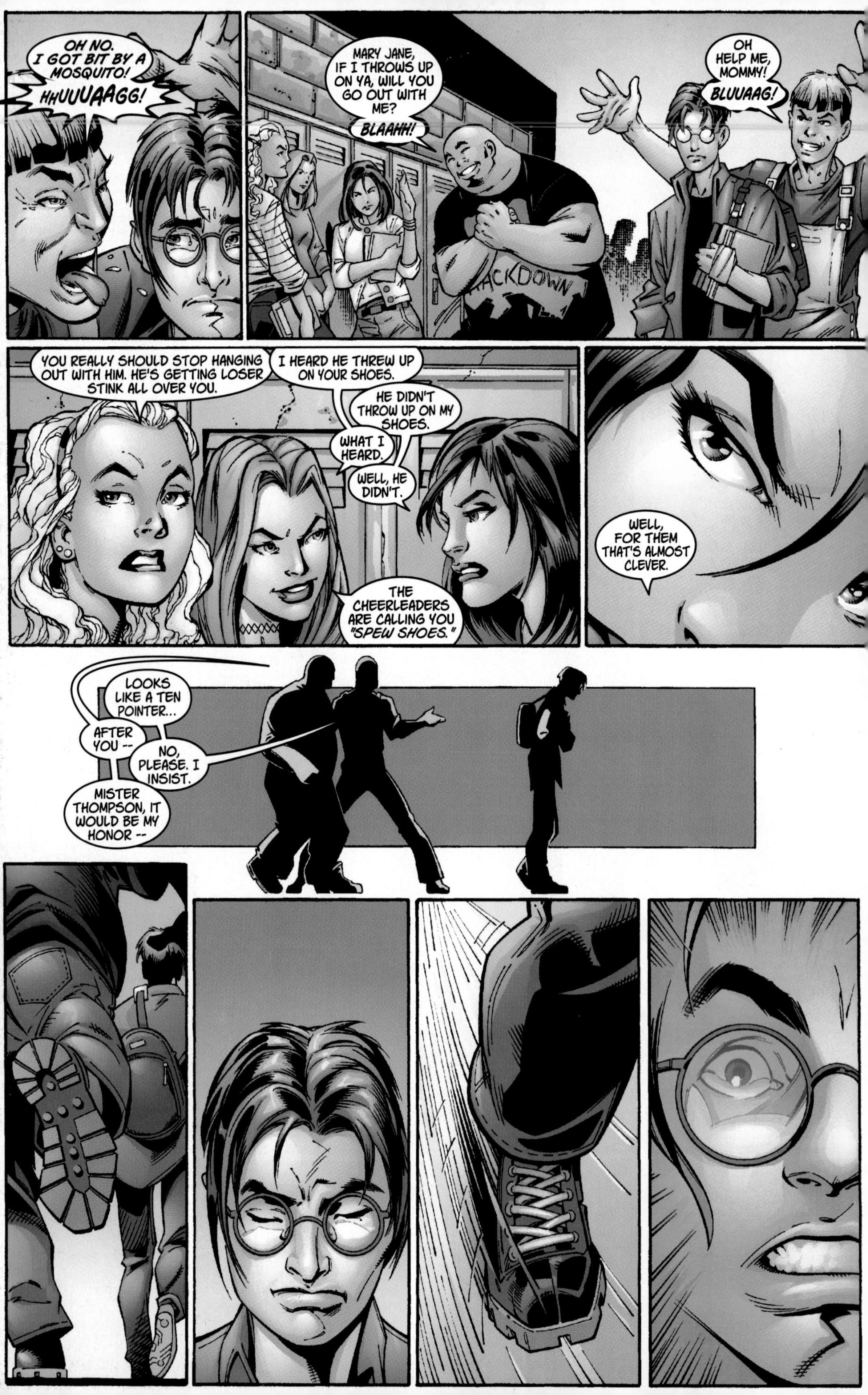
OH NO. I GOT BIT BY A MOSQUITO!
HHUUUAAGG!
MARY JANE, IF I THROWS UP ON YA, WILL YOU GO OUT WITH ME?
BLAAHH!
OH HELP ME, MOMMY!
BLUUAAG!
ACKDOWN
YOU REALLY SHOULD STOP HANGING OUT WITH HIM. HE'S GETTING LOSER STINK ALL OVER YOU.
I HEARD HE THREW UP ON YOUR SHOES.
HE DIDN'T THROW UP ON MY SHOES.
WHAT I HEARD.
WELL, HE DIDN'T.
THE CHEERLEADERS ARE CALLING YOU "SPEW SHOES."
WELL, FOR THEM THAT'S ALMOST CLEVER.
LOOKS LIKE A TEN POINTER...
AFTER YOU --
NO, PLEASE. I INSIST.
MISTER THOMPSON, IT WOULD BE MY HONOR --

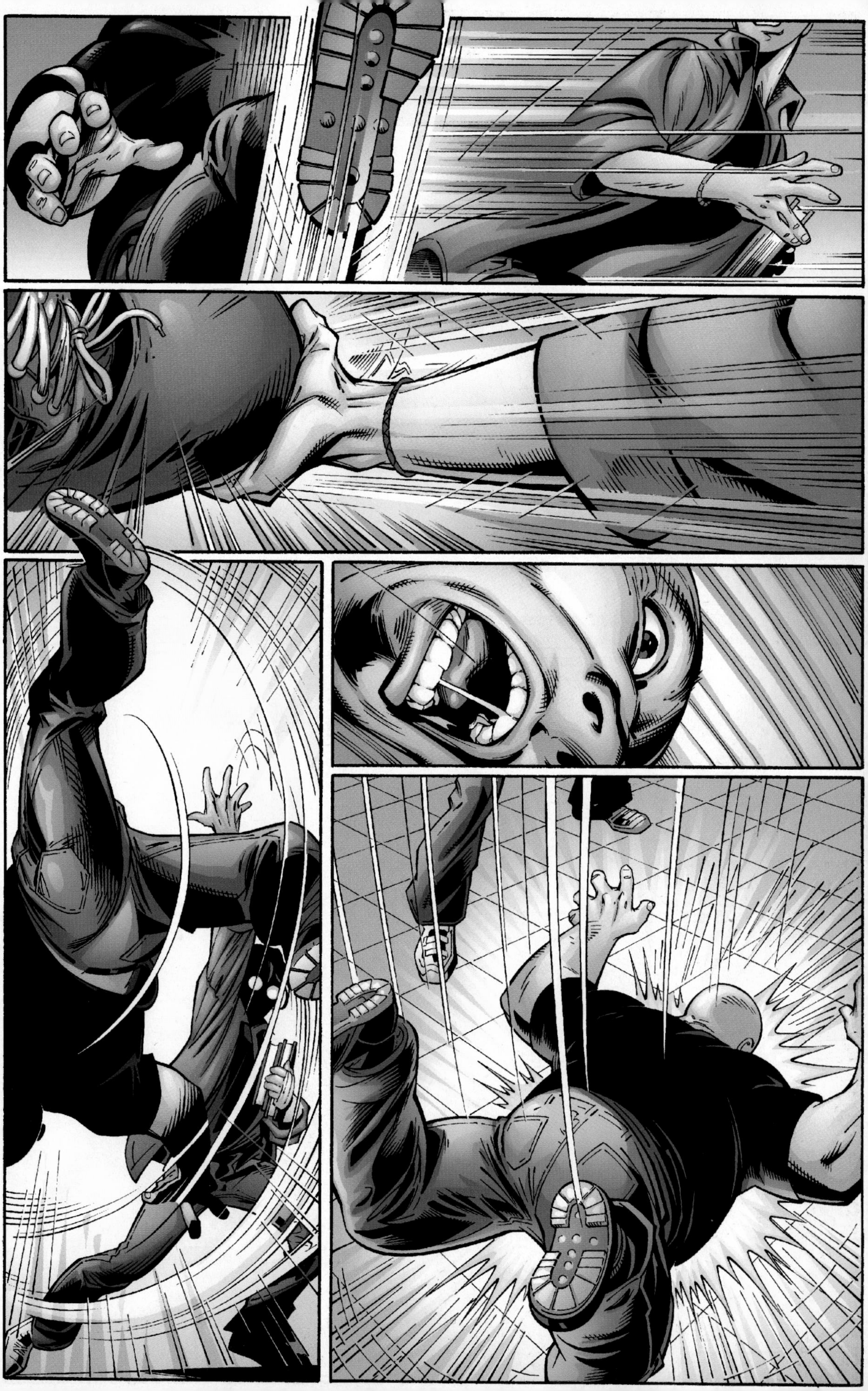

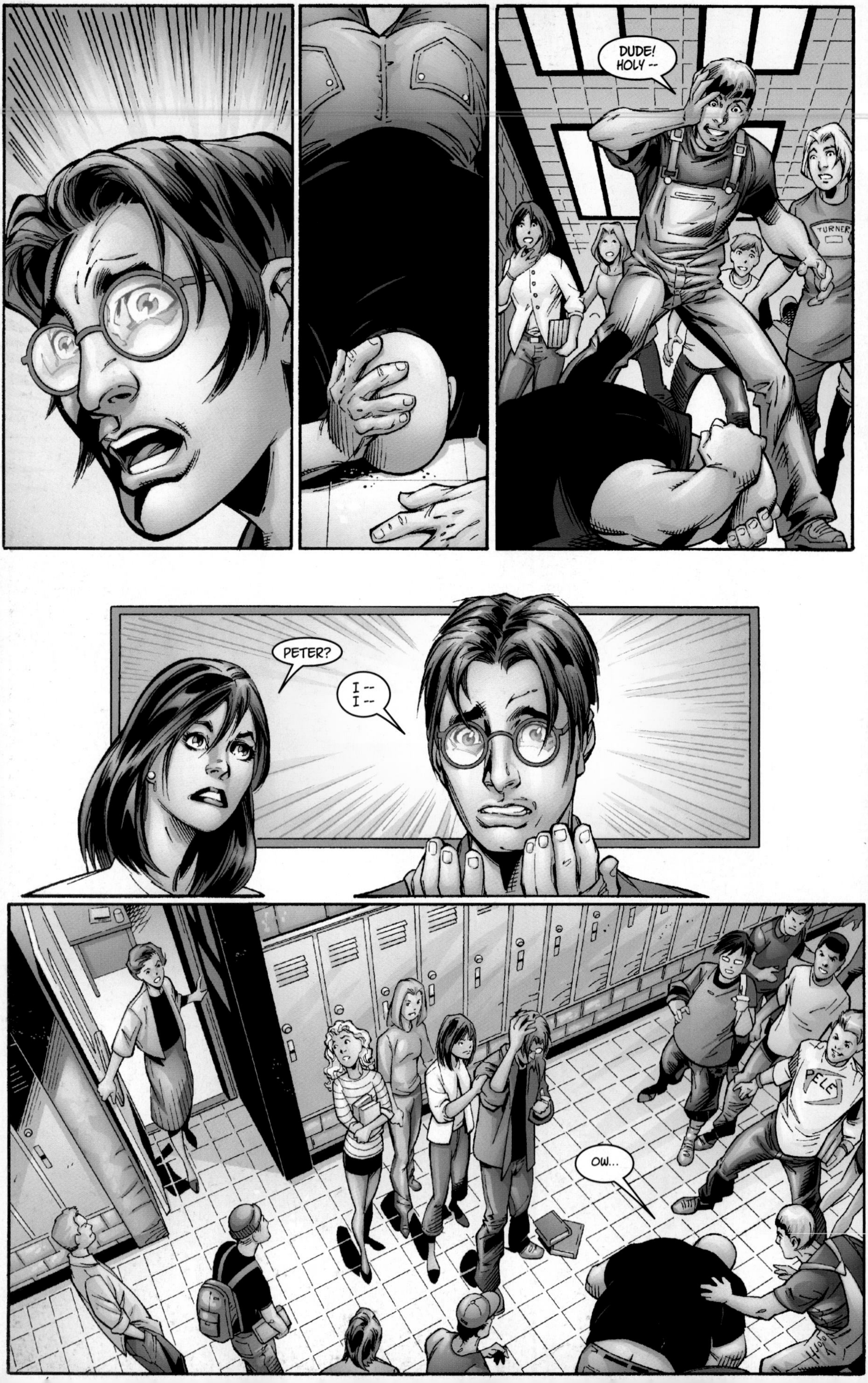
DUDE! HOLY --
TURNER
PETER?
I --
I --
PELE
OW...

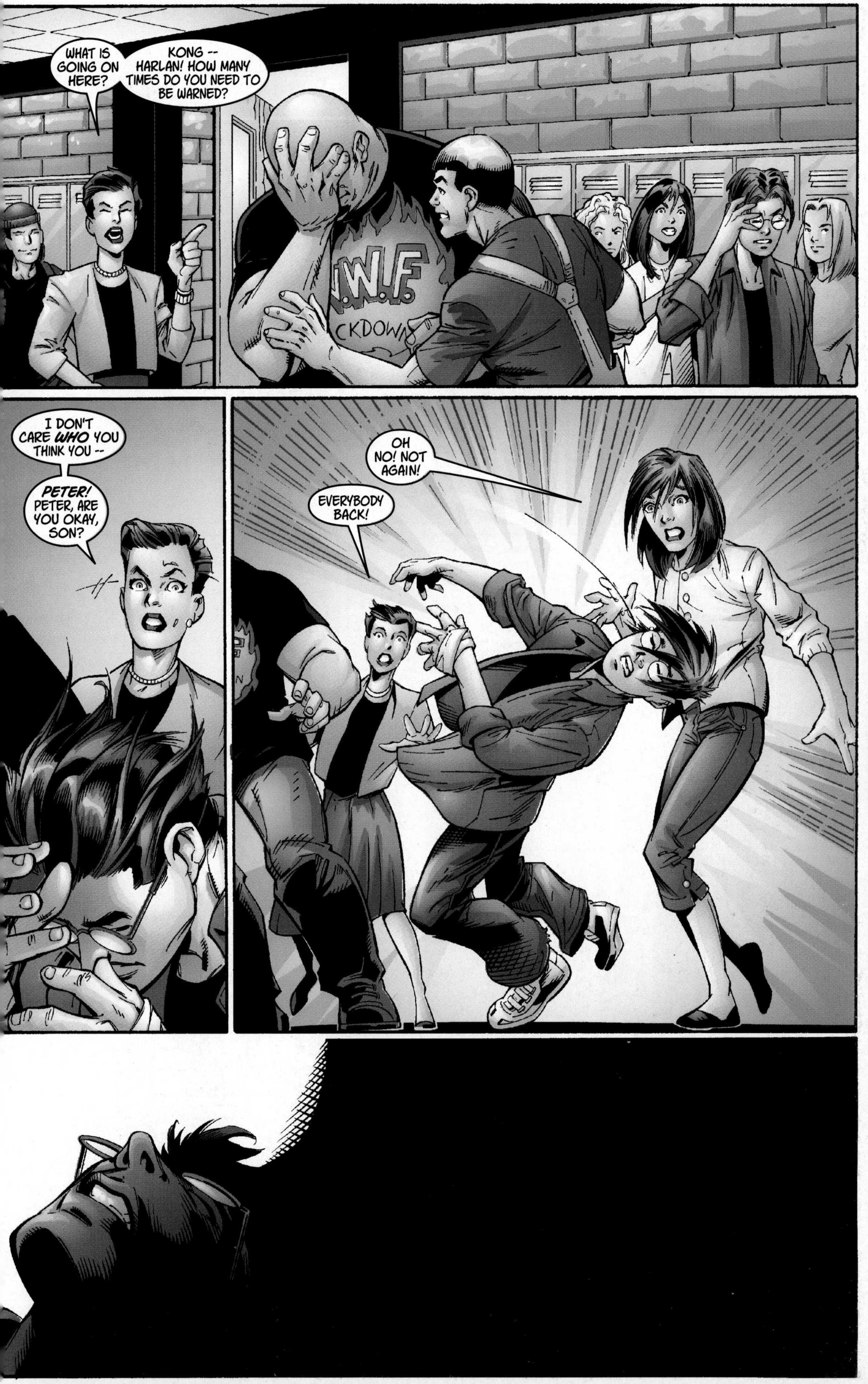

WHAT IS GOING ON HERE?
KONG -- HARLAN! HOW MANY TIMES DO YOU NEED TO BE WARNED?
I DON'T CARE **WHO** YOU THINK YOU --
PETER! PETER, ARE YOU OKAY, SON?
OH NO! NOT AGAIN!
EVERYBODY BACK!

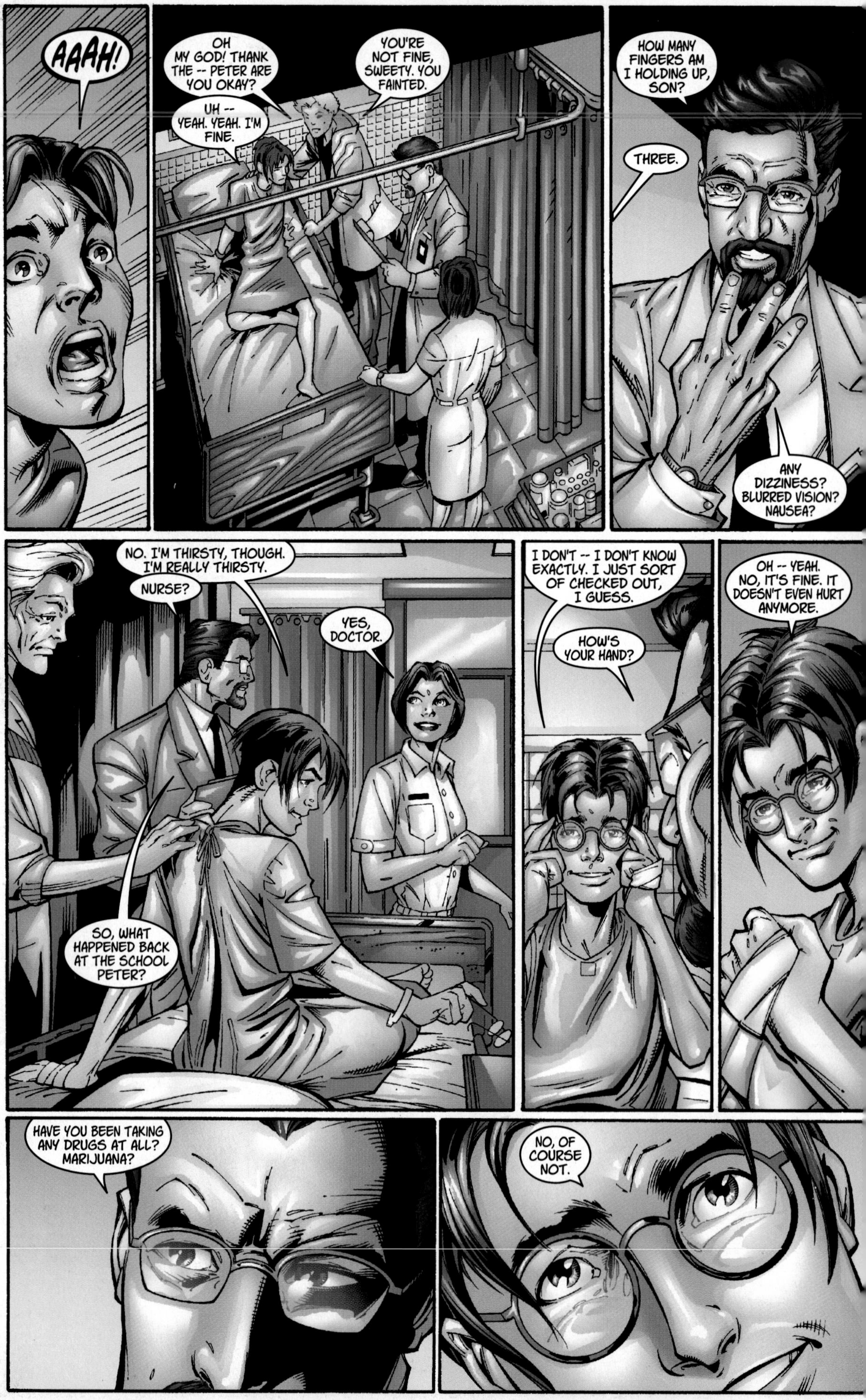
AAAH!
OH MY GOD! THANK THE -- PETER ARE YOU OKAY?
UH -- YEAH. YEAH. I'M FINE.
YOU'RE NOT FINE, SWEETY. YOU FAINTED.
HOW MANY FINGERS AM I HOLDING UP, SON?
THREE.
ANY DIZZINESS? BLURRED VISION? NAUSEA?
NO. I'M THIRSTY, THOUGH. I'M REALLY THIRSTY.
NURSE?
YES, DOCTOR.
SO, WHAT HAPPENED BACK AT THE SCHOOL PETER?
I DON'T -- I DON'T KNOW EXACTLY. I JUST SORT OF CHECKED OUT, I GUESS.
HOW'S YOUR HAND?
OH -- YEAH. NO, IT'S FINE. IT DOESN'T EVEN HURT ANYMORE.
HAVE YOU BEEN TAKING ANY DRUGS AT ALL? MARIJUANA?
NO, OF COURSE NOT.

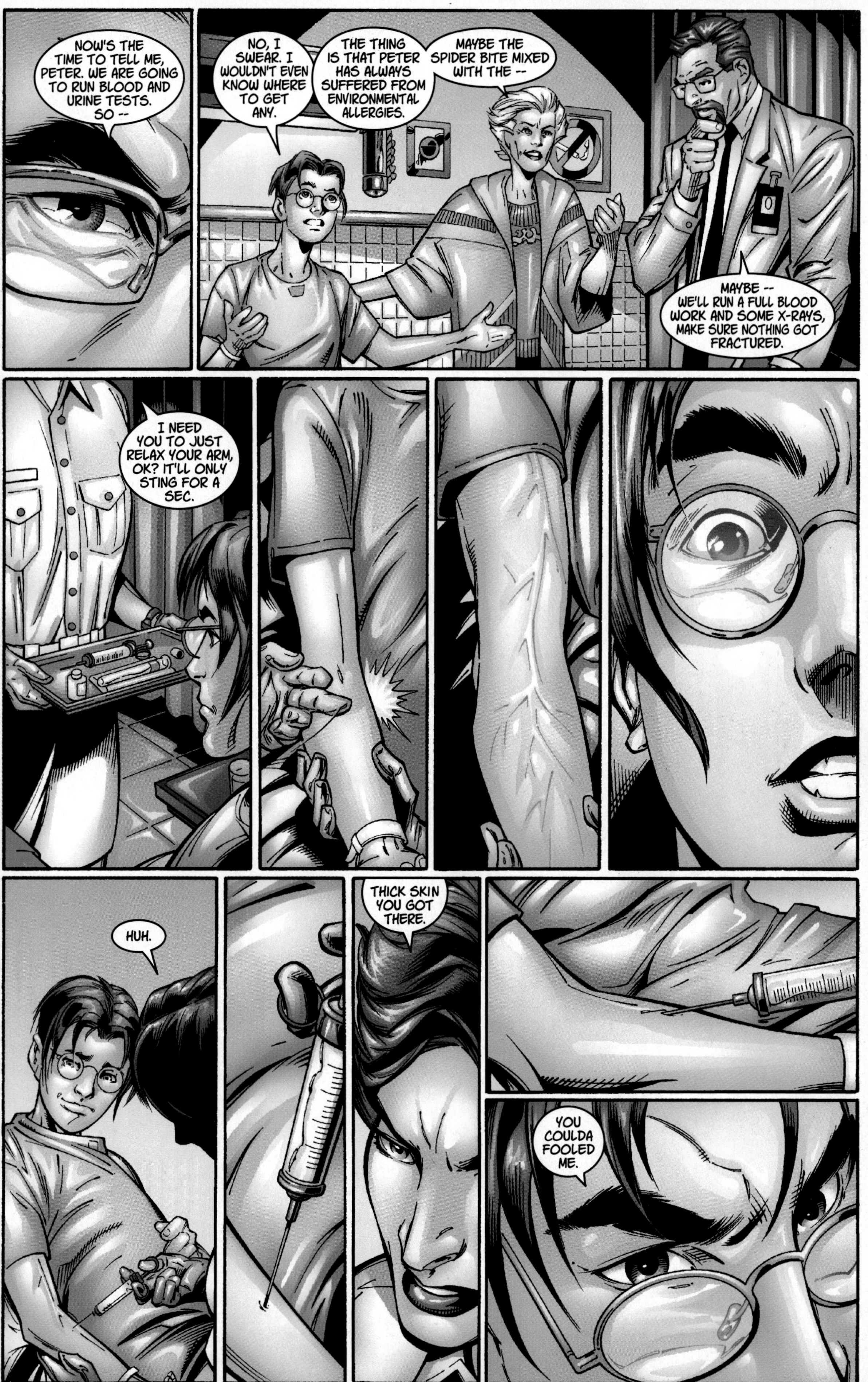
NOW'S THE TIME TO TELL ME, PETER. WE ARE GOING TO RUN BLOOD AND URINE TESTS. SO --
NO, I SWEAR. I WOULDN'T EVEN KNOW WHERE TO GET ANY.
THE THING IS THAT PETER HAS ALWAYS SUFFERED FROM ENVIRONMENTAL ALLERGIES.
MAYBE THE SPIDER BITE MIXED WITH THE --
MAYBE -- WE'LL RUN A FULL BLOOD WORK AND SOME X-RAYS, MAKE SURE NOTHING GOT FRACTURED.
I NEED YOU TO JUST RELAX YOUR ARM, OK? IT'LL ONLY STING FOR A SEC.
HUH.
THICK SKIN YOU GOT THERE.
YOU COULDA FOOLED ME.

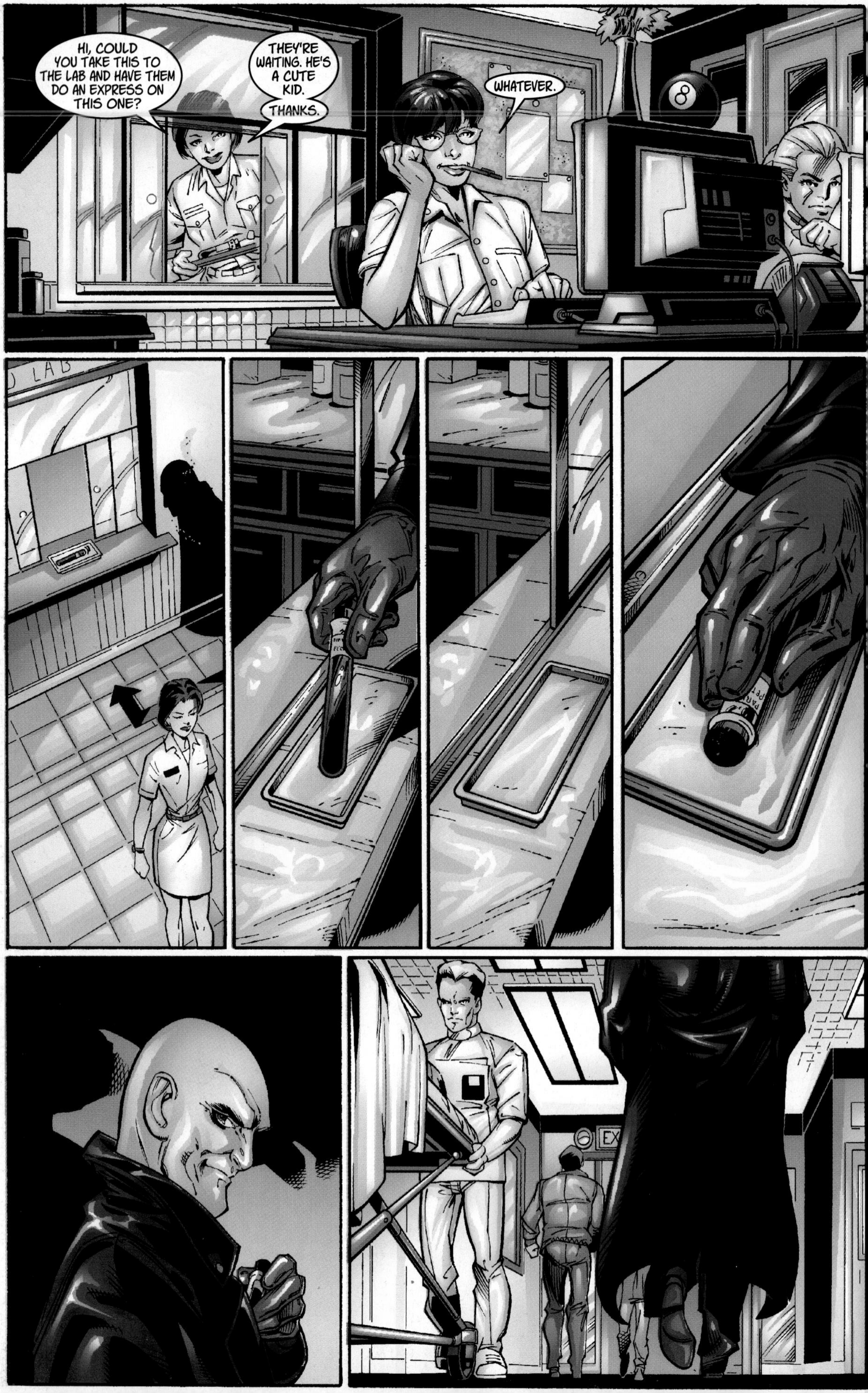
HI, COULD YOU TAKE THIS TO THE LAB AND HAVE THEM DO AN EXPRESS ON THIS ONE?
THEY'RE WAITING. HE'S A CUTE KID.
THANKS.
WHATEVER.
LAB

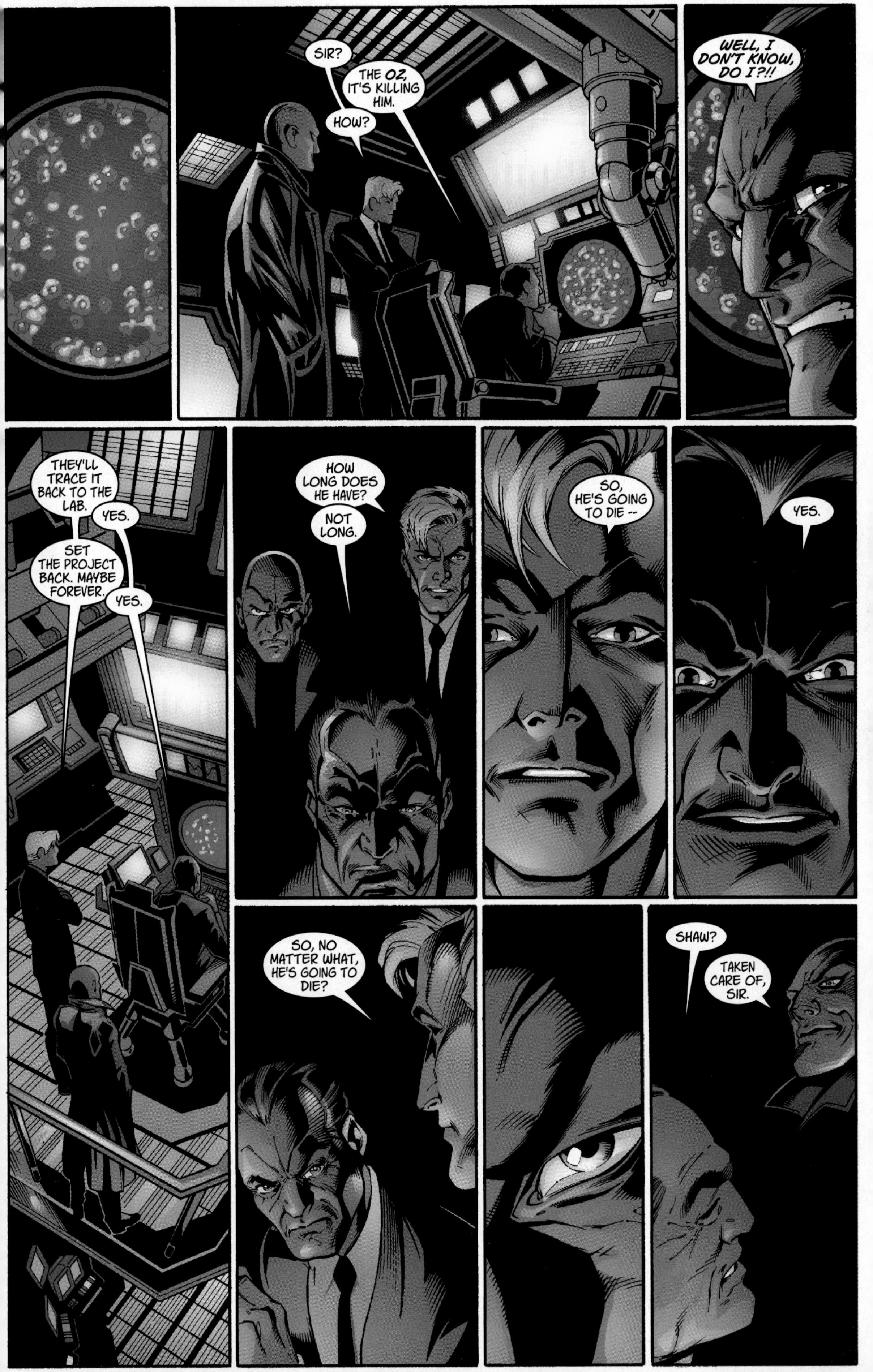
SIR?
THE OZ, IT'S KILLING HIM.
HOW?
WELL, I DON'T KNOW, DO I?!!
THEY'LL TRACE IT BACK TO THE LAB.
YES.
SET THE PROJECT BACK. MAYBE FOREVER.
YES.
HOW LONG DOES HE HAVE?
NOT LONG.
SO, HE'S GOING TO DIE --
YES.
SO, NO MATTER WHAT, HE'S GOING TO DIE?
SHAW?
TAKEN CARE OF, SIR.

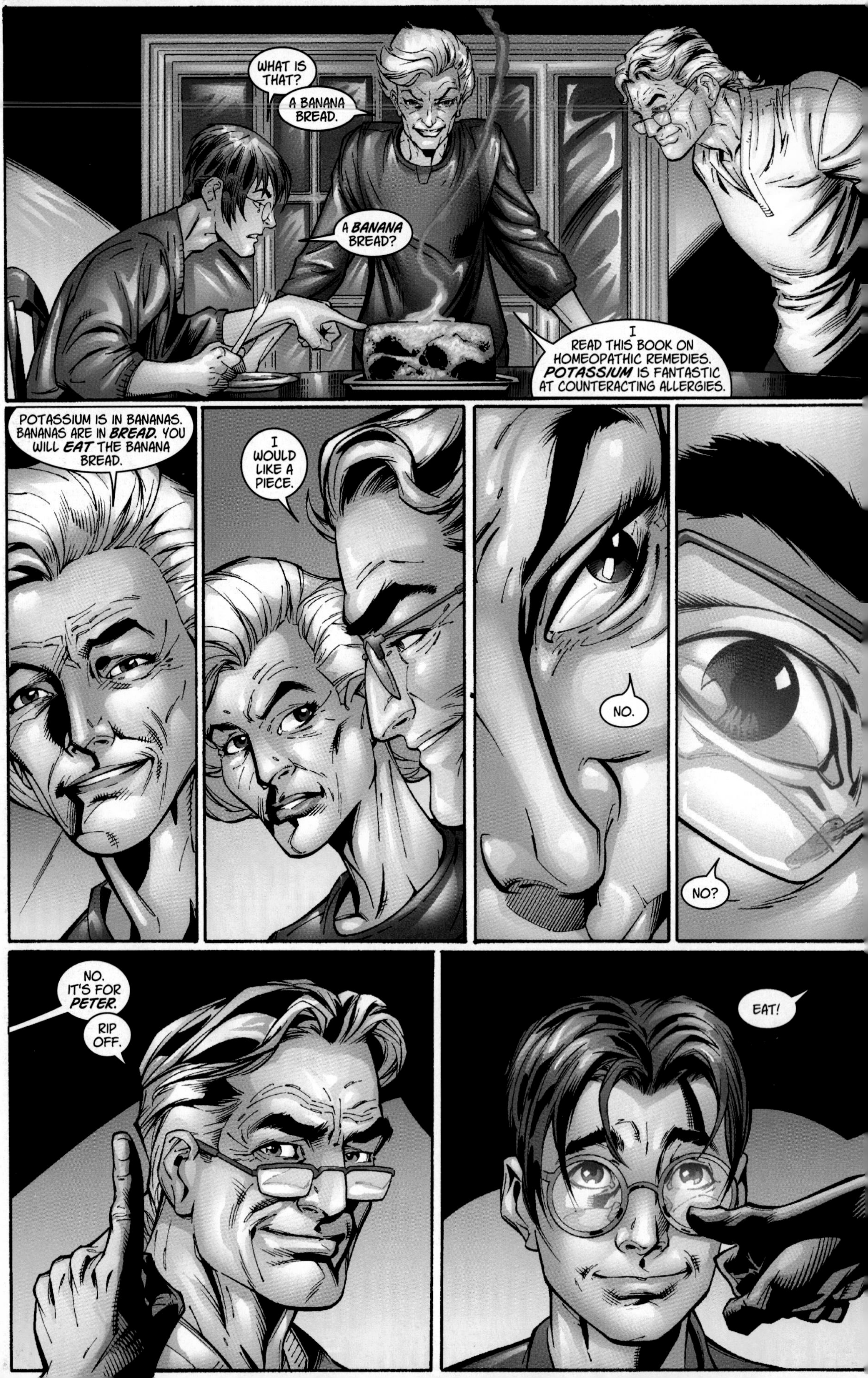
WHAT IS THAT?
A BANANA BREAD.
A *BANANA* BREAD?
I READ THIS BOOK ON HOMEOPATHIC REMEDIES. *POTASSIUM* IS FANTASTIC AT COUNTERACTING ALLERGIES.
POTASSIUM IS IN BANANAS. BANANAS ARE IN *BREAD*. YOU WILL *EAT* THE BANANA BREAD.
I WOULD LIKE A PIECE.
NO.
NO?
NO. IT'S FOR *PETER*.
RIP OFF.
EAT!

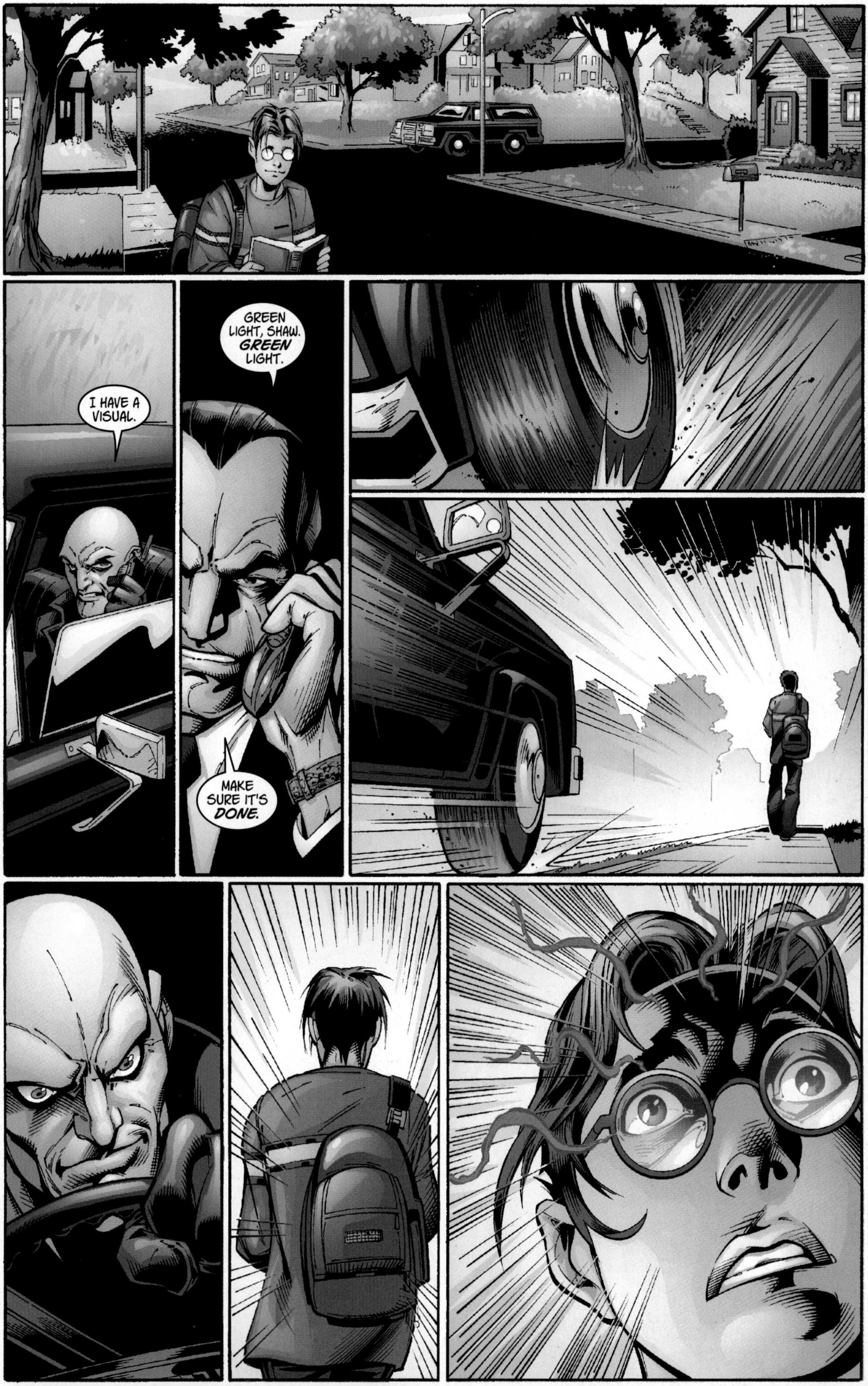
I HAVE A VISUAL.
GREEN LIGHT, SHAW. GREEN LIGHT.
MAKE SURE IT'S DONE.

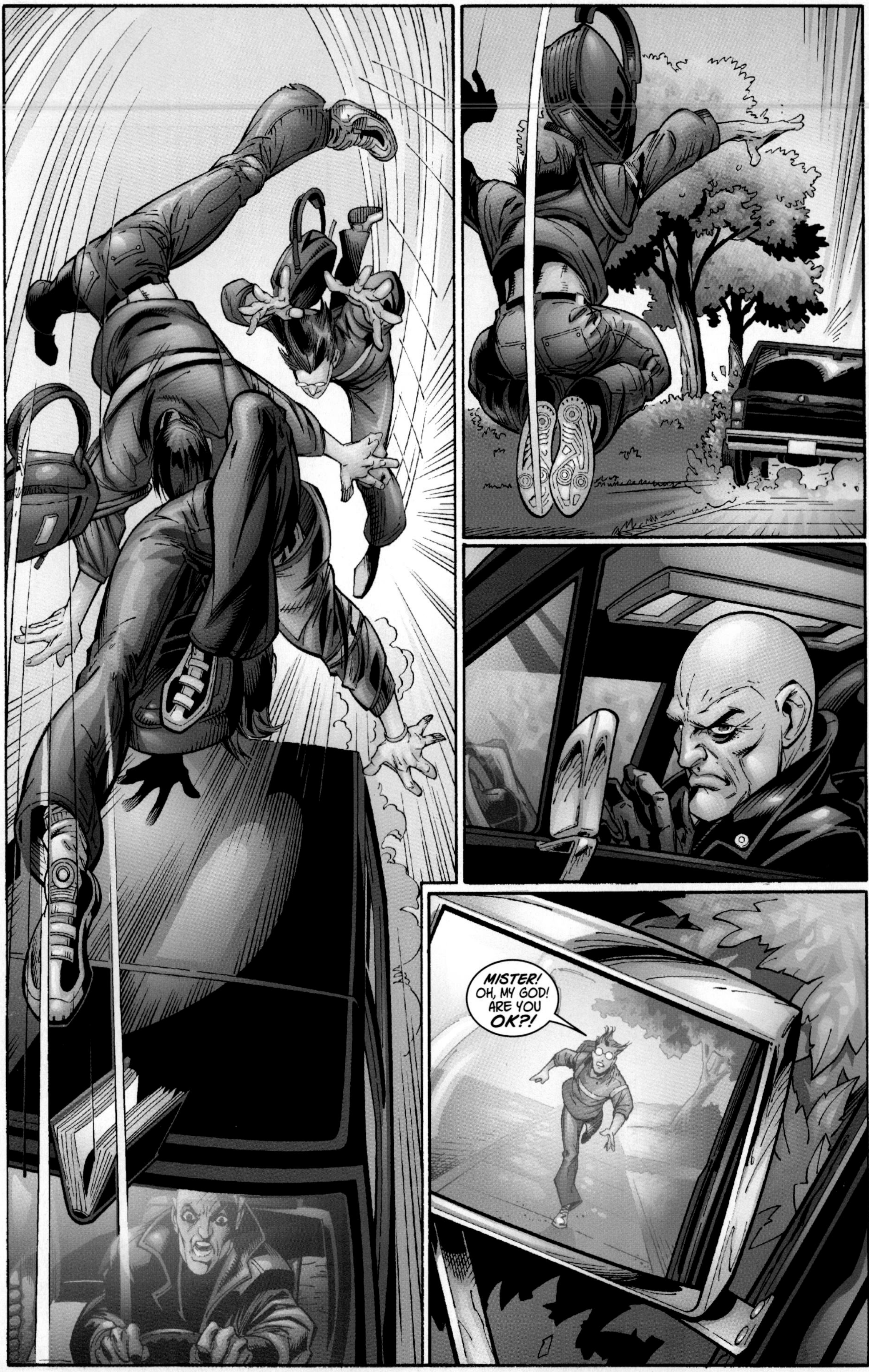
MISTER! OH, MY GOD! ARE YOU OK?!

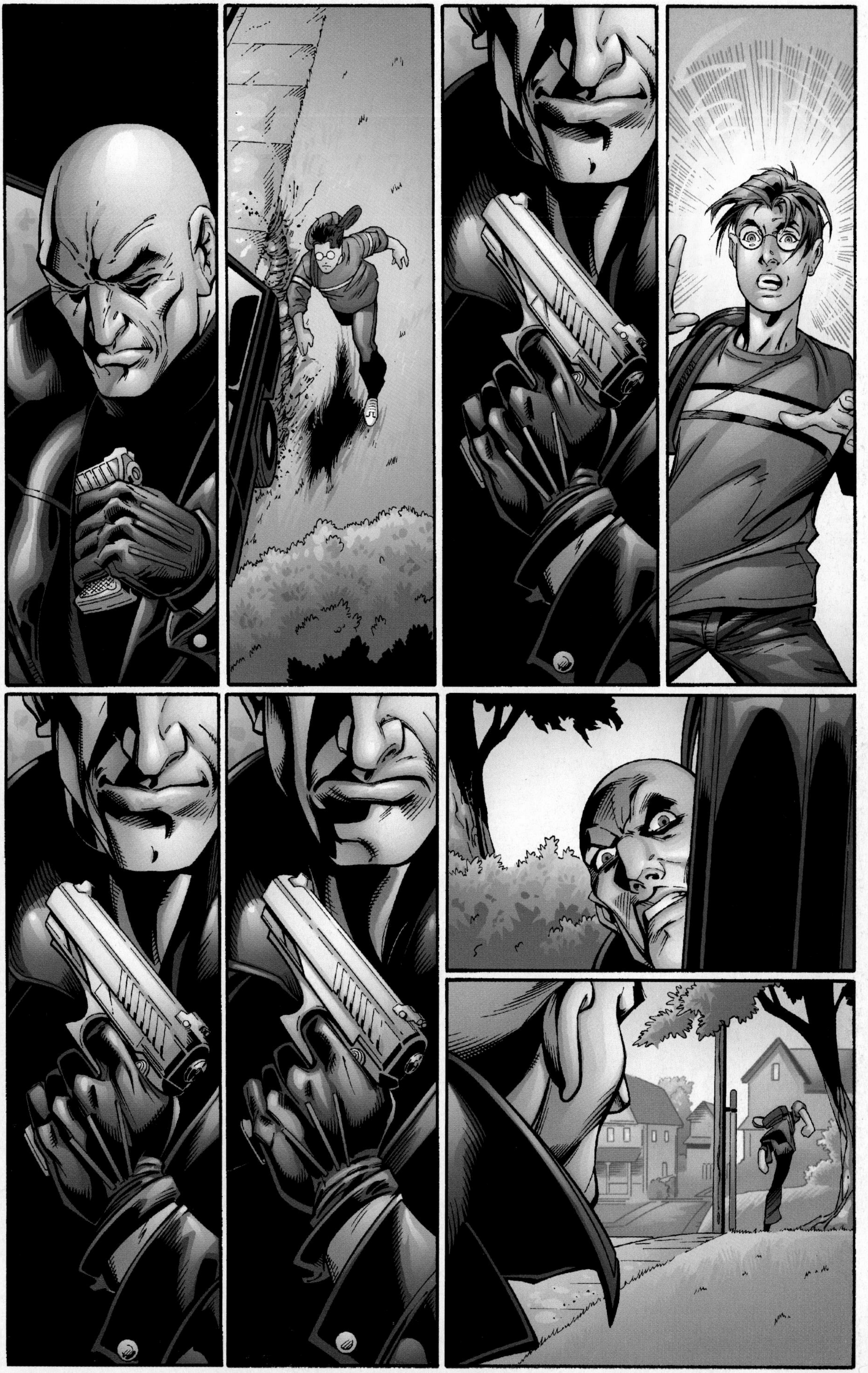

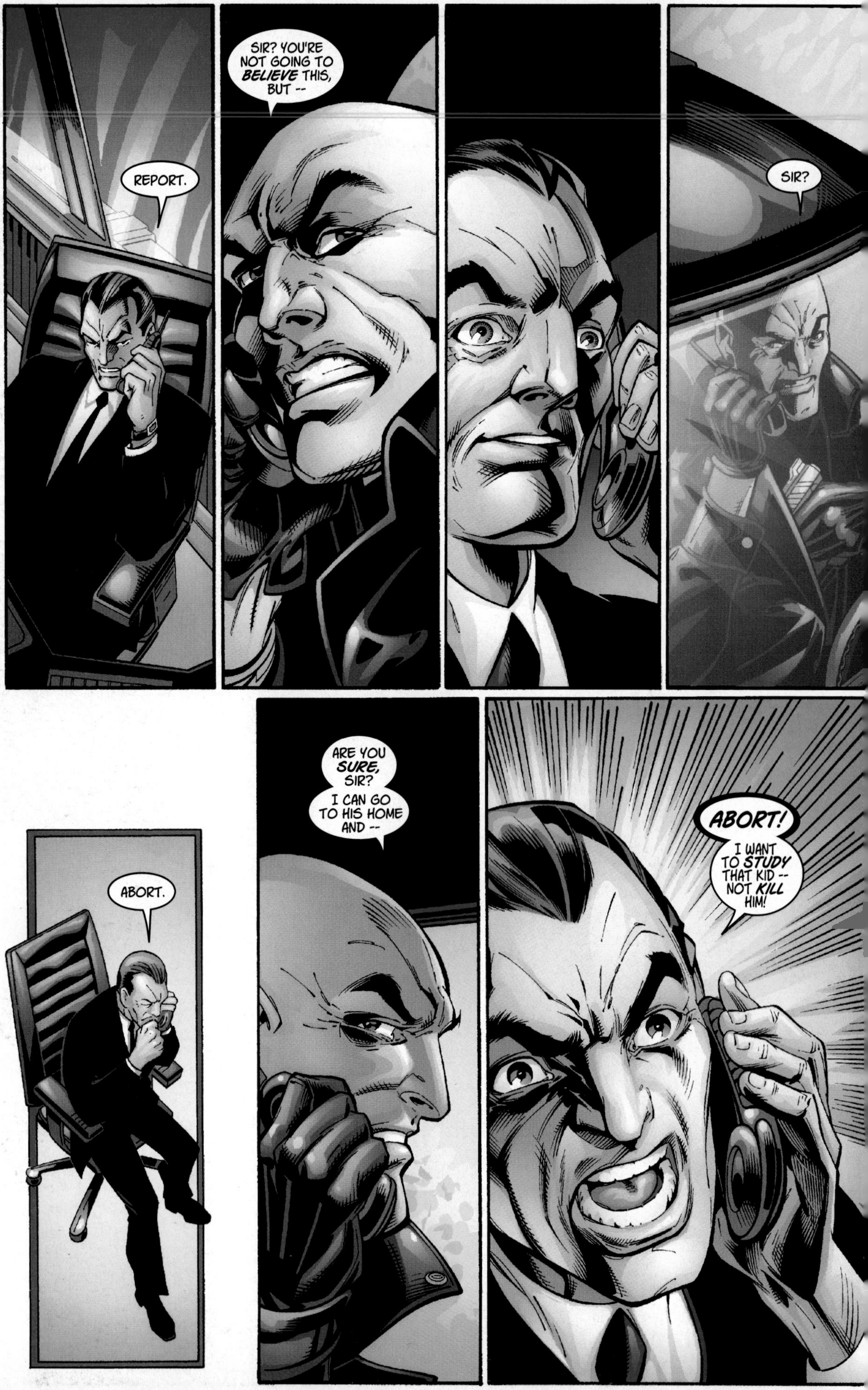
REPORT.
SIR? YOU'RE NOT GOING TO BELIEVE THIS, BUT --
SIR?
ABORT.
ARE YOU SURE, SIR?
I CAN GO TO HIS HOME AND --
ABORT!
I WANT TO STUDY THAT KID -- NOT KILL HIM!

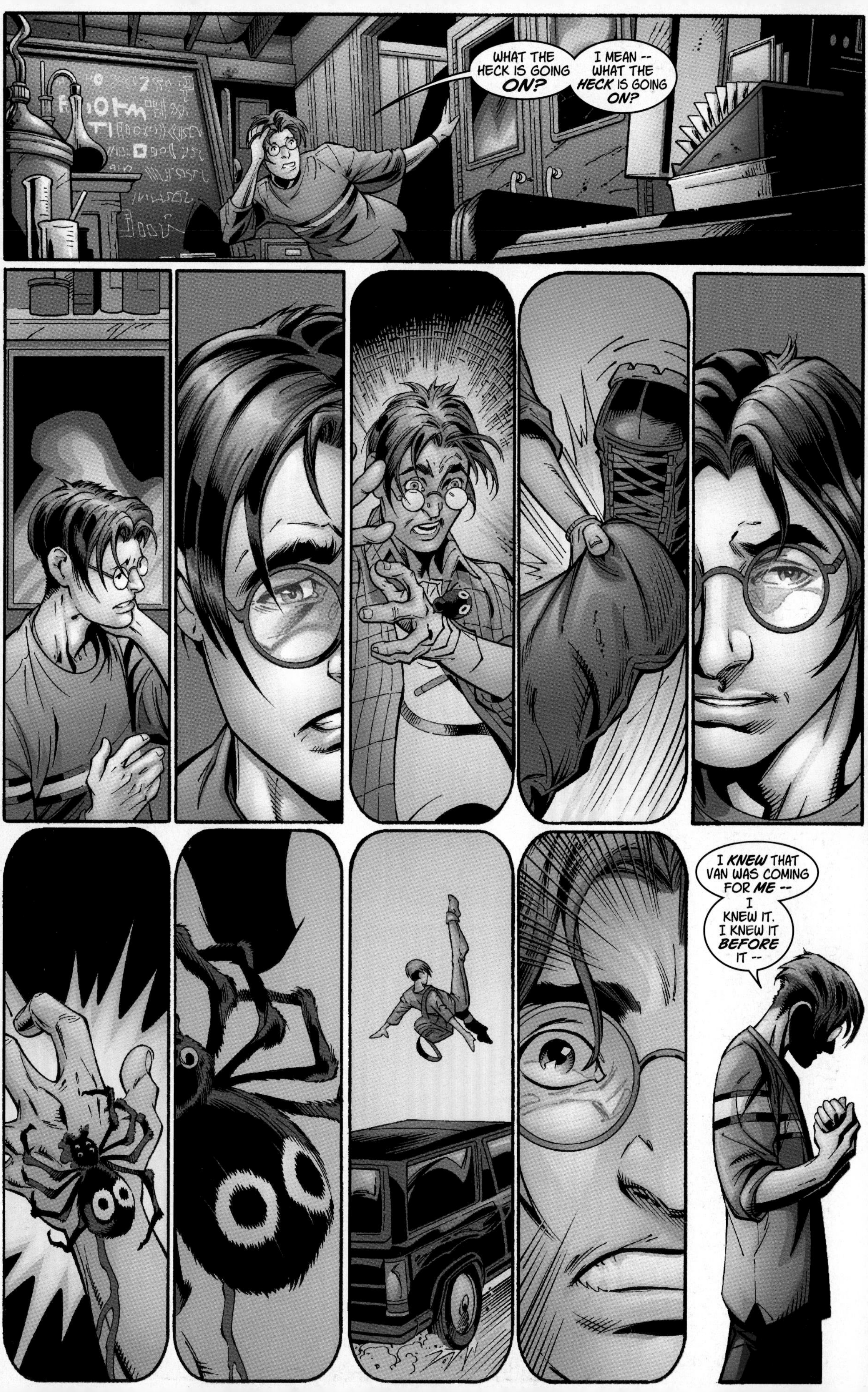
WHAT THE HECK IS GOING ON?
I MEAN -- WHAT THE HECK IS GOING ON?
I KNEW THAT VAN WAS COMING FOR ME --
I KNEW IT. I KNEW IT BEFORE IT --

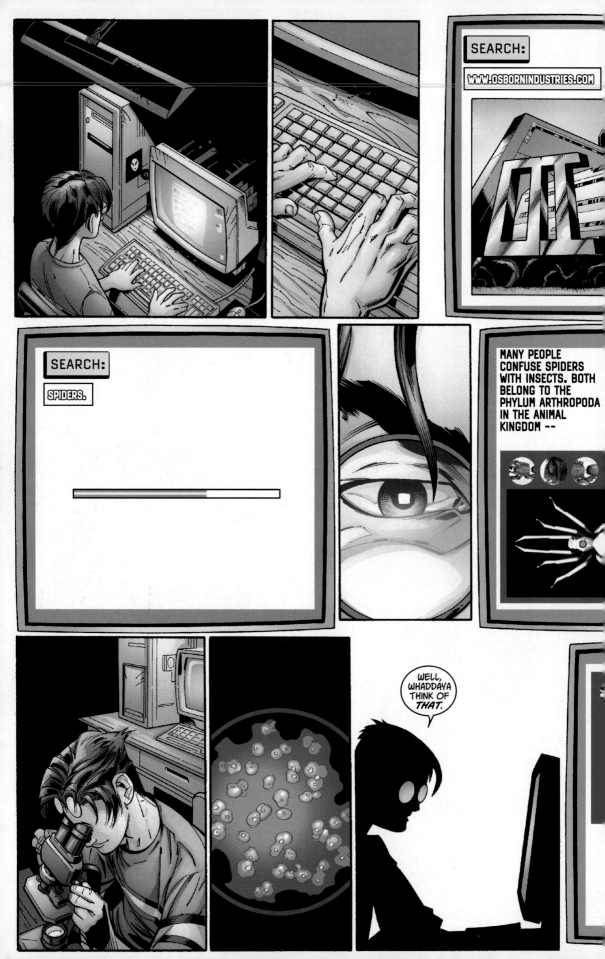

SEARCH:

WWW.OSBORNINDUSTRIES.COM

SEARCH:

SPIDERS.

MANY PEOPLE CONFUSE SPIDERS WITH INSECTS. BOTH BELONG TO THE PHYLUM ARTHROPODA IN THE ANIMAL KINGDOM --

WELL, WHADDAYA THINK OF *THAT.*

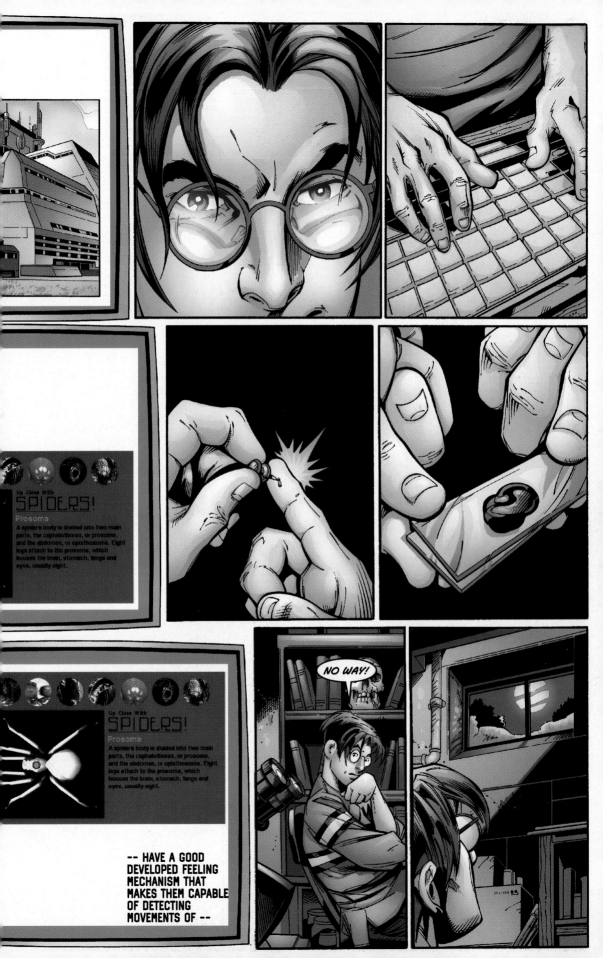

Up Close With
SPIDERS!
Prosoma
A spider's body is divided into two main parts, the cephalothorax, or prosoma, and the abdomen, or opisthosoma. Eight legs attach to the prosoma, which houses the brain, stomach, fangs and eyes, usually eight.

Up Close With
SPIDERS!
Prosoma
A spider's body is divided into two main parts, the cephalothorax, or prosoma, and the abdomen, or opisthosoma. Eight legs attach to the prosoma, which houses the brain, stomach, fangs and eyes, usually eight.

NO WAY!

-- HAVE A GOOD DEVELOPED FEELING MECHANISM THAT MAKES THEM CAPABLE OF DETECTING MOVEMENTS OF --

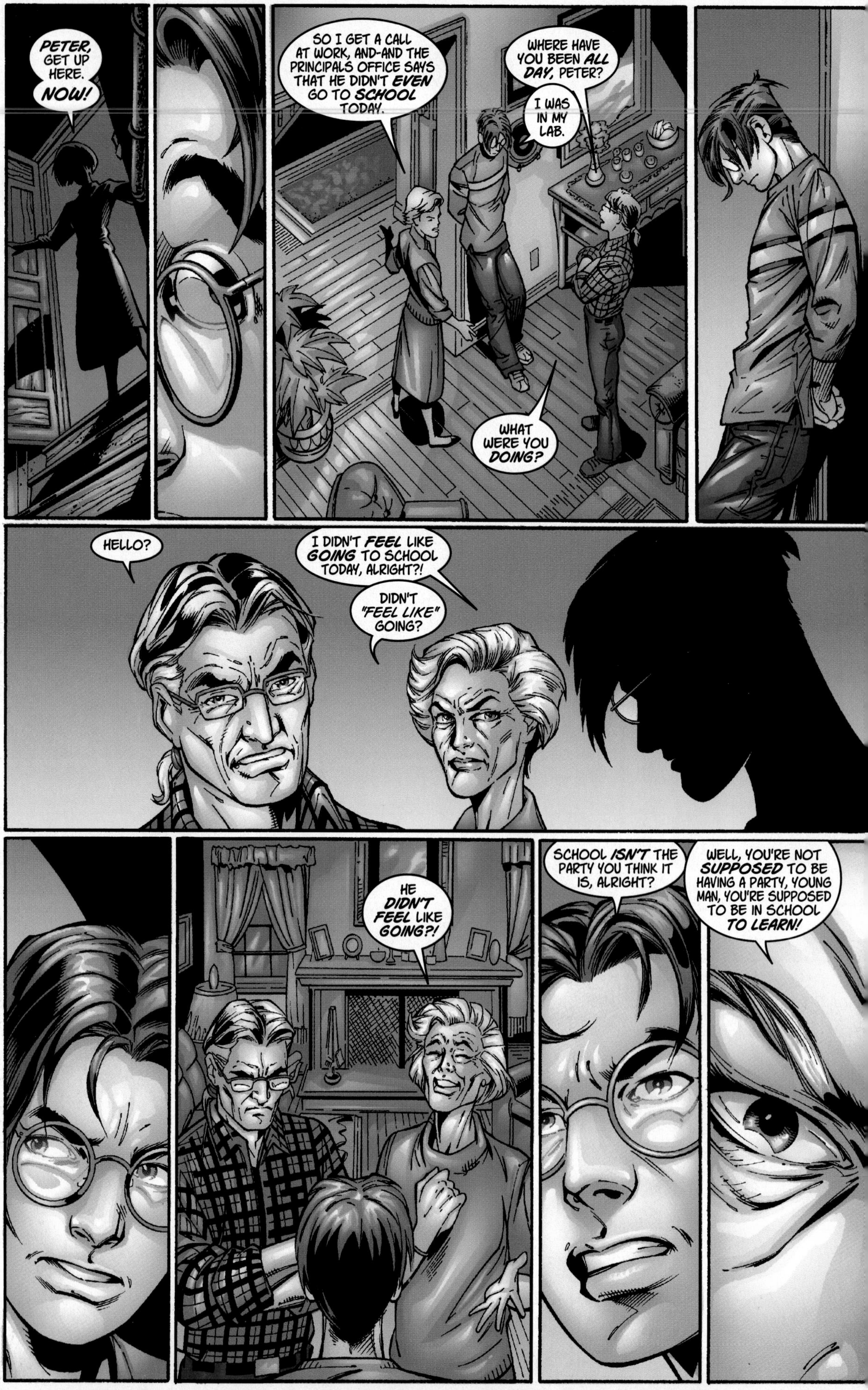
PETER, GET UP HERE. NOW!
SO I GET A CALL AT WORK, AND-AND THE PRINCIPALS OFFICE SAYS THAT HE DIDN'T EVEN GO TO SCHOOL TODAY.
WHERE HAVE YOU BEEN ALL DAY, PETER?
I WAS IN MY LAB.
WHAT WERE YOU DOING?
HELLO?
I DIDN'T FEEL LIKE GOING TO SCHOOL TODAY, ALRIGHT?!
DIDN'T "FEEL LIKE" GOING?
HE DIDN'T FEEL LIKE GOING?!
SCHOOL ISN'T THE PARTY YOU THINK IT IS, ALRIGHT?
WELL, YOU'RE NOT SUPPOSED TO BE HAVING A PARTY, YOUNG MAN, YOU'RE SUPPOSED TO BE IN SCHOOL TO LEARN!

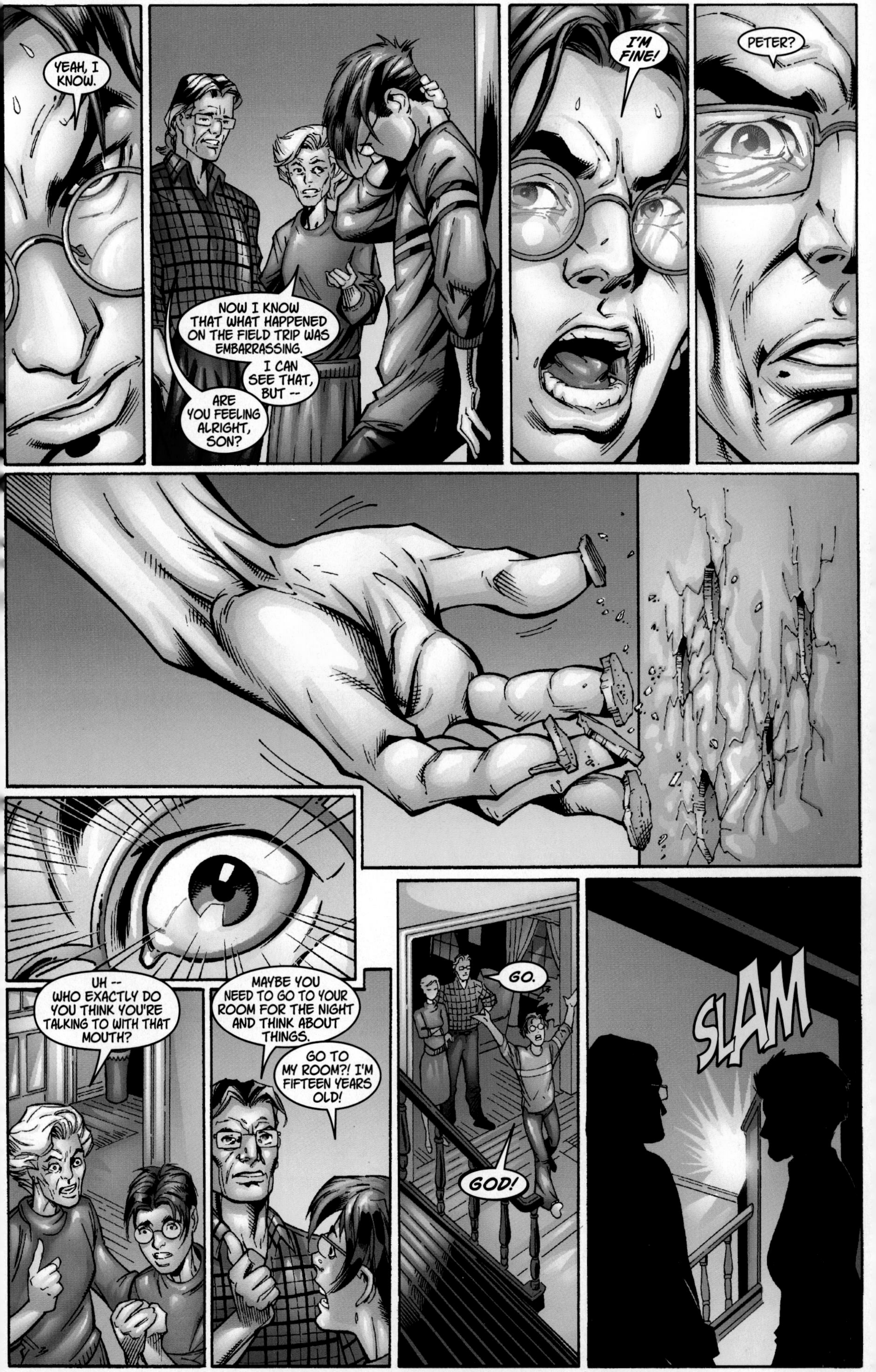
YEAH, I KNOW.
NOW I KNOW THAT WHAT HAPPENED ON THE FIELD TRIP WAS EMBARRASSING.
I CAN SEE THAT, BUT --
ARE YOU FEELING ALRIGHT, SON?
I'M FINE!
PETER?
UH -- WHO EXACTLY DO YOU THINK YOU'RE TALKING TO WITH THAT MOUTH?
MAYBE YOU NEED TO GO TO YOUR ROOM FOR THE NIGHT AND THINK ABOUT THINGS.
GO TO MY ROOM?! I'M FIFTEEN YEARS OLD!
GO.
GOD!
SLAM

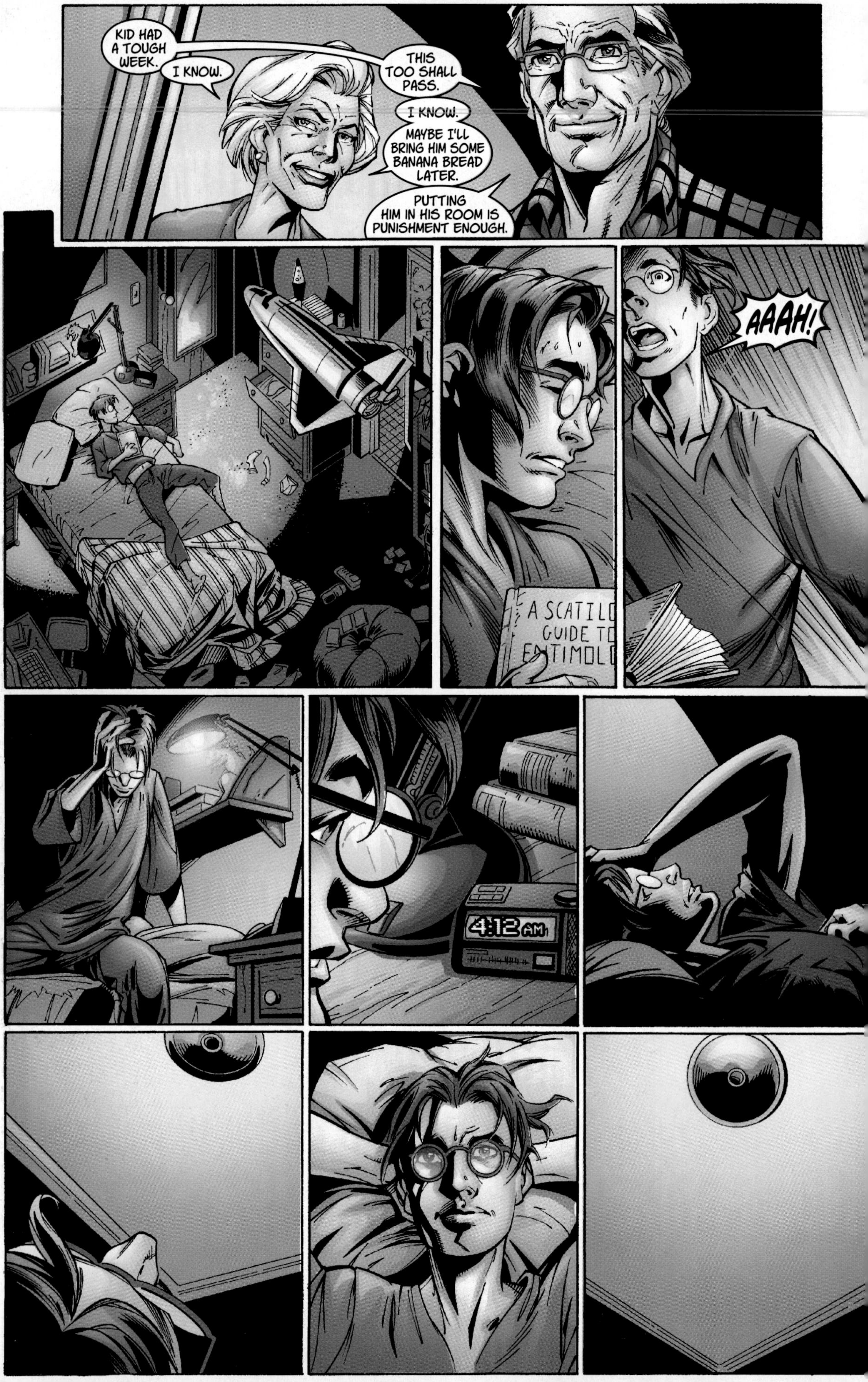

KID HAD A TOUGH WEEK.
I KNOW.
THIS TOO SHALL PASS.
I KNOW.
MAYBE I'LL BRING HIM SOME BANANA BREAD LATER.
PUTTING HIM IN HIS ROOM IS PUNISHMENT ENOUGH.
A SCATILO GUIDE TO ENTIMOLO
AAAH!
4:12 AM

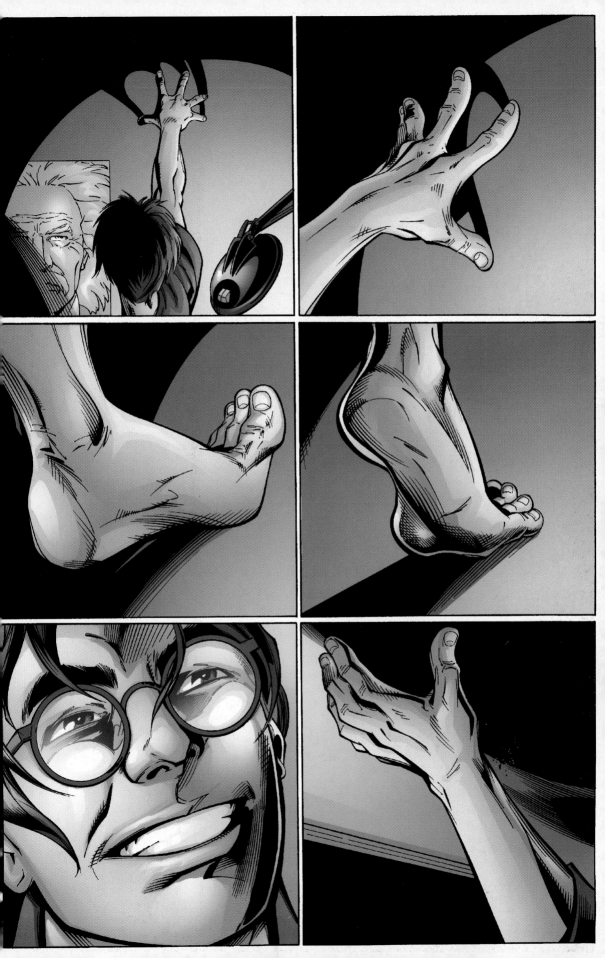

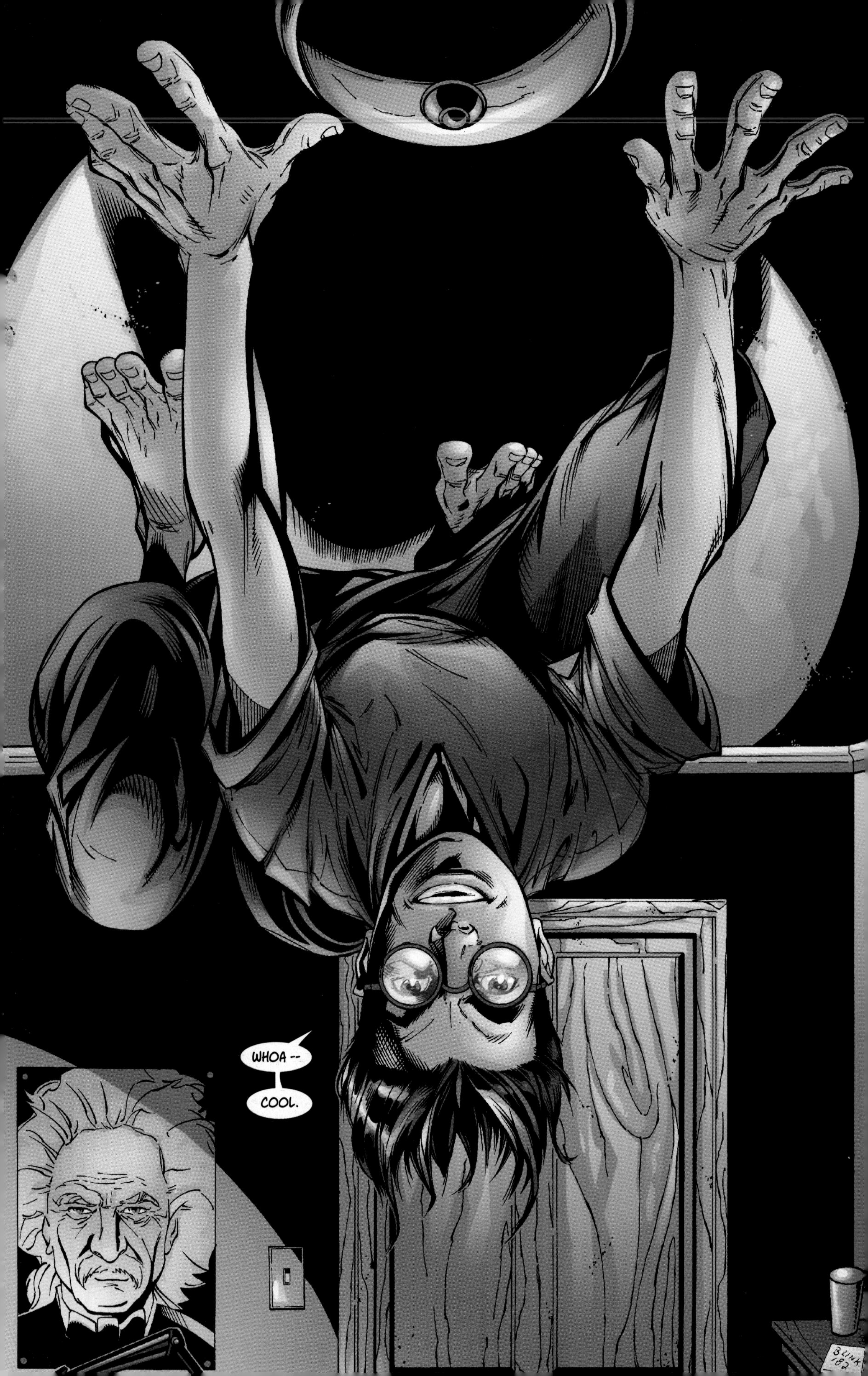
WHOA --
COOL.

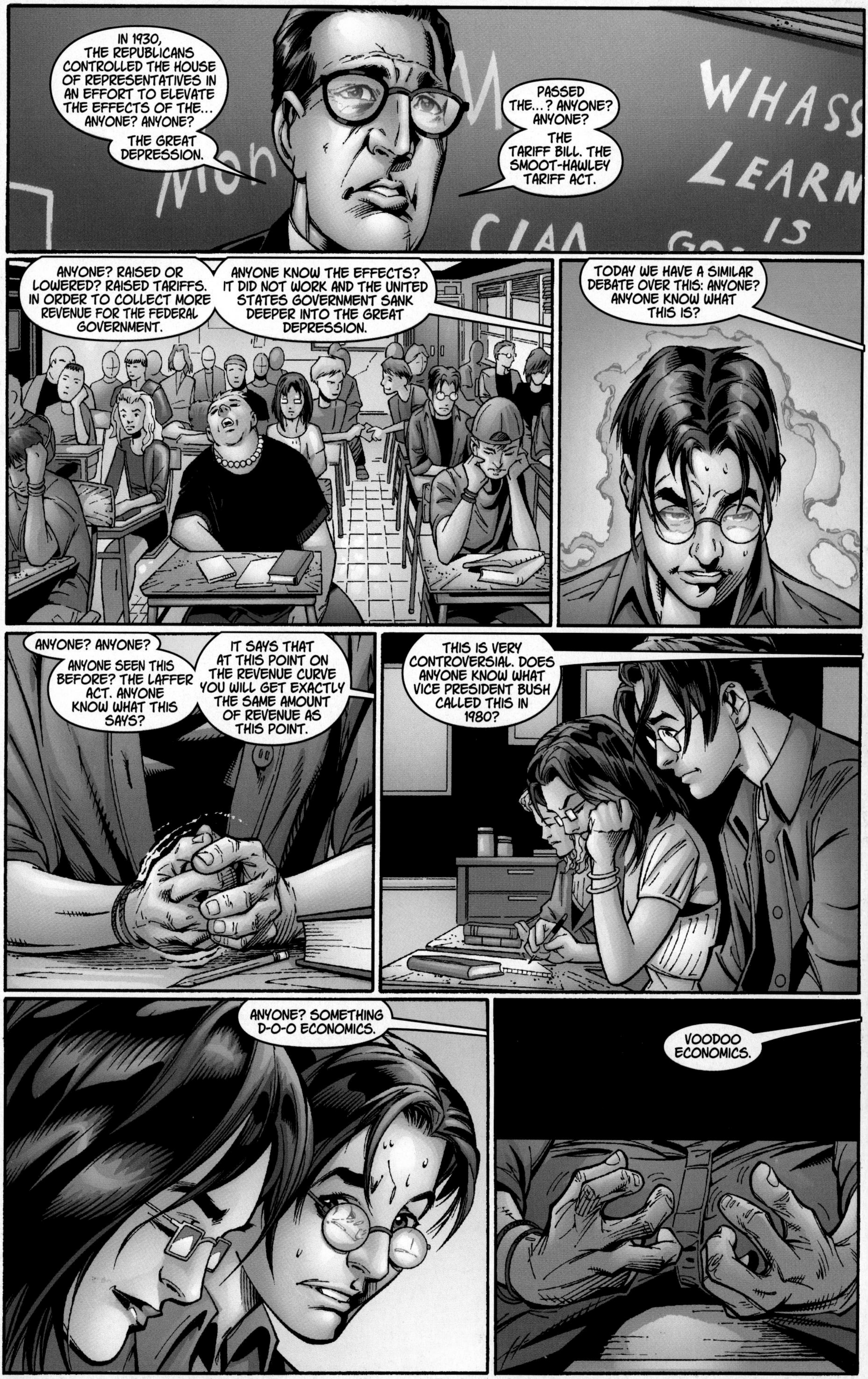
IN 1930, THE REPUBLICANS CONTROLLED THE HOUSE OF REPRESENTATIVES IN AN EFFORT TO ELEVATE THE EFFECTS OF THE... ANYONE? ANYONE?
THE GREAT DEPRESSION.
PASSED THE...? ANYONE? ANYONE?
THE TARIFF BILL. THE SMOOT-HAWLEY TARIFF ACT.
WHASS
LEARN
IS
ANYONE? RAISED OR LOWERED? RAISED TARIFFS. IN ORDER TO COLLECT MORE REVENUE FOR THE FEDERAL GOVERNMENT.
ANYONE KNOW THE EFFECTS? IT DID NOT WORK AND THE UNITED STATES GOVERNMENT SANK DEEPER INTO THE GREAT DEPRESSION.
TODAY WE HAVE A SIMILAR DEBATE OVER THIS: ANYONE? ANYONE KNOW WHAT THIS IS?
ANYONE? ANYONE?
ANYONE SEEN THIS BEFORE? THE LAFFER ACT. ANYONE KNOW WHAT THIS SAYS?
IT SAYS THAT AT THIS POINT ON THE REVENUE CURVE YOU WILL GET EXACTLY THE SAME AMOUNT OF REVENUE AS THIS POINT.
THIS IS VERY CONTROVERSIAL. DOES ANYONE KNOW WHAT VICE PRESIDENT BUSH CALLED THIS IN 1980?
ANYONE? SOMETHING D-O-O ECONOMICS.
VOODOO ECONOMICS.

CHAPTER 2

GROWING PAINS

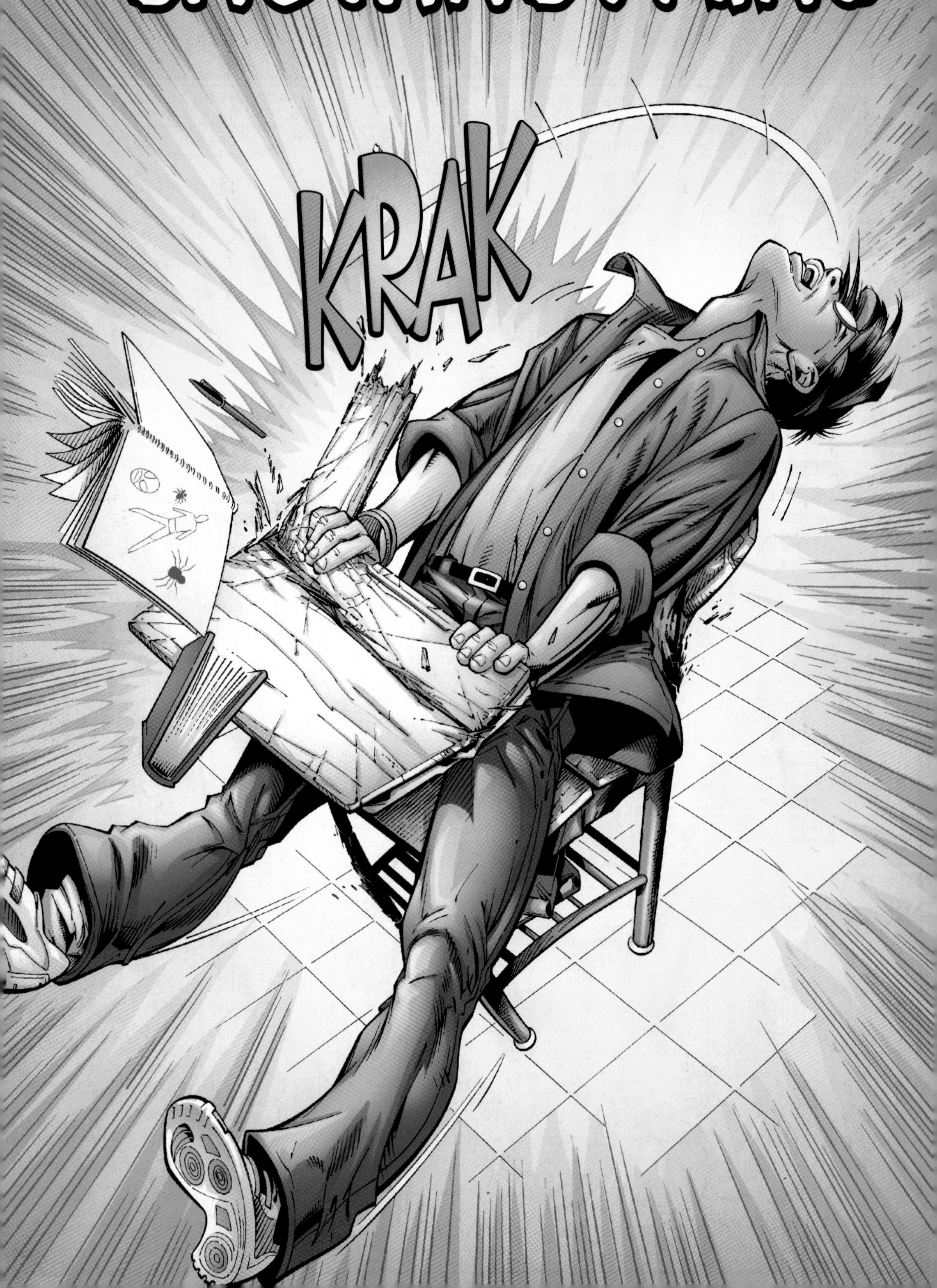

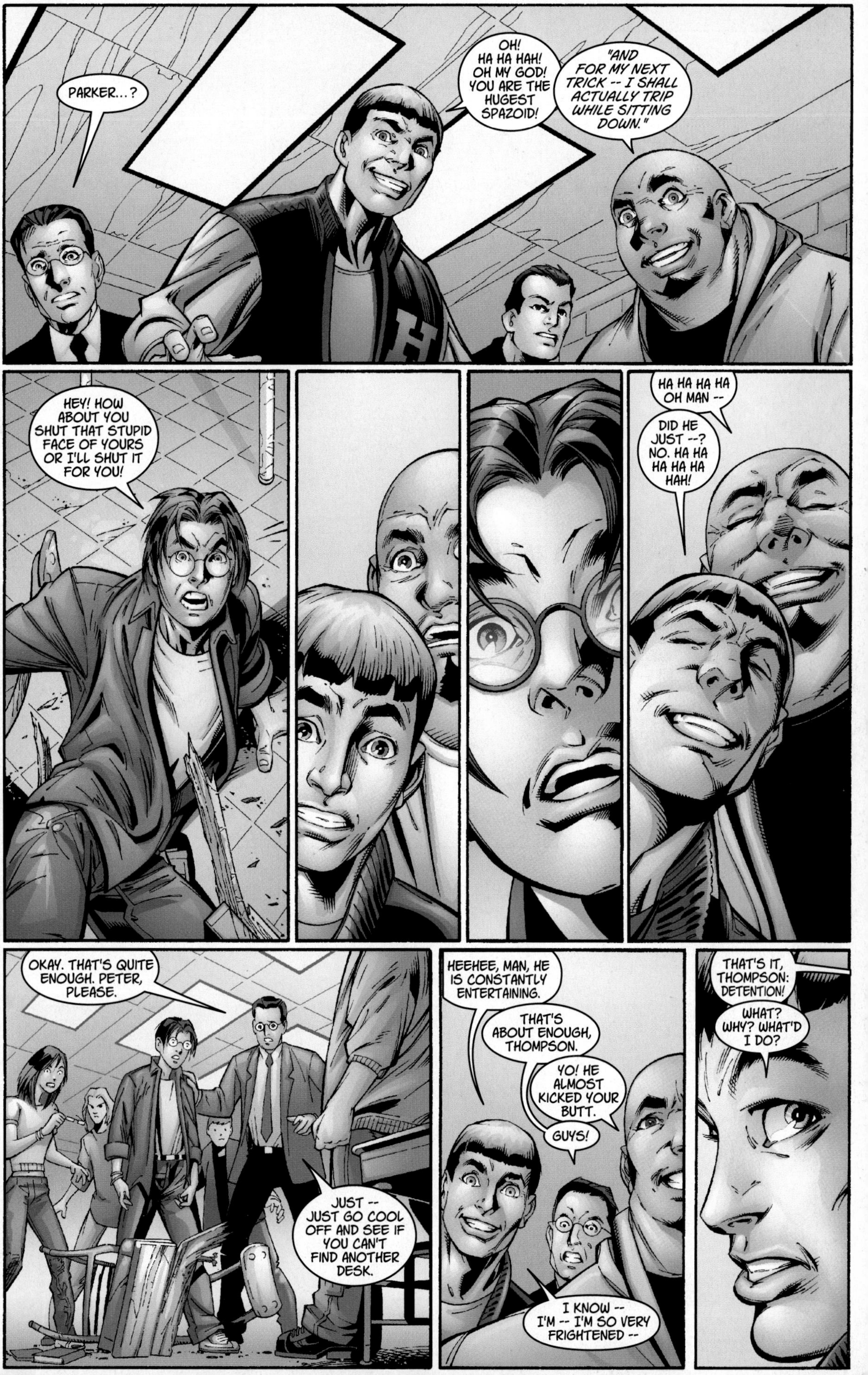
PARKER...?
OH! HA HA HAH! OH MY GOD! YOU ARE THE HUGEST SPAZOID!
"AND FOR MY NEXT TRICK -- I SHALL ACTUALLY TRIP WHILE SITTING DOWN."
HEY! HOW ABOUT YOU SHUT THAT STUPID FACE OF YOURS OR I'LL SHUT IT FOR YOU!
HA HA HA HA OH MAN --
DID HE JUST --? NO. HA HA HA HA HA HAH!
OKAY. THAT'S QUITE ENOUGH. PETER, PLEASE.
JUST -- JUST GO COOL OFF AND SEE IF YOU CAN'T FIND ANOTHER DESK.
HEEHEE, MAN, HE IS CONSTANTLY ENTERTAINING.
THAT'S ABOUT ENOUGH, THOMPSON.
YO! HE ALMOST KICKED YOUR BUTT.
GUYS!
I KNOW -- I'M -- I'M SO VERY FRIGHTENED --
THAT'S IT, THOMPSON: DETENTION!
WHAT? WHY? WHAT'D I DO?

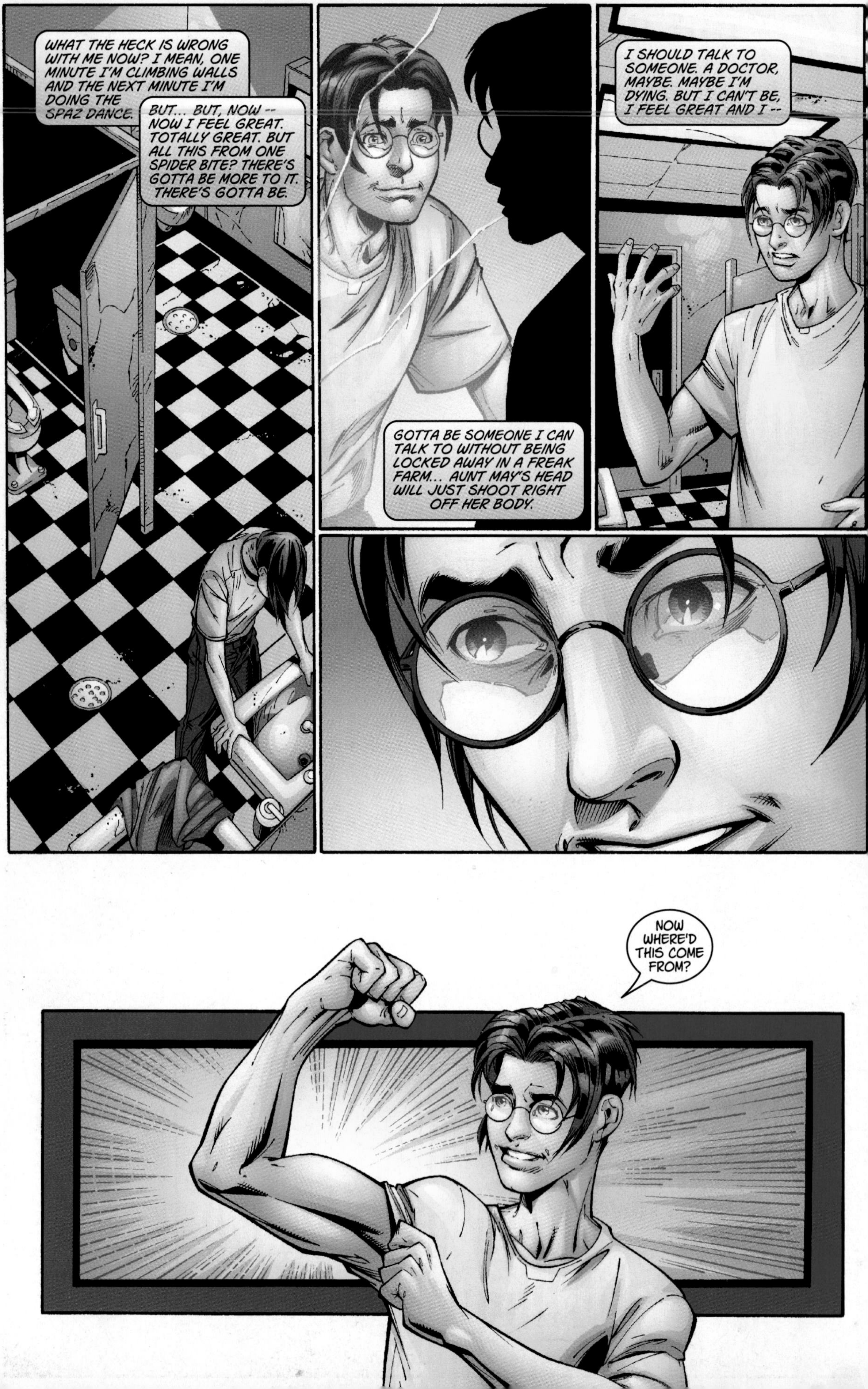
WHAT THE HECK IS WRONG WITH ME NOW? I MEAN, ONE MINUTE I'M CLIMBING WALLS AND THE NEXT MINUTE I'M DOING THE SPAZ DANCE.
BUT... BUT, NOW -- NOW I FEEL GREAT. TOTALLY GREAT. BUT ALL THIS FROM ONE SPIDER BITE? THERE'S GOTTA BE MORE TO IT. THERE'S GOTTA BE.
GOTTA BE SOMEONE I CAN TALK TO WITHOUT BEING LOCKED AWAY IN A FREAK FARM... AUNT MAY'S HEAD WILL JUST SHOOT RIGHT OFF HER BODY.
I SHOULD TALK TO SOMEONE. A DOCTOR, MAYBE. MAYBE I'M DYING. BUT I CAN'T BE, I FEEL GREAT AND I --
NOW WHERE'D THIS COME FROM?

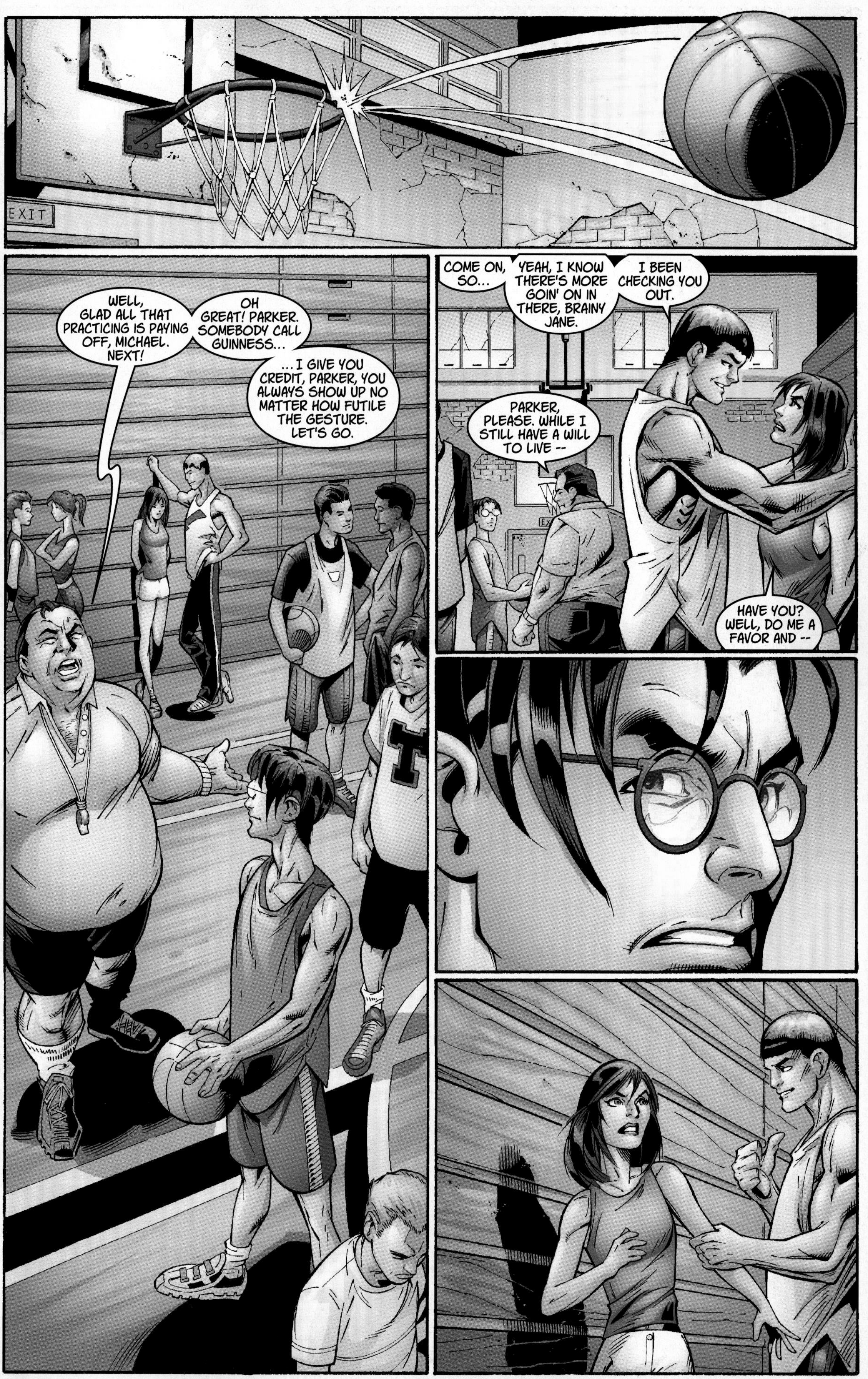
EXIT
WELL, GLAD ALL THAT PRACTICING IS PAYING OFF, MICHAEL. NEXT!
OH GREAT! PARKER. SOMEBODY CALL GUINNESS...
...I GIVE YOU CREDIT, PARKER, YOU ALWAYS SHOW UP NO MATTER HOW FUTILE THE GESTURE. LET'S GO.
COME ON, SO...
YEAH, I KNOW THERE'S MORE GOIN' ON IN THERE, BRAINY JANE.
I BEEN CHECKING YOU OUT.
PARKER, PLEASE. WHILE I STILL HAVE A WILL TO LIVE --
HAVE YOU? WELL, DO ME A FAVOR AND --

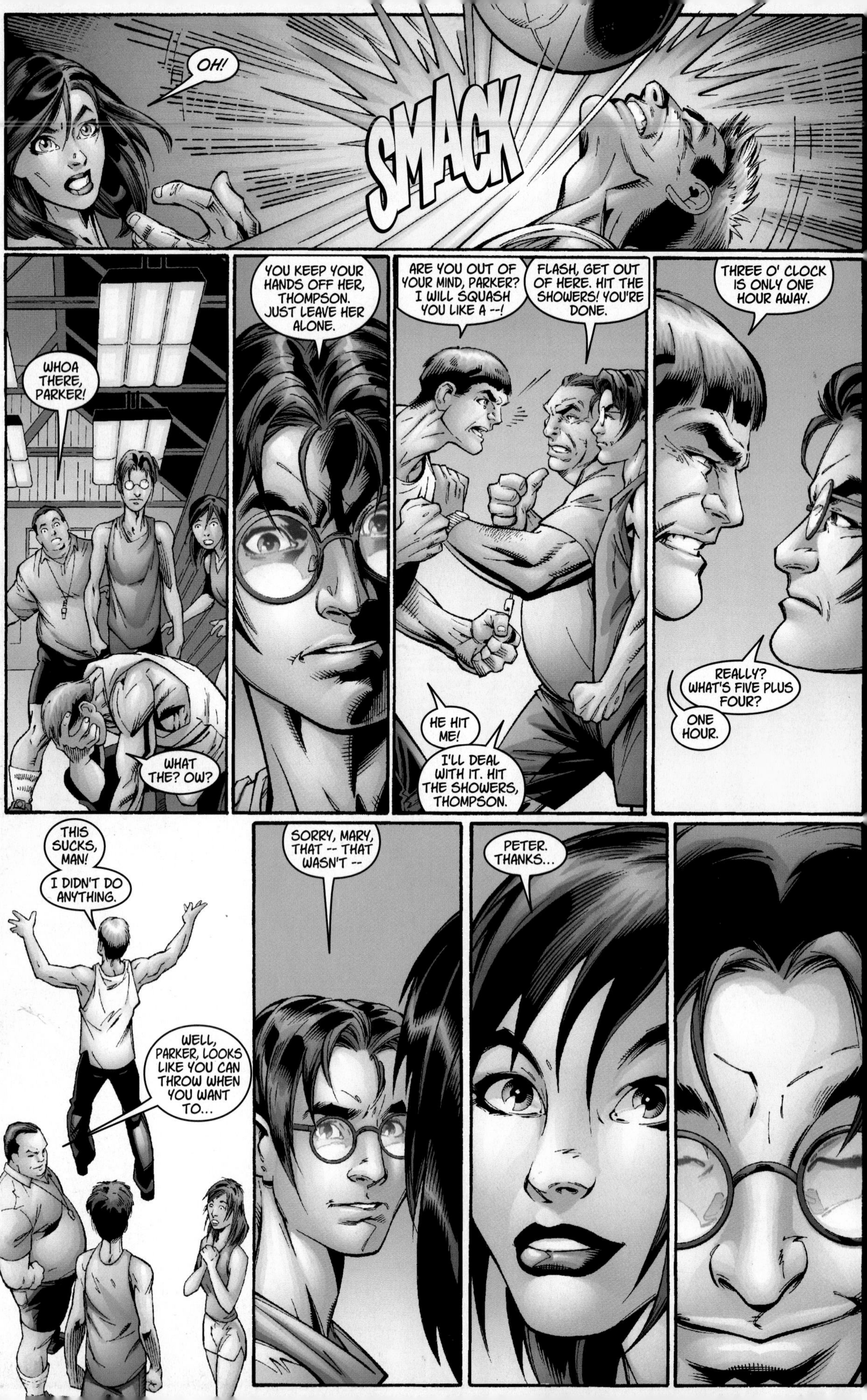
OH!
SMACK
WHOA THERE, PARKER!
WHAT THE? OW?
YOU KEEP YOUR HANDS OFF HER, THOMPSON. JUST LEAVE HER ALONE.
ARE YOU OUT OF YOUR MIND, PARKER? I WILL SQUASH YOU LIKE A --!
FLASH, GET OUT OF HERE. HIT THE SHOWERS! YOU'RE DONE.
HE HIT ME!
I'LL DEAL WITH IT. HIT THE SHOWERS, THOMPSON.
THREE O' CLOCK IS ONLY ONE HOUR AWAY.
REALLY? WHAT'S FIVE PLUS FOUR?
ONE HOUR.
THIS SUCKS, MAN!
I DIDN'T DO ANYTHING.
WELL, PARKER, LOOKS LIKE YOU CAN THROW WHEN YOU WANT TO...
SORRY, MARY, THAT -- THAT WASN'T --
PETER. THANKS...

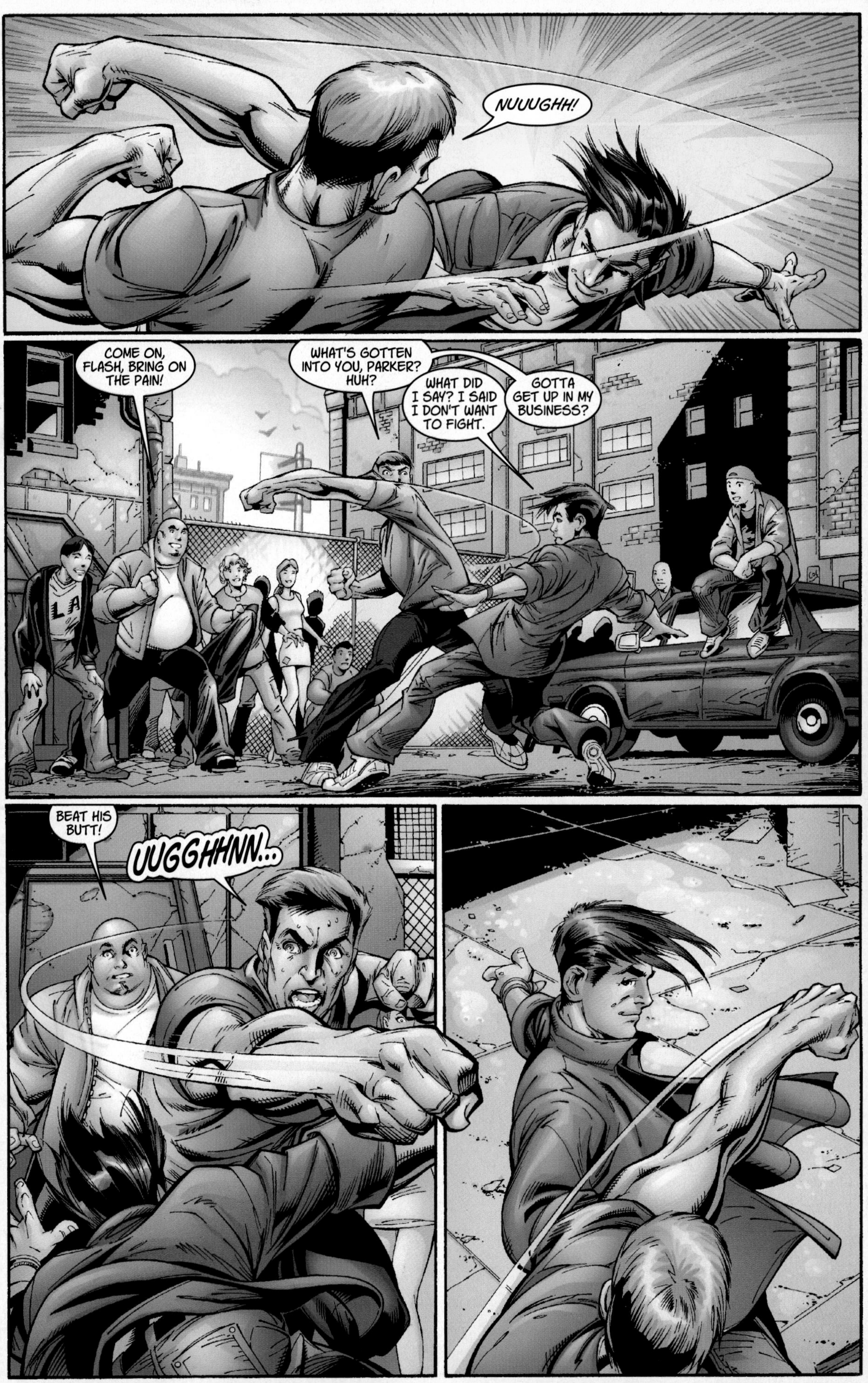
NUUUGHH!
COME ON, FLASH, BRING ON THE PAIN!
WHAT'S GOTTEN INTO YOU, PARKER? HUH?
GOTTA GET UP IN MY BUSINESS?
WHAT DID I SAY? I SAID I DON'T WANT TO FIGHT.
BEAT HIS BUTT!
UUGGHHNN...

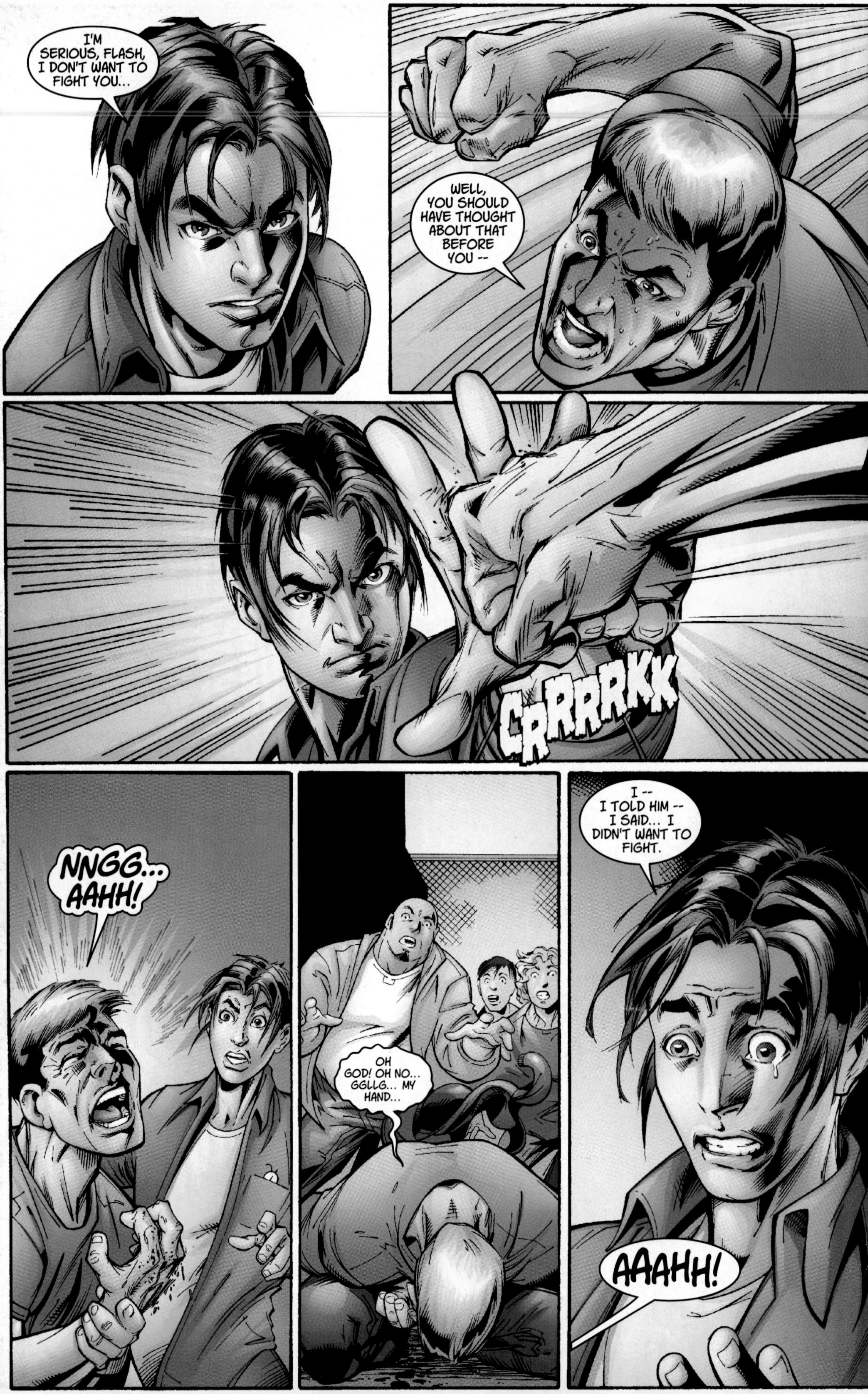
I'M SERIOUS, FLASH, I DON'T WANT TO FIGHT YOU...
WELL, YOU SHOULD HAVE THOUGHT ABOUT THAT BEFORE YOU --
CRRRRKK
NNGG... AAHH!
OH GOD! OH NO... GGLLG... MY HAND...
I -- I TOLD HIM -- I SAID... I DIDN'T WANT TO FIGHT.
AAAHH!

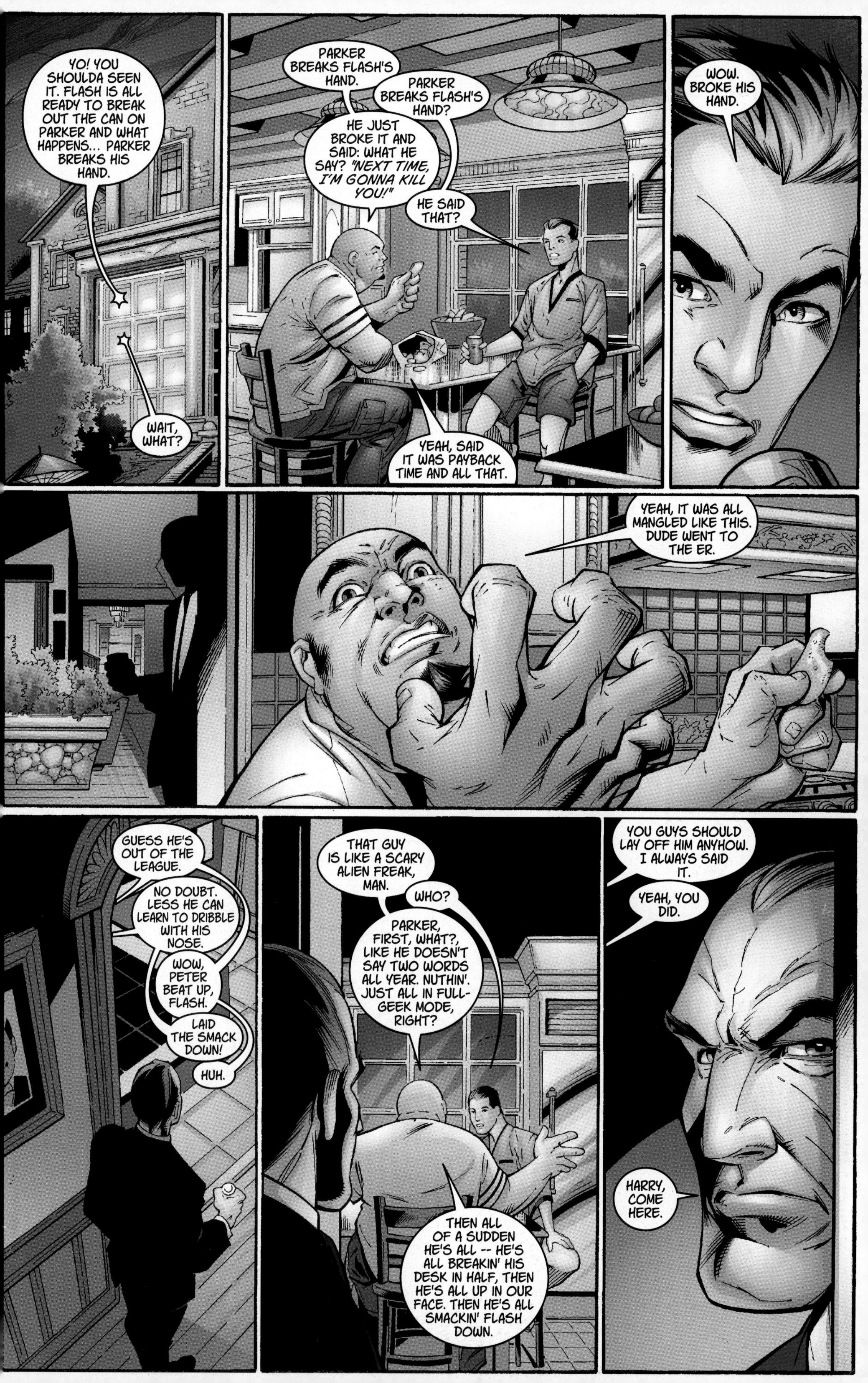
YO! YOU SHOULDA SEEN IT. FLASH IS ALL READY TO BREAK OUT THE CAN ON PARKER AND WHAT HAPPENS... PARKER BREAKS HIS HAND.
WAIT, WHAT?
PARKER BREAKS FLASH'S HAND.
PARKER BREAKS FLASH'S HAND?
HE JUST BROKE IT AND SAID: WHAT HE SAY? "NEXT TIME, I'M GONNA KILL YOU!"
HE SAID THAT?
YEAH, SAID IT WAS PAYBACK TIME AND ALL THAT.
WOW. BROKE HIS HAND.
YEAH, IT WAS ALL MANGLED LIKE THIS. DUDE WENT TO THE ER.
GUESS HE'S OUT OF THE LEAGUE.
NO DOUBT. LESS HE CAN LEARN TO DRIBBLE WITH HIS NOSE.
WOW, PETER BEAT UP, FLASH.
LAID THE SMACK DOWN!
HUH.
THAT GUY IS LIKE A SCARY ALIEN FREAK, MAN.
WHO?
PARKER, FIRST, WHAT?, LIKE HE DOESN'T SAY TWO WORDS ALL YEAR. NUTHIN'. JUST ALL IN FULL-GEEK MODE, RIGHT?
THEN ALL OF A SUDDEN HE'S ALL -- HE'S ALL BREAKIN' HIS DESK IN HALF, THEN HE'S ALL UP IN OUR FACE. THEN HE'S ALL SMACKIN' FLASH DOWN.
YOU GUYS SHOULD LAY OFF HIM ANYHOW. I ALWAYS SAID IT.
YEAH, YOU DID.
HARRY, COME HERE.

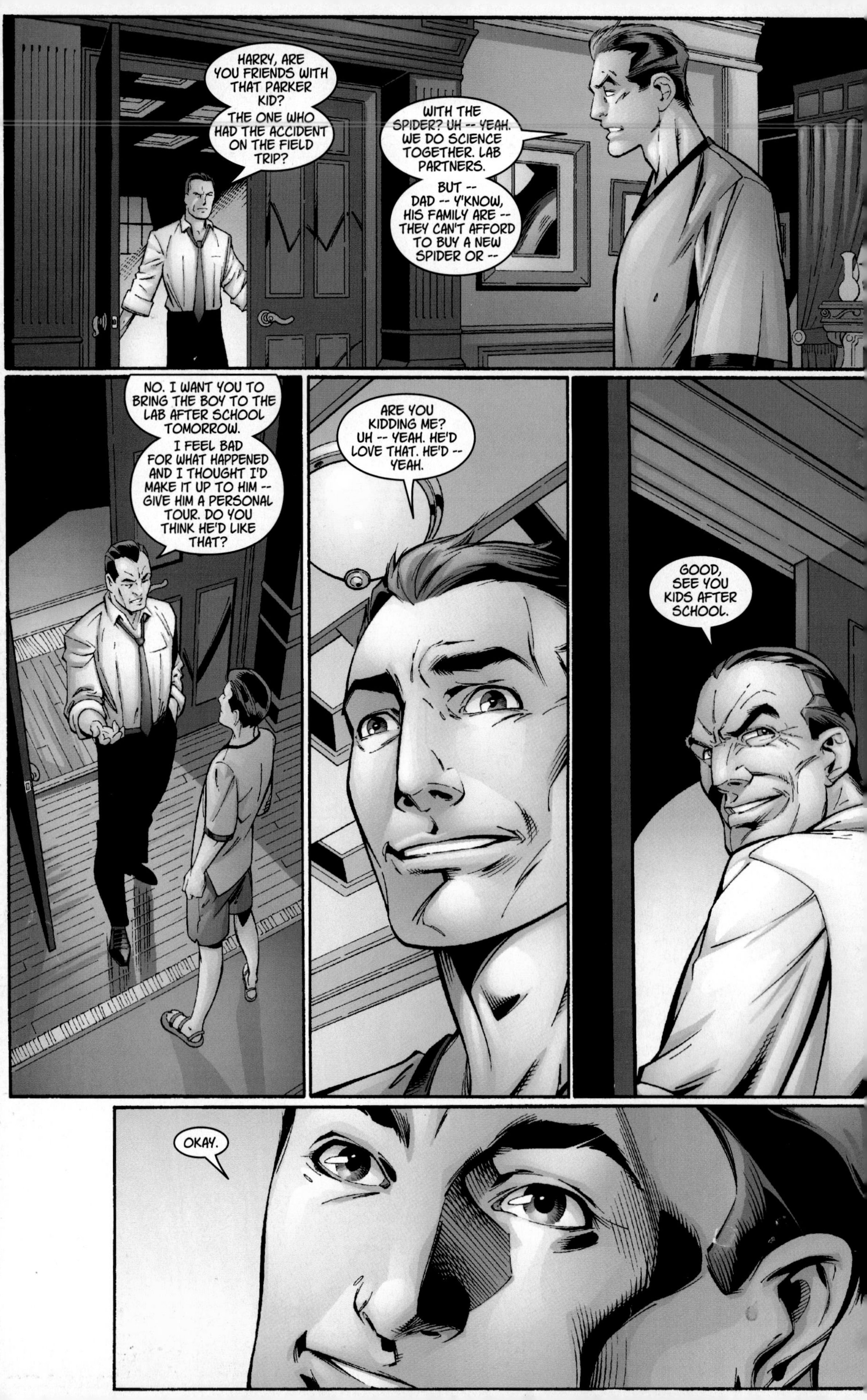

HARRY, ARE YOU FRIENDS WITH THAT PARKER KID?
THE ONE WHO HAD THE ACCIDENT ON THE FIELD TRIP?
WITH THE SPIDER? UH -- YEAH. WE DO SCIENCE TOGETHER. LAB PARTNERS.
BUT -- DAD -- Y'KNOW, HIS FAMILY ARE -- THEY CAN'T AFFORD TO BUY A NEW SPIDER OR --
NO. I WANT YOU TO BRING THE BOY TO THE LAB AFTER SCHOOL TOMORROW.
I FEEL BAD FOR WHAT HAPPENED AND I THOUGHT I'D MAKE IT UP TO HIM -- GIVE HIM A PERSONAL TOUR. DO YOU THINK HE'D LIKE THAT?
ARE YOU KIDDING ME? UH -- YEAH. HE'D LOVE THAT. HE'D -- YEAH.
GOOD, SEE YOU KIDS AFTER SCHOOL.
OKAY.

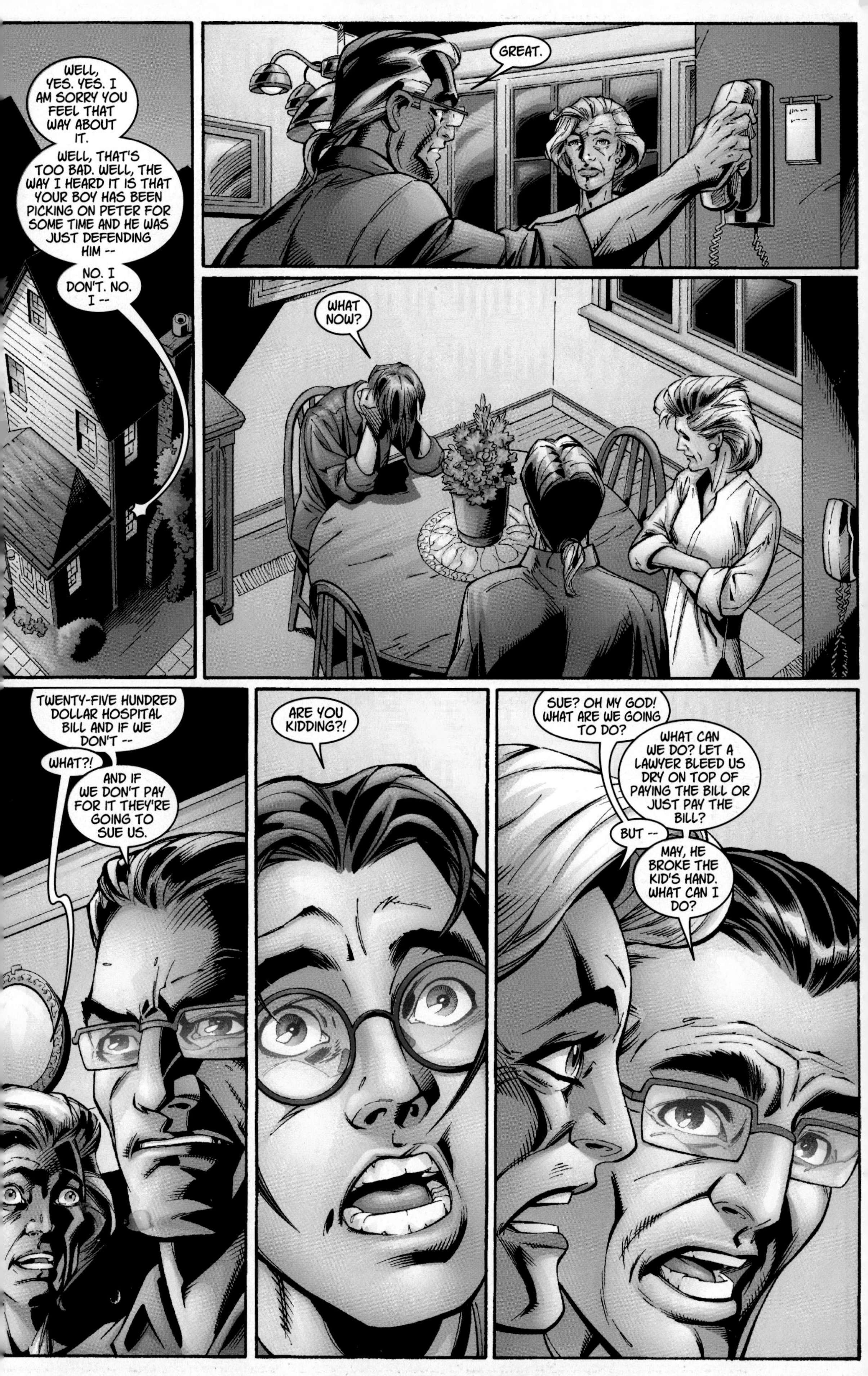
WELL, YES. YES. I AM SORRY YOU FEEL THAT WAY ABOUT IT.
WELL, THAT'S TOO BAD. WELL, THE WAY I HEARD IT IS THAT YOUR BOY HAS BEEN PICKING ON PETER FOR SOME TIME AND HE WAS JUST DEFENDING HIM --
NO. I DON'T. NO. I --
GREAT.
WHAT NOW?
TWENTY-FIVE HUNDRED DOLLAR HOSPITAL BILL AND IF WE DON'T --
WHAT?!
AND IF WE DON'T PAY FOR IT THEY'RE GOING TO SUE US.
ARE YOU KIDDING?!
SUE? OH MY GOD! WHAT ARE WE GOING TO DO?
WHAT CAN WE DO? LET A LAWYER BLEED US DRY ON TOP OF PAYING THE BILL OR JUST PAY THE BILL?
BUT --
MAY, HE BROKE THE KID'S HAND. WHAT CAN I DO?

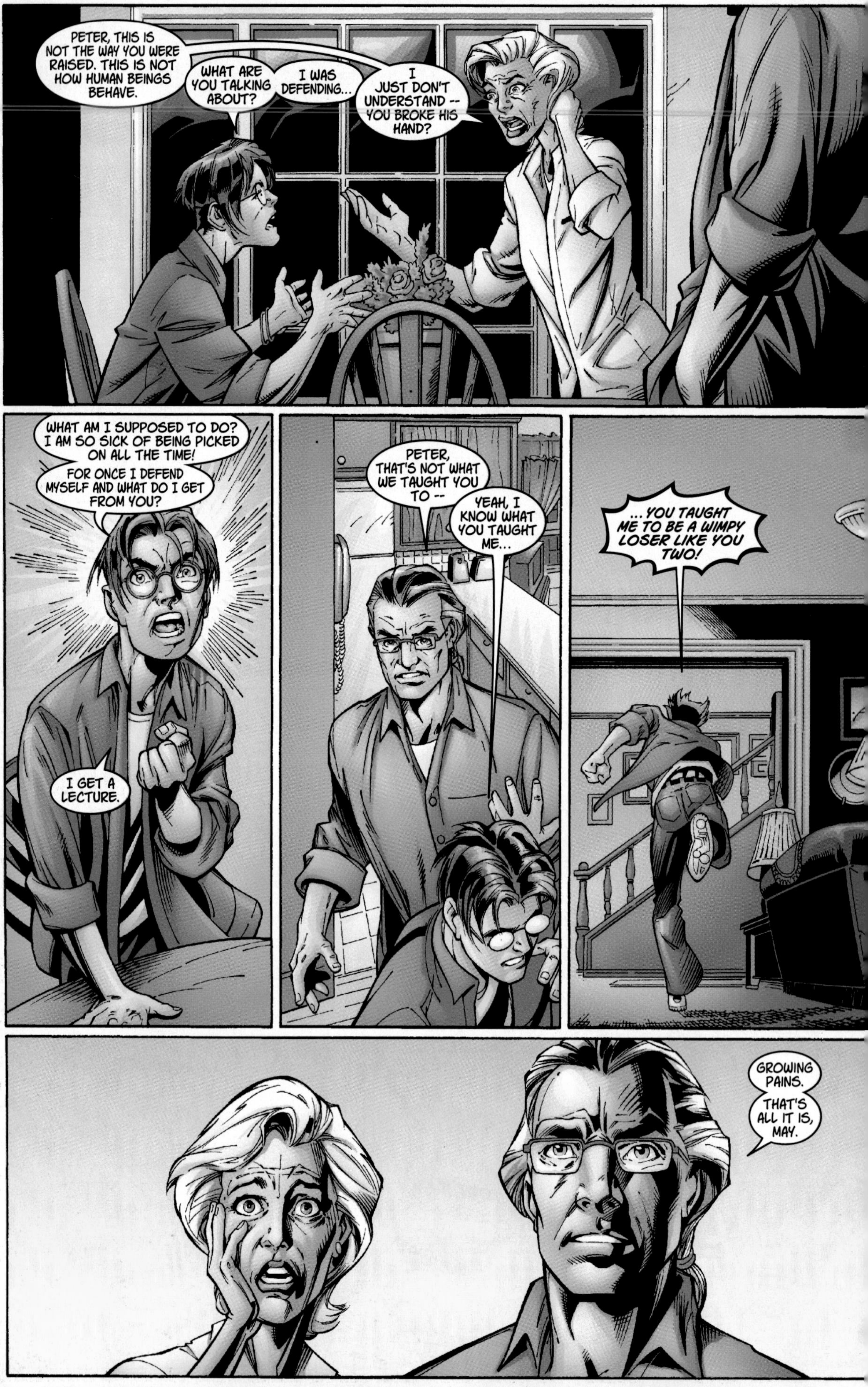

PETER, THIS IS NOT THE WAY YOU WERE RAISED. THIS IS NOT HOW HUMAN BEINGS BEHAVE.
WHAT ARE YOU TALKING ABOUT?
I WAS DEFENDING...
I JUST DON'T UNDERSTAND -- YOU BROKE HIS HAND?
WHAT AM I SUPPOSED TO DO? I AM SO SICK OF BEING PICKED ON ALL THE TIME!
FOR ONCE I DEFEND MYSELF AND WHAT DO I GET FROM YOU?
I GET A LECTURE.
PETER, THAT'S NOT WHAT WE TAUGHT YOU TO --
YEAH, I KNOW WHAT YOU TAUGHT ME...
...YOU TAUGHT ME TO BE A WIMPY LOSER LIKE YOU TWO!
GROWING PAINS.
THAT'S ALL IT IS, MAY.

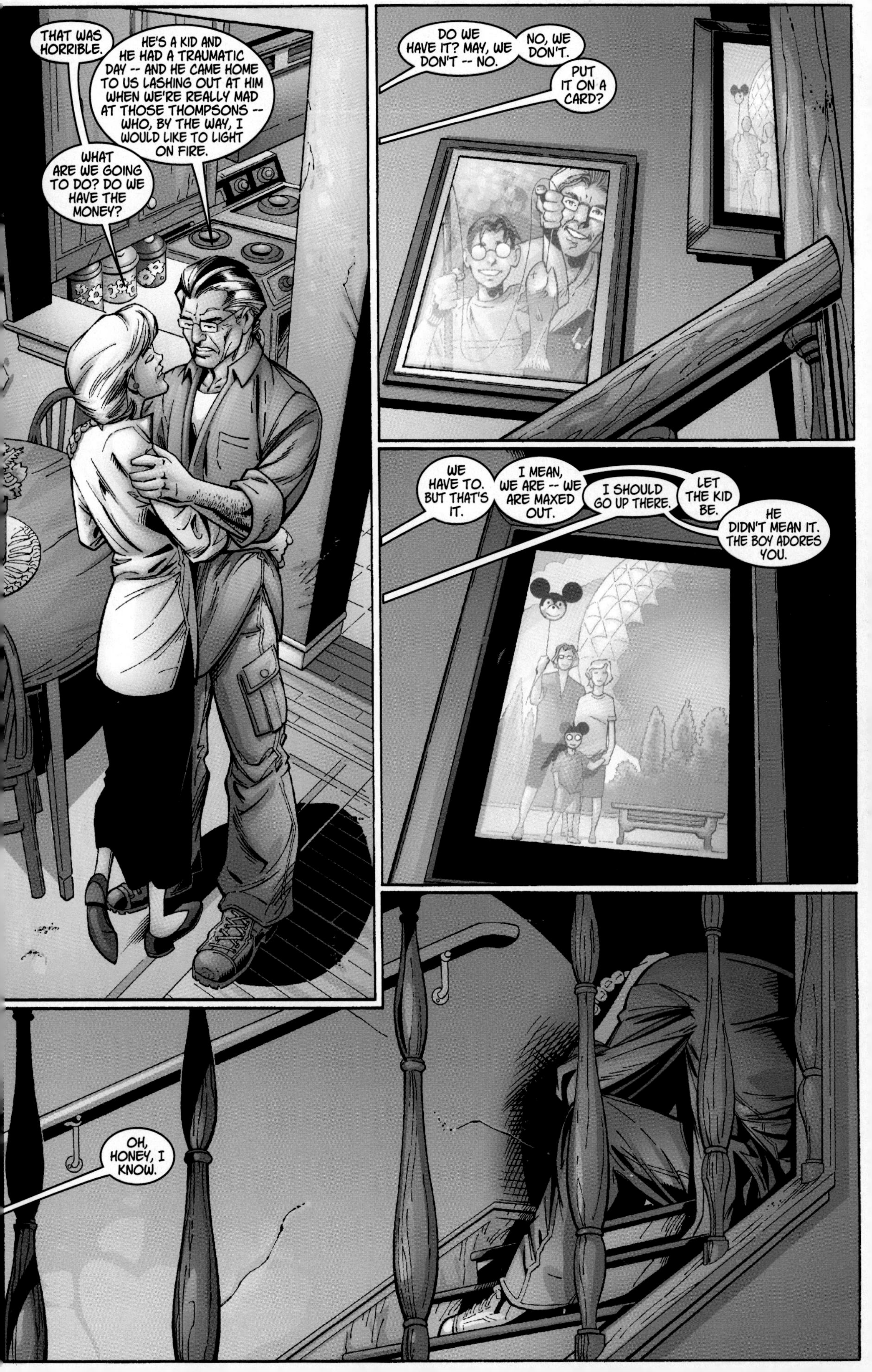
THAT WAS HORRIBLE.
HE'S A KID AND HE HAD A TRAUMATIC DAY -- AND HE CAME HOME TO US LASHING OUT AT HIM WHEN WE'RE REALLY MAD AT THOSE THOMPSONS -- WHO, BY THE WAY, I WOULD LIKE TO LIGHT ON FIRE.
WHAT ARE WE GOING TO DO? DO WE HAVE THE MONEY?
DO WE HAVE IT? MAY, WE DON'T -- NO.
NO, WE DON'T.
PUT IT ON A CARD?
WE HAVE TO. BUT THAT'S IT.
I MEAN, WE ARE -- WE ARE MAXED OUT.
I SHOULD GO UP THERE.
LET THE KID BE.
HE DIDN'T MEAN IT. THE BOY ADORES YOU.
OH, HONEY, I KNOW.

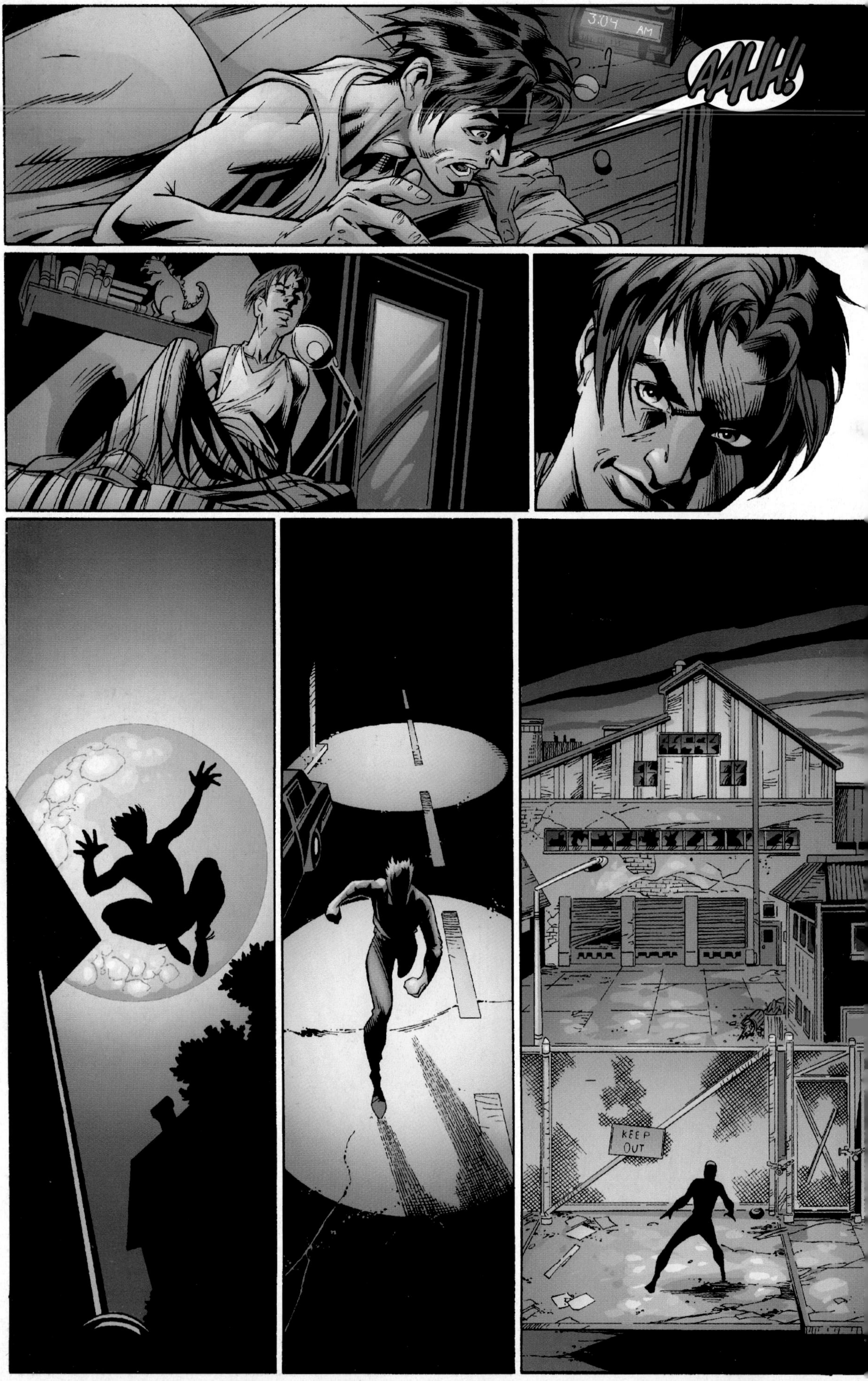
3:04 AM
AAHH!
KEEP OUT

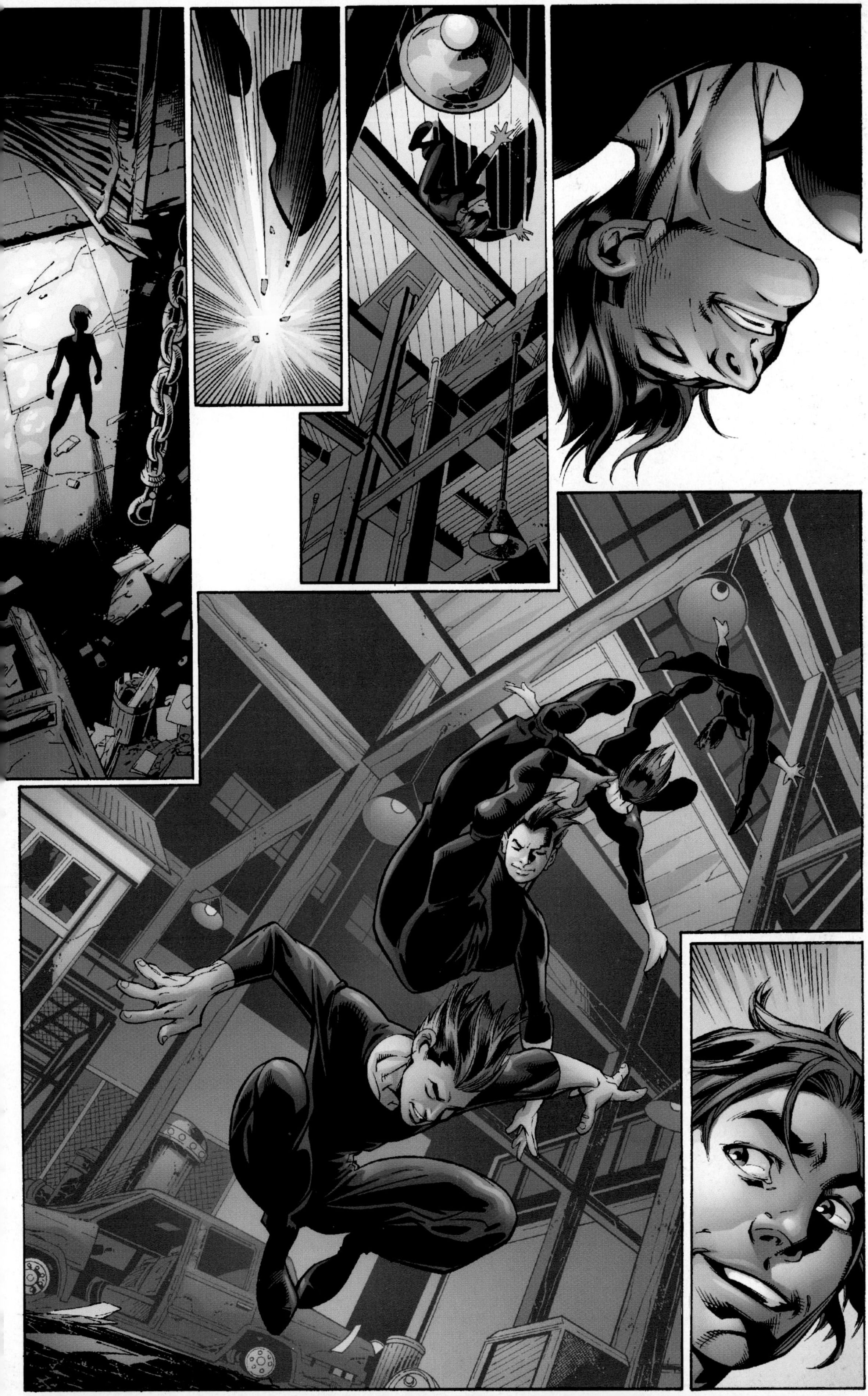

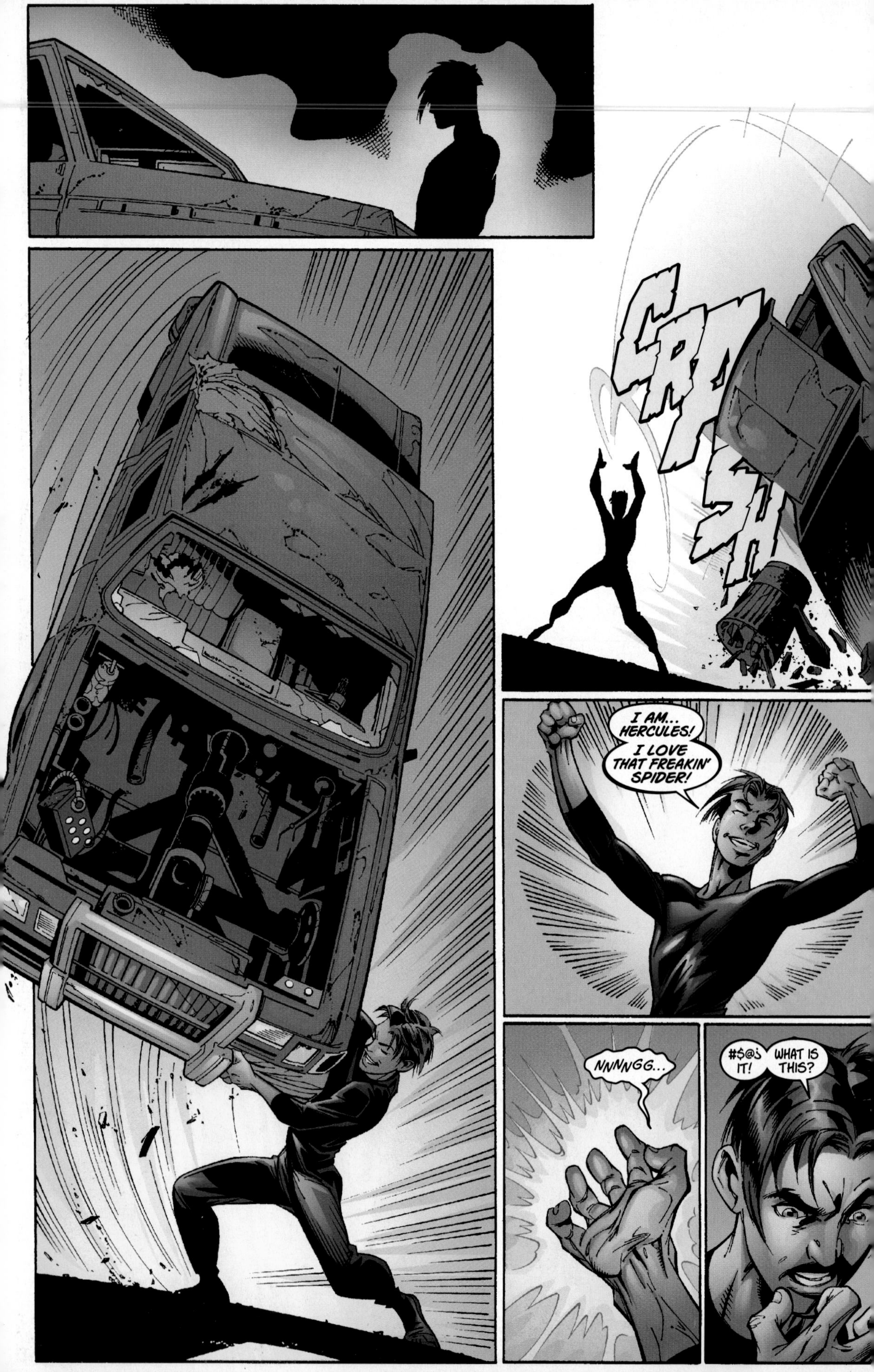
CRASH
I AM... HERCULES! I LOVE THAT FREAKIN' SPIDER!
NNNNGG...
#$@¿ IT!
WHAT IS THIS?

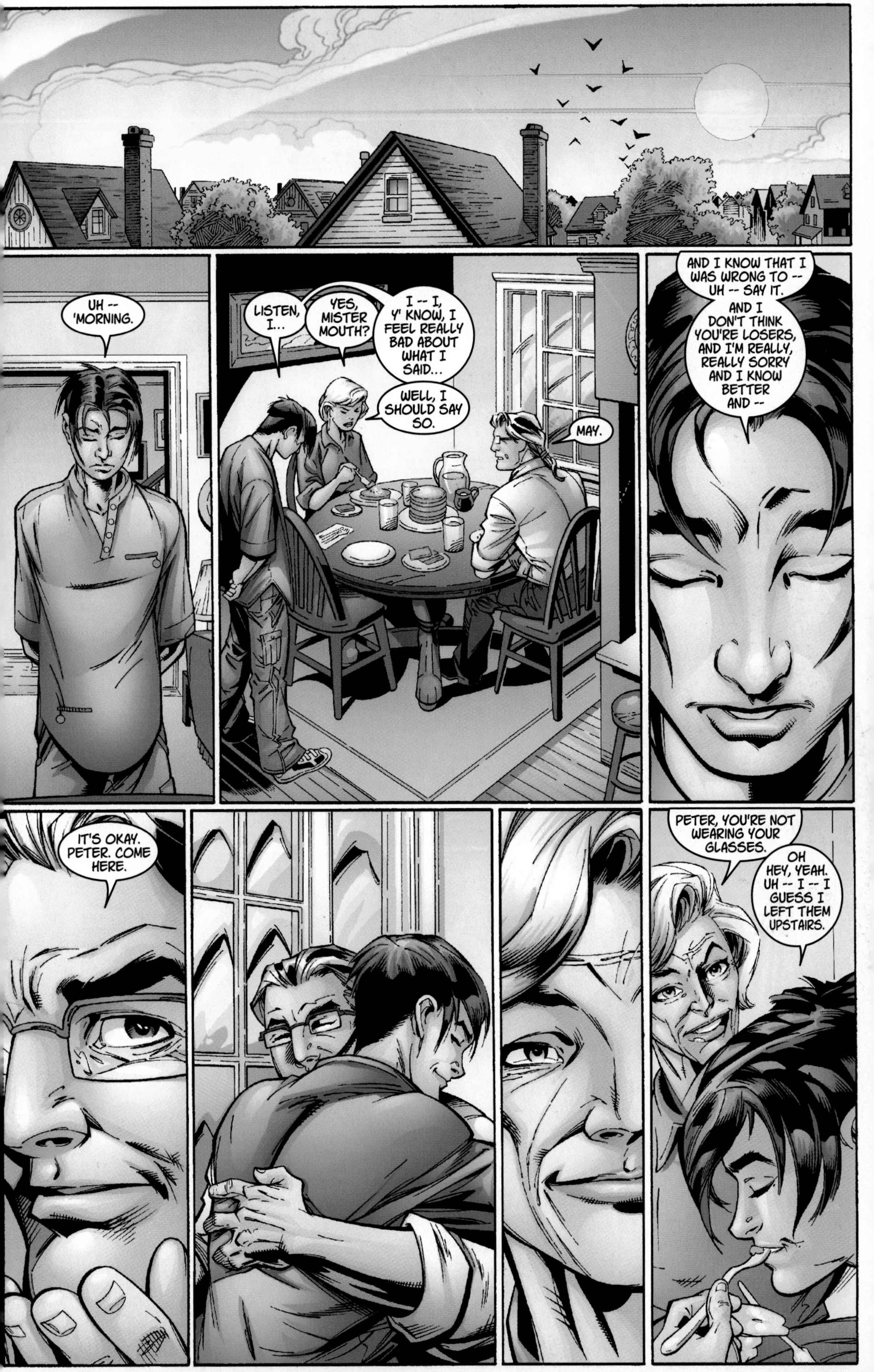
UH -- 'MORNING.
LISTEN, I...
YES, MISTER MOUTH?
I -- I, Y' KNOW, I FEEL REALLY BAD ABOUT WHAT I SAID...
WELL, I SHOULD SAY SO.
MAY.
AND I KNOW THAT I WAS WRONG TO -- UH -- SAY IT.
AND I DON'T THINK YOU'RE LOSERS, AND I'M REALLY, REALLY SORRY AND I KNOW BETTER AND --
IT'S OKAY. PETER. COME HERE.
PETER, YOU'RE NOT WEARING YOUR GLASSES.
OH HEY, YEAH. UH -- I -- I GUESS I LEFT THEM UPSTAIRS.

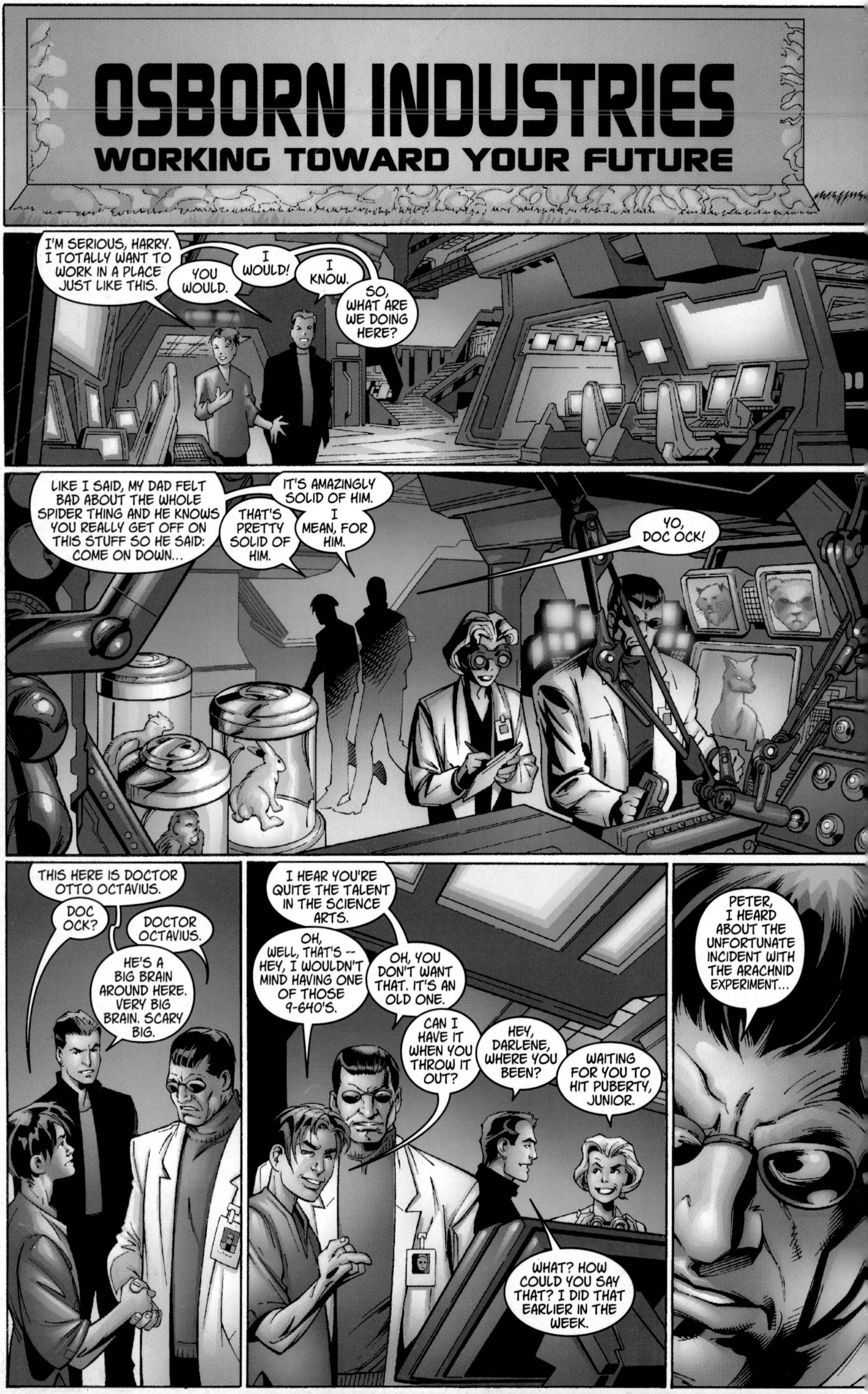
OSBORN INDUSTRIES
WORKING TOWARD YOUR FUTURE
I'M SERIOUS, HARRY. I TOTALLY WANT TO WORK IN A PLACE JUST LIKE THIS.
YOU WOULD.
I WOULD!
I KNOW.
SO, WHAT ARE WE DOING HERE?
LIKE I SAID, MY DAD FELT BAD ABOUT THE WHOLE SPIDER THING AND HE KNOWS YOU REALLY GET OFF ON THIS STUFF SO HE SAID: COME ON DOWN...
THAT'S PRETTY SOLID OF HIM.
IT'S AMAZINGLY SOLID OF HIM.
I MEAN, FOR HIM.
YO, DOC OCK!
THIS HERE IS DOCTOR OTTO OCTAVIUS.
DOC OCK?
DOCTOR OCTAVIUS.
HE'S A BIG BRAIN AROUND HERE. VERY BIG BRAIN. SCARY BIG.
I HEAR YOU'RE QUITE THE TALENT IN THE SCIENCE ARTS.
OH, WELL, THAT'S -- HEY, I WOULDN'T MIND HAVING ONE OF THOSE 9-640'S.
OH, YOU DON'T WANT THAT. IT'S AN OLD ONE.
CAN I HAVE IT WHEN YOU THROW IT OUT?
HEY, DARLENE, WHERE YOU BEEN?
WAITING FOR YOU TO HIT PUBERTY, JUNIOR.
WHAT? HOW COULD YOU SAY THAT? I DID THAT EARLIER IN THE WEEK.
PETER, I HEARD ABOUT THE UNFORTUNATE INCIDENT WITH THE ARACHNID EXPERIMENT...

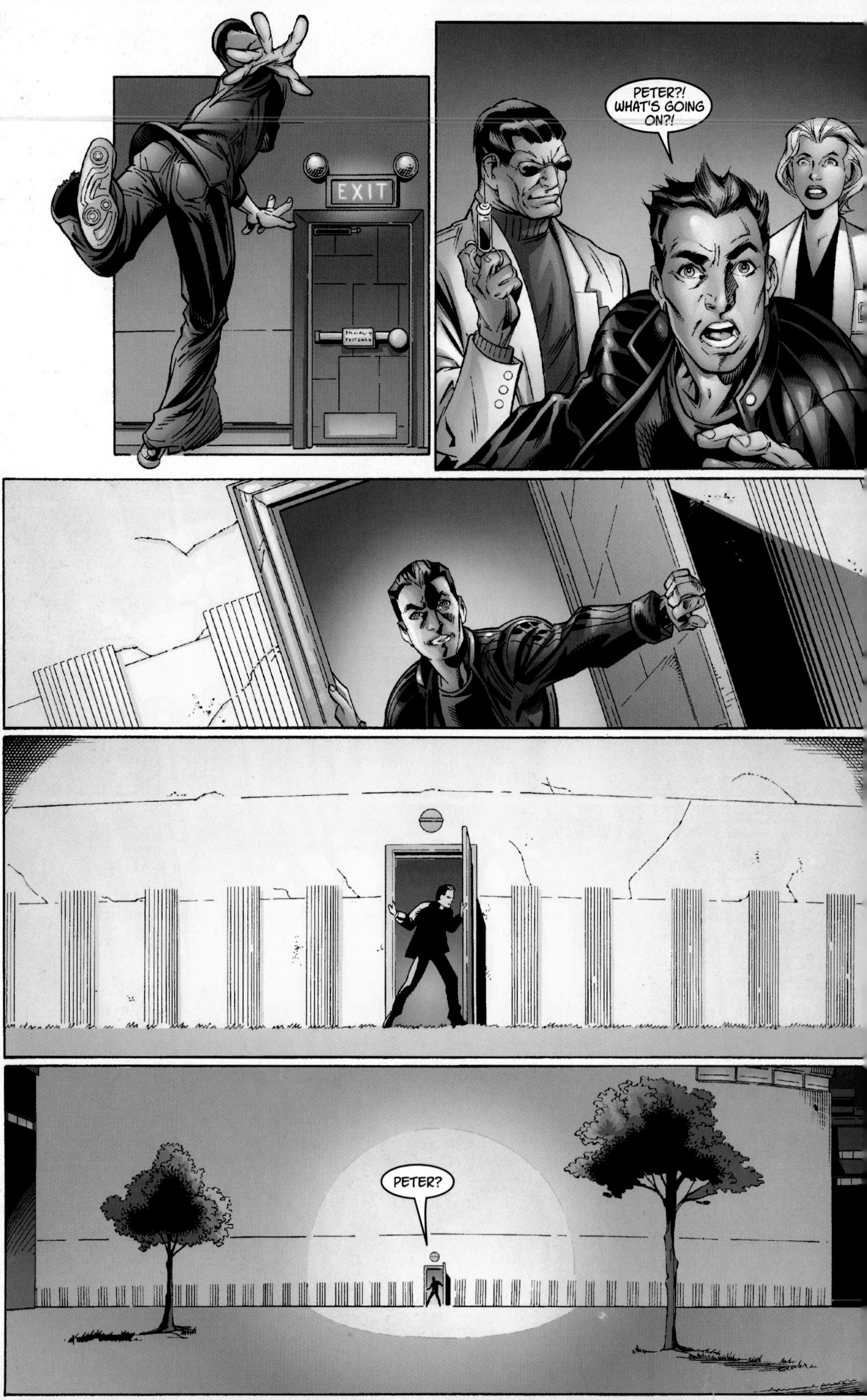
EXIT
PETER?! WHAT'S GOING ON?!
PETER?

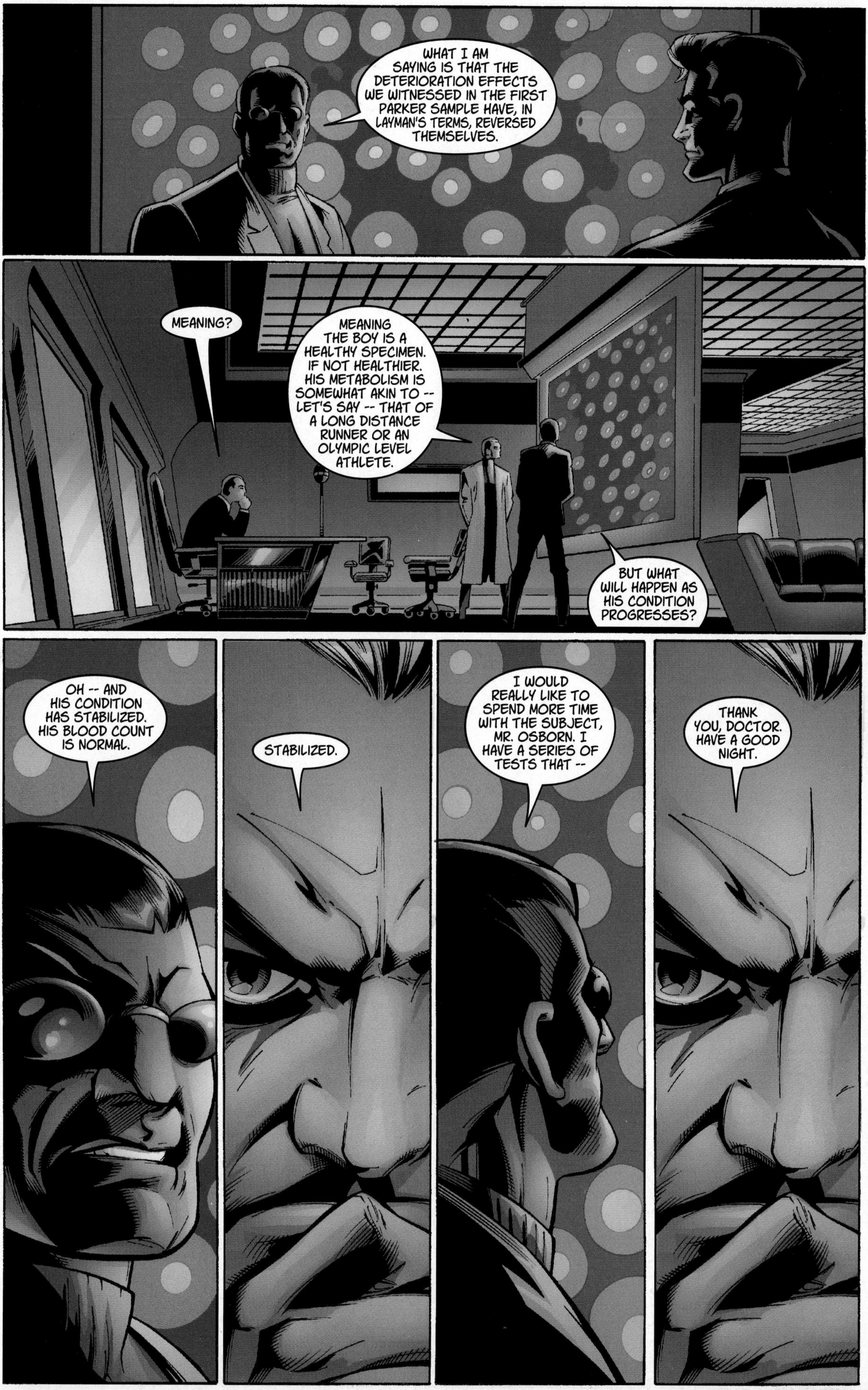
WHAT I AM SAYING IS THAT THE DETERIORATION EFFECTS WE WITNESSED IN THE FIRST PARKER SAMPLE HAVE, IN LAYMAN'S TERMS, REVERSED THEMSELVES.
MEANING?
MEANING THE BOY IS A HEALTHY SPECIMEN. IF NOT HEALTHIER. HIS METABOLISM IS SOMEWHAT AKIN TO -- LET'S SAY -- THAT OF A LONG DISTANCE RUNNER OR AN OLYMPIC LEVEL ATHLETE.
BUT WHAT WILL HAPPEN AS HIS CONDITION PROGRESSES?
OH -- AND HIS CONDITION HAS STABILIZED. HIS BLOOD COUNT IS NORMAL.
STABILIZED.
I WOULD REALLY LIKE TO SPEND MORE TIME WITH THE SUBJECT, MR. OSBORN. I HAVE A SERIES OF TESTS THAT --
THANK YOU, DOCTOR. HAVE A GOOD NIGHT.

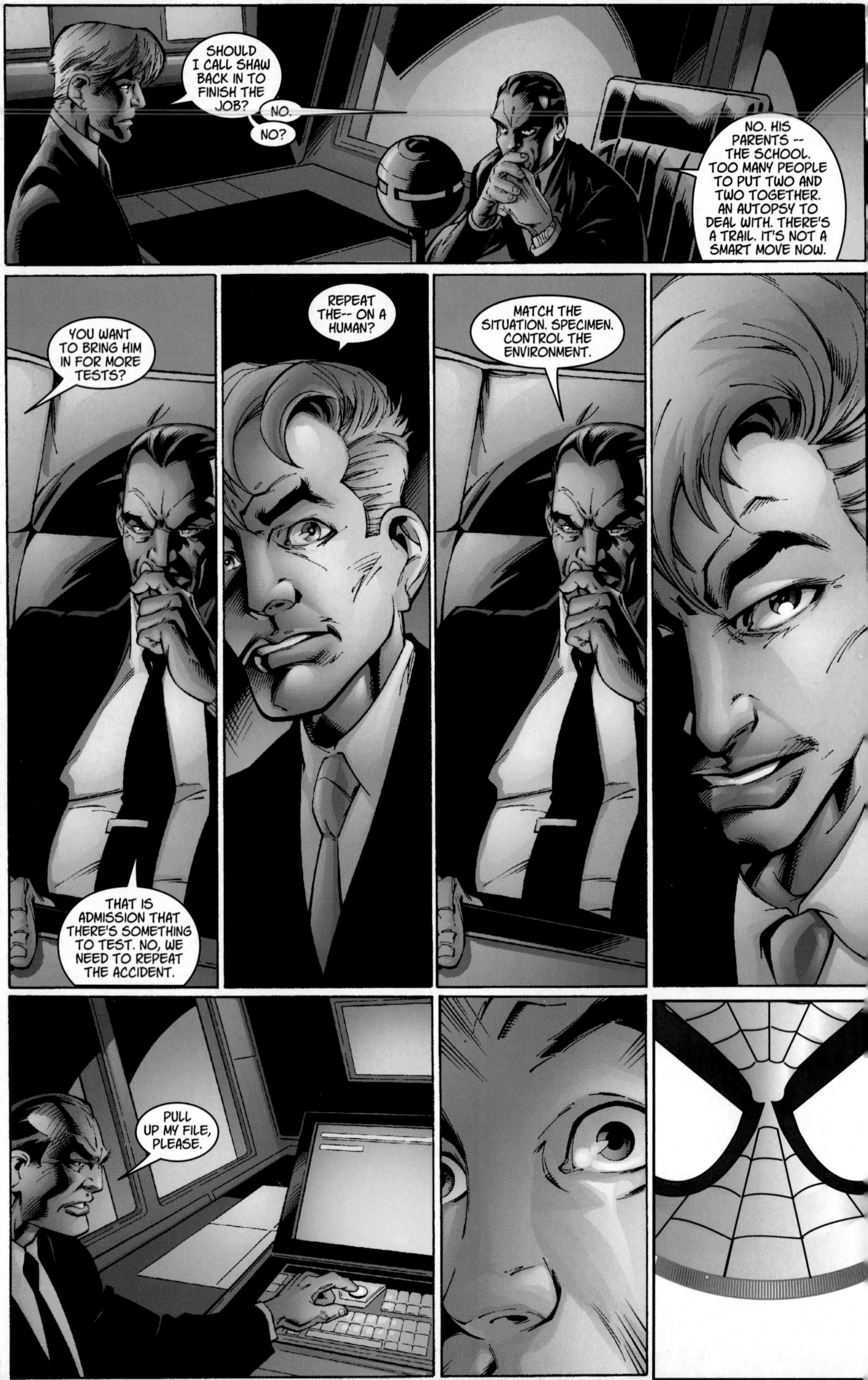
SHOULD I CALL SHAW BACK IN TO FINISH THE JOB?
NO.
NO?
NO. HIS PARENTS -- THE SCHOOL. TOO MANY PEOPLE TO PUT TWO AND TWO TOGETHER. AN AUTOPSY TO DEAL WITH. THERE'S A TRAIL. IT'S NOT A SMART MOVE NOW.
YOU WANT TO BRING HIM IN FOR MORE TESTS?
THAT IS ADMISSION THAT THERE'S SOMETHING TO TEST. NO, WE NEED TO REPEAT THE ACCIDENT.
REPEAT THE-- ON A HUMAN?
MATCH THE SITUATION. SPECIMEN. CONTROL THE ENVIRONMENT.
PULL UP MY FILE, PLEASE.

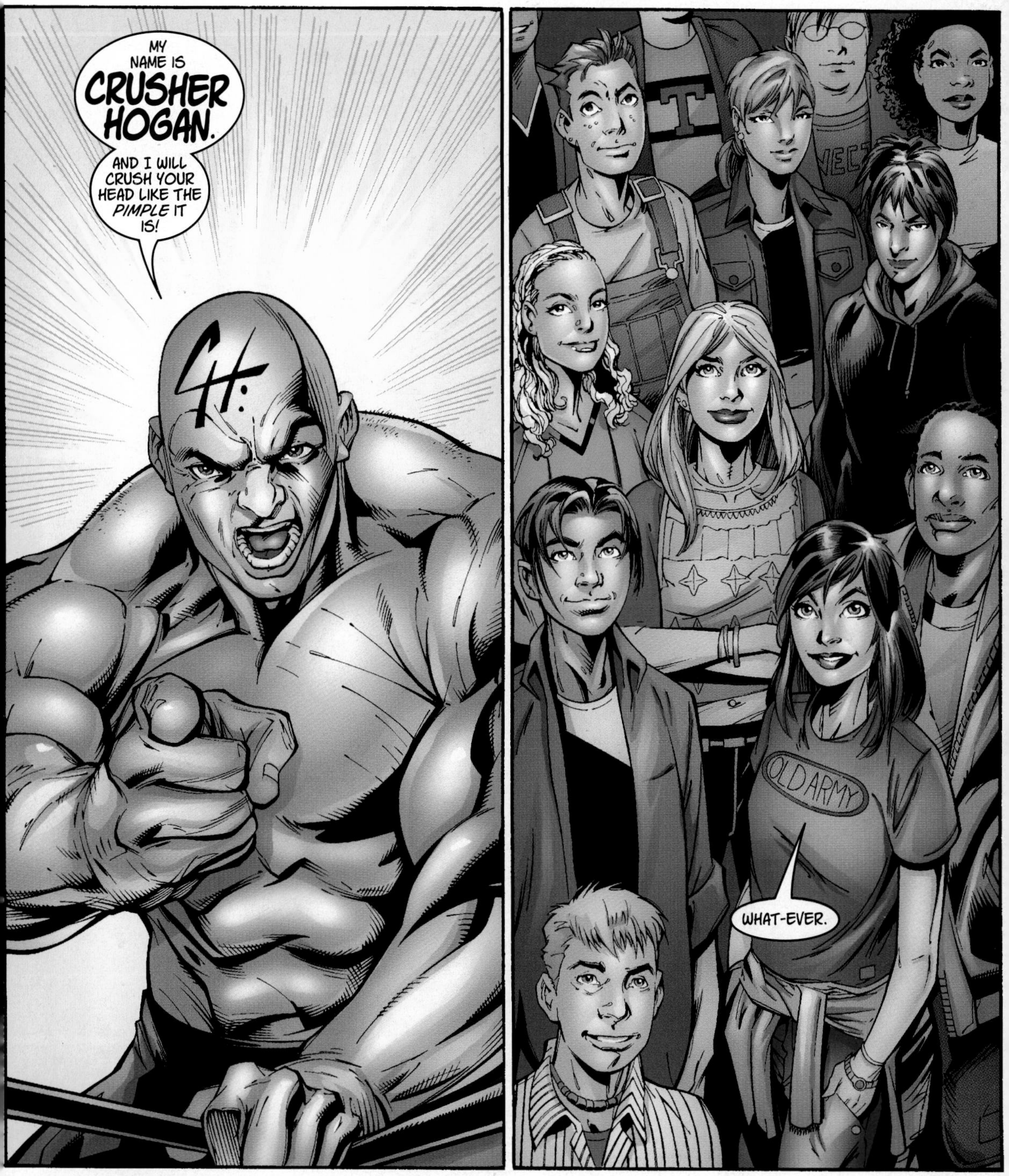
MY NAME IS CRUSHER HOGAN.
AND I WILL CRUSH YOUR HEAD LIKE THE *PIMPLE* IT IS!
OLD ARMY
WHAT-EVER.

CHAPTER 3

WANNABE

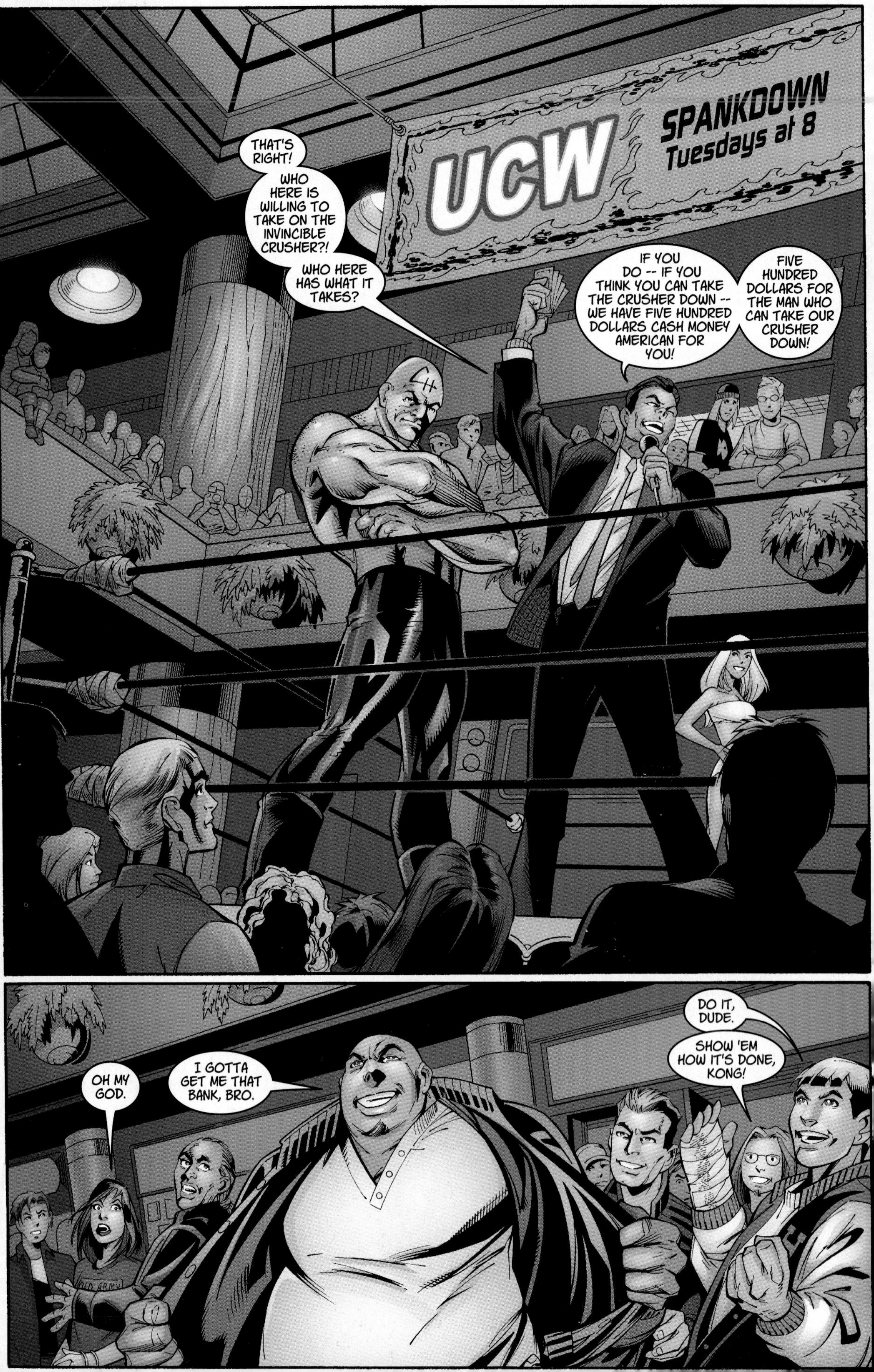
UCW
SPANKDOWN Tuesdays at 8
THAT'S RIGHT!
WHO HERE IS WILLING TO TAKE ON THE INVINCIBLE CRUSHER?!
WHO HERE HAS WHAT IT TAKES?
IF YOU DO -- IF YOU THINK YOU CAN TAKE THE CRUSHER DOWN -- WE HAVE FIVE HUNDRED DOLLARS CASH MONEY AMERICAN FOR YOU!
FIVE HUNDRED DOLLARS FOR THE MAN WHO CAN TAKE OUR CRUSHER DOWN!
DO IT, DUDE.
SHOW 'EM HOW IT'S DONE, KONG!
I GOTTA GET ME THAT BANK, BRO.
OH MY GOD.

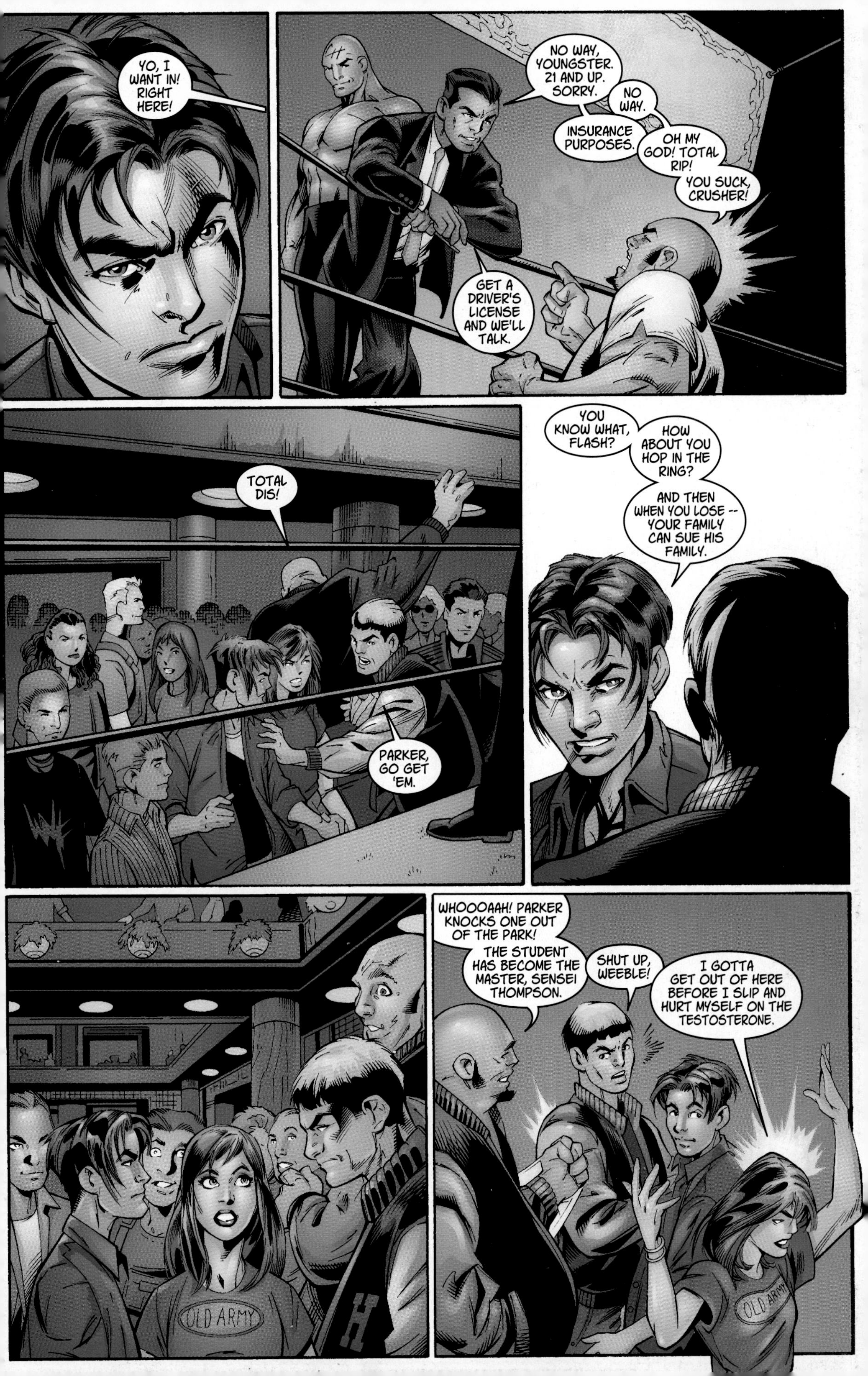
YO, I WANT IN! RIGHT HERE!
NO WAY, YOUNGSTER. 21 AND UP. SORRY.
INSURANCE PURPOSES.
NO WAY.
OH MY GOD! TOTAL RIP!
YOU SUCK, CRUSHER!
GET A DRIVER'S LICENSE AND WE'LL TALK.
TOTAL DIS!
PARKER, GO GET 'EM.
YOU KNOW WHAT, FLASH?
HOW ABOUT YOU HOP IN THE RING?
AND THEN WHEN YOU LOSE -- YOUR FAMILY CAN SUE HIS FAMILY.
OLD ARMY
WHOOOAAH! PARKER KNOCKS ONE OUT OF THE PARK!
THE STUDENT HAS BECOME THE MASTER, SENSEI THOMPSON.
SHUT UP, WEEBLE!
I GOTTA GET OUT OF HERE BEFORE I SLIP AND HURT MYSELF ON THE TESTOSTERONE.
OLD ARMY

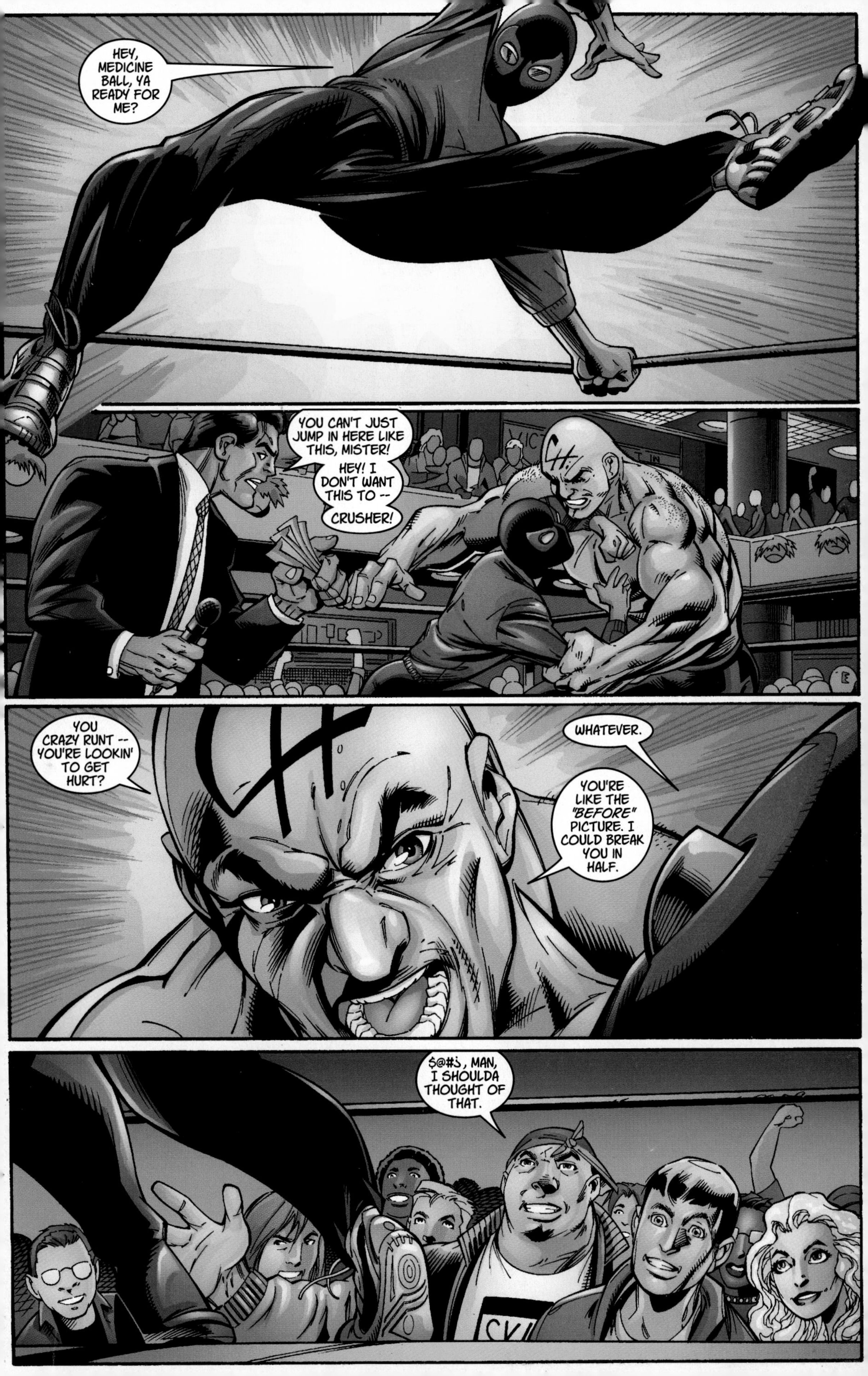
HEY, MEDICINE BALL, YA READY FOR ME?
YOU CAN'T JUST JUMP IN HERE LIKE THIS, MISTER!
HEY! I DON'T WANT THIS TO --
CRUSHER!
YOU CRAZY RUNT -- YOU'RE LOOKIN' TO GET HURT?
WHATEVER.
YOU'RE LIKE THE "BEFORE" PICTURE. I COULD BREAK YOU IN HALF.
$@#Ś, MAN, I SHOULDA THOUGHT OF THAT.

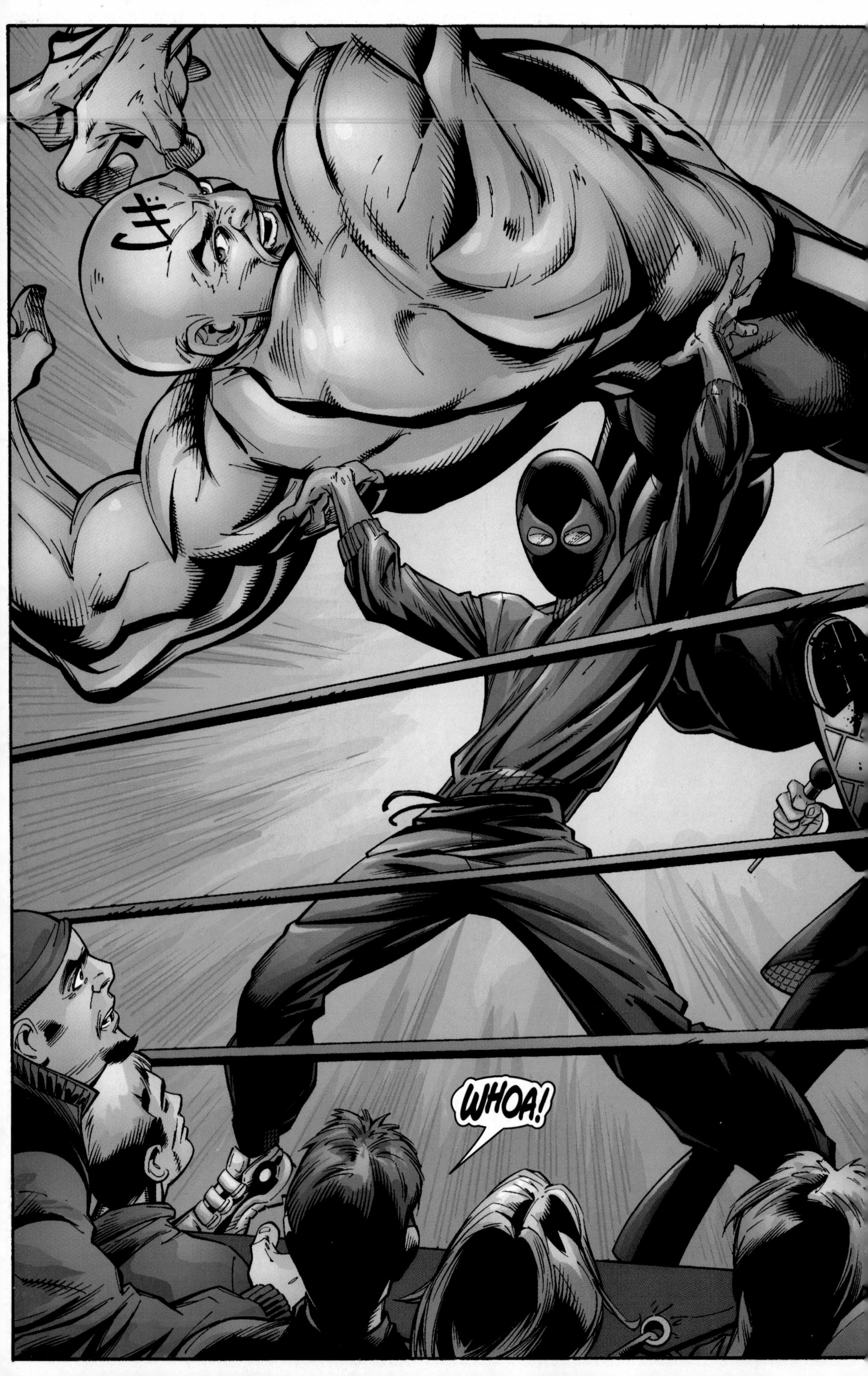
WHOA!

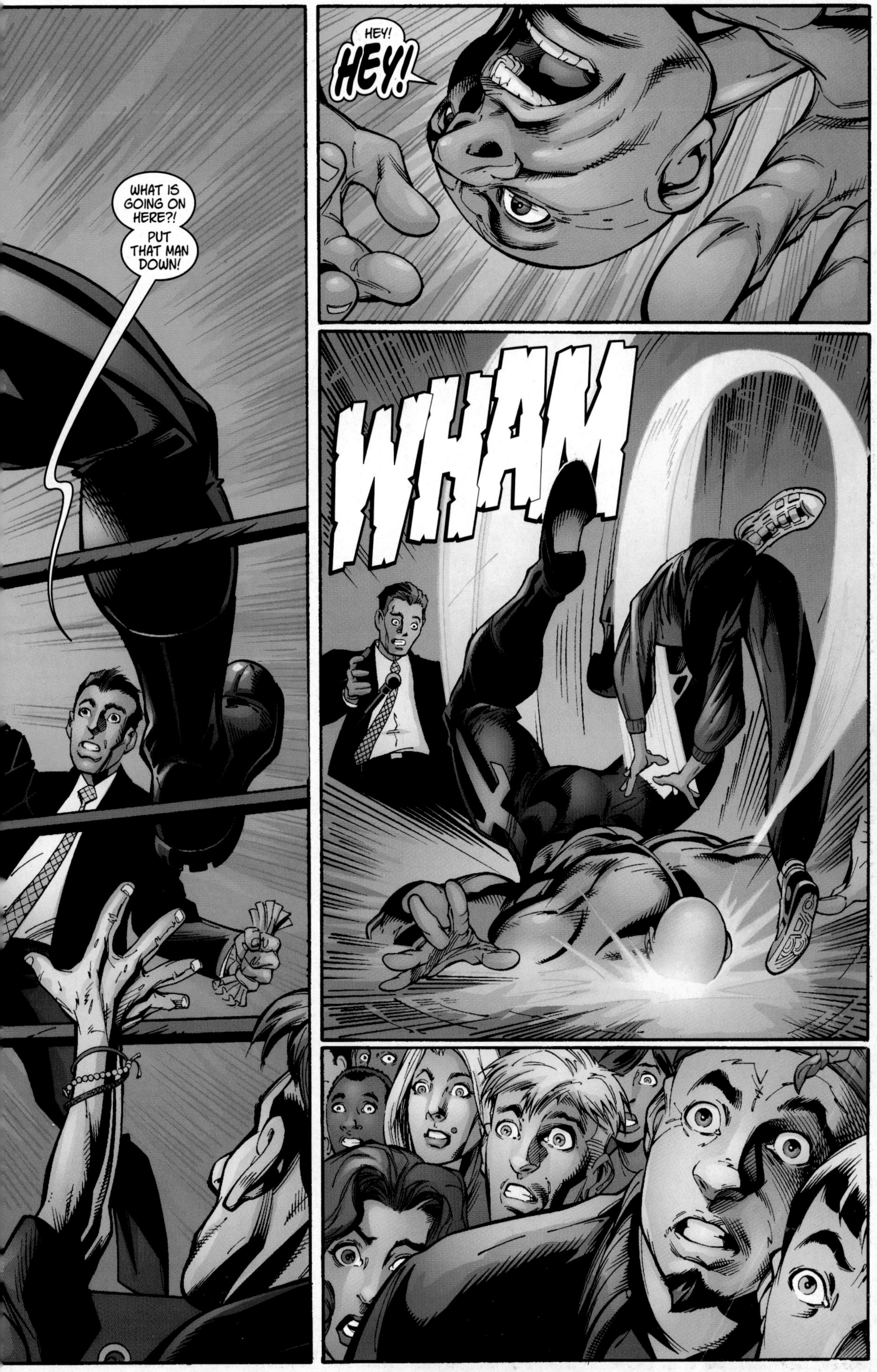
HEY! HEY!
WHAT IS GOING ON HERE?! PUT THAT MAN DOWN!
WHAM

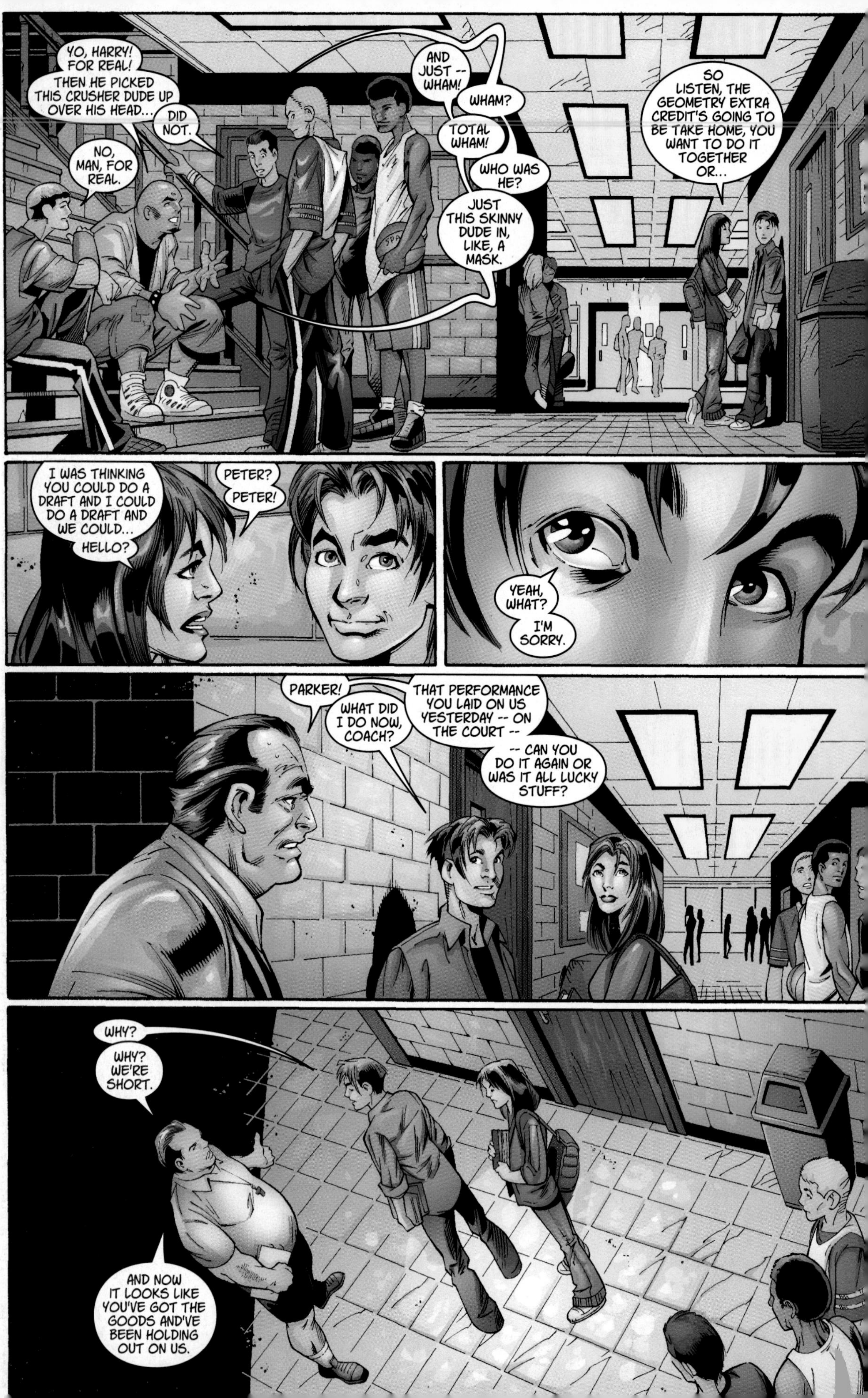

YO, HARRY! FOR REAL!
THEN HE PICKED THIS CRUSHER DUDE UP OVER HIS HEAD...
DID NOT.
NO, MAN, FOR REAL.
AND JUST -- WHAM!
WHAM?
TOTAL WHAM!
WHO WAS HE?
JUST THIS SKINNY DUDE IN, LIKE, A MASK.
SO LISTEN, THE GEOMETRY EXTRA CREDIT'S GOING TO BE TAKE HOME, YOU WANT TO DO IT TOGETHER OR...
I WAS THINKING YOU COULD DO A DRAFT AND I COULD DO A DRAFT AND WE COULD...
HELLO?
PETER?
PETER!
YEAH, WHAT?
I'M SORRY.
PARKER!
WHAT DID I DO NOW, COACH?
THAT PERFORMANCE YOU LAID ON US YESTERDAY -- ON THE COURT --
-- CAN YOU DO IT AGAIN OR WAS IT ALL LUCKY STUFF?
WHY?
WHY? WE'RE SHORT.
AND NOW IT LOOKS LIKE YOU'VE GOT THE GOODS AND'VE BEEN HOLDING OUT ON US.

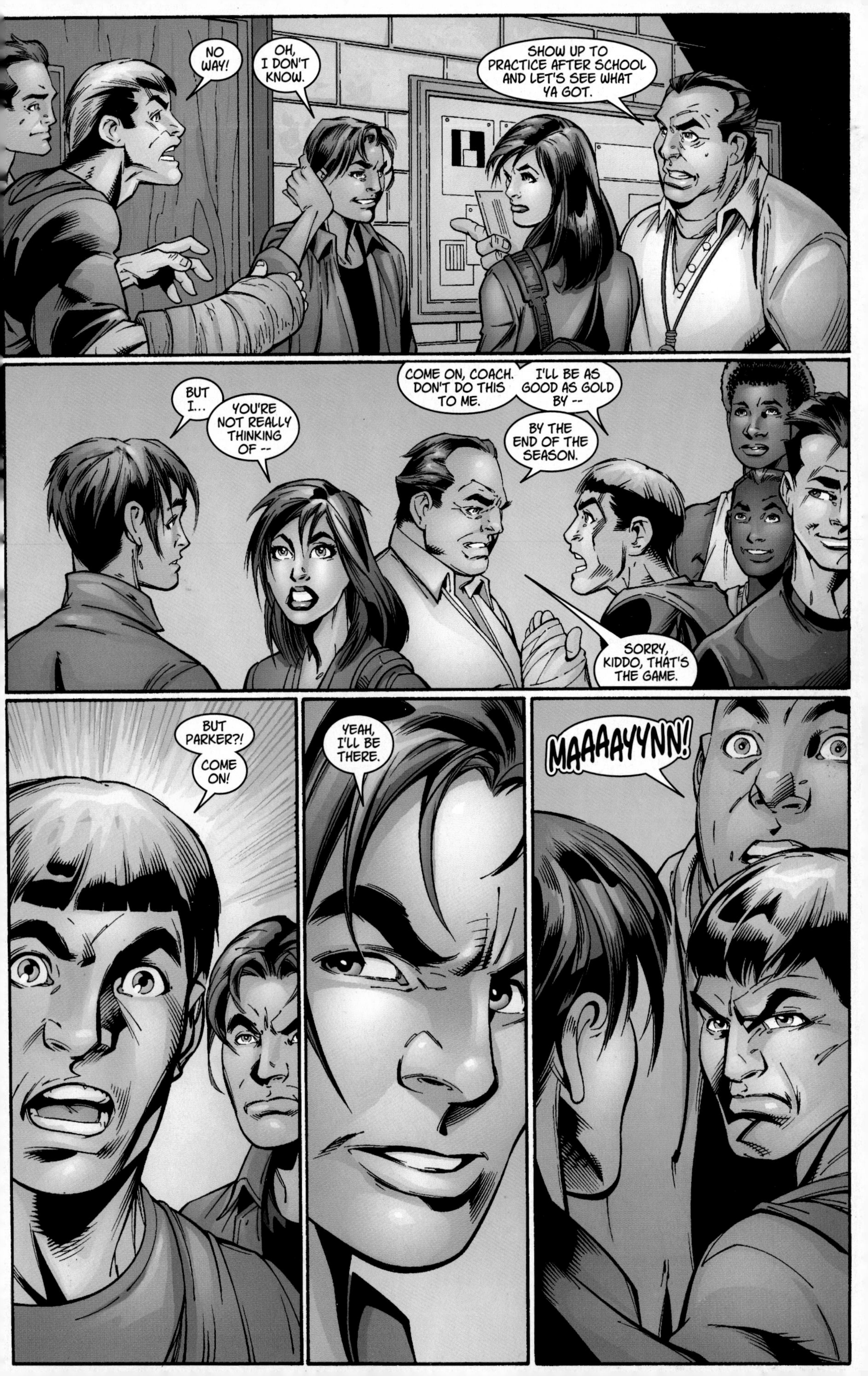
NO WAY!
OH, I DON'T KNOW.
SHOW UP TO PRACTICE AFTER SCHOOL AND LET'S SEE WHAT YA GOT.
BUT I...
YOU'RE NOT REALLY THINKING OF --
COME ON, COACH. DON'T DO THIS TO ME.
I'LL BE AS GOOD AS GOLD BY --
BY THE END OF THE SEASON.
SORRY, KIDDO, THAT'S THE GAME.
BUT PARKER?!
COME ON!
YEAH, I'LL BE THERE.
MAAAAYYNN!

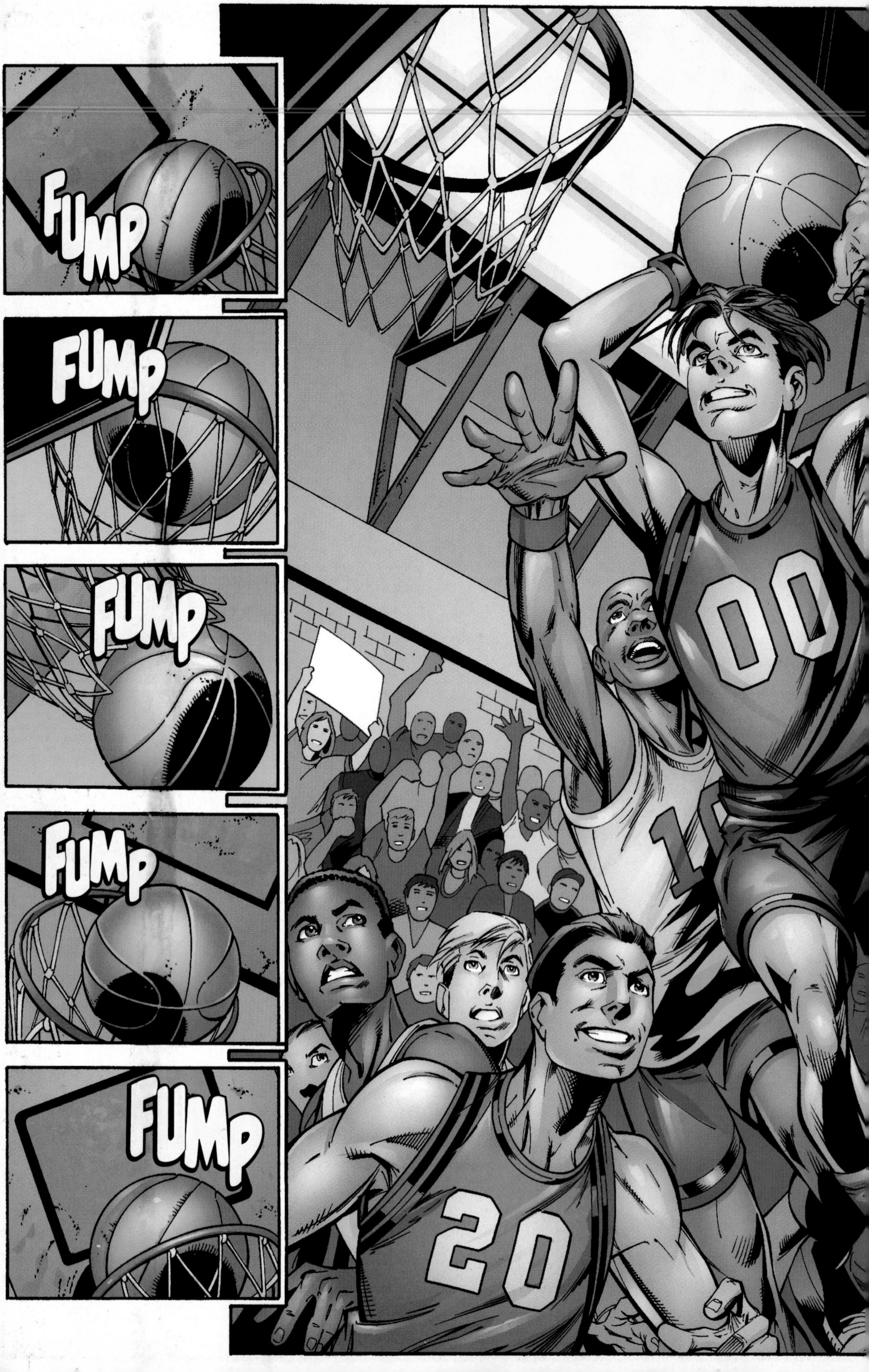
FUMP
FUMP
FUMP
FUMP
FUMP

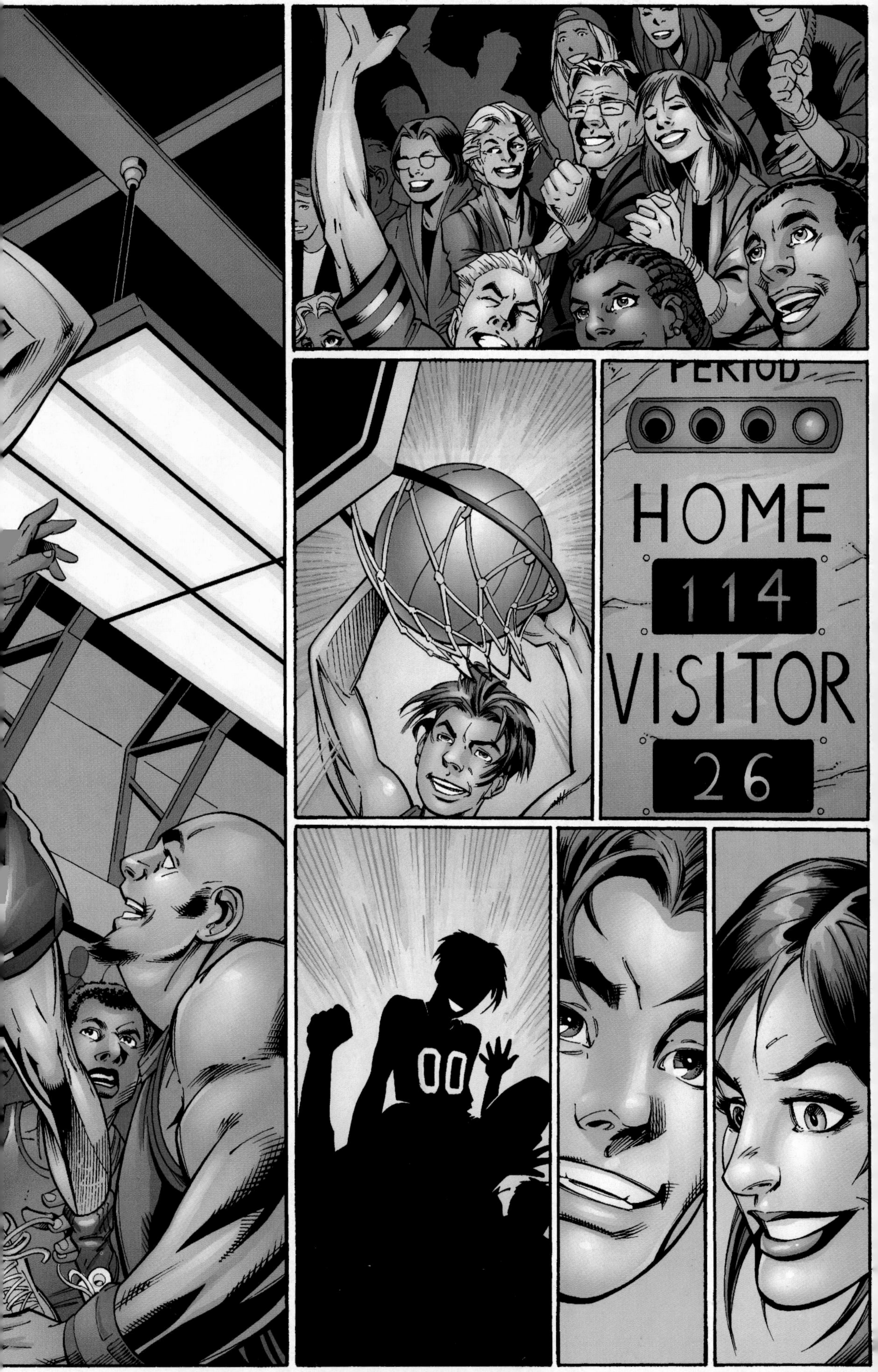
PERIOD
HOME
114
VISITOR
26
00

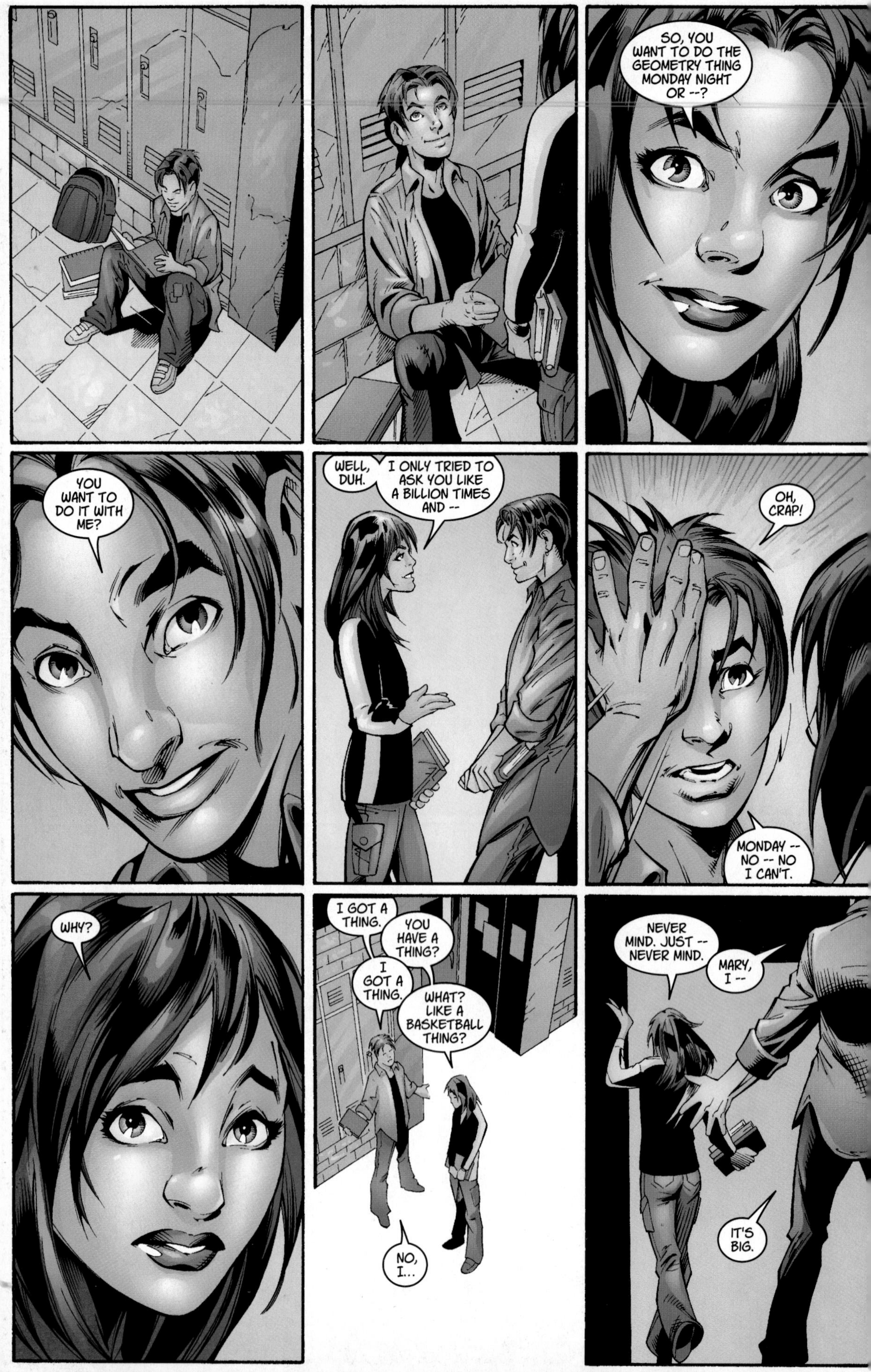
SO, YOU WANT TO DO THE GEOMETRY THING MONDAY NIGHT OR --?
YOU WANT TO DO IT WITH ME?
WELL, DUH.
I ONLY TRIED TO ASK YOU LIKE A BILLION TIMES AND --
OH, CRAP!
MONDAY -- NO -- NO I CAN'T.
WHY?
I GOT A THING.
YOU HAVE A THING?
I GOT A THING.
WHAT? LIKE A BASKETBALL THING?
NO, I...
NEVER MIND. JUST -- NEVER MIND.
MARY, I --
IT'S BIG.

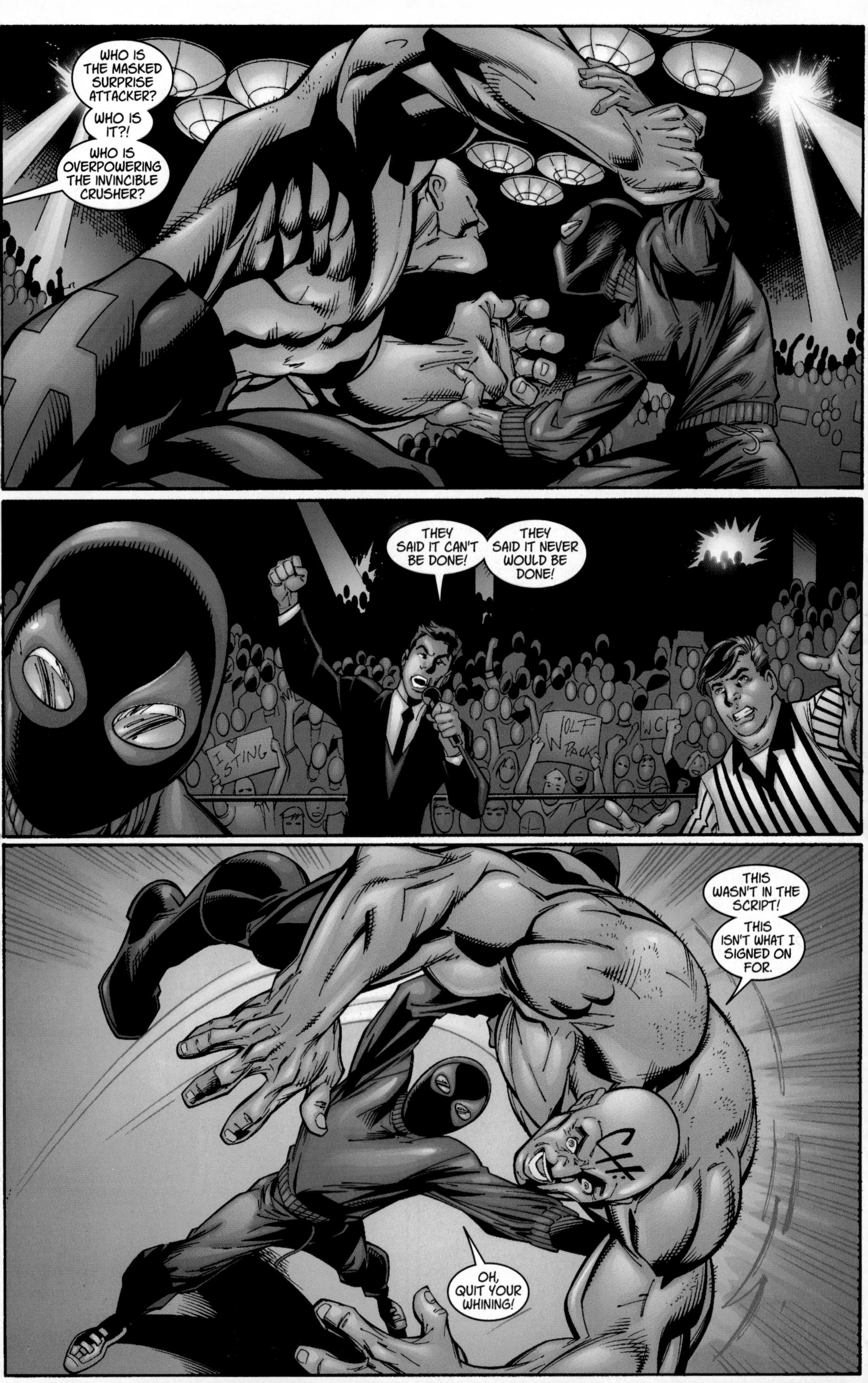
WHO IS THE MASKED SURPRISE ATTACKER?
WHO IS IT?!
WHO IS OVERPOWERING THE INVINCIBLE CRUSHER?
THEY SAID IT CAN'T BE DONE!
THEY SAID IT NEVER WOULD BE DONE!
I ♥ STING
WOLF PACK
WCF
THIS WASN'T IN THE SCRIPT!
THIS ISN'T WHAT I SIGNED ON FOR.
OH, QUIT YOUR WHINING!

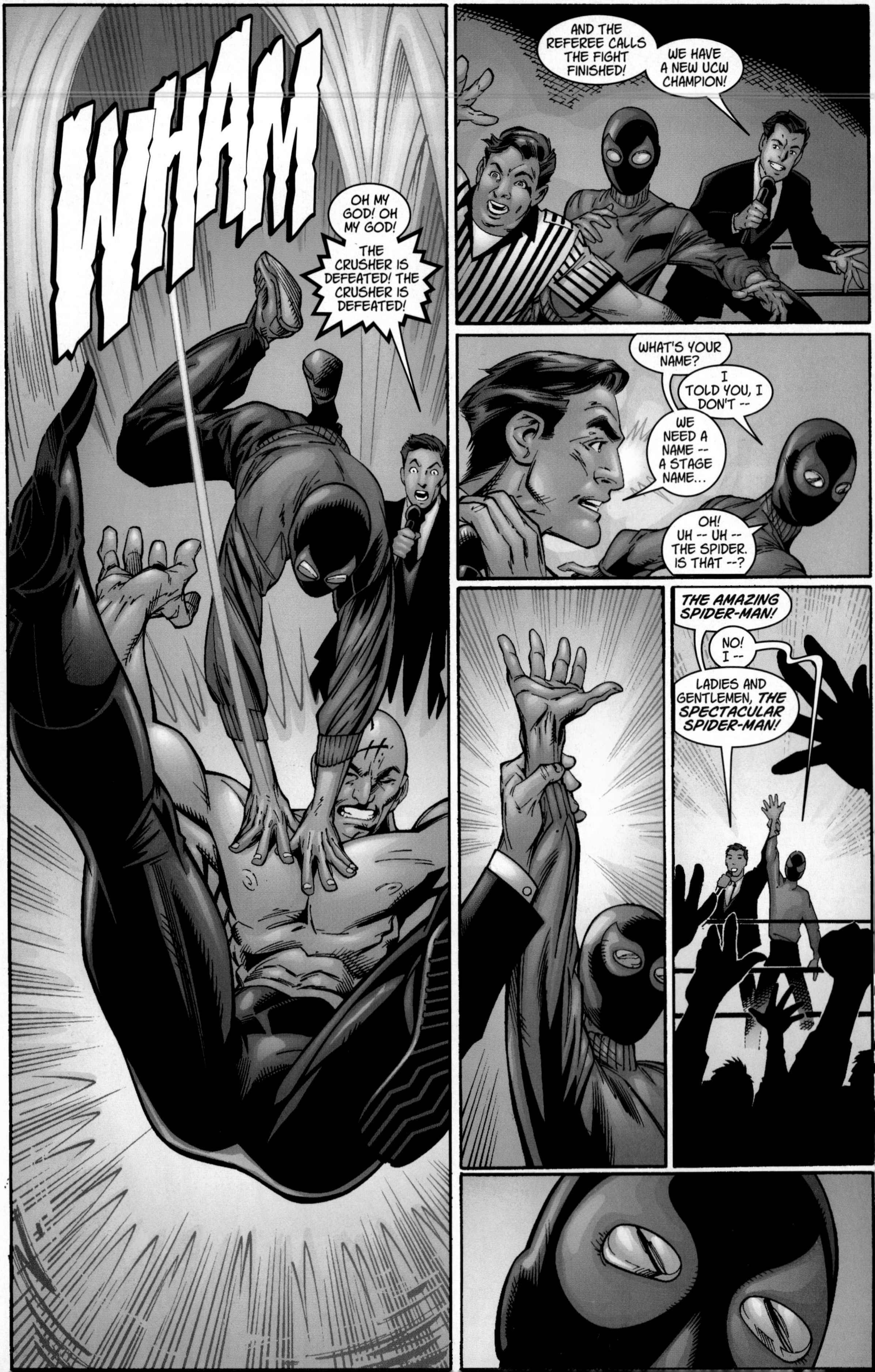
WHAM
OH MY GOD! OH MY GOD!
THE CRUSHER IS DEFEATED! THE CRUSHER IS DEFEATED!
AND THE REFEREE CALLS THE FIGHT FINISHED!
WE HAVE A NEW UCW CHAMPION!
WHAT'S YOUR NAME?
I TOLD YOU, I DON'T --
WE NEED A NAME -- A STAGE NAME...
OH! UH -- UH -- THE SPIDER. IS THAT --?
THE AMAZING SPIDER-MAN!
NO! I --
LADIES AND GENTLEMEN, THE SPECTACULAR SPIDER-MAN!

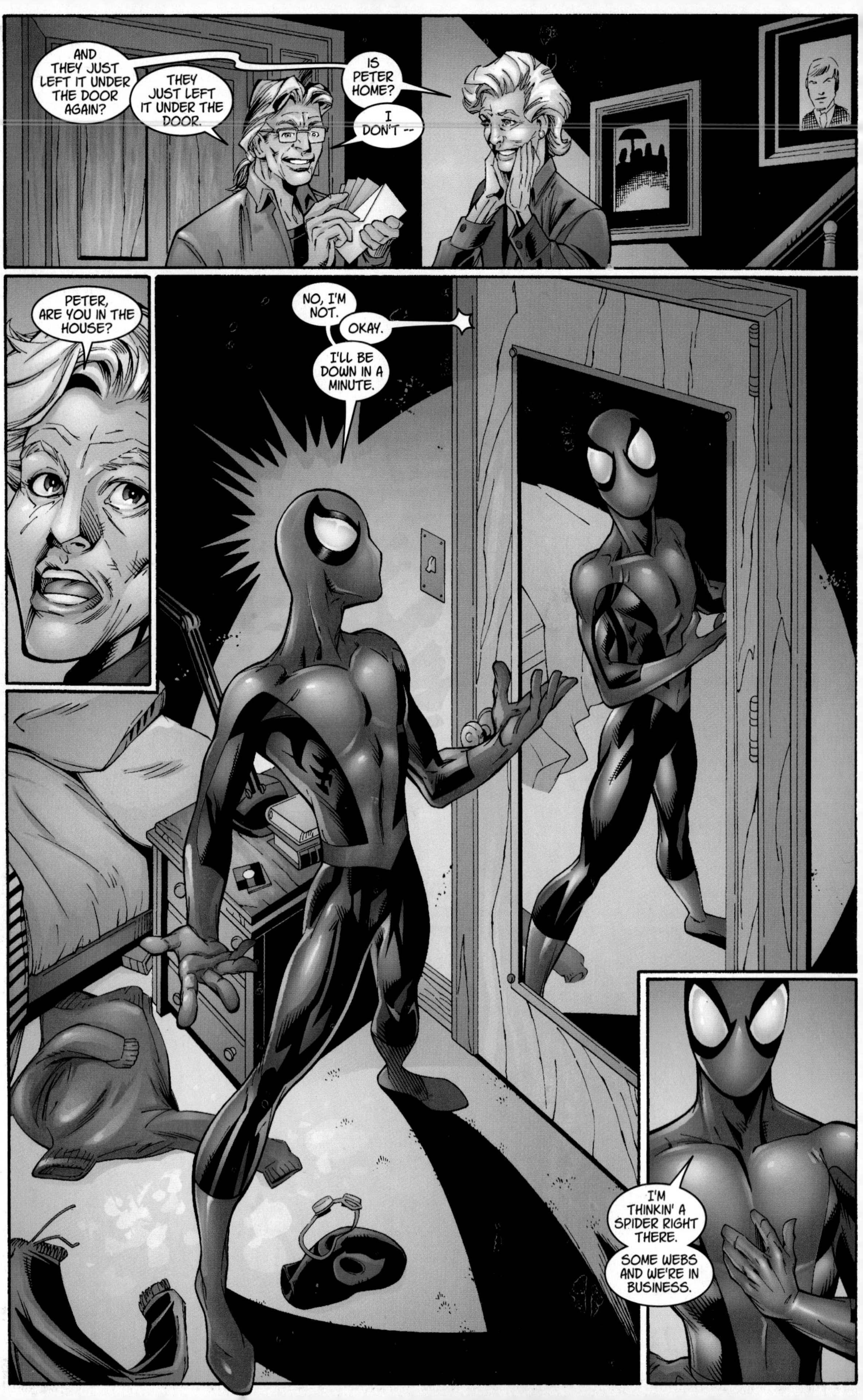
AND THEY JUST LEFT IT UNDER THE DOOR AGAIN?
THEY JUST LEFT IT UNDER THE DOOR.
IS PETER HOME?
I DON'T --
PETER, ARE YOU IN THE HOUSE?
NO, I'M NOT.
OKAY.
I'LL BE DOWN IN A MINUTE.
I'M THINKIN' A SPIDER RIGHT THERE.
SOME WEBS AND WE'RE IN BUSINESS.

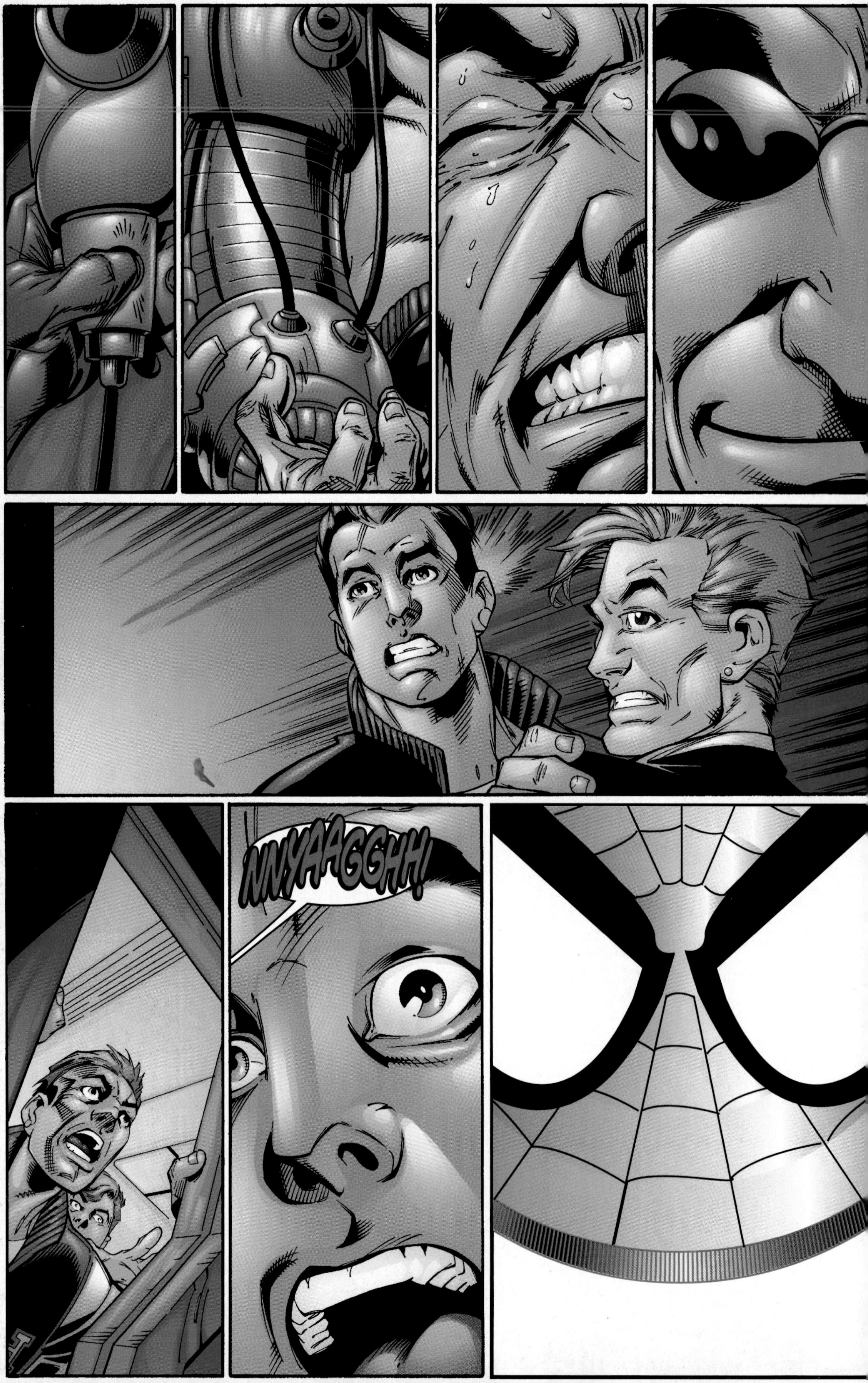
NNYAAGGHH!

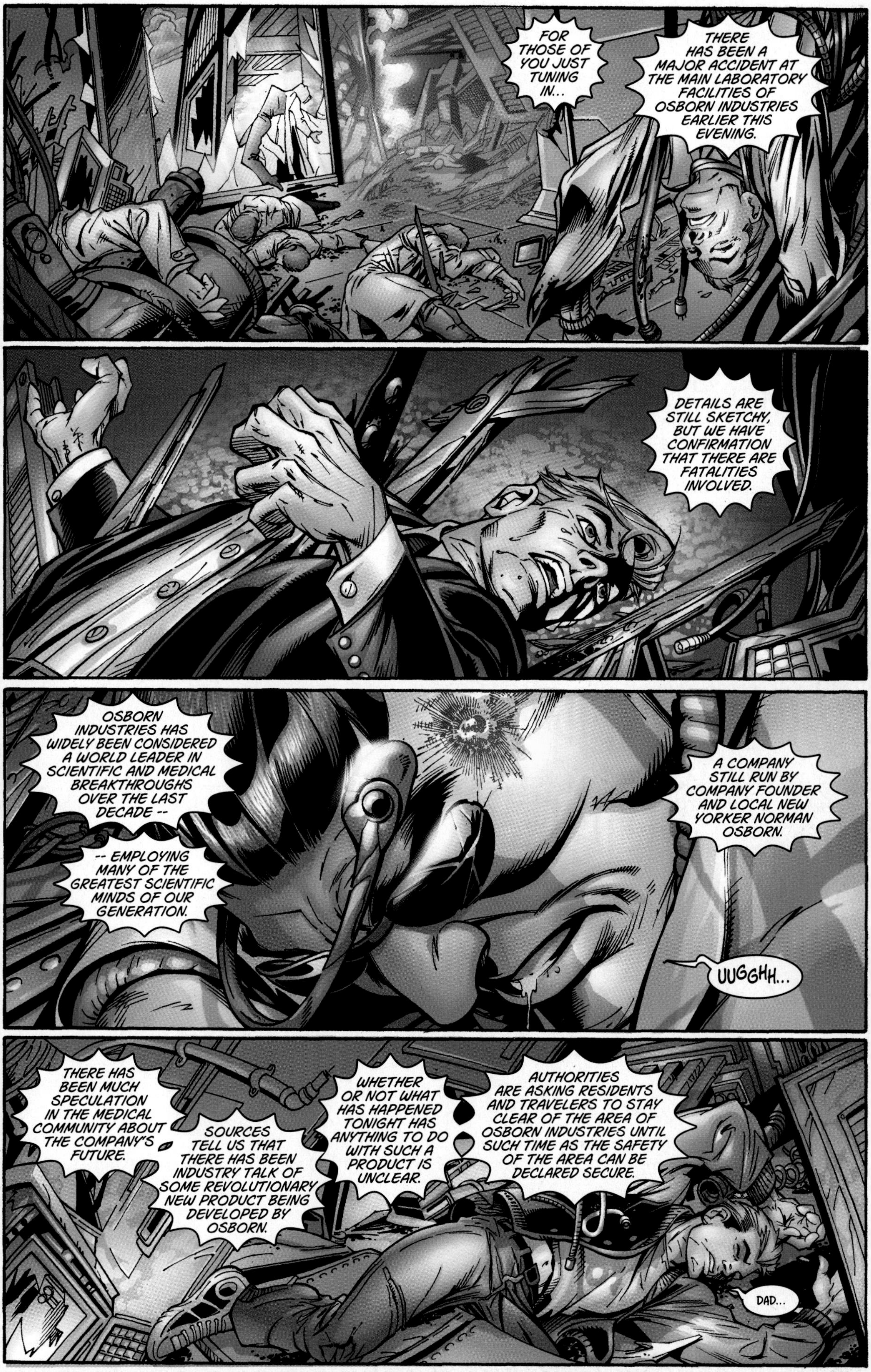
FOR THOSE OF YOU JUST TUNING IN...
THERE HAS BEEN A MAJOR ACCIDENT AT THE MAIN LABORATORY FACILITIES OF OSBORN INDUSTRIES EARLIER THIS EVENING.
DETAILS ARE STILL SKETCHY, BUT WE HAVE CONFIRMATION THAT THERE ARE FATALITIES INVOLVED.
OSBORN INDUSTRIES HAS WIDELY BEEN CONSIDERED A WORLD LEADER IN SCIENTIFIC AND MEDICAL BREAKTHROUGHS OVER THE LAST DECADE --
-- EMPLOYING MANY OF THE GREATEST SCIENTIFIC MINDS OF OUR GENERATION.
A COMPANY STILL RUN BY COMPANY FOUNDER AND LOCAL NEW YORKER NORMAN OSBORN.
UUGGHH...
THERE HAS BEEN MUCH SPECULATION IN THE MEDICAL COMMUNITY ABOUT THE COMPANY'S FUTURE.
SOURCES TELL US THAT THERE HAS BEEN INDUSTRY TALK OF SOME REVOLUTIONARY NEW PRODUCT BEING DEVELOPED BY OSBORN.
WHETHER OR NOT WHAT HAS HAPPENED TONIGHT HAS ANYTHING TO DO WITH SUCH A PRODUCT IS UNCLEAR.
AUTHORITIES ARE ASKING RESIDENTS AND TRAVELERS TO STAY CLEAR OF THE AREA OF OSBORN INDUSTRIES UNTIL SUCH TIME AS THE SAFETY OF THE AREA CAN BE DECLARED SECURE.
DAD...

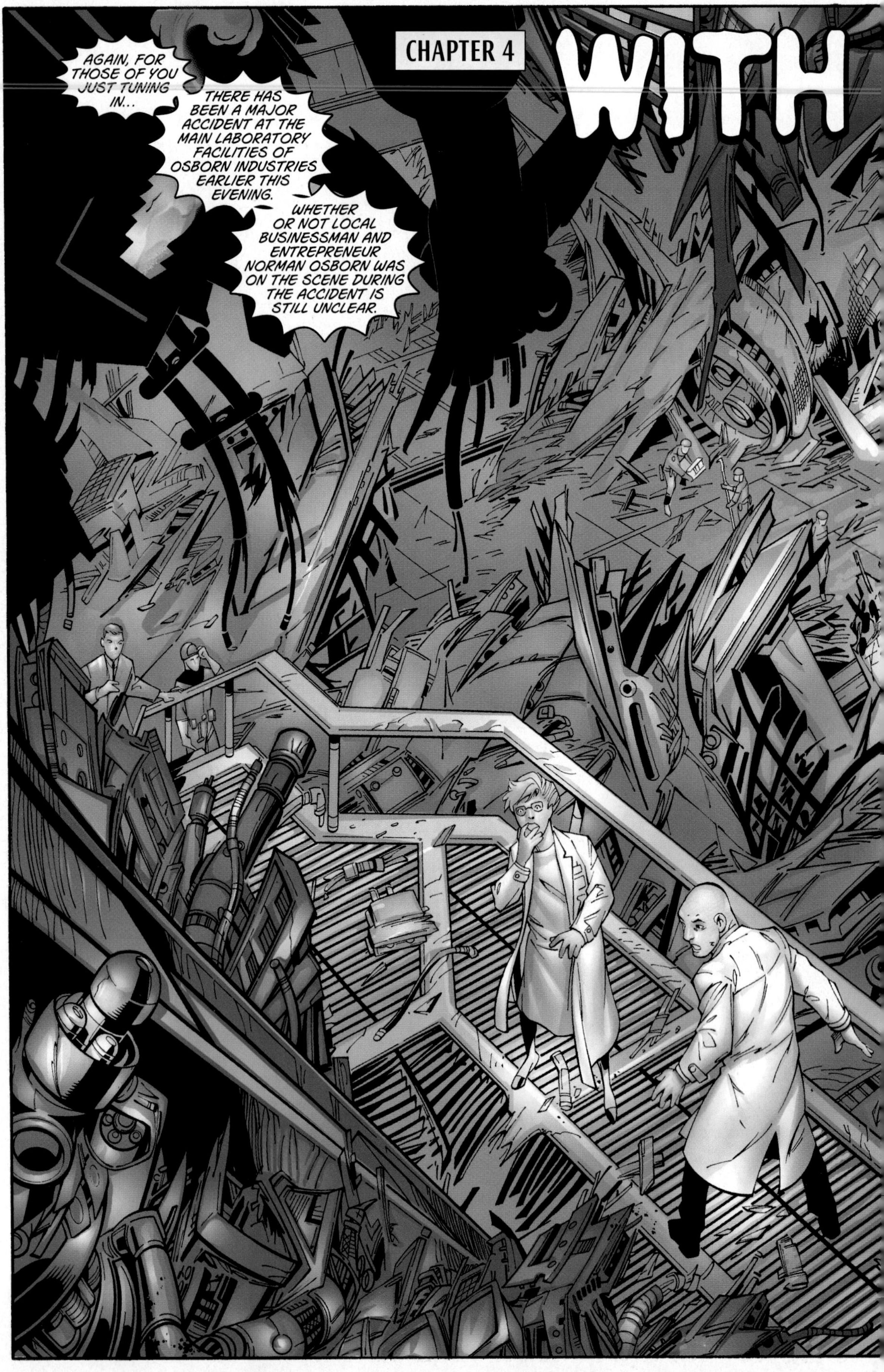
CHAPTER 4
WITH
AGAIN, FOR THOSE OF YOU JUST TUNING IN...
THERE HAS BEEN A MAJOR ACCIDENT AT THE MAIN LABORATORY FACILITIES OF OSBORN INDUSTRIES EARLIER THIS EVENING.
WHETHER OR NOT LOCAL BUSINESSMAN AND ENTREPRENEUR NORMAN OSBORN WAS ON THE SCENE DURING THE ACCIDENT IS STILL UNCLEAR.

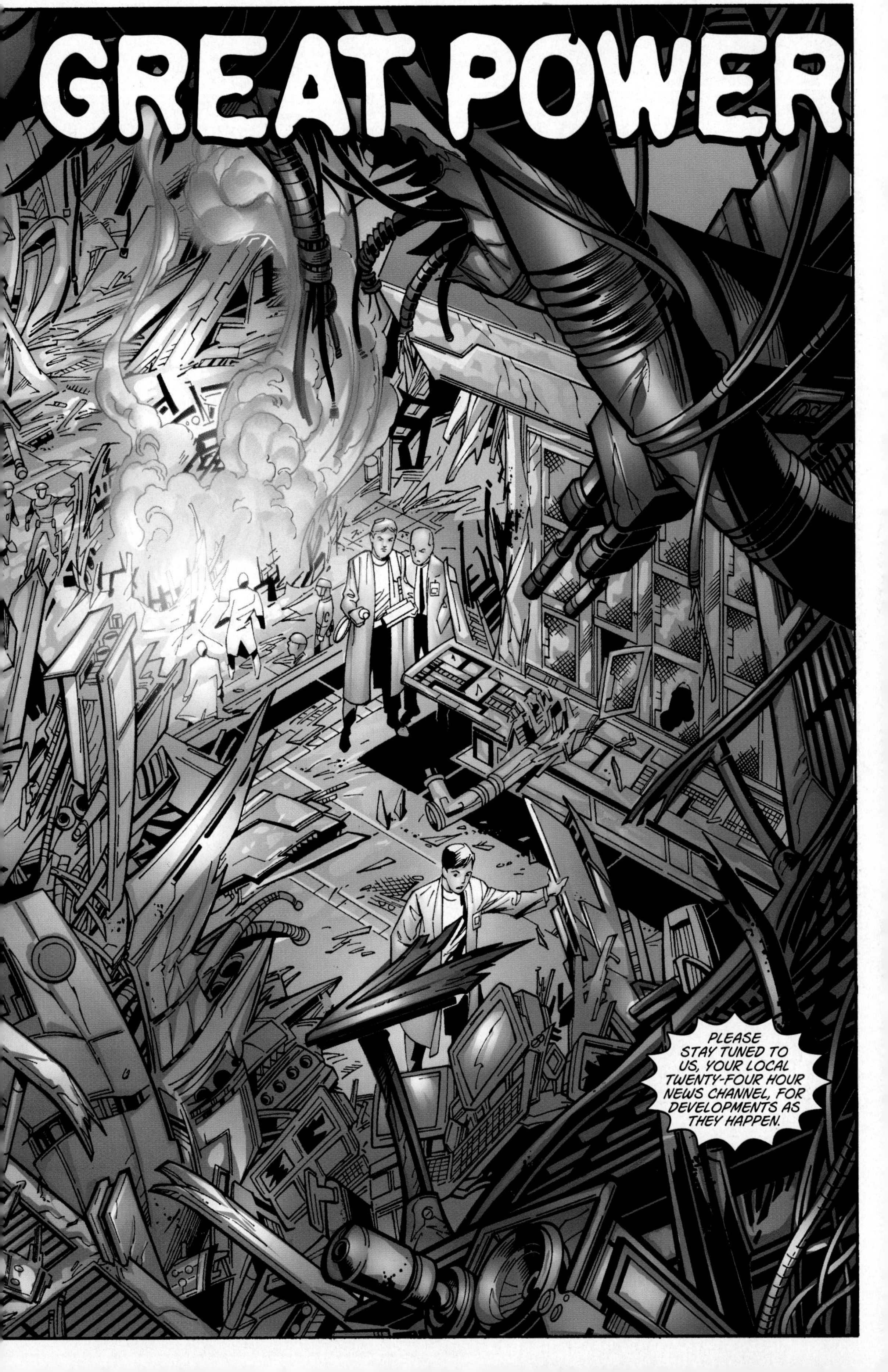
GREAT POWER
PLEASE STAY TUNED TO US, YOUR LOCAL TWENTY-FOUR HOUR NEWS CHANNEL, FOR DEVELOPMENTS AS THEY HAPPEN.

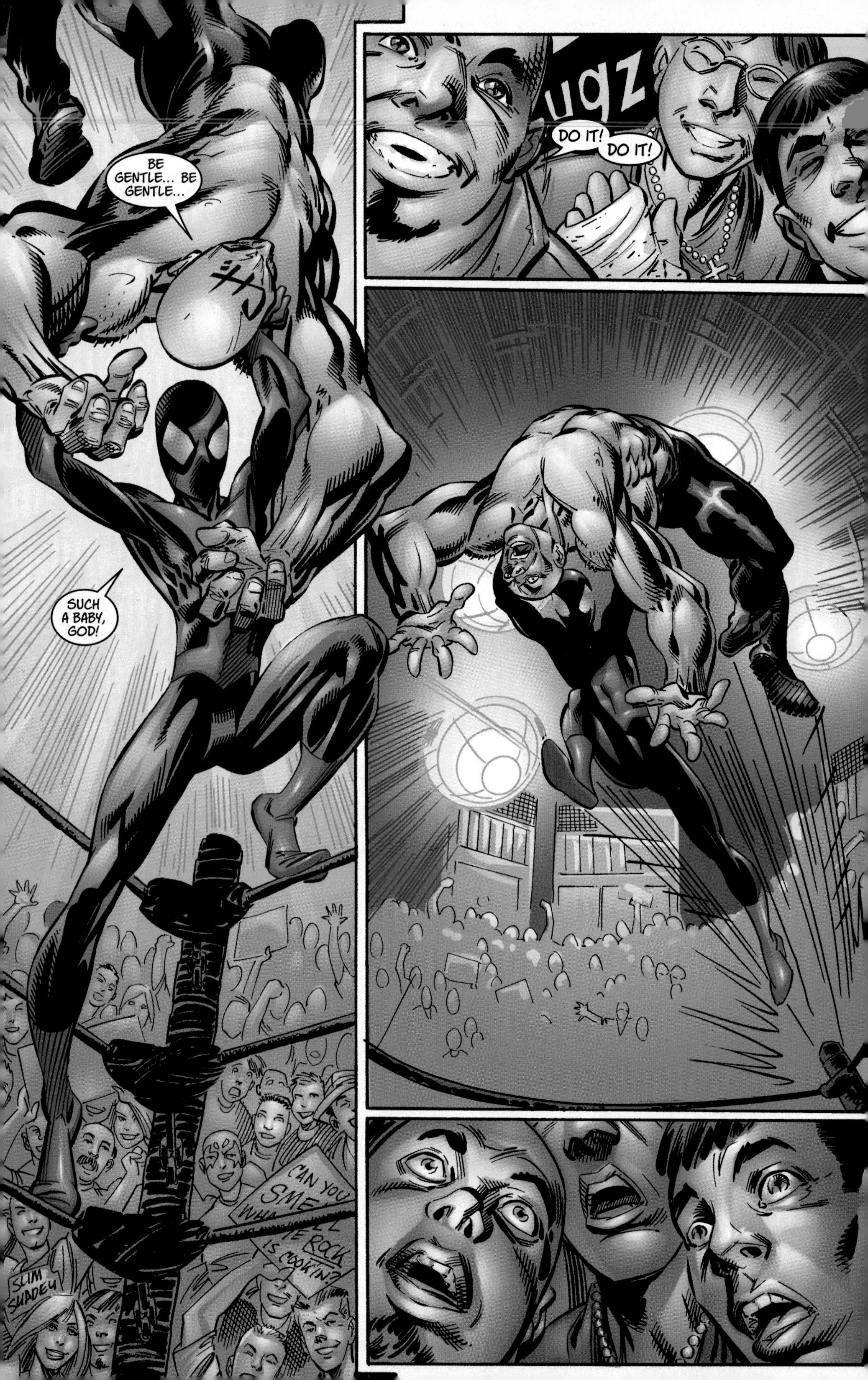
BE GENTLE... BE GENTLE...
SUCH A BABY, GOD!
DO IT!
DO IT!
CAN YOU
IS COOKIN'?
SLIM SHADEY

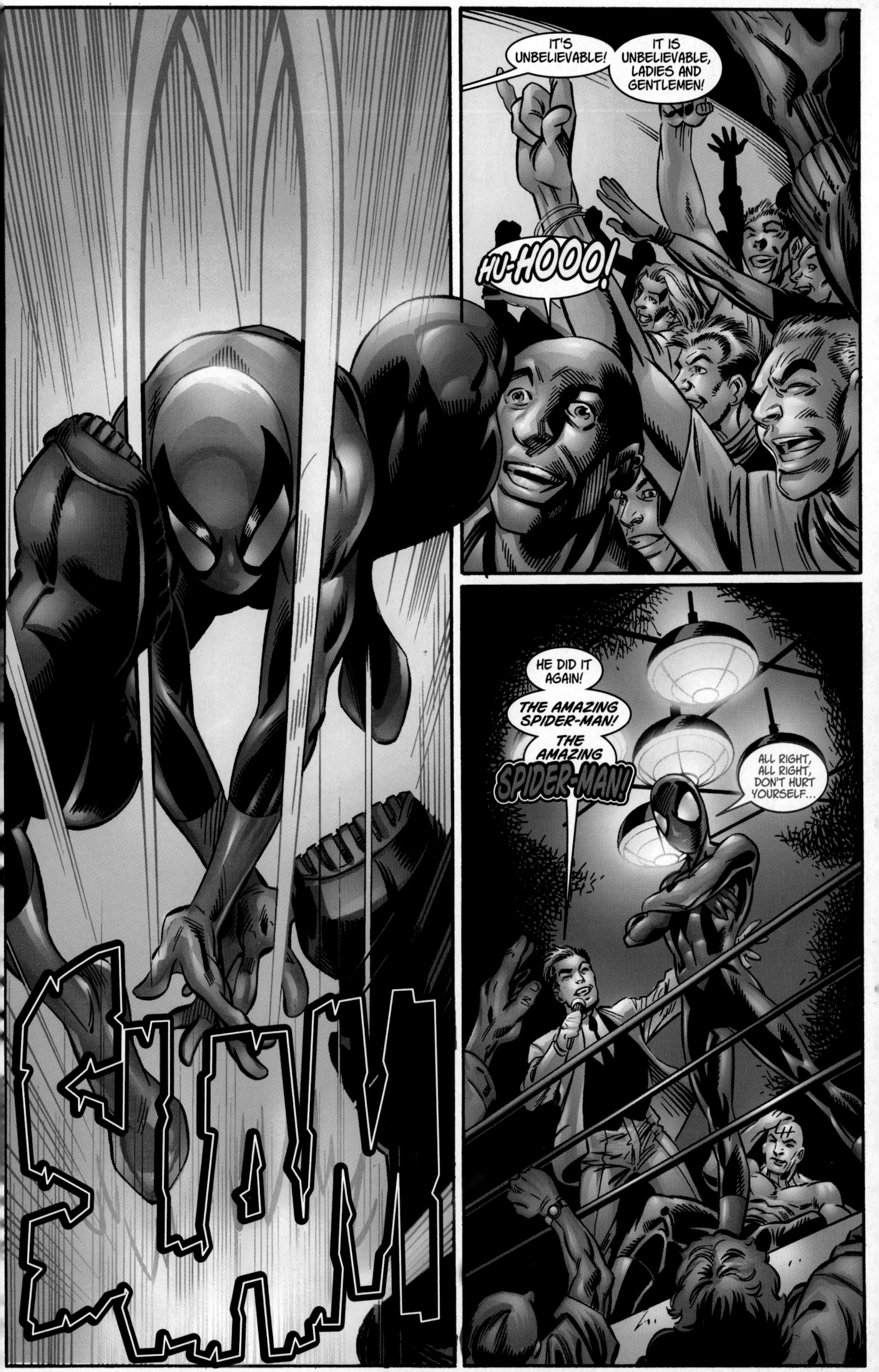
SLAM
IT'S UNBELIEVABLE!
IT IS UNBELIEVABLE, LADIES AND GENTLEMEN!
HU-HOOO!
HE DID IT AGAIN!
THE AMAZING SPIDER-MAN!
THE AMAZING SPIDER-MAN!
ALL RIGHT, ALL RIGHT, DON'T HURT YOURSELF...

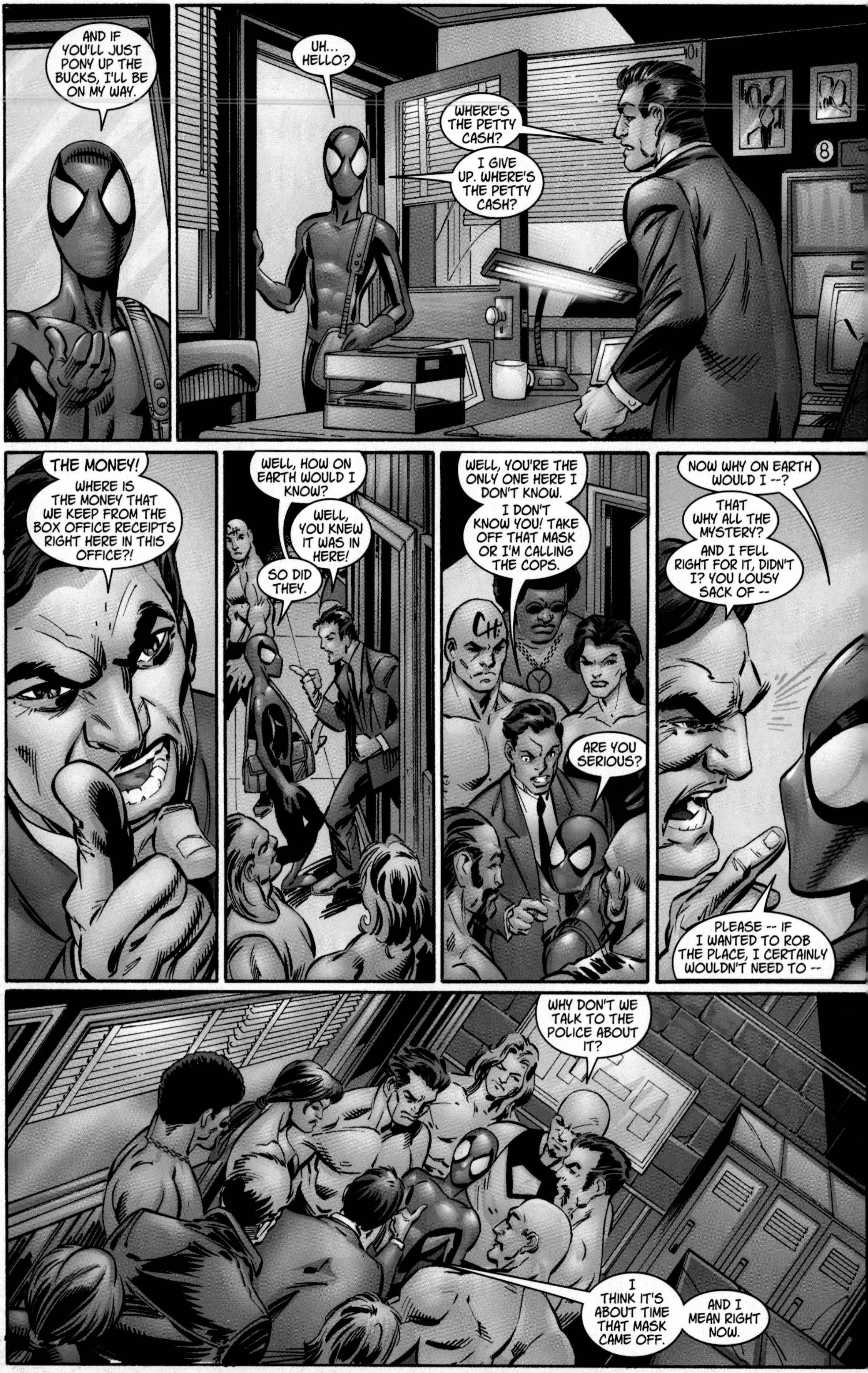
AND IF YOU'LL JUST PONY UP THE BUCKS, I'LL BE ON MY WAY.
UH... HELLO?
WHERE'S THE PETTY CASH?
I GIVE UP. WHERE'S THE PETTY CASH?
THE MONEY!
WHERE IS THE MONEY THAT WE KEEP FROM THE BOX OFFICE RECEIPTS RIGHT HERE IN THIS OFFICE?!
WELL, HOW ON EARTH WOULD I KNOW?
WELL, YOU KNEW IT WAS IN HERE!
SO DID THEY.
WELL, YOU'RE THE ONLY ONE HERE I DON'T KNOW.
I DON'T KNOW YOU! TAKE OFF THAT MASK OR I'M CALLING THE COPS.
ARE YOU SERIOUS?
NOW WHY ON EARTH WOULD I --?
THAT WHY ALL THE MYSTERY?
AND I FELL RIGHT FOR IT, DIDN'T I? YOU LOUSY SACK OF --
PLEASE -- IF I WANTED TO ROB THE PLACE, I CERTAINLY WOULDN'T NEED TO --
WHY DON'T WE TALK TO THE POLICE ABOUT IT?
I THINK IT'S ABOUT TIME THAT MASK CAME OFF.
AND I MEAN RIGHT NOW.

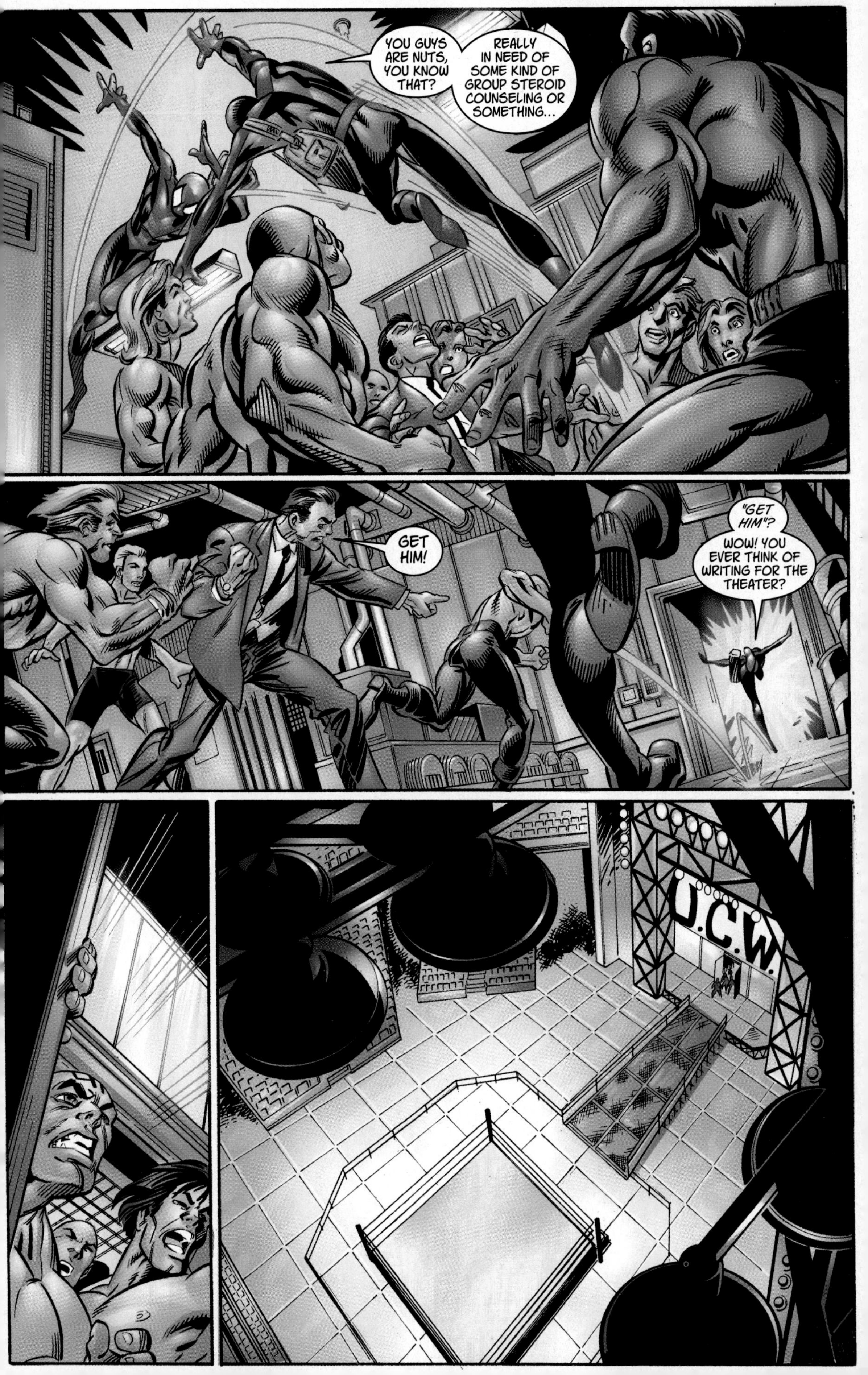
YOU GUYS ARE NUTS, YOU KNOW THAT?
REALLY IN NEED OF SOME KIND OF GROUP STEROID COUNSELING OR SOMETHING...
GET HIM!
"GET HIM"?
WOW! YOU EVER THINK OF WRITING FOR THE THEATER?
U.C.W.

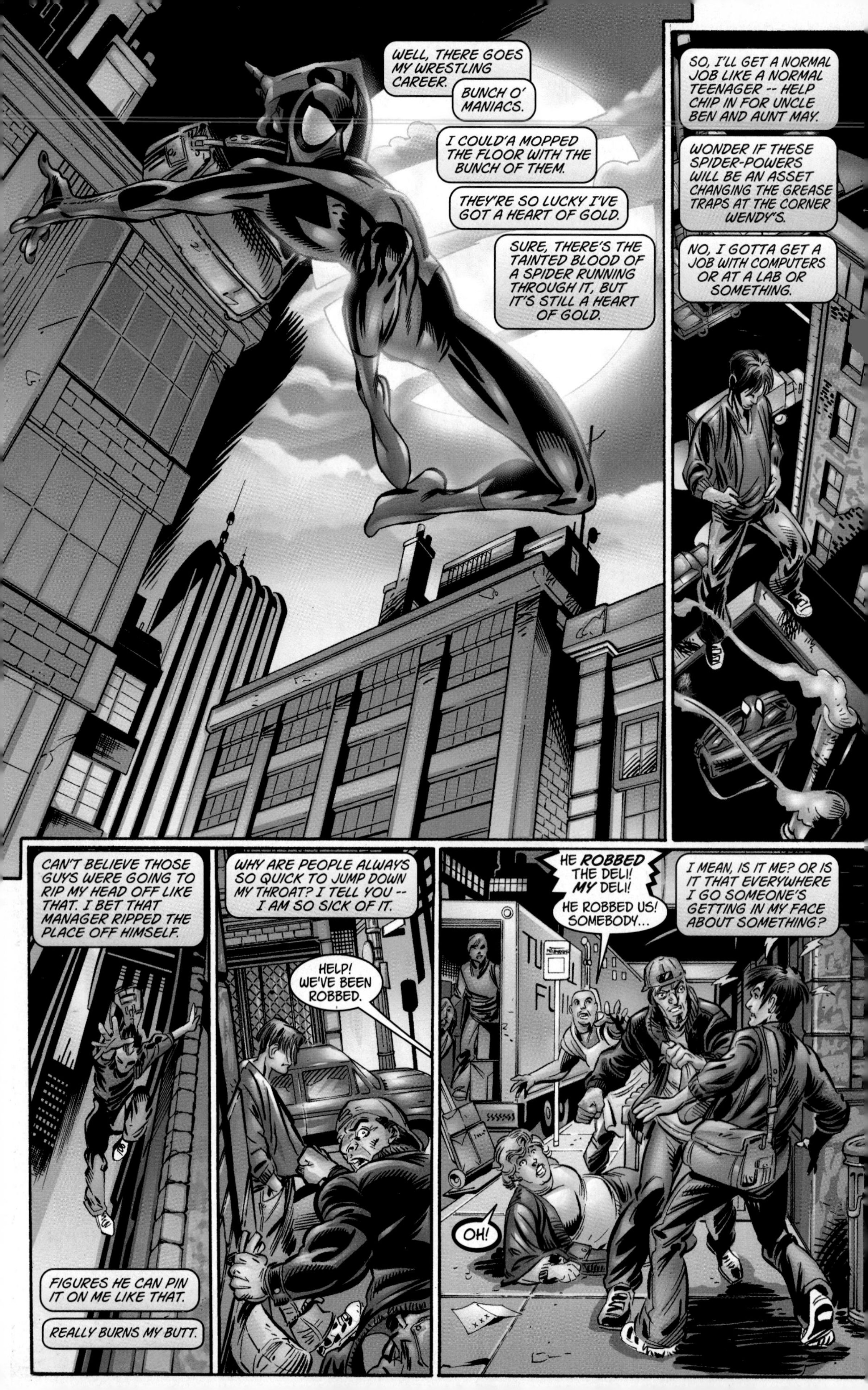
WELL, THERE GOES MY WRESTLING CAREER.
BUNCH O' MANIACS.
I COULD'A MOPPED THE FLOOR WITH THE BUNCH OF THEM.
THEY'RE SO LUCKY I'VE GOT A HEART OF GOLD.
SURE, THERE'S THE TAINTED BLOOD OF A SPIDER RUNNING THROUGH IT, BUT IT'S STILL A HEART OF GOLD.
SO, I'LL GET A NORMAL JOB LIKE A NORMAL TEENAGER -- HELP CHIP IN FOR UNCLE BEN AND AUNT MAY.
WONDER IF THESE SPIDER-POWERS WILL BE AN ASSET CHANGING THE GREASE TRAPS AT THE CORNER WENDY'S.
NO, I GOTTA GET A JOB WITH COMPUTERS OR AT A LAB OR SOMETHING.
CAN'T BELIEVE THOSE GUYS WERE GOING TO RIP MY HEAD OFF LIKE THAT. I BET THAT MANAGER RIPPED THE PLACE OFF HIMSELF.
FIGURES HE CAN PIN IT ON ME LIKE THAT.
REALLY BURNS MY BUTT.
WHY ARE PEOPLE ALWAYS SO QUICK TO JUMP DOWN MY THROAT? I TELL YOU -- I AM SO SICK OF IT.
HELP! WE'VE BEEN ROBBED.
HE ROBBED THE DELI! MY DELI!
HE ROBBED US! SOMEBODY...
I MEAN, IS IT ME? OR IS IT THAT EVERYWHERE I GO SOMEONE'S GETTING IN MY FACE ABOUT SOMETHING?
OH!

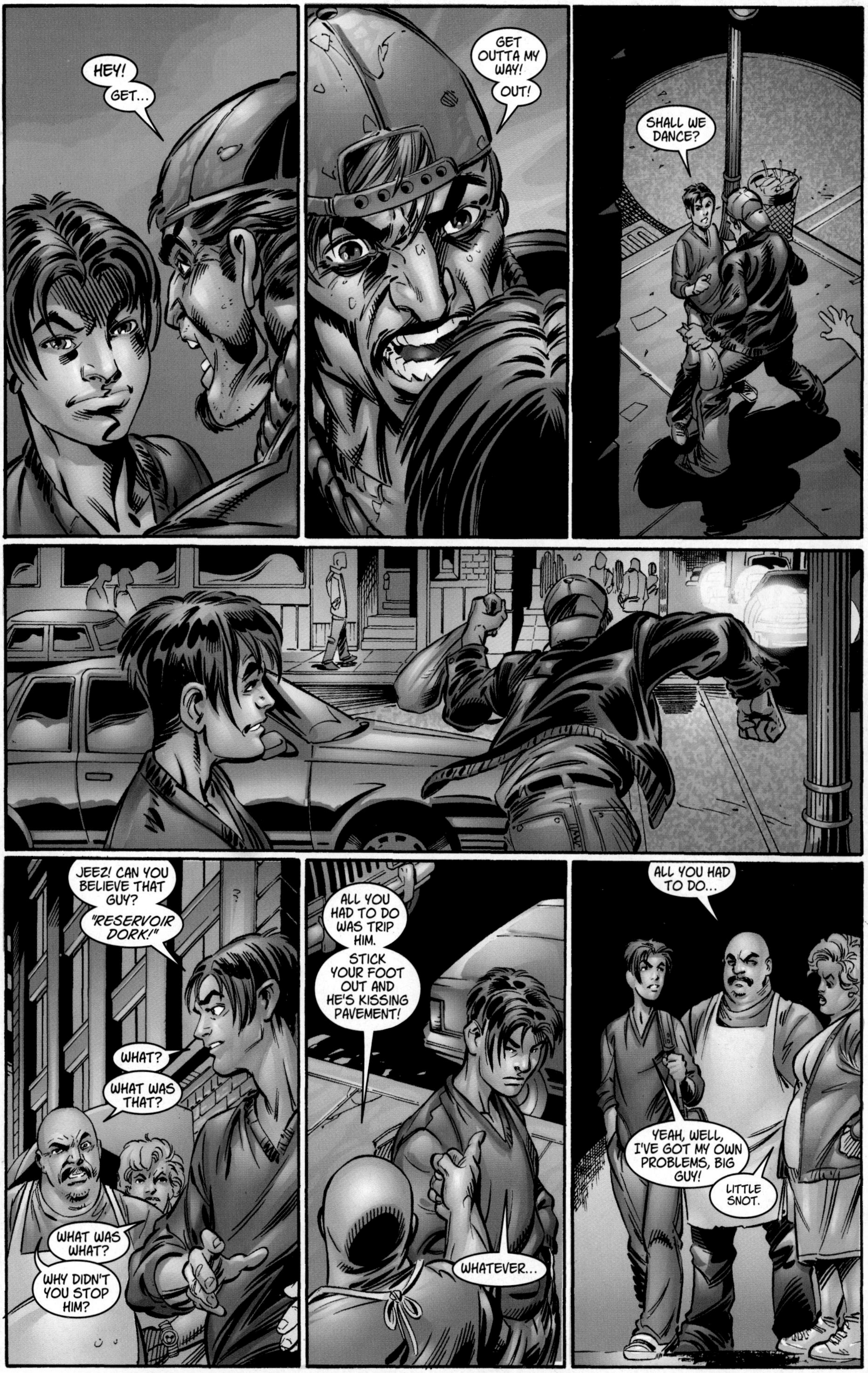
HEY!
GET...
GET OUTTA MY WAY!
OUT!
SHALL WE DANCE?
JEEZ! CAN YOU BELIEVE THAT GUY? "RESERVOIR DORK!"
WHAT?
WHAT WAS THAT?
WHAT WAS WHAT?
WHY DIDN'T YOU STOP HIM?
ALL YOU HAD TO DO WAS TRIP HIM.
STICK YOUR FOOT OUT AND HE'S KISSING PAVEMENT!
WHATEVER...
ALL YOU HAD TO DO...
YEAH, WELL, I'VE GOT MY OWN PROBLEMS, BIG GUY!
LITTLE SNOT.

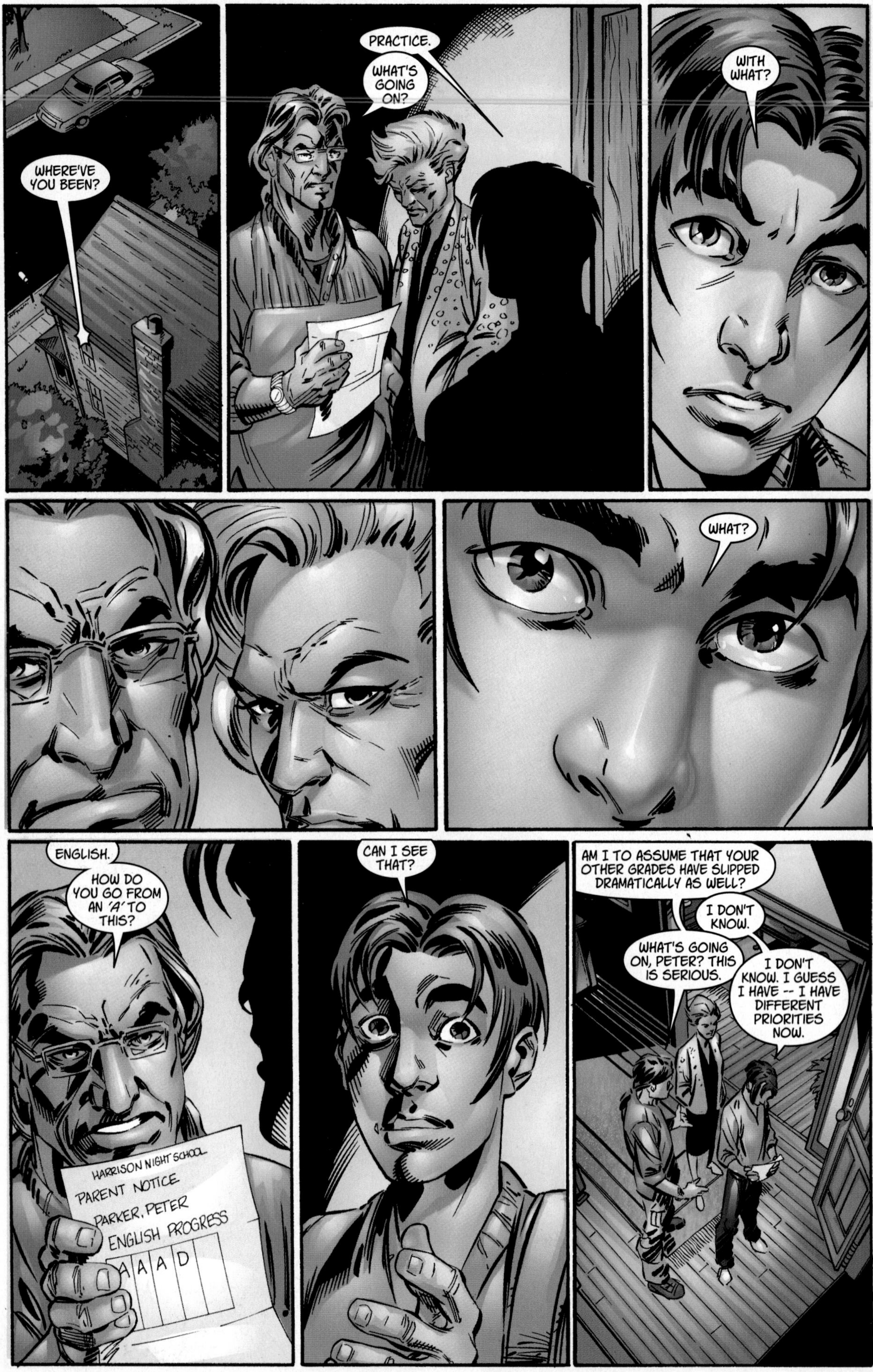
WHERE'VE YOU BEEN?
PRACTICE.
WHAT'S GOING ON?
WITH WHAT?
WHAT?
ENGLISH.
HOW DO YOU GO FROM AN 'A' TO THIS?
HARRISON NIGHT SCHOOL
PARENT NOTICE
PARKER, PETER
ENGLISH PROGRESS
A A A D
CAN I SEE THAT?
AM I TO ASSUME THAT YOUR OTHER GRADES HAVE SLIPPED DRAMATICALLY AS WELL?
I DON'T KNOW.
WHAT'S GOING ON, PETER? THIS IS SERIOUS.
I DON'T KNOW. I GUESS I HAVE -- I HAVE DIFFERENT PRIORITIES NOW.

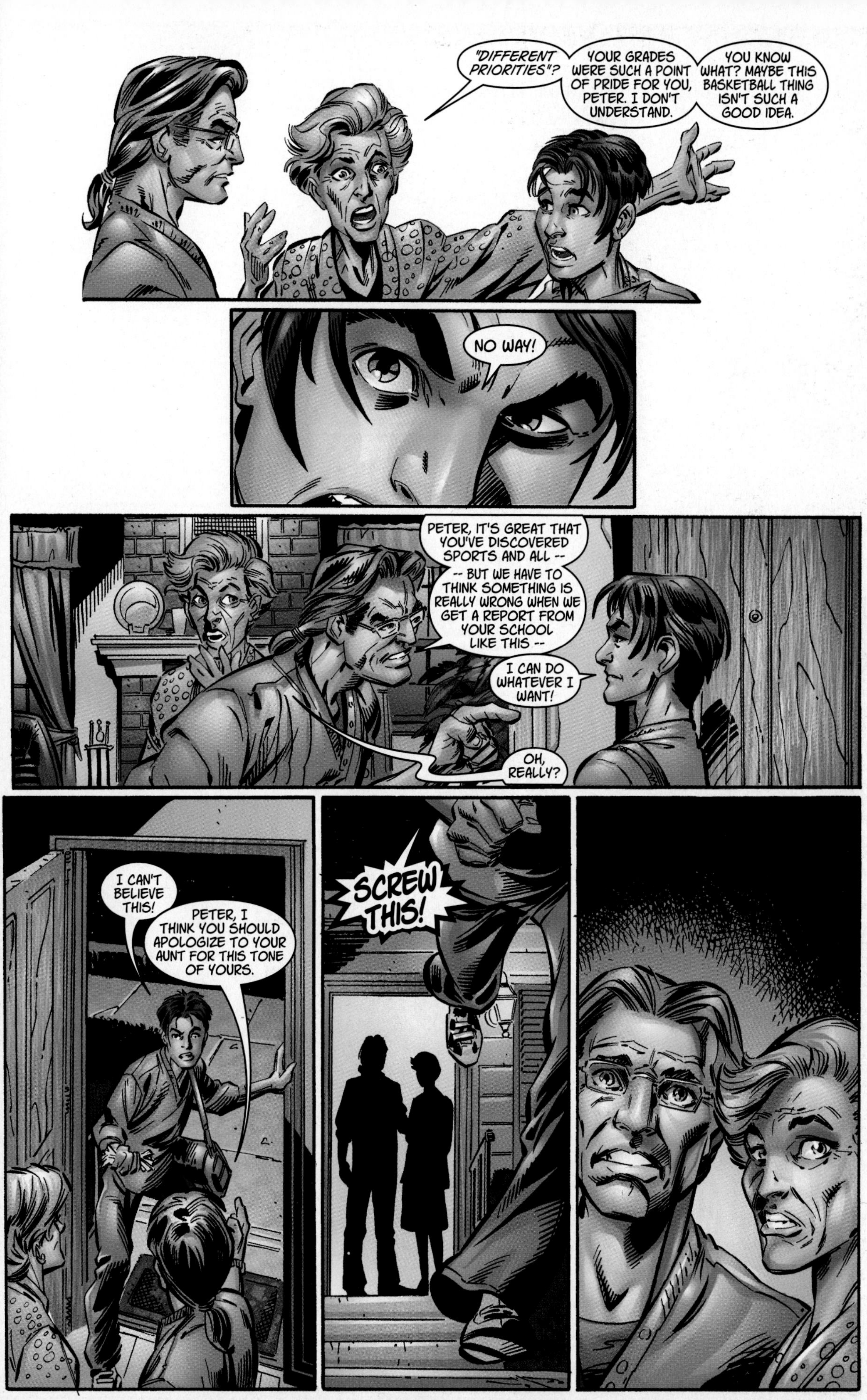
"DIFFERENT PRIORITIES"?
YOUR GRADES WERE SUCH A POINT OF PRIDE FOR YOU, PETER. I DON'T UNDERSTAND.
YOU KNOW WHAT? MAYBE THIS BASKETBALL THING ISN'T SUCH A GOOD IDEA.
NO WAY!
PETER, IT'S GREAT THAT YOU'VE DISCOVERED SPORTS AND ALL --
-- BUT WE HAVE TO THINK SOMETHING IS REALLY WRONG WHEN WE GET A REPORT FROM YOUR SCHOOL LIKE THIS --
I CAN DO WHATEVER I WANT!
OH, REALLY?
I CAN'T BELIEVE THIS!
PETER, I THINK YOU SHOULD APOLOGIZE TO YOUR AUNT FOR THIS TONE OF YOURS.
SCREW THIS!

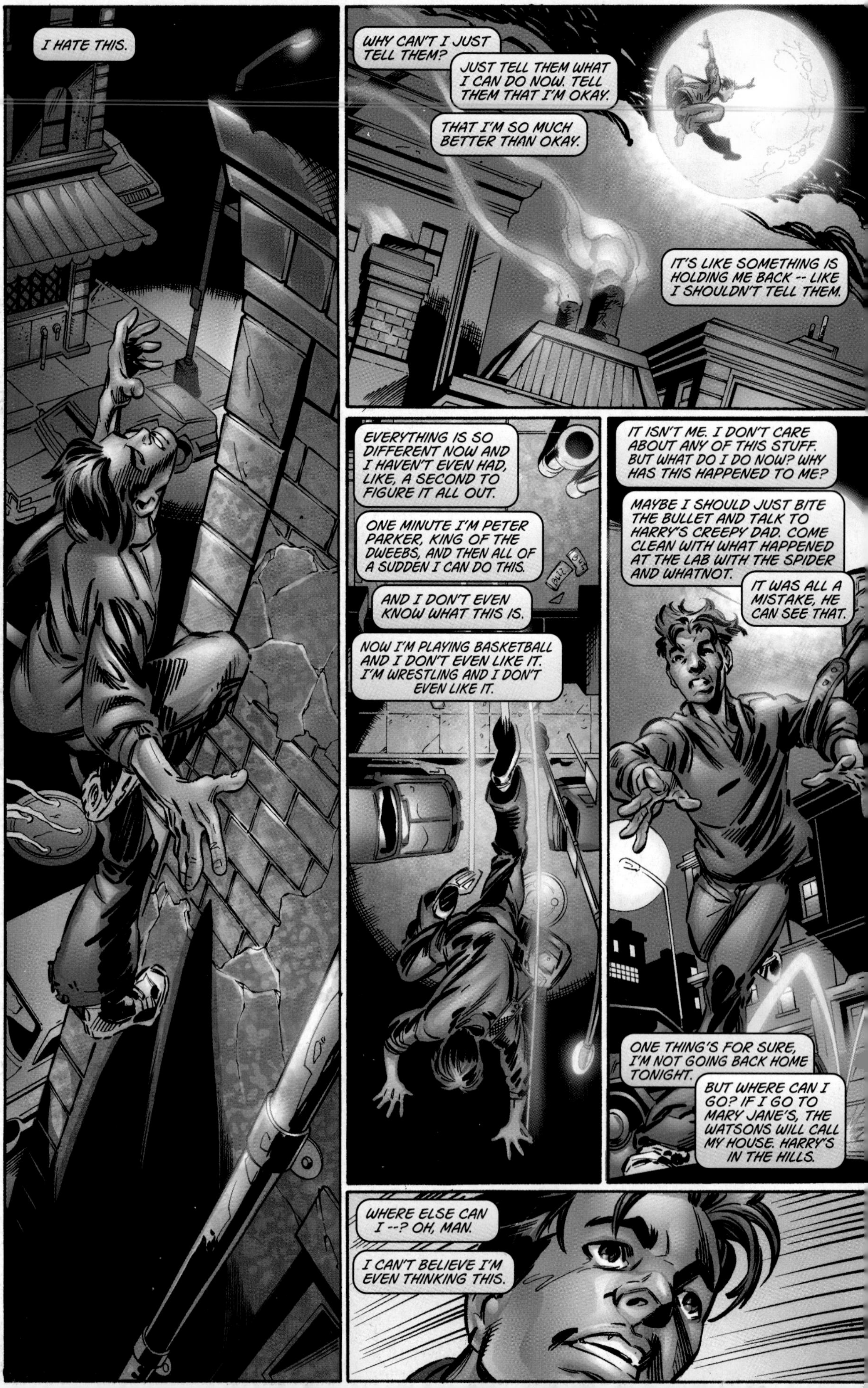
I HATE THIS.
WHY CAN'T I JUST TELL THEM?
JUST TELL THEM WHAT I CAN DO NOW. TELL THEM THAT I'M OKAY.
THAT I'M SO MUCH BETTER THAN OKAY.
IT'S LIKE SOMETHING IS HOLDING ME BACK -- LIKE I SHOULDN'T TELL THEM.
EVERYTHING IS SO DIFFERENT NOW AND I HAVEN'T EVEN HAD, LIKE, A SECOND TO FIGURE IT ALL OUT.
ONE MINUTE I'M PETER PARKER, KING OF THE DWEEBS, AND THEN ALL OF A SUDDEN I CAN DO THIS.
AND I DON'T EVEN KNOW WHAT THIS IS.
NOW I'M PLAYING BASKETBALL AND I DON'T EVEN LIKE IT. I'M WRESTLING AND I DON'T EVEN LIKE IT.
IT ISN'T ME. I DON'T CARE ABOUT ANY OF THIS STUFF. BUT WHAT DO I DO NOW? WHY HAS THIS HAPPENED TO ME?
MAYBE I SHOULD JUST BITE THE BULLET AND TALK TO HARRY'S CREEPY DAD. COME CLEAN WITH WHAT HAPPENED AT THE LAB WITH THE SPIDER AND WHATNOT.
IT WAS ALL A MISTAKE, HE CAN SEE THAT.
ONE THING'S FOR SURE, I'M NOT GOING BACK HOME TONIGHT.
BUT WHERE CAN I GO? IF I GO TO MARY JANE'S, THE WATSONS WILL CALL MY HOUSE. HARRY'S IN THE HILLS.
WHERE ELSE CAN I --? OH, MAN.
I CAN'T BELIEVE I'M EVEN THINKING THIS.

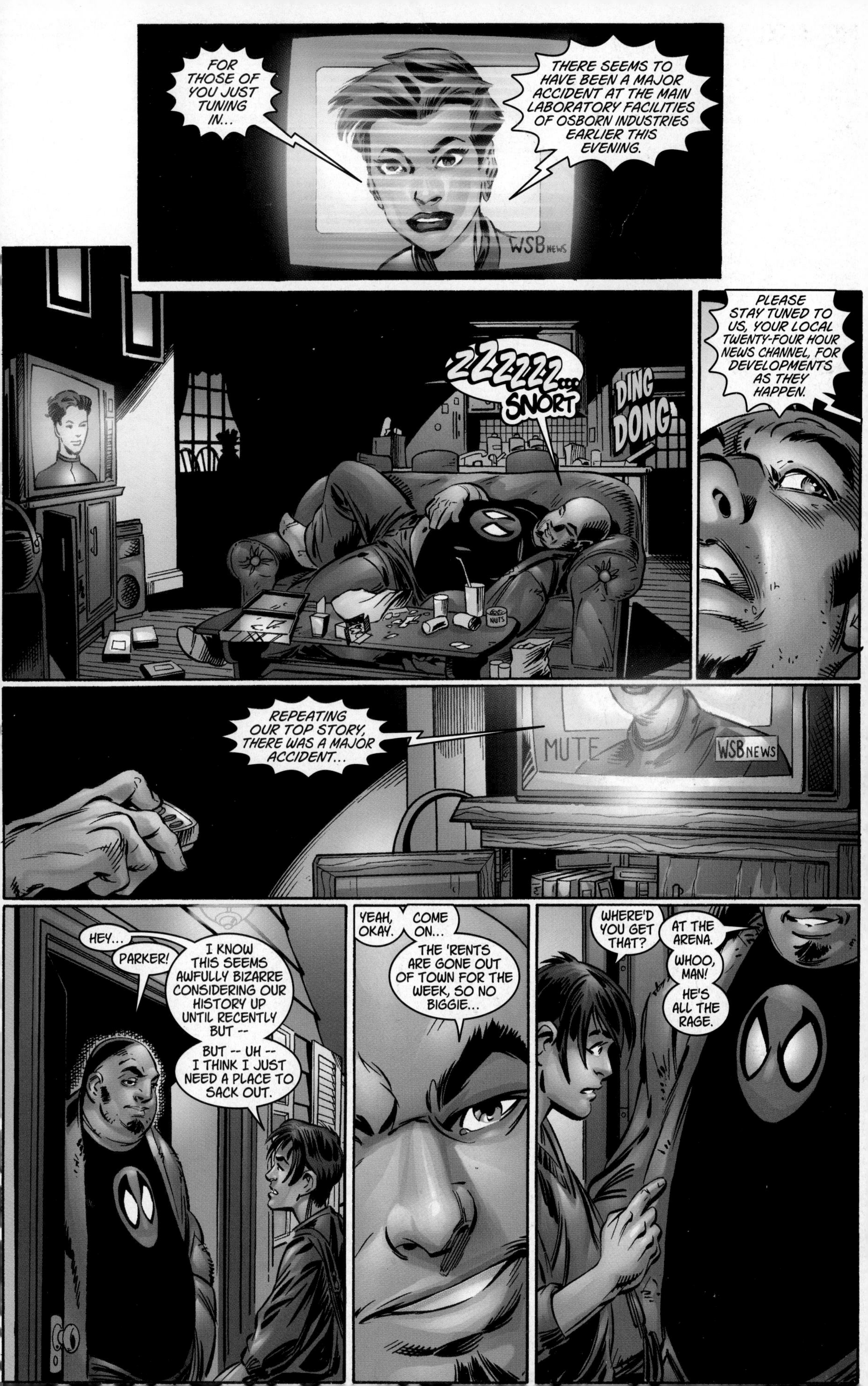

FOR THOSE OF YOU JUST TUNING IN...
THERE SEEMS TO HAVE BEEN A MAJOR ACCIDENT AT THE MAIN LABORATORY FACILITIES OF OSBORN INDUSTRIES EARLIER THIS EVENING.
WSB NEWS
ZZZZZZZ... SNORT
DING DONG
PLEASE STAY TUNED TO US, YOUR LOCAL TWENTY-FOUR HOUR NEWS CHANNEL, FOR DEVELOPMENTS AS THEY HAPPEN.
REPEATING OUR TOP STORY, THERE WAS A MAJOR ACCIDENT...
MUTE
WSB NEWS
HEY...
PARKER!
I KNOW THIS SEEMS AWFULLY BIZARRE CONSIDERING OUR HISTORY UP UNTIL RECENTLY BUT --
BUT -- UH -- I THINK I JUST NEED A PLACE TO SACK OUT.
YEAH, OKAY.
COME ON...
THE 'RENTS ARE GONE OUT OF TOWN FOR THE WEEK, SO NO BIGGIE...
WHERE'D YOU GET THAT?
AT THE ARENA.
WHOO, MAN!
HE'S ALL THE RAGE.

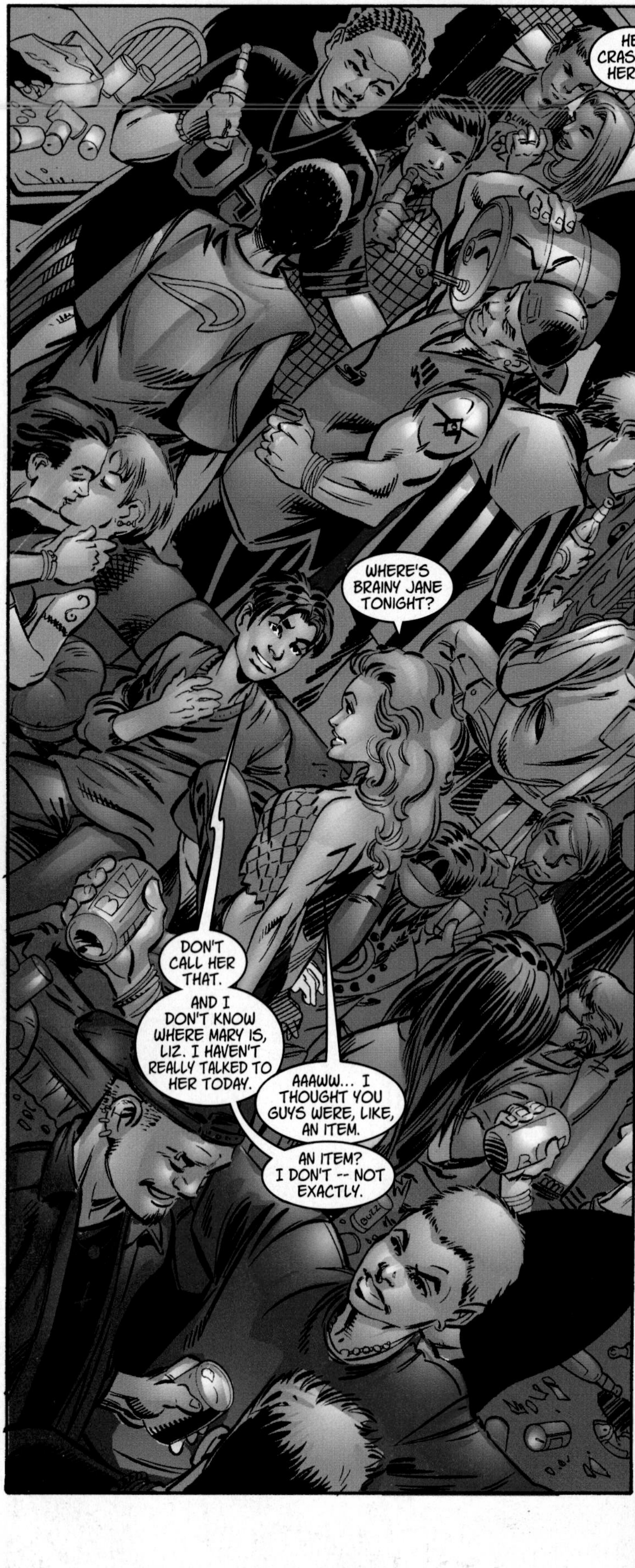
HE CRASHED HERE?
HE DID.
IN YOUR PAD?
RIGHT THERE ON THAT COUCH.
AND YOU LET HIM.
SURE.
PUNY PARKER?
WHAT ARE YOU -- SIX YEARS OLD?
YOU GUYS HEAR WHAT HAPPENED TO HARRY'S DAD?
WHERE'S BRAINY JANE TONIGHT?
DON'T CALL HER THAT.
AND I DON'T KNOW WHERE MARY IS, LIZ. I HAVEN'T REALLY TALKED TO HER TODAY.
AAAWW... I THOUGHT YOU GUYS WERE, LIKE, AN ITEM.
AN ITEM? I DON'T -- NOT EXACTLY.

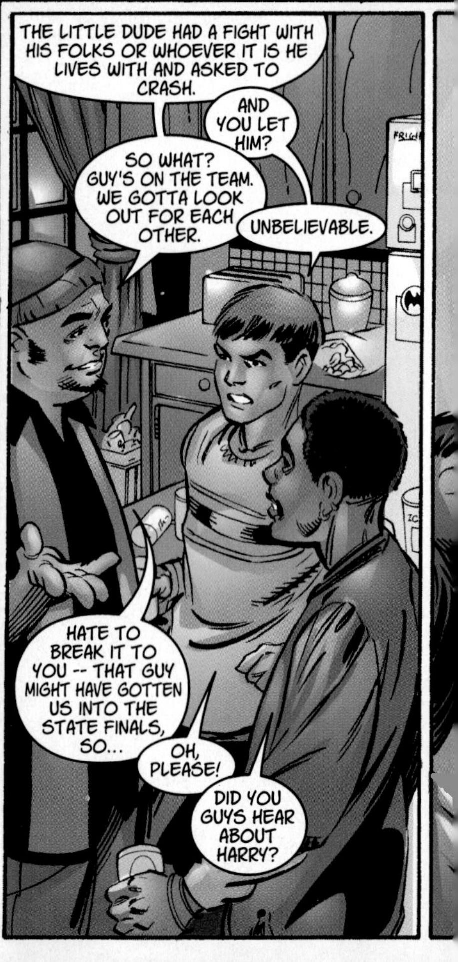
THE LITTLE DUDE HAD A FIGHT WITH HIS FOLKS OR WHOEVER IT IS HE LIVES WITH AND ASKED TO CRASH.
AND YOU LET HIM?
SO WHAT? GUY'S ON THE TEAM. WE GOTTA LOOK OUT FOR EACH OTHER.
UNBELIEVABLE.
HATE TO BREAK IT TO YOU -- THAT GUY MIGHT HAVE GOTTEN US INTO THE STATE FINALS, SO...
OH, PLEASE!
DID YOU GUYS HEAR ABOUT HARRY?

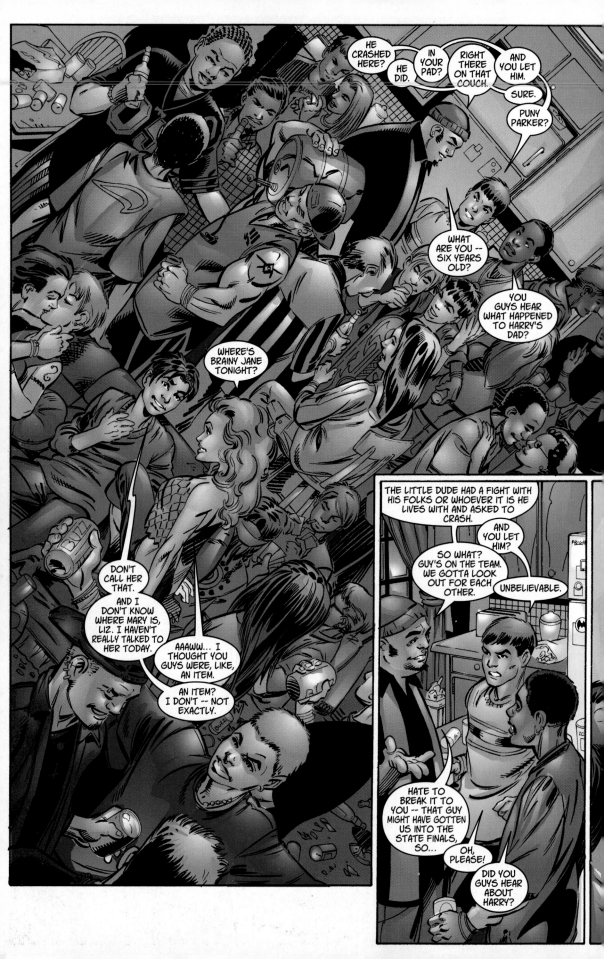

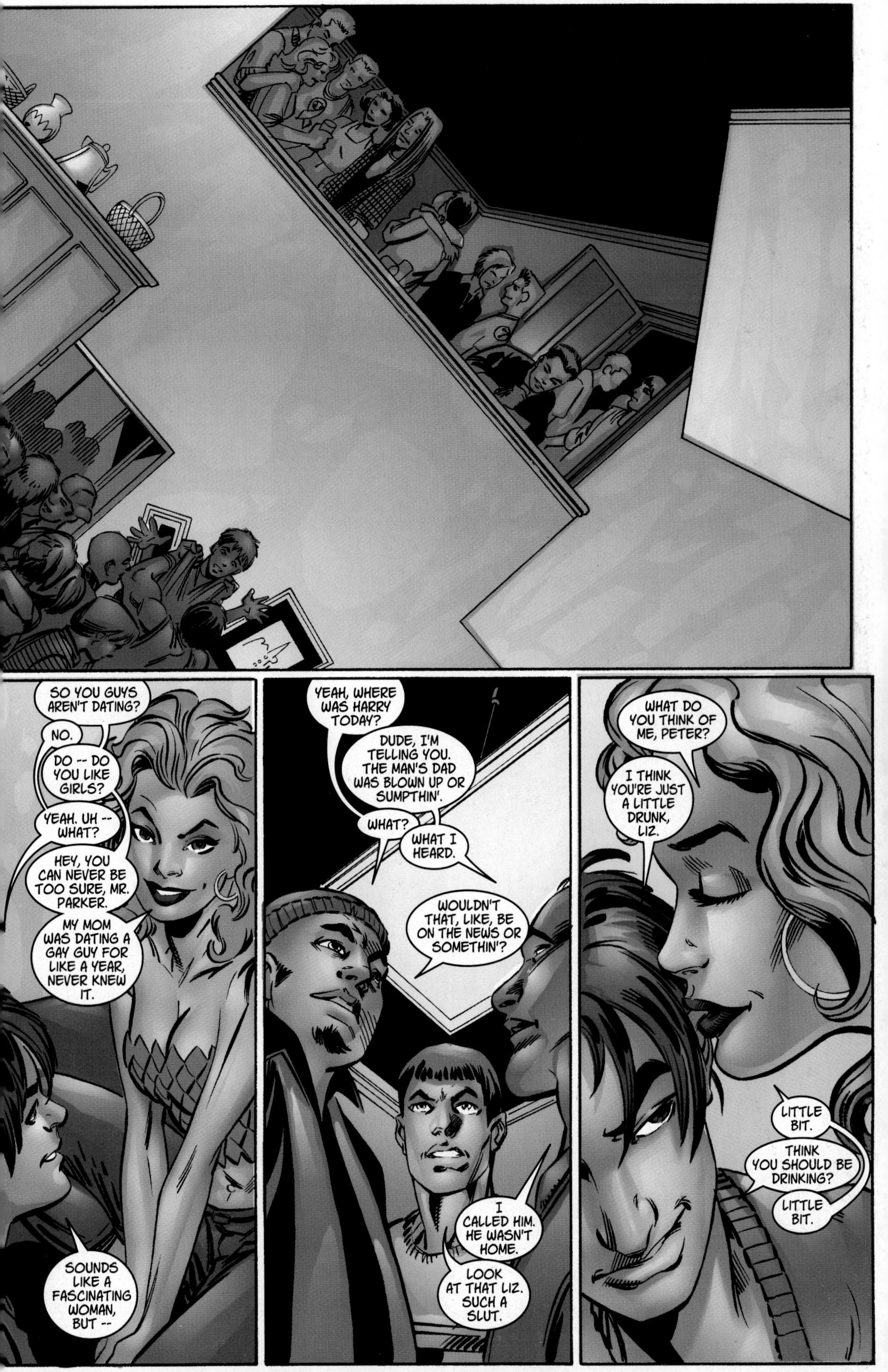
SO YOU GUYS AREN'T DATING?
NO.
DO -- DO YOU LIKE GIRLS?
YEAH. UH -- WHAT?
HEY, YOU CAN NEVER BE TOO SURE, MR. PARKER.
MY MOM WAS DATING A GAY GUY FOR LIKE A YEAR, NEVER KNEW IT.
SOUNDS LIKE A FASCINATING WOMAN, BUT --
YEAH, WHERE WAS HARRY TODAY?
DUDE, I'M TELLING YOU. THE MAN'S DAD WAS BLOWN UP OR SUMPTHIN'.
WHAT?
WHAT I HEARD.
WOULDN'T THAT, LIKE, BE ON THE NEWS OR SOMETHIN'?
I CALLED HIM. HE WASN'T HOME.
LOOK AT THAT LIZ. SUCH A SLUT.
WHAT DO YOU THINK OF ME, PETER?
I THINK YOU'RE JUST A LITTLE DRUNK, LIZ.
LITTLE BIT.
THINK YOU SHOULD BE DRINKING?
LITTLE BIT.

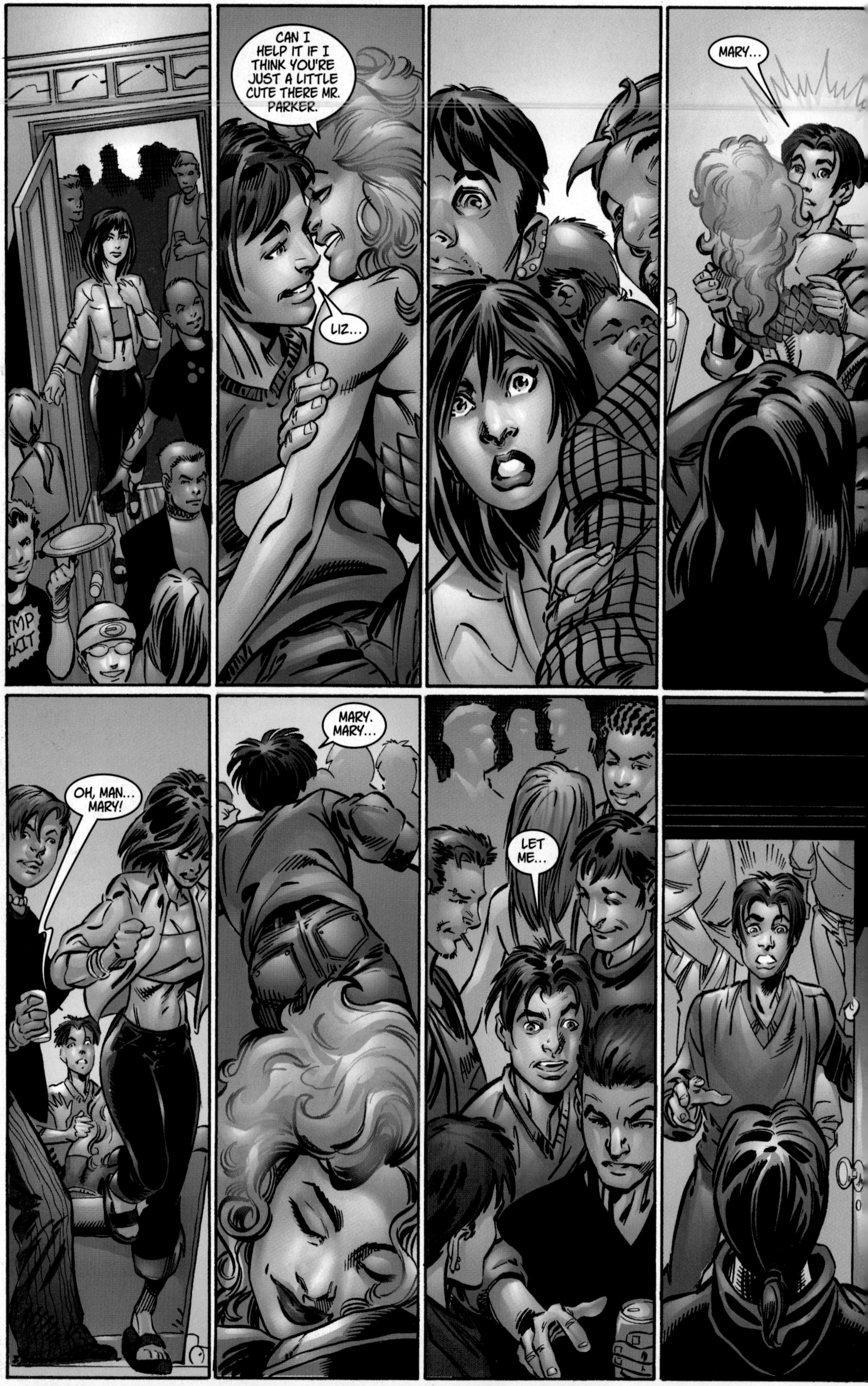
CAN I HELP IT IF I THINK YOU'RE JUST A LITTLE CUTE THERE MR. PARKER.
LIZ...
MARY...
OH, MAN... MARY!
MARY. MARY...
LET ME...

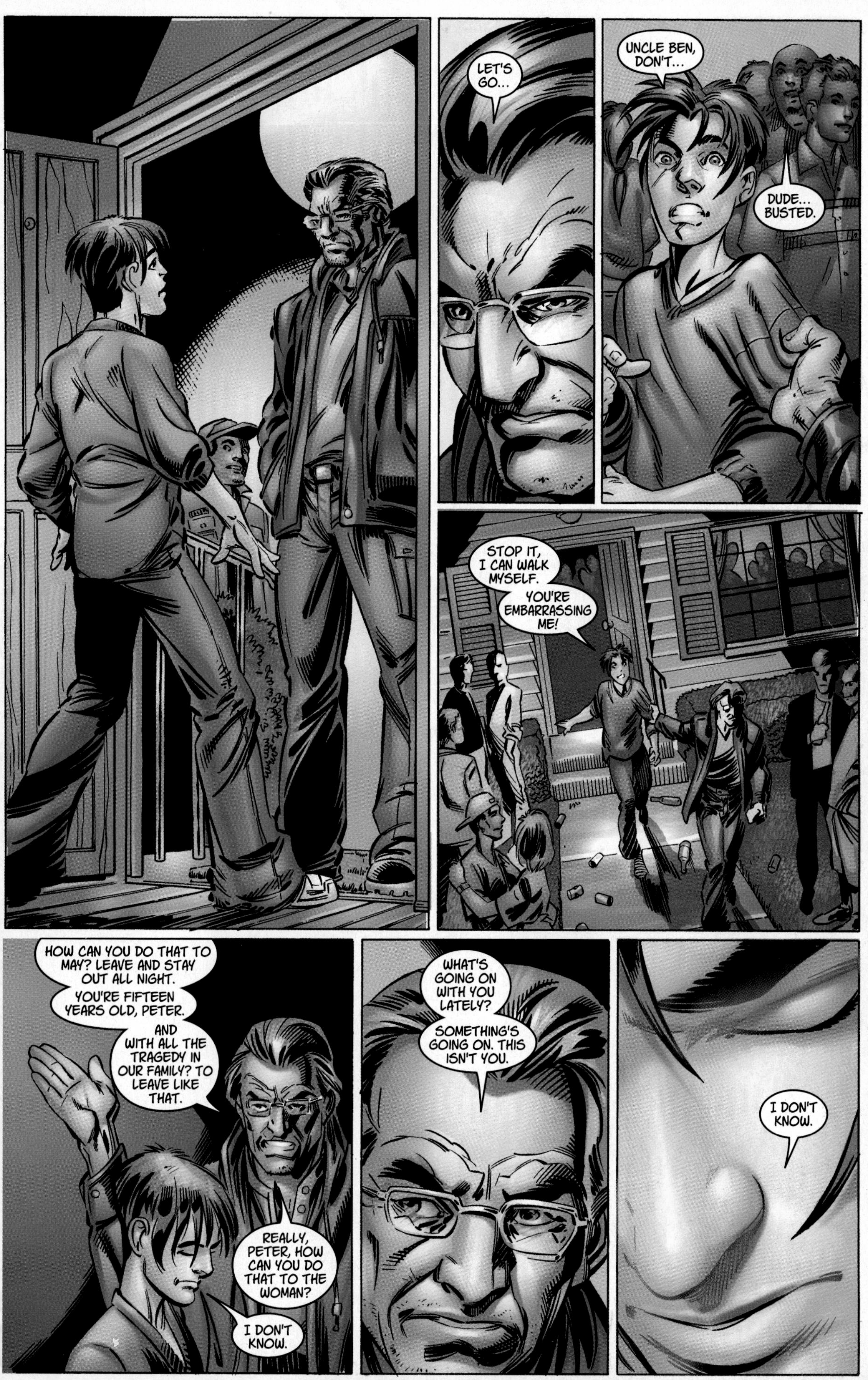
LET'S GO...
UNCLE BEN, DON'T...
DUDE... BUSTED.
STOP IT, I CAN WALK MYSELF.
YOU'RE EMBARRASSING ME!
HOW CAN YOU DO THAT TO MAY? LEAVE AND STAY OUT ALL NIGHT.
YOU'RE FIFTEEN YEARS OLD, PETER.
AND WITH ALL THE TRAGEDY IN OUR FAMILY? TO LEAVE LIKE THAT.
REALLY, PETER, HOW CAN YOU DO THAT TO THE WOMAN?
I DON'T KNOW.
WHAT'S GOING ON WITH YOU LATELY?
SOMETHING'S GOING ON. THIS ISN'T YOU.
I DON'T KNOW.

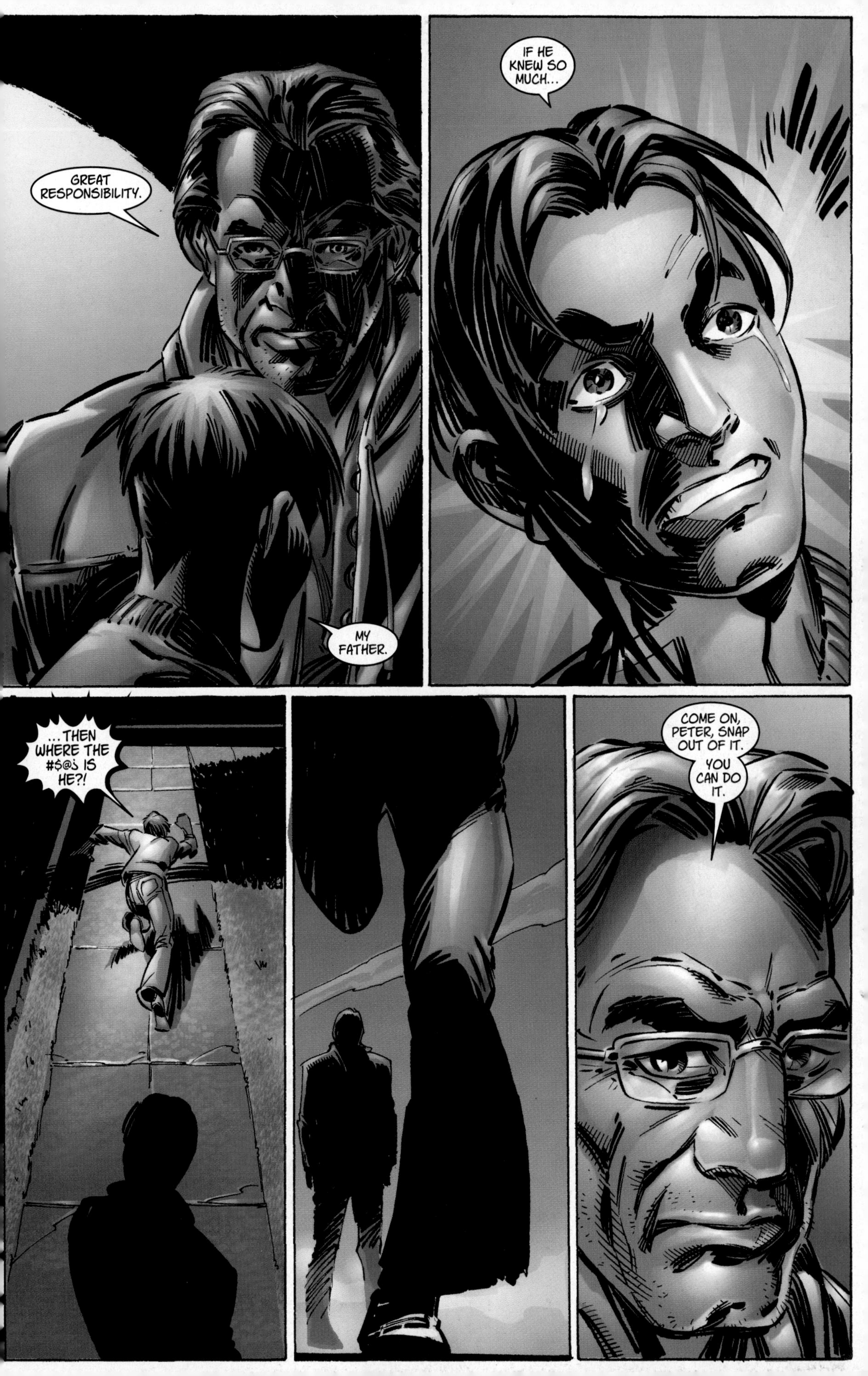
GREAT RESPONSIBILITY.
MY FATHER.
IF HE KNEW SO MUCH...
...THEN WHERE THE #$@¿ IS HE?!
COME ON, PETER, SNAP OUT OF IT.
YOU CAN DO IT.

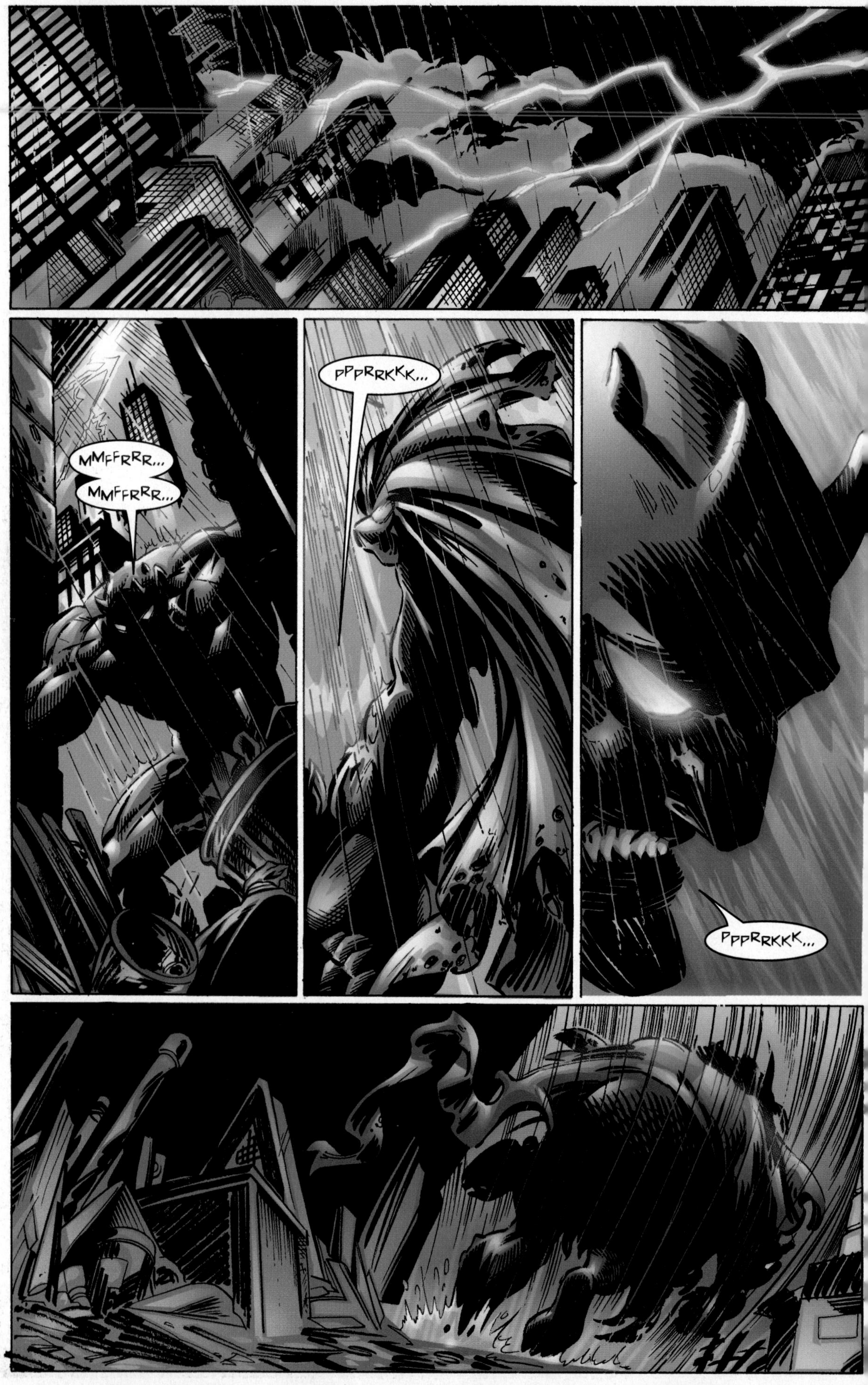
MMFFRRR...
MMFFRRR...
PPPRRKKK...
PPPRRKKK...

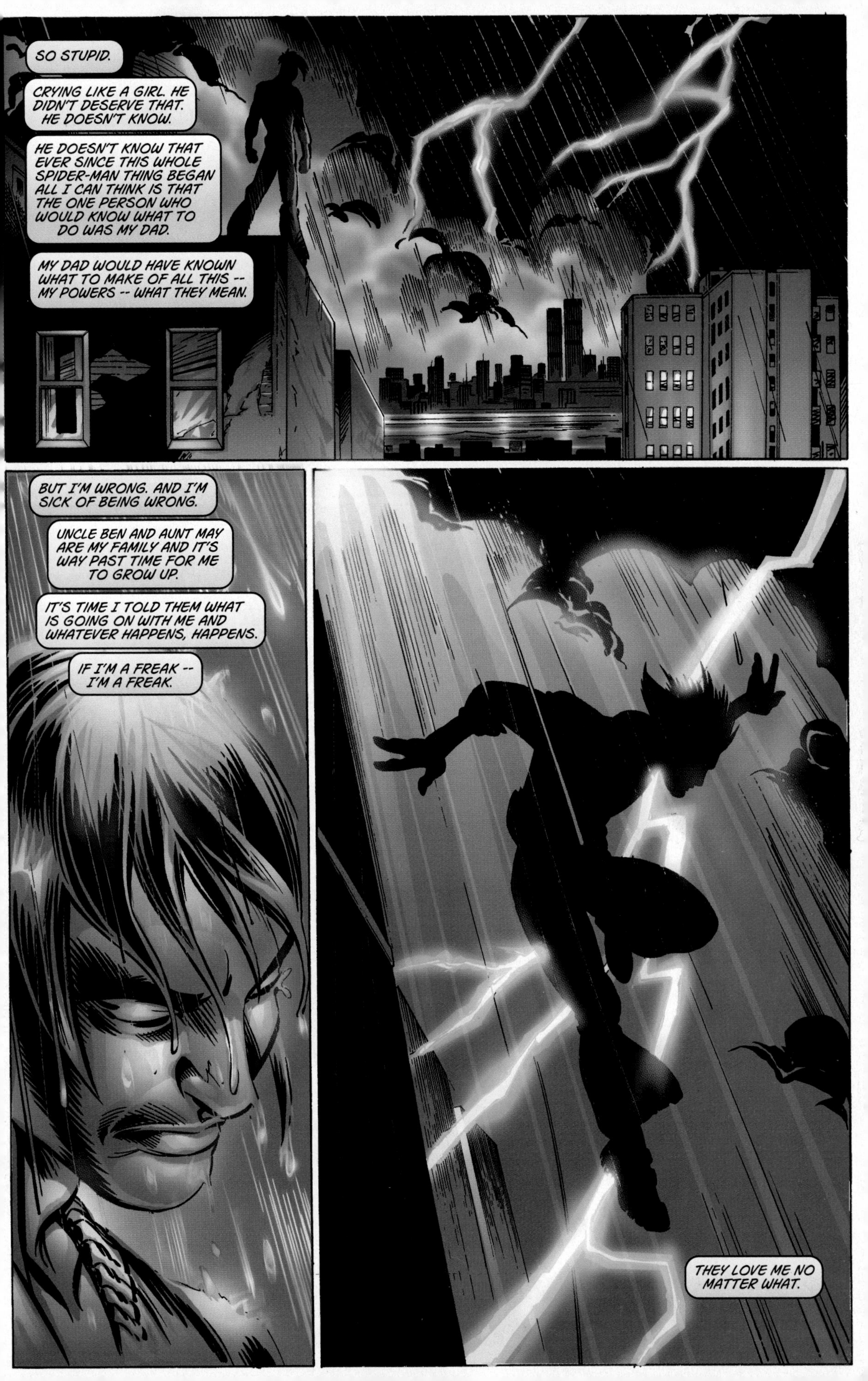
SO STUPID.
CRYING LIKE A GIRL. HE DIDN'T DESERVE THAT. HE DOESN'T KNOW.
HE DOESN'T KNOW THAT EVER SINCE THIS WHOLE SPIDER-MAN THING BEGAN ALL I CAN THINK IS THAT THE ONE PERSON WHO WOULD KNOW WHAT TO DO WAS MY DAD.
MY DAD WOULD HAVE KNOWN WHAT TO MAKE OF ALL THIS -- MY POWERS -- WHAT THEY MEAN.
BUT I'M WRONG. AND I'M SICK OF BEING WRONG.
UNCLE BEN AND AUNT MAY ARE MY FAMILY AND IT'S WAY PAST TIME FOR ME TO GROW UP.
IT'S TIME I TOLD THEM WHAT IS GOING ON WITH ME AND WHATEVER HAPPENS, HAPPENS.
IF I'M A FREAK -- I'M A FREAK.
THEY LOVE ME NO MATTER WHAT.

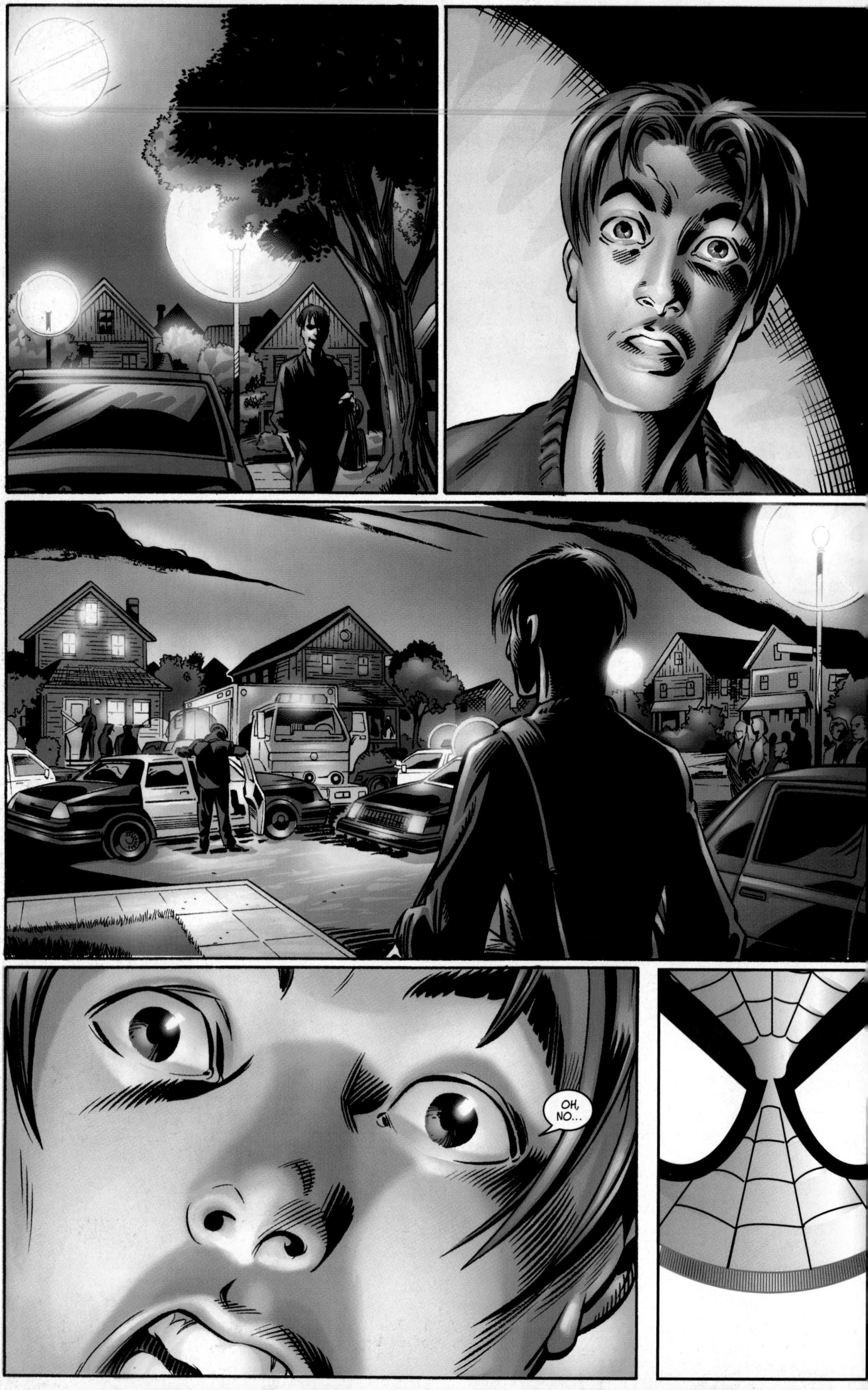
OH, NO...

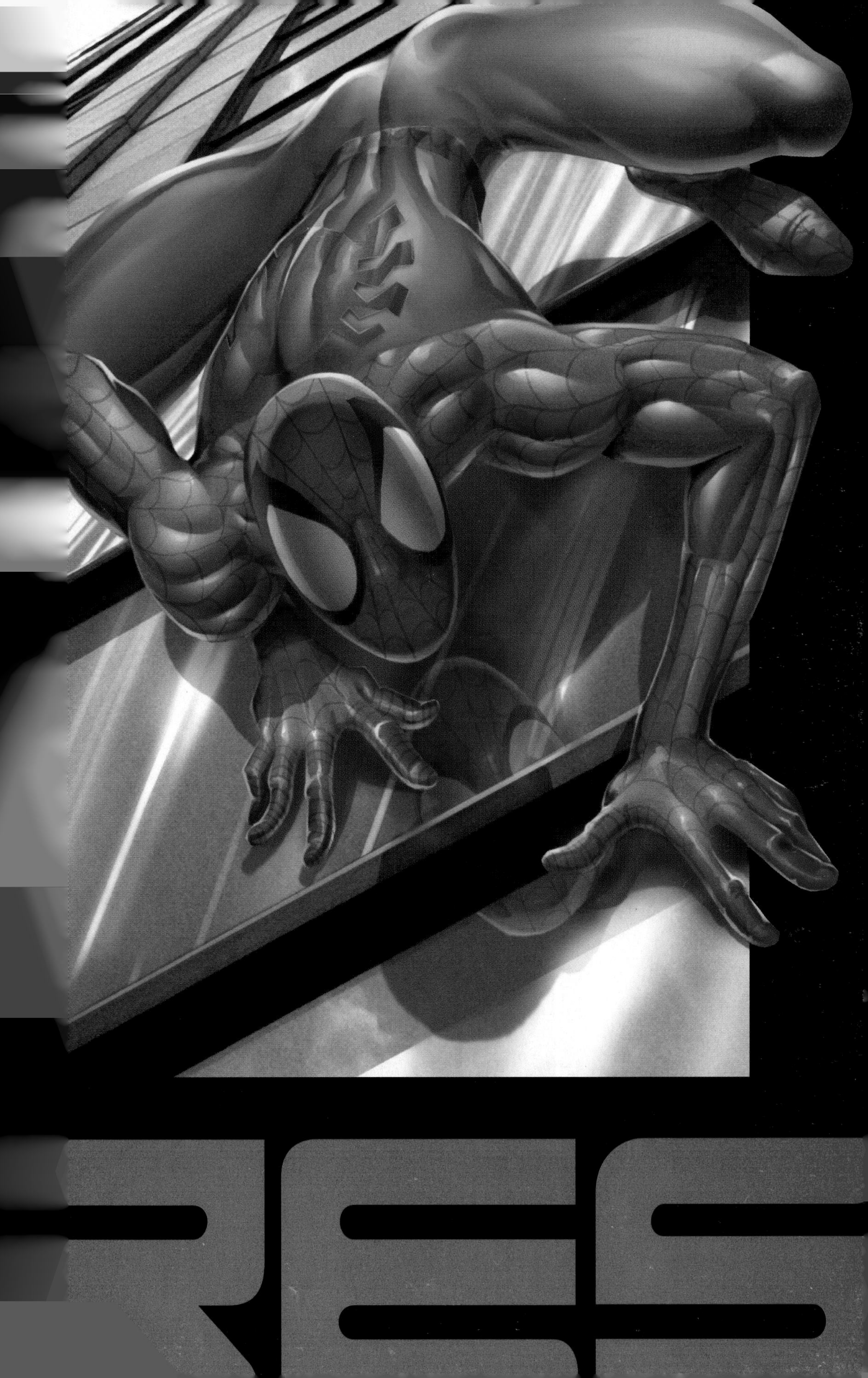

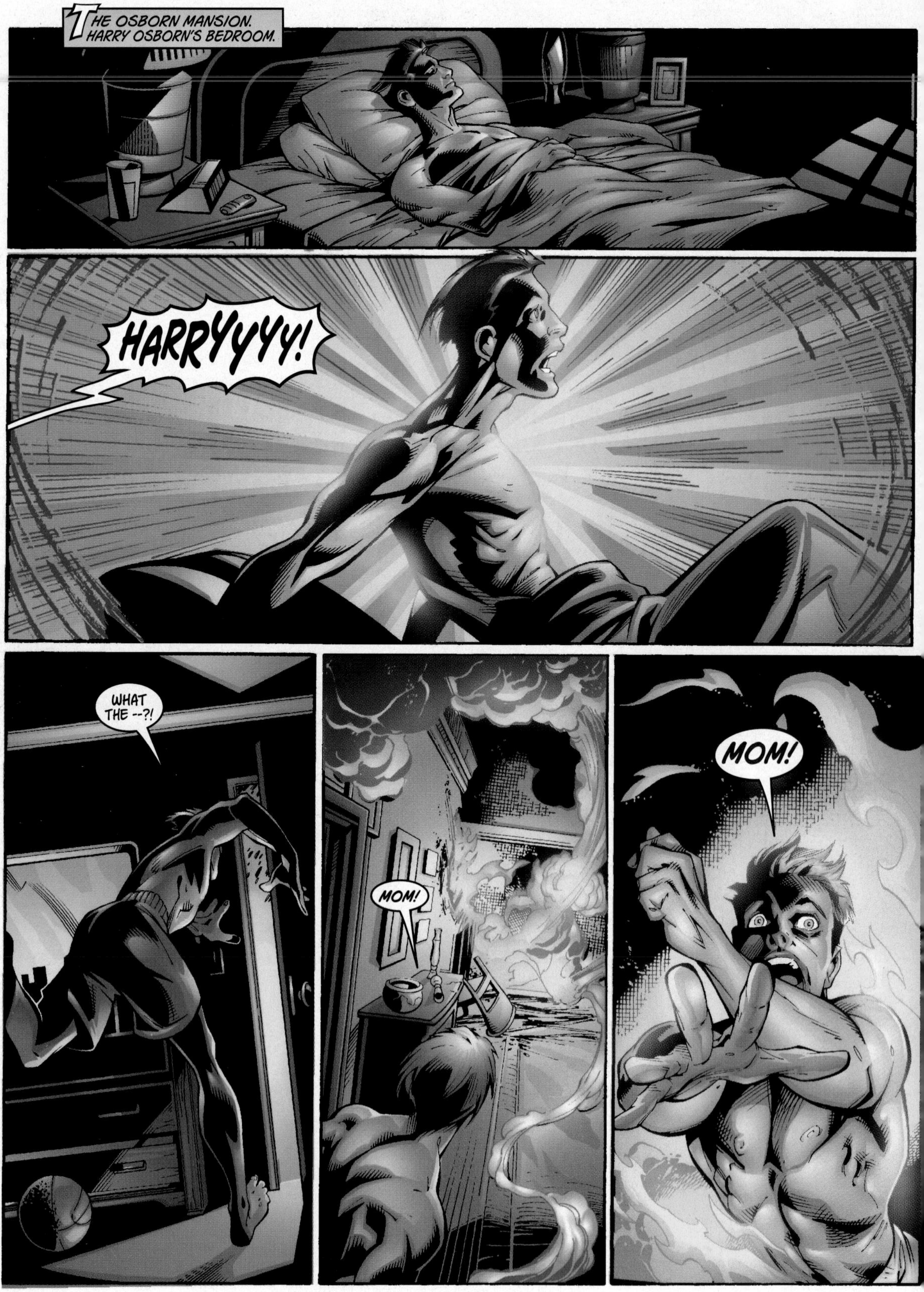
THE OSBORN MANSION. HARRY OSBORN'S BEDROOM.
HARRYYYY!
WHAT THE --?!
MOM!
MOM!

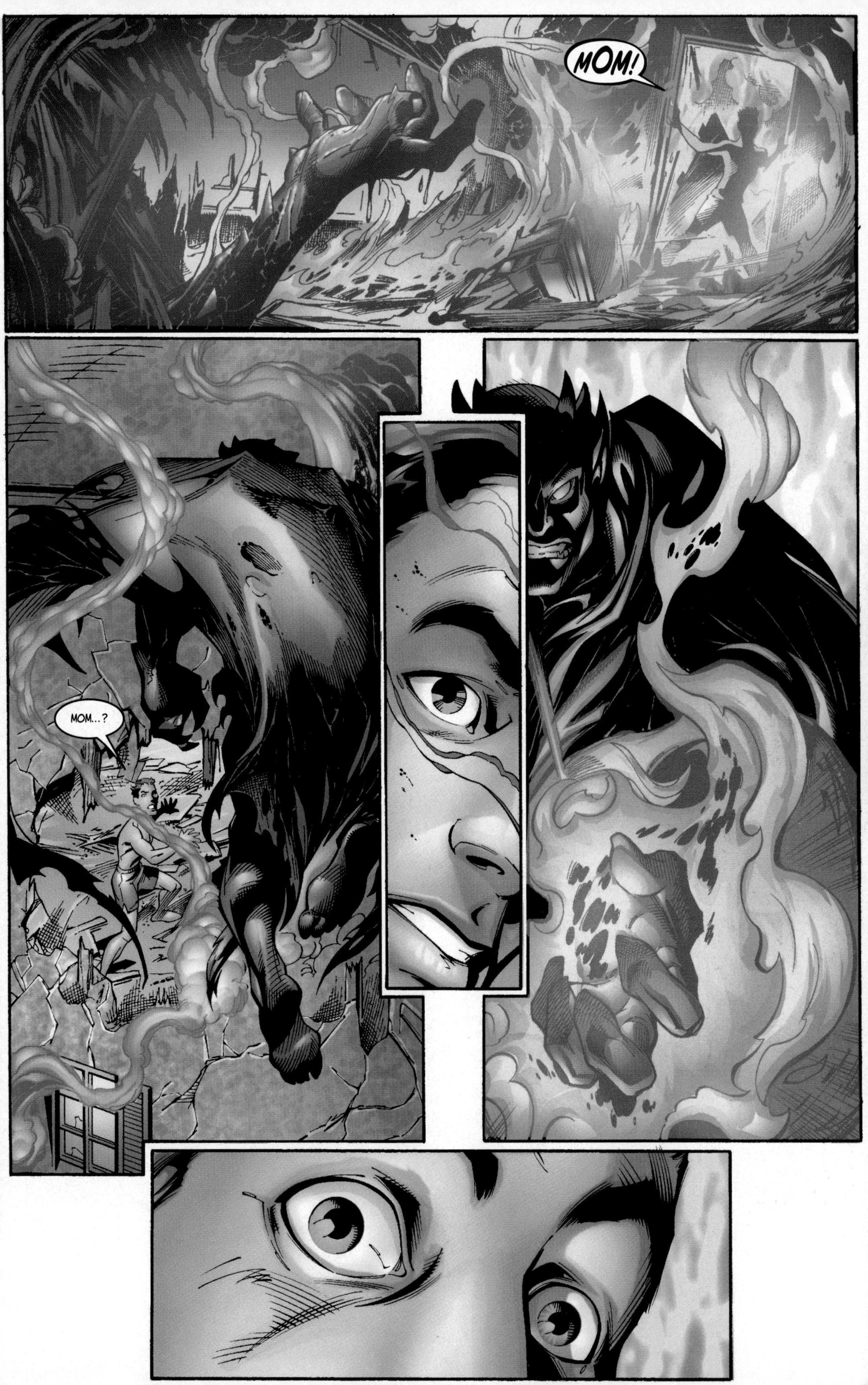
MOM!
MOM...?

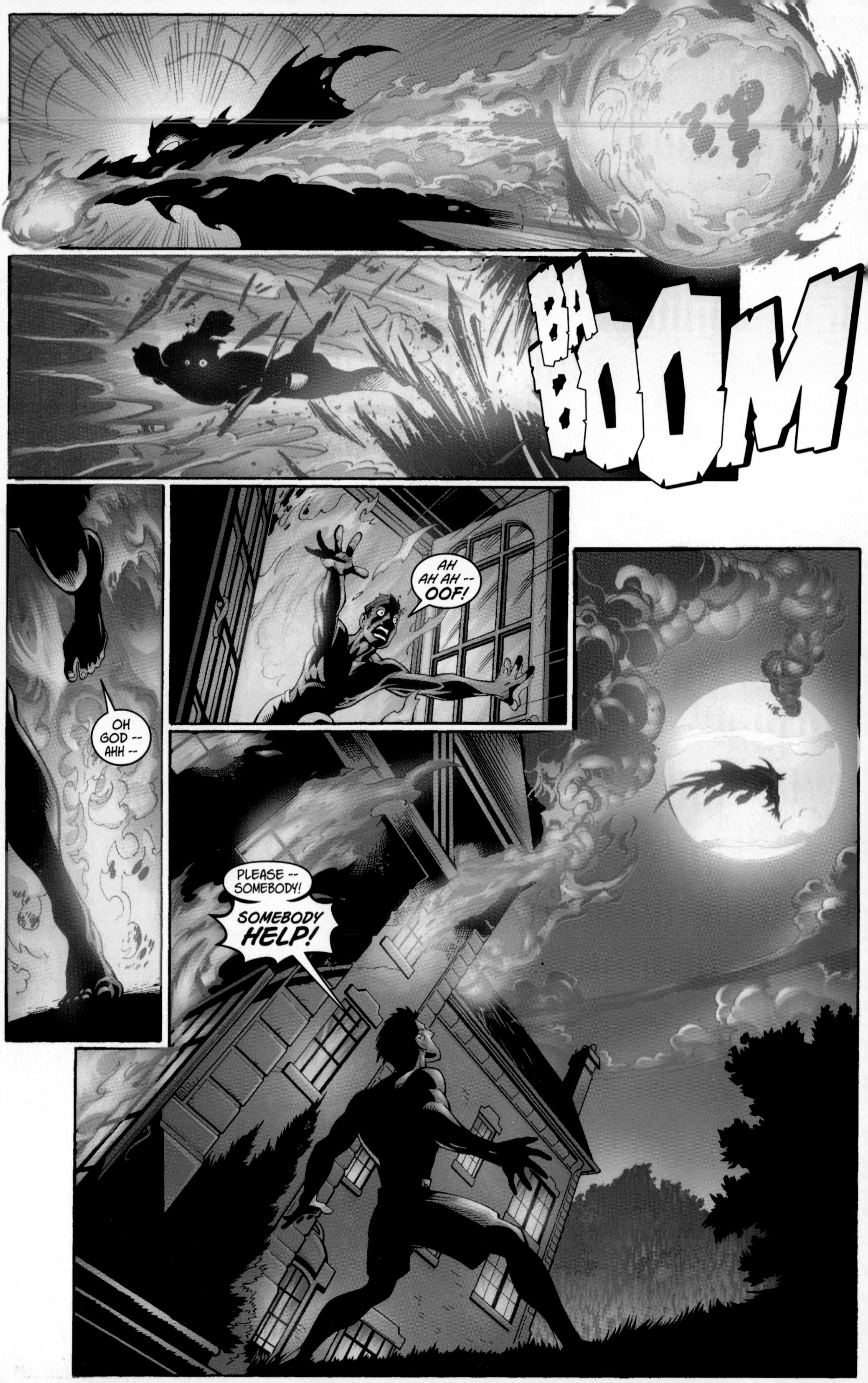
BA BOOM
AH AH AH -- OOF!
OH GOD -- AHH --
PLEASE -- SOMEBODY!
SOMEBODY HELP!

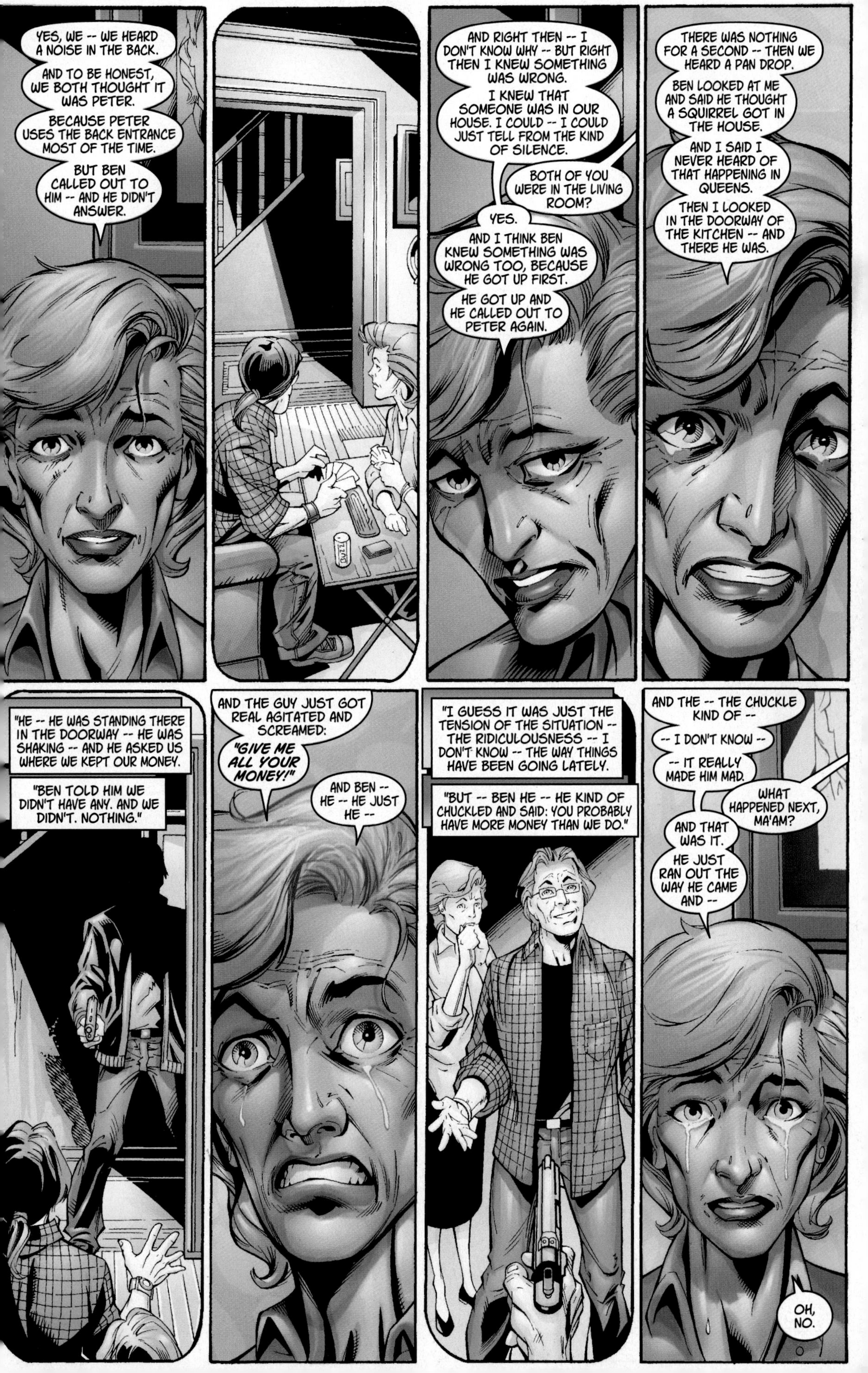
YES, WE -- WE HEARD A NOISE IN THE BACK.
AND TO BE HONEST, WE BOTH THOUGHT IT WAS PETER.
BECAUSE PETER USES THE BACK ENTRANCE MOST OF THE TIME.
BUT BEN CALLED OUT TO HIM -- AND HE DIDN'T ANSWER.
BUZZ
AND RIGHT THEN -- I DON'T KNOW WHY -- BUT RIGHT THEN I KNEW SOMETHING WAS WRONG.
I KNEW THAT SOMEONE WAS IN OUR HOUSE. I COULD -- I COULD JUST TELL FROM THE KIND OF SILENCE.
BOTH OF YOU WERE IN THE LIVING ROOM?
YES.
AND I THINK BEN KNEW SOMETHING WAS WRONG TOO, BECAUSE HE GOT UP FIRST.
HE GOT UP AND HE CALLED OUT TO PETER AGAIN.
THERE WAS NOTHING FOR A SECOND -- THEN WE HEARD A PAN DROP.
BEN LOOKED AT ME AND SAID HE THOUGHT A SQUIRREL GOT IN THE HOUSE.
AND I SAID I NEVER HEARD OF THAT HAPPENING IN QUEENS.
THEN I LOOKED IN THE DOORWAY OF THE KITCHEN -- AND THERE HE WAS.
"HE -- HE WAS STANDING THERE IN THE DOORWAY -- HE WAS SHAKING -- AND HE ASKED US WHERE WE KEPT OUR MONEY.
"BEN TOLD HIM WE DIDN'T HAVE ANY. AND WE DIDN'T. NOTHING."
AND THE GUY JUST GOT REAL AGITATED AND SCREAMED: *"GIVE ME ALL YOUR MONEY!"*
AND BEN -- HE -- HE JUST HE --
"I GUESS IT WAS JUST THE TENSION OF THE SITUATION -- THE RIDICULOUSNESS -- I DON'T KNOW -- THE WAY THINGS HAVE BEEN GOING LATELY.
"BUT -- BEN HE -- HE KIND OF CHUCKLED AND SAID: YOU PROBABLY HAVE MORE MONEY THAN WE DO."
AND THE -- THE CHUCKLE KIND OF --
-- I DON'T KNOW --
-- IT REALLY MADE HIM MAD.
WHAT HAPPENED NEXT, MA'AM?
AND THAT WAS IT.
HE JUST RAN OUT THE WAY HE CAME AND --
OH, NO.

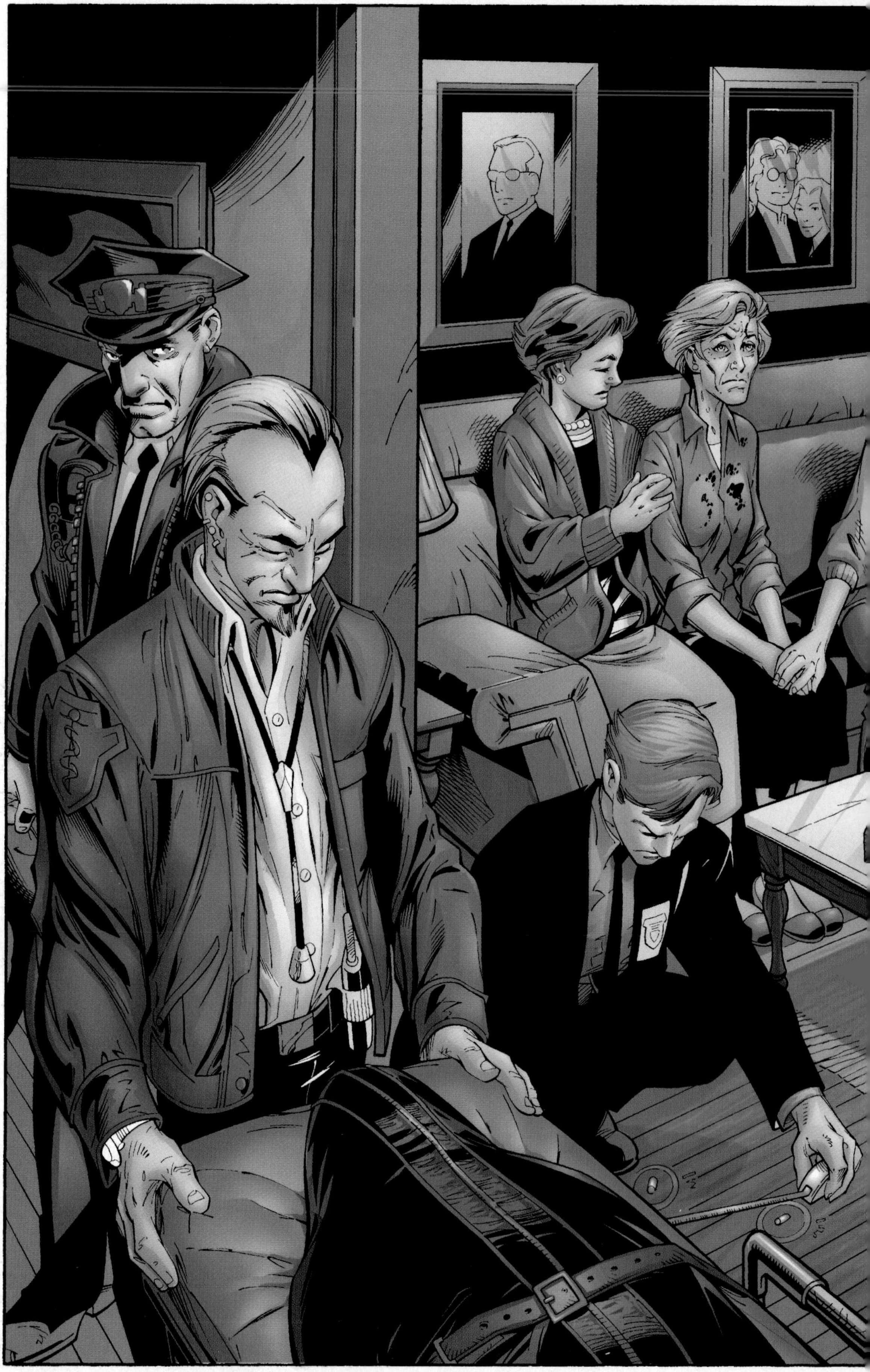

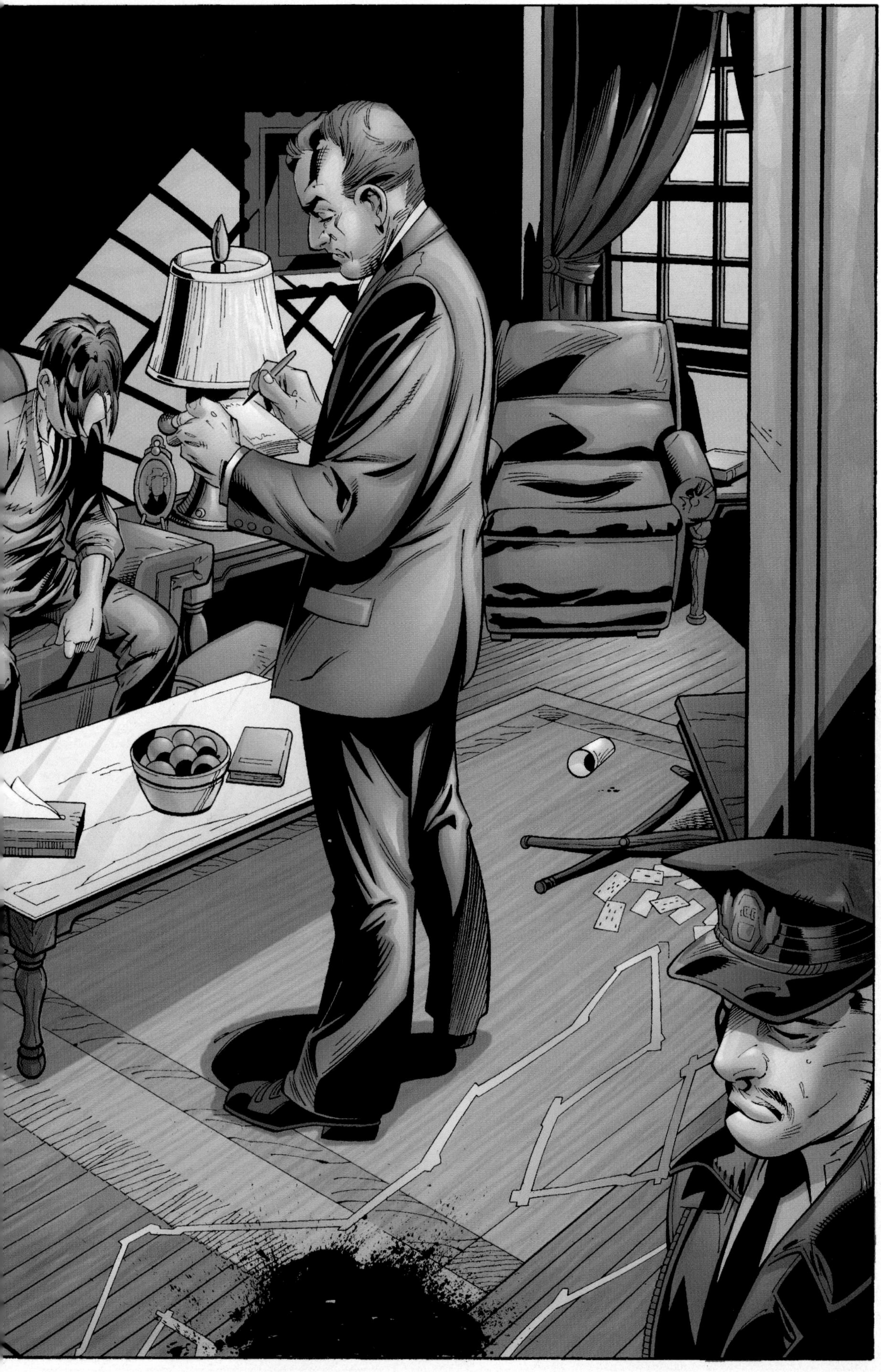

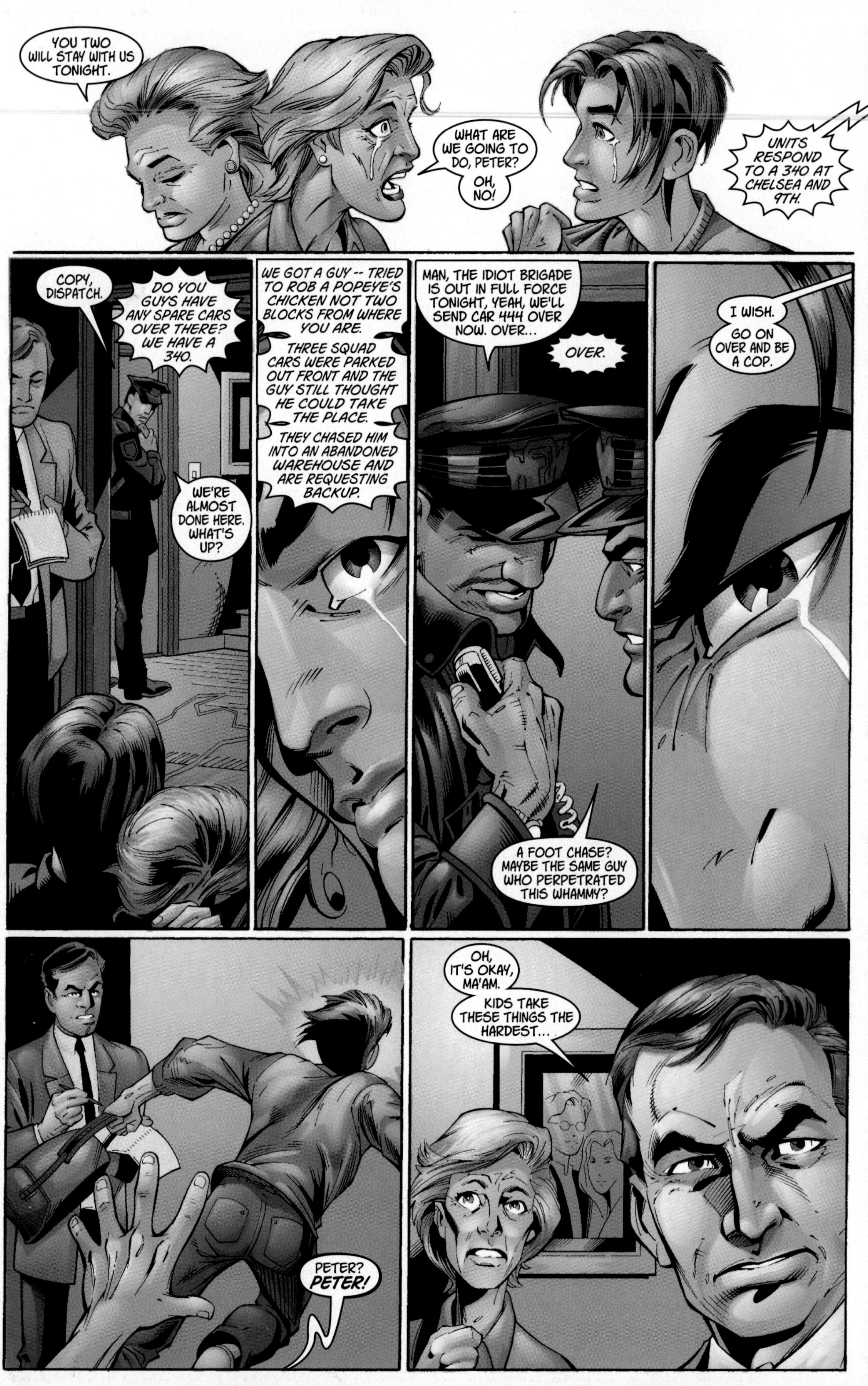
YOU TWO WILL STAY WITH US TONIGHT.
WHAT ARE WE GOING TO DO, PETER?
OH, NO!
UNITS RESPOND TO A 340 AT CHELSEA AND 9TH.
COPY, DISPATCH.
DO YOU GUYS HAVE ANY SPARE CARS OVER THERE? WE HAVE A 340.
WE'RE ALMOST DONE HERE. WHAT'S UP?
WE GOT A GUY -- TRIED TO ROB A POPEYE'S CHICKEN NOT TWO BLOCKS FROM WHERE YOU ARE.
THREE SQUAD CARS WERE PARKED OUT FRONT AND THE GUY STILL THOUGHT HE COULD TAKE THE PLACE.
THEY CHASED HIM INTO AN ABANDONED WAREHOUSE AND ARE REQUESTING BACKUP.
MAN, THE IDIOT BRIGADE IS OUT IN FULL FORCE TONIGHT, YEAH, WE'LL SEND CAR 444 OVER NOW. OVER...
OVER.
A FOOT CHASE? MAYBE THE SAME GUY WHO PERPETRATED THIS WHAMMY?
I WISH.
GO ON OVER AND BE A COP.
PETER? PETER!
OH, IT'S OKAY, MA'AM.
KIDS TAKE THESE THINGS THE HARDEST...

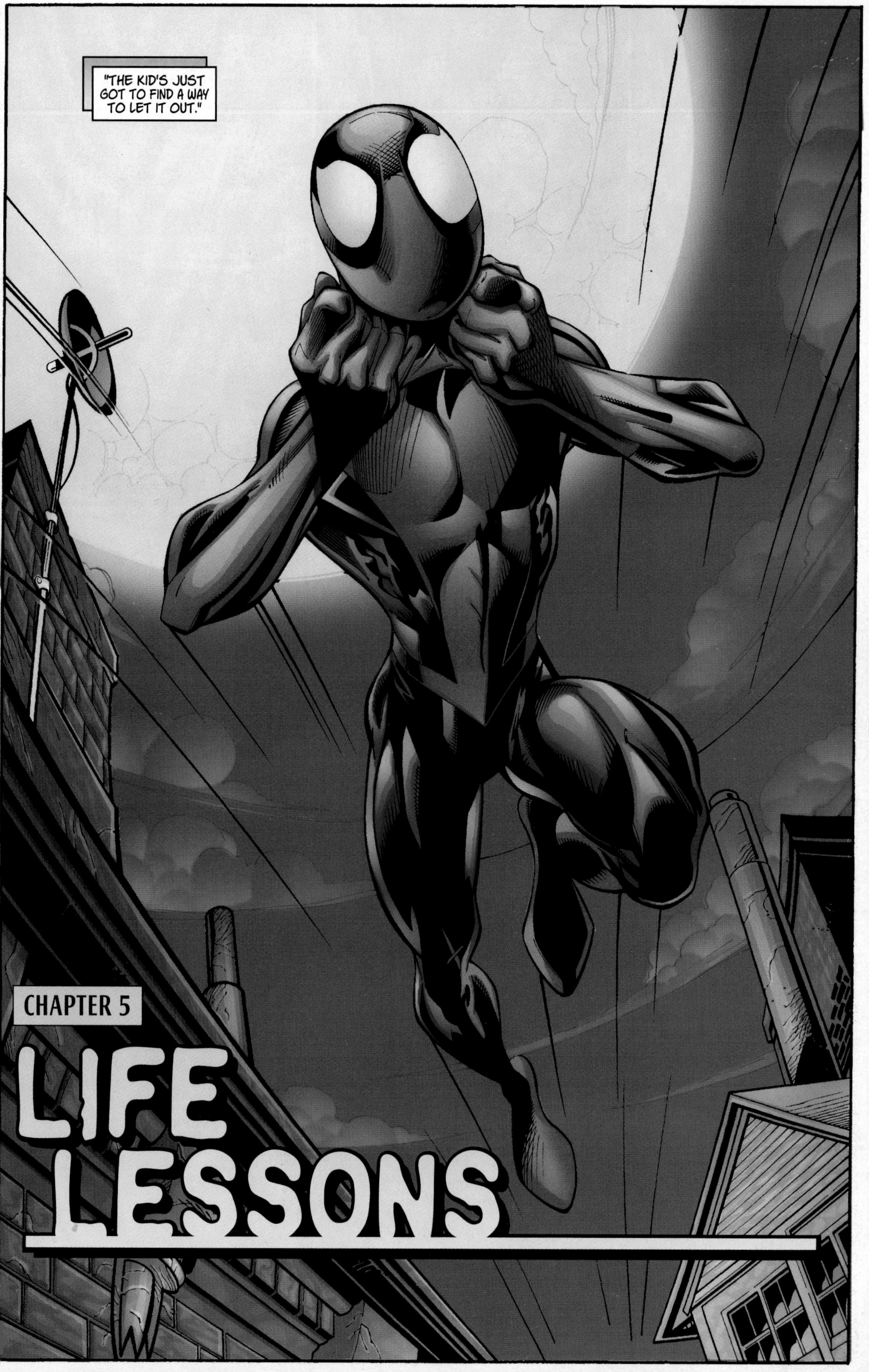
"THE KID'S JUST GOT TO FIND A WAY TO LET IT OUT."
CHAPTER 5
LIFE LESSONS

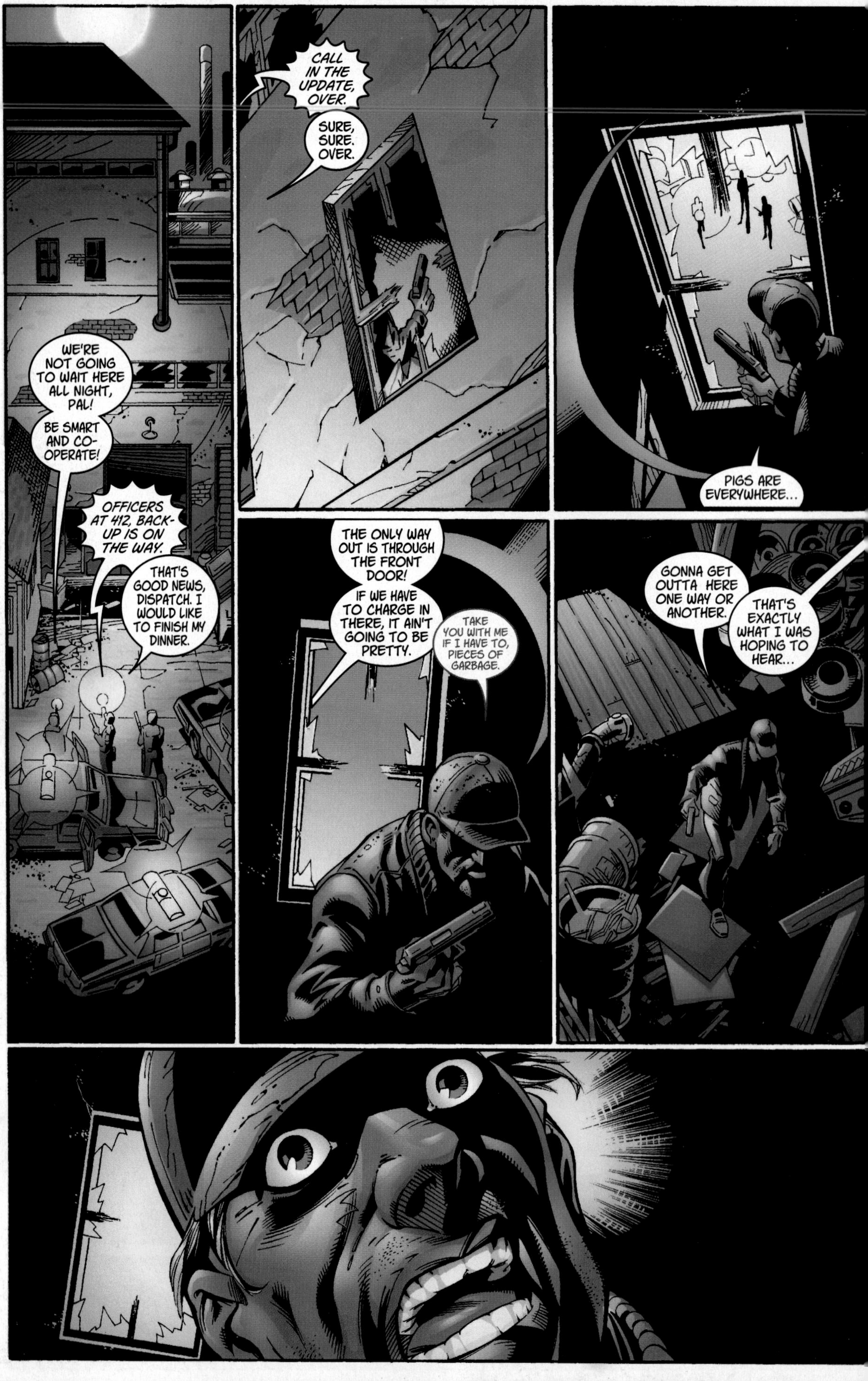

WE'RE NOT GOING TO WAIT HERE ALL NIGHT, PAL!
BE SMART AND CO-OPERATE!
OFFICERS AT 412, BACK-UP IS ON THE WAY.
THAT'S GOOD NEWS, DISPATCH. I WOULD LIKE TO FINISH MY DINNER.
CALL IN THE UPDATE, OVER.
SURE, SURE. OVER.
PIGS ARE EVERYWHERE...
THE ONLY WAY OUT IS THROUGH THE FRONT DOOR!
IF WE HAVE TO CHARGE IN THERE, IT AIN'T GOING TO BE PRETTY.
TAKE YOU WITH ME IF I HAVE TO, PIECES OF GARBAGE.
GONNA GET OUTTA HERE ONE WAY OR ANOTHER.
THAT'S EXACTLY WHAT I WAS HOPING TO HEAR...

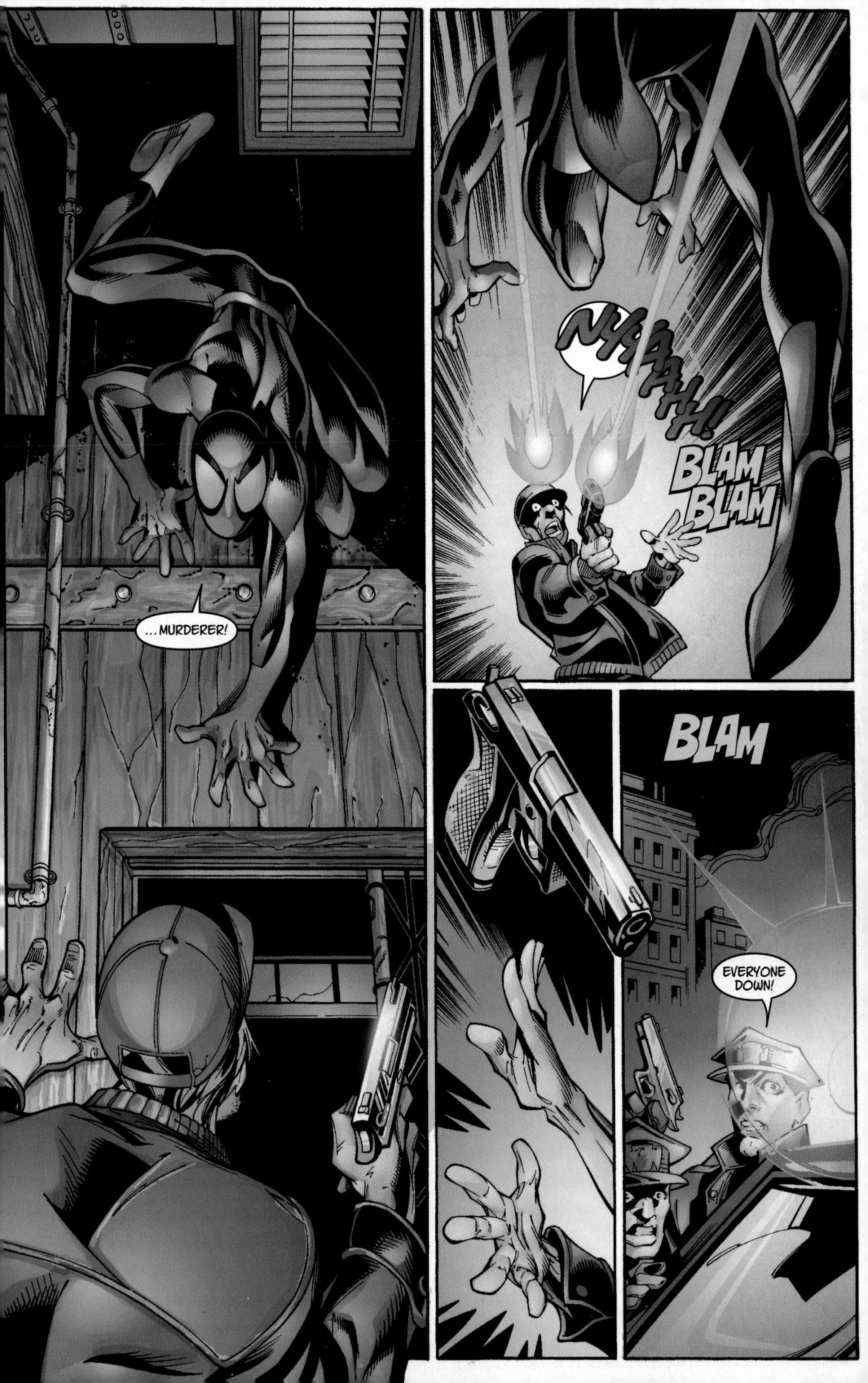
...MURDERER!
NYAAAHH!
BLAM
BLAM
BLAM
EVERYONE DOWN!

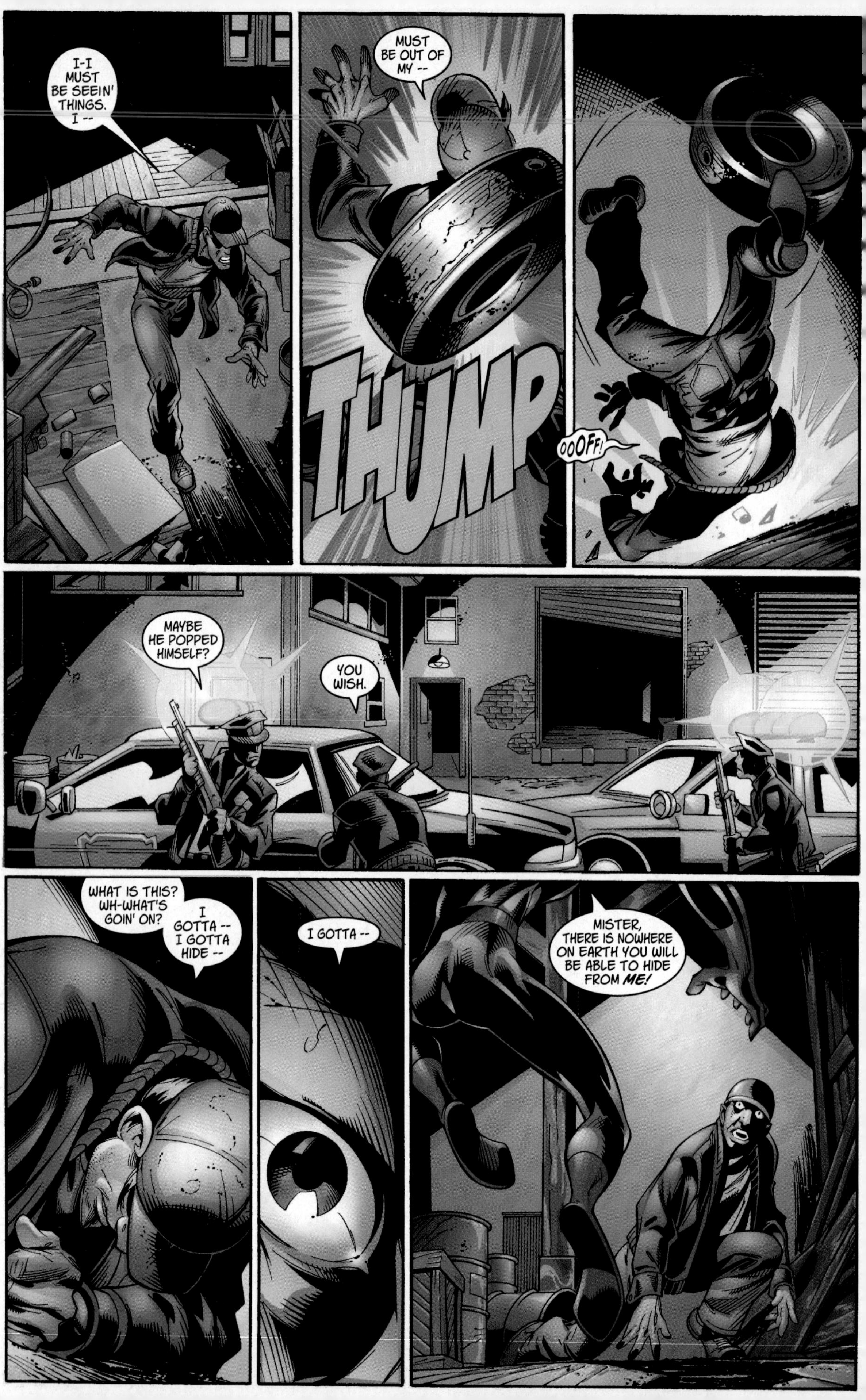
I-I MUST BE SEEIN' THINGS. I --
MUST BE OUT OF MY --
THUMP
OOOFF!
MAYBE HE POPPED HIMSELF?
YOU WISH.
WHAT IS THIS? WH-WHAT'S GOIN' ON?
I GOTTA -- I GOTTA HIDE --
I GOTTA --
MISTER, THERE IS NOWHERE ON EARTH YOU WILL BE ABLE TO HIDE FROM *ME!*

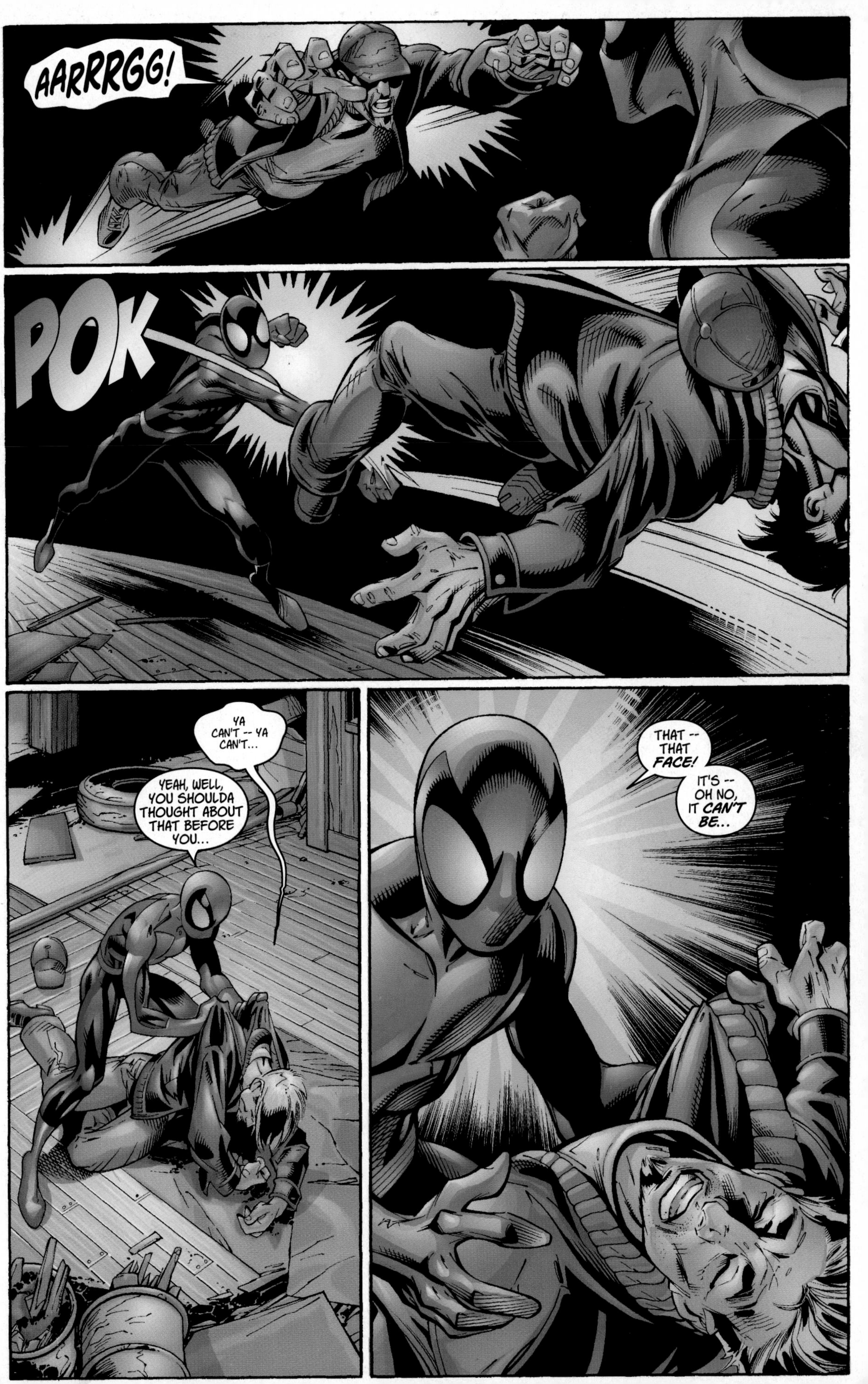
AARRRGG!
POK
YA CAN'T -- YA CAN'T...
YEAH, WELL, YOU SHOULDA THOUGHT ABOUT THAT BEFORE YOU...
THAT -- THAT FACE!
IT'S -- OH NO, IT CAN'T BE...

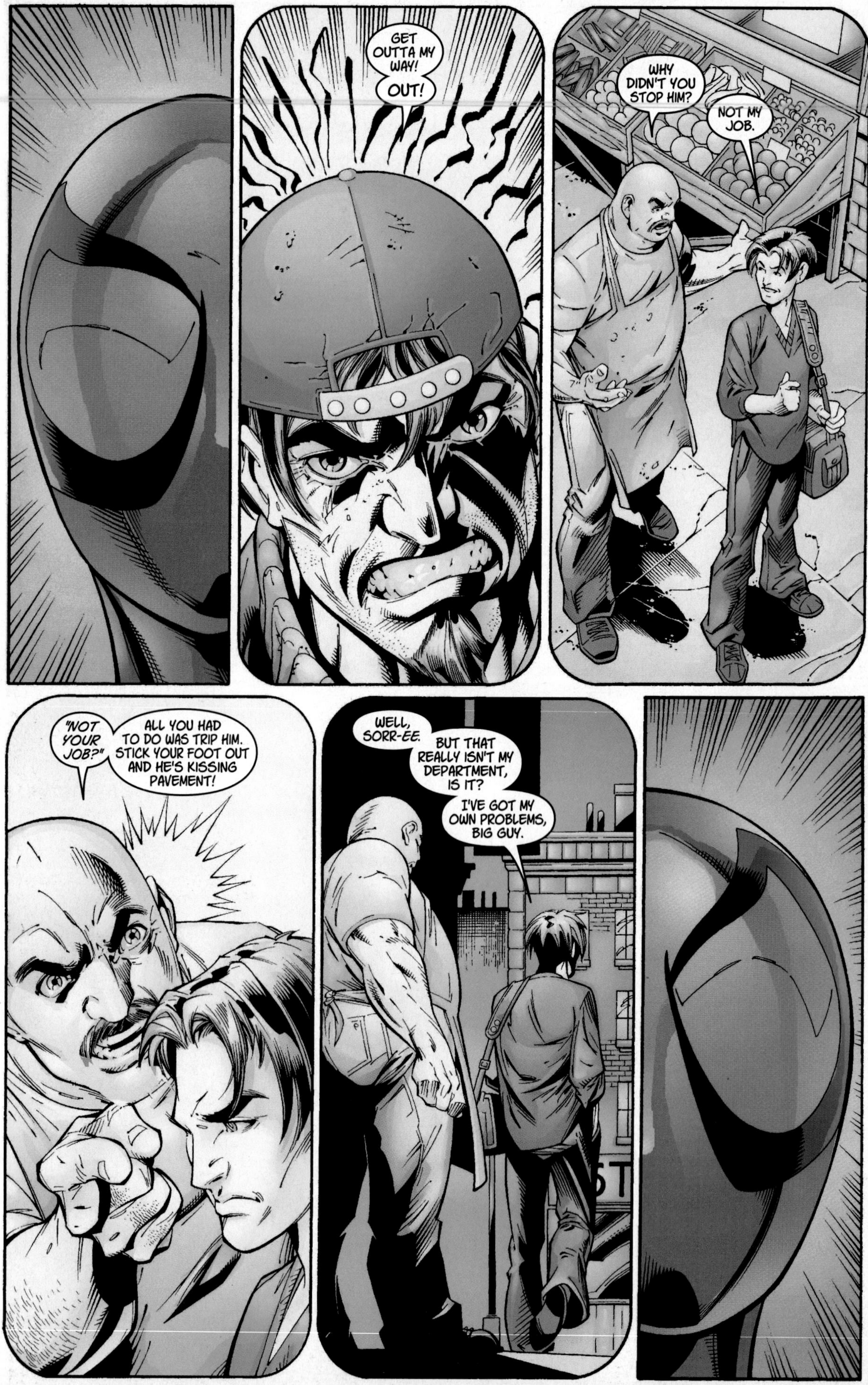
GET OUTTA MY WAY!
OUT!
WHY DIDN'T YOU STOP HIM?
NOT MY JOB.
"NOT YOUR JOB?"
ALL YOU HAD TO DO WAS TRIP HIM. STICK YOUR FOOT OUT AND HE'S KISSING PAVEMENT!
WELL, SORR-EE.
BUT THAT REALLY ISN'T MY DEPARTMENT, IS IT?
I'VE GOT MY OWN PROBLEMS, BIG GUY.

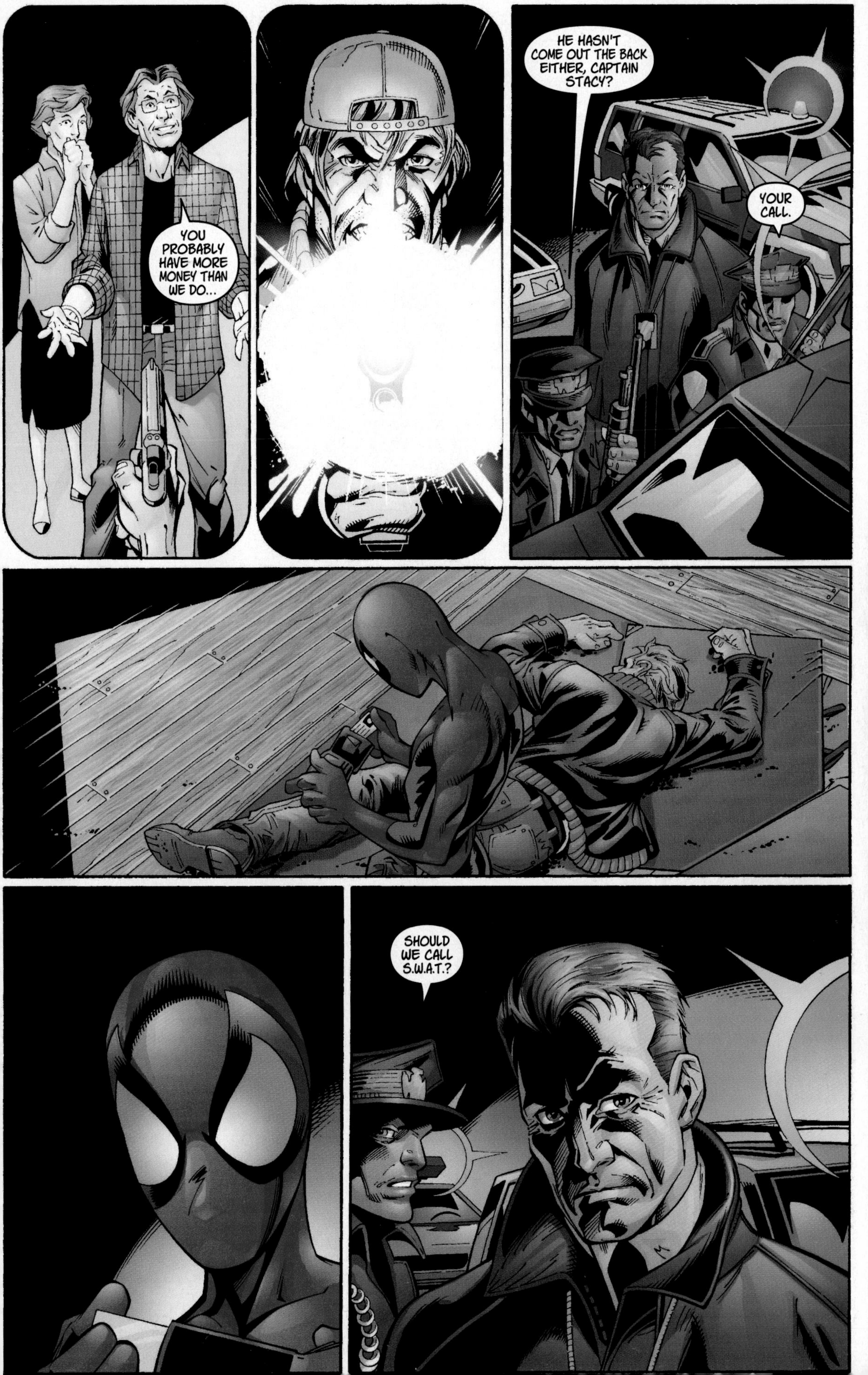
YOU PROBABLY HAVE MORE MONEY THAN WE DO...
HE HASN'T COME OUT THE BACK EITHER, CAPTAIN STACY?
YOUR CALL.
SHOULD WE CALL S.W.A.T.?

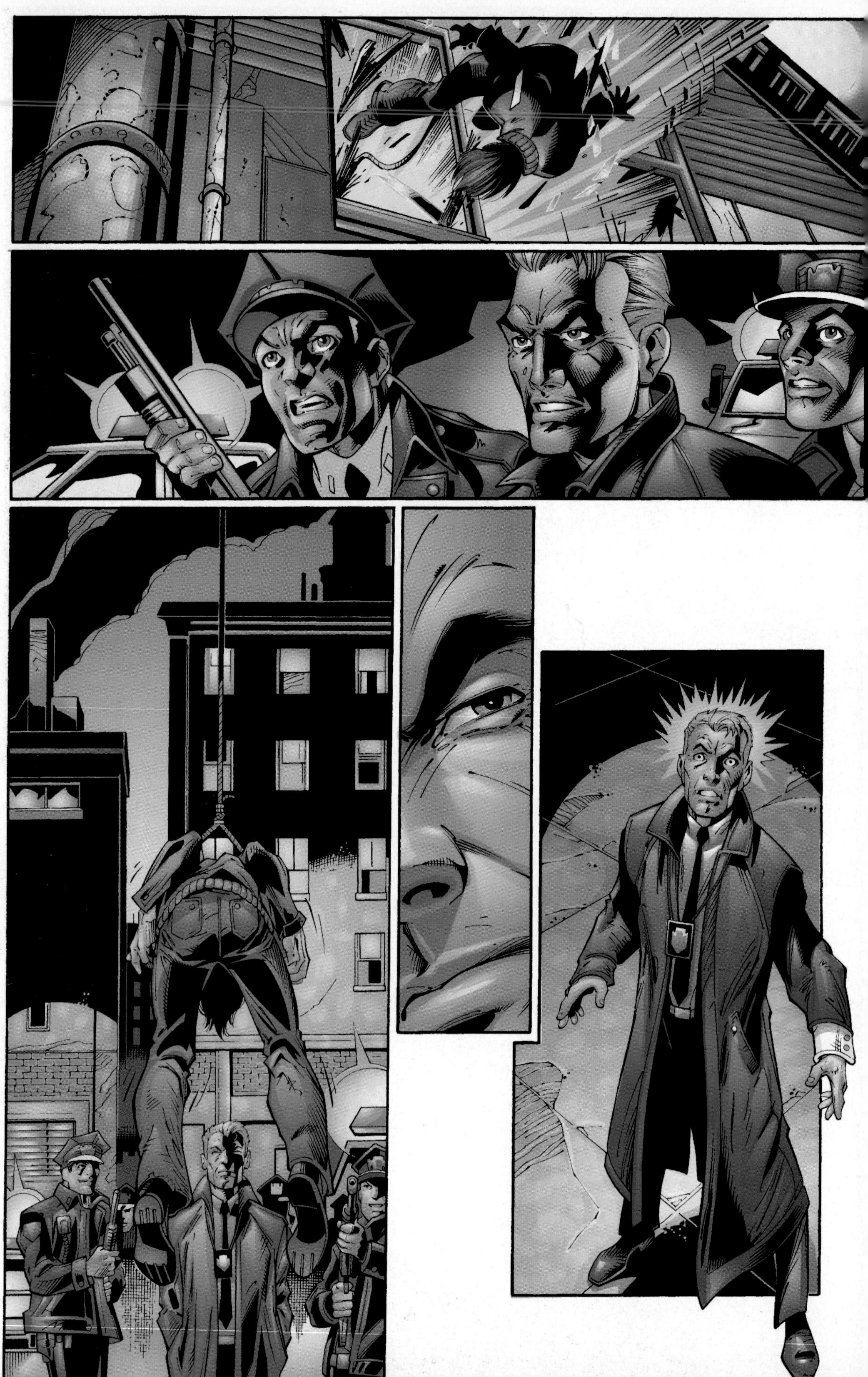

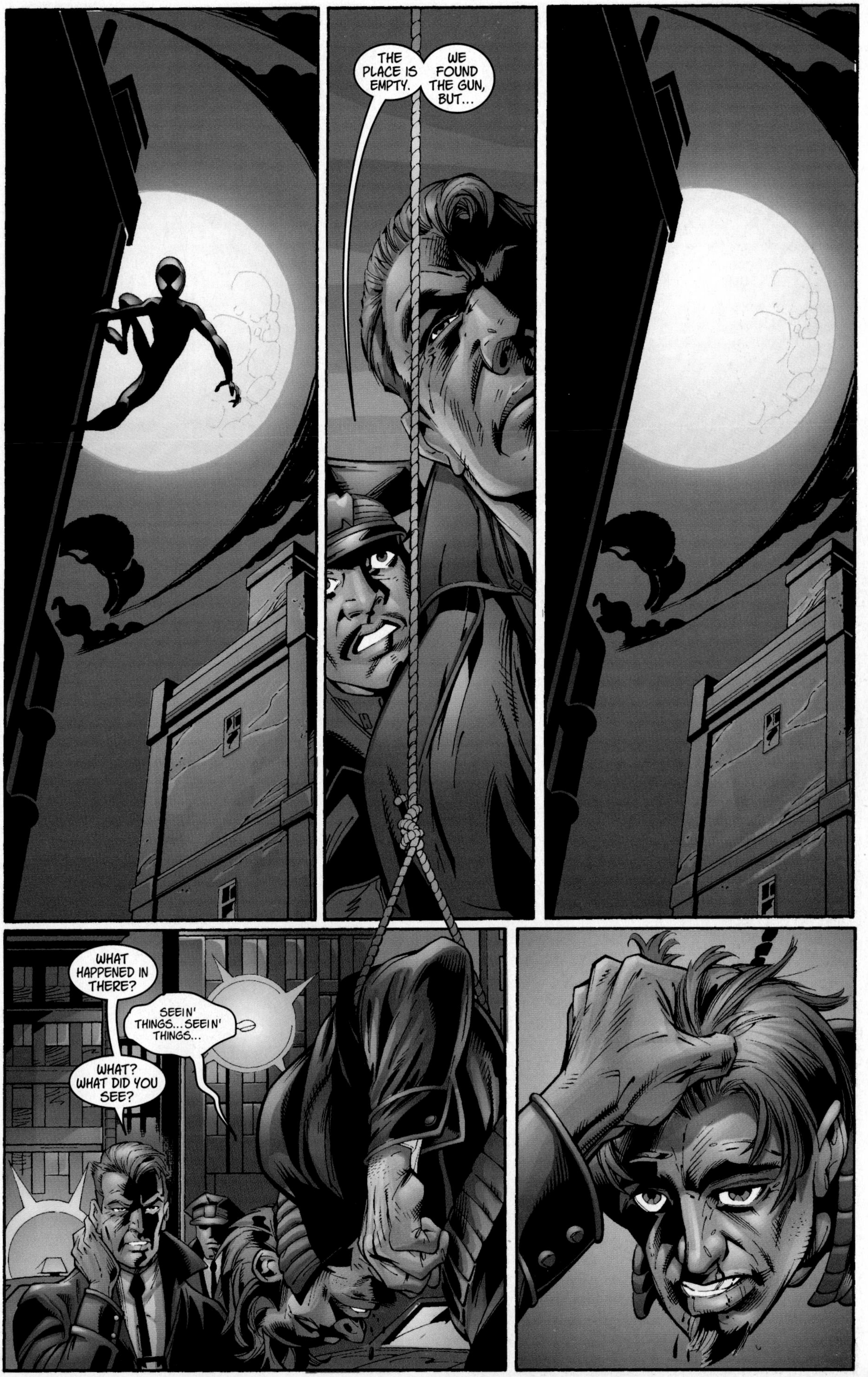
THE PLACE IS EMPTY.
WE FOUND THE GUN, BUT...
WHAT HAPPENED IN THERE?
SEEIN' THINGS... SEEIN' THINGS...
WHAT? WHAT DID YOU SEE?

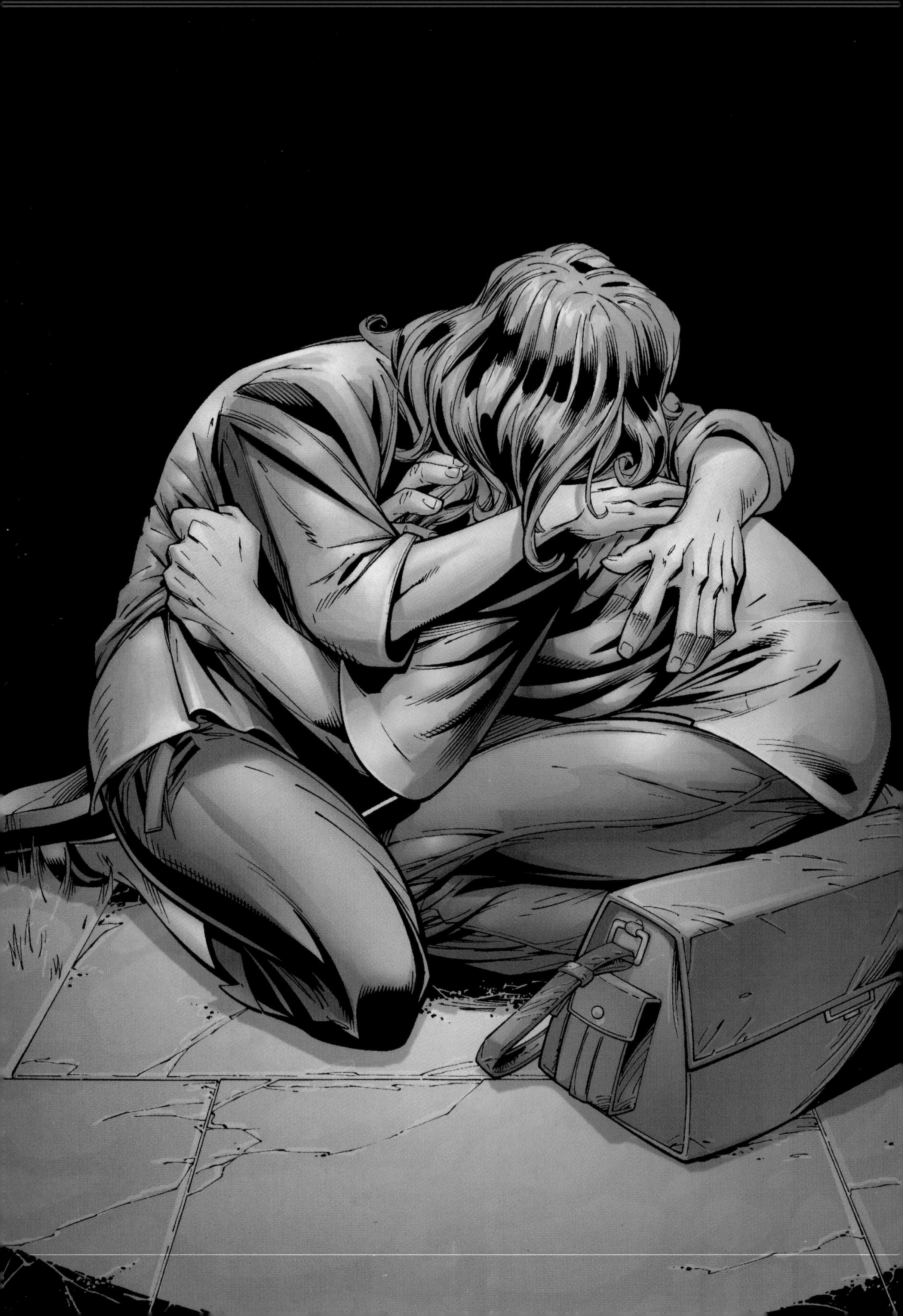

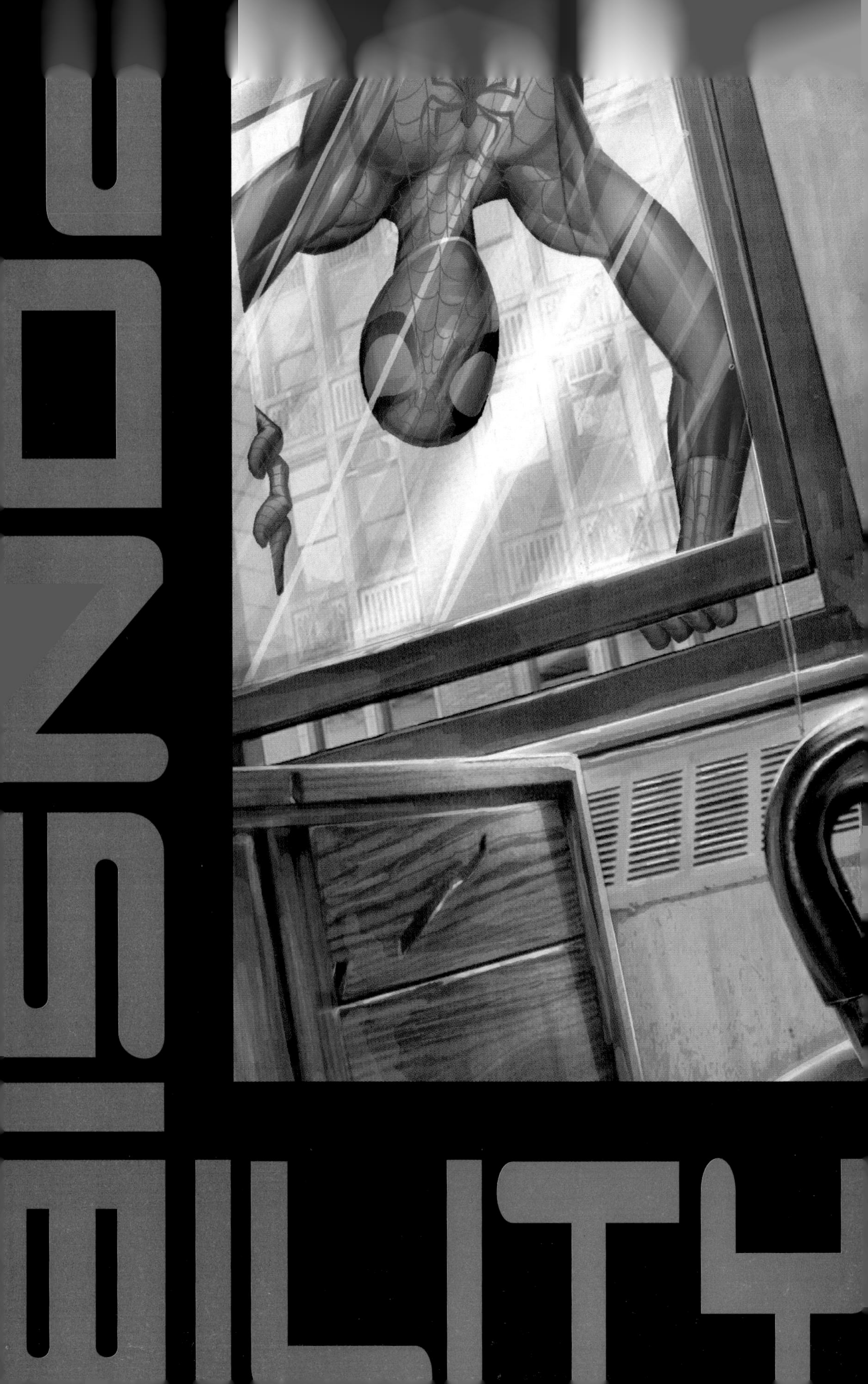

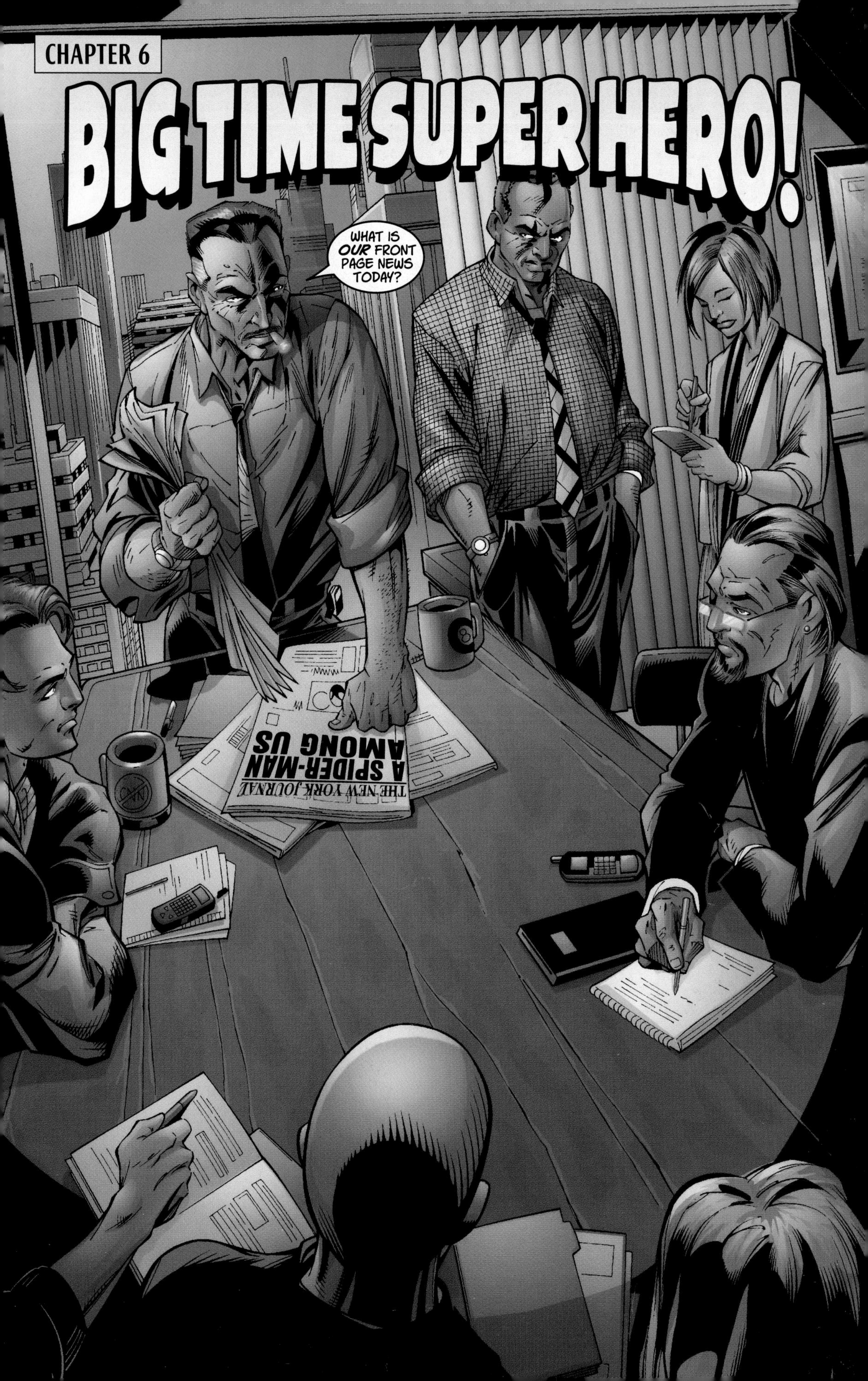
CHAPTER 6
BIG TIME SUPER HERO!
WHAT IS OUR FRONT PAGE NEWS TODAY?
THE NEW YORK JOURNAL
A SPIDER-MAN AMONG US

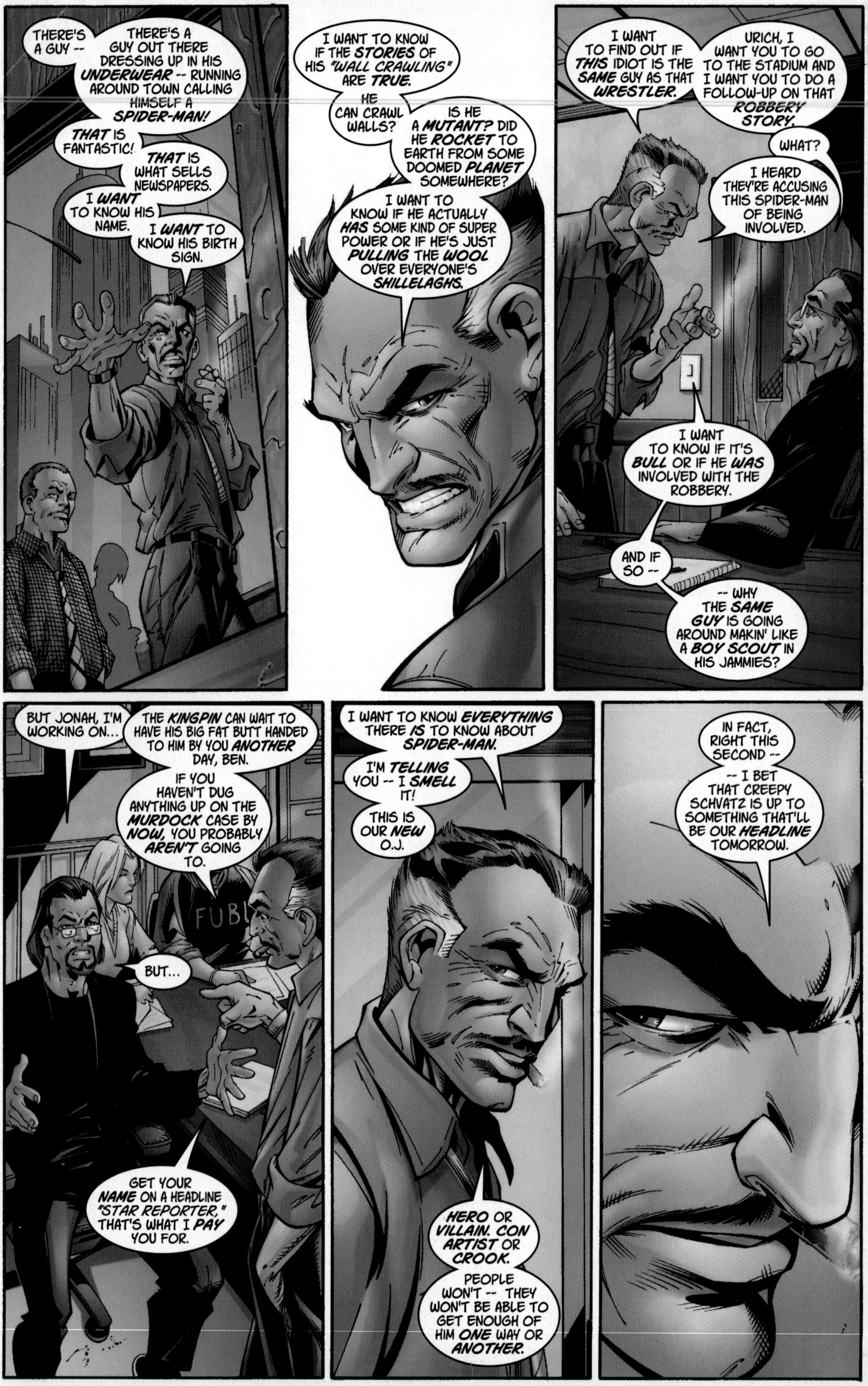
THERE'S A GUY --
THERE'S A GUY OUT THERE DRESSING UP IN HIS UNDERWEAR -- RUNNING AROUND TOWN CALLING HIMSELF A SPIDER-MAN!
THAT IS FANTASTIC!
THAT IS WHAT SELLS NEWSPAPERS.
I WANT TO KNOW HIS NAME.
I WANT TO KNOW HIS BIRTH SIGN.
I WANT TO KNOW IF THE STORIES OF HIS "WALL CRAWLING" ARE TRUE.
HE CAN CRAWL WALLS?
IS HE A MUTANT? DID HE ROCKET TO EARTH FROM SOME DOOMED PLANET SOMEWHERE?
I WANT TO KNOW IF HE ACTUALLY HAS SOME KIND OF SUPER POWER OR IF HE'S JUST PULLING THE WOOL OVER EVERYONE'S SHILLELAGHS.
I WANT TO FIND OUT IF THIS IDIOT IS THE SAME GUY AS THAT WRESTLER.
URICH, I WANT YOU TO GO TO THE STADIUM AND I WANT YOU TO DO A FOLLOW-UP ON THAT ROBBERY STORY.
WHAT?
I HEARD THEY'RE ACCUSING THIS SPIDER-MAN OF BEING INVOLVED.
I WANT TO KNOW IF IT'S BULL OR IF HE WAS INVOLVED WITH THE ROBBERY.
AND IF SO --
-- WHY THE SAME GUY IS GOING AROUND MAKIN' LIKE A BOY SCOUT IN HIS JAMMIES?
BUT JONAH, I'M WORKING ON...
THE KINGPIN CAN WAIT TO HAVE HIS BIG FAT BUTT HANDED TO HIM BY YOU ANOTHER DAY, BEN.
IF YOU HAVEN'T DUG ANYTHING UP ON THE MURDOCK CASE BY NOW, YOU PROBABLY AREN'T GOING TO.
FUBU
BUT...
GET YOUR NAME ON A HEADLINE "STAR REPORTER," THAT'S WHAT I PAY YOU FOR.
I WANT TO KNOW EVERYTHING THERE IS TO KNOW ABOUT SPIDER-MAN.
I'M TELLING YOU -- I SMELL IT!
THIS IS OUR NEW O.J.
HERO OR VILLAIN. CON ARTIST OR CROOK.
PEOPLE WON'T -- THEY WON'T BE ABLE TO GET ENOUGH OF HIM ONE WAY OR ANOTHER.
IN FACT, RIGHT THIS SECOND --
-- I BET THAT CREEPY SCHVATZ IS UP TO SOMETHING THAT'LL BE OUR HEADLINE TOMORROW.

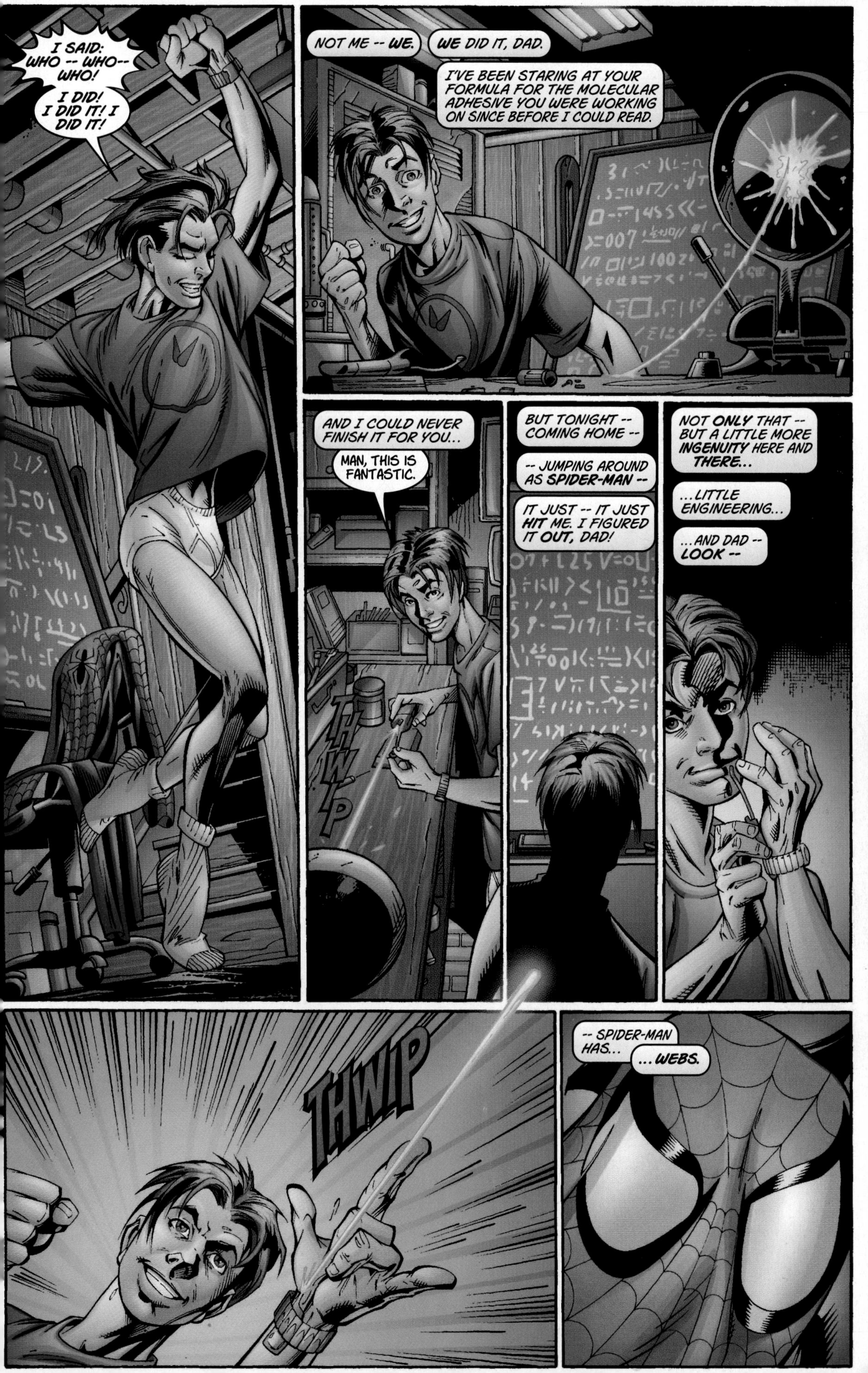
I SAID: WHO -- WHO-- WHO!
I DID! I DID IT! I DID IT!
NOT ME -- WE.
WE DID IT, DAD.
I'VE BEEN STARING AT YOUR FORMULA FOR THE MOLECULAR ADHESIVE YOU WERE WORKING ON SINCE BEFORE I COULD READ.
AND I COULD NEVER FINISH IT FOR YOU...
MAN, THIS IS FANTASTIC.
THWIP
BUT TONIGHT -- COMING HOME --
-- JUMPING AROUND AS SPIDER-MAN --
IT JUST -- IT JUST HIT ME. I FIGURED IT OUT, DAD!
NOT ONLY THAT -- BUT A LITTLE MORE INGENUITY HERE AND THERE...
...LITTLE ENGINEERING...
...AND DAD -- LOOK --
THWIP
-- SPIDER-MAN HAS...
...WEBS.

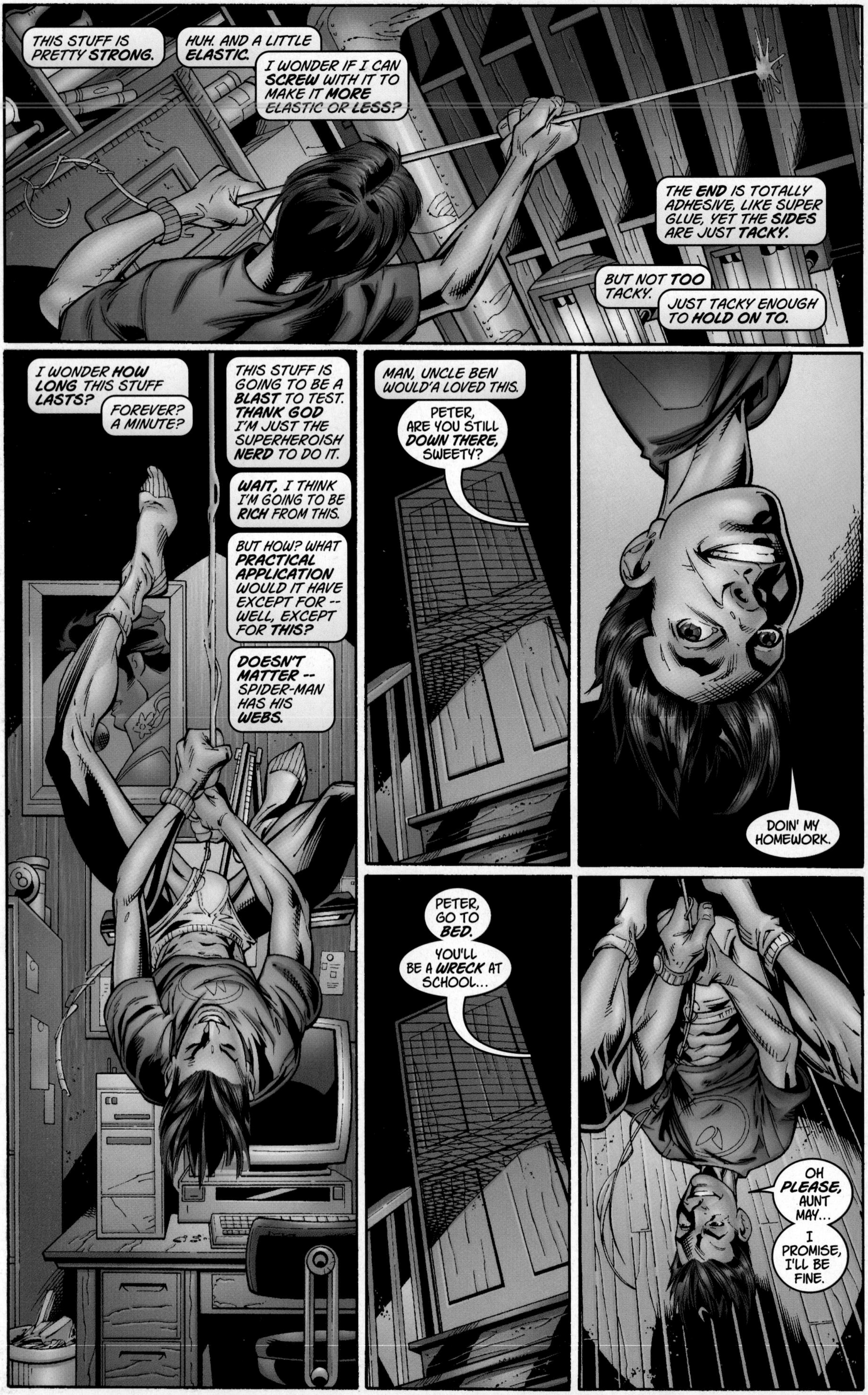
THIS STUFF IS PRETTY STRONG.
HUH. AND A LITTLE ELASTIC.
I WONDER IF I CAN SCREW WITH IT TO MAKE IT MORE ELASTIC OR LESS?
THE END IS TOTALLY ADHESIVE, LIKE SUPER GLUE, YET THE SIDES ARE JUST TACKY.
BUT NOT TOO TACKY.
JUST TACKY ENOUGH TO HOLD ON TO.
I WONDER HOW LONG THIS STUFF LASTS?
FOREVER? A MINUTE?
THIS STUFF IS GOING TO BE A BLAST TO TEST. THANK GOD I'M JUST THE SUPERHEROISH NERD TO DO IT.
WAIT, I THINK I'M GOING TO BE RICH FROM THIS.
BUT HOW? WHAT PRACTICAL APPLICATION WOULD IT HAVE EXCEPT FOR -- WELL, EXCEPT FOR THIS?
DOESN'T MATTER -- SPIDER-MAN HAS HIS WEBS.
MAN, UNCLE BEN WOULD'A LOVED THIS.
PETER, ARE YOU STILL DOWN THERE, SWEETY?
DOIN' MY HOMEWORK.
PETER, GO TO BED.
YOU'LL BE A WRECK AT SCHOOL...
OH PLEASE, AUNT MAY...
I PROMISE, I'LL BE FINE.

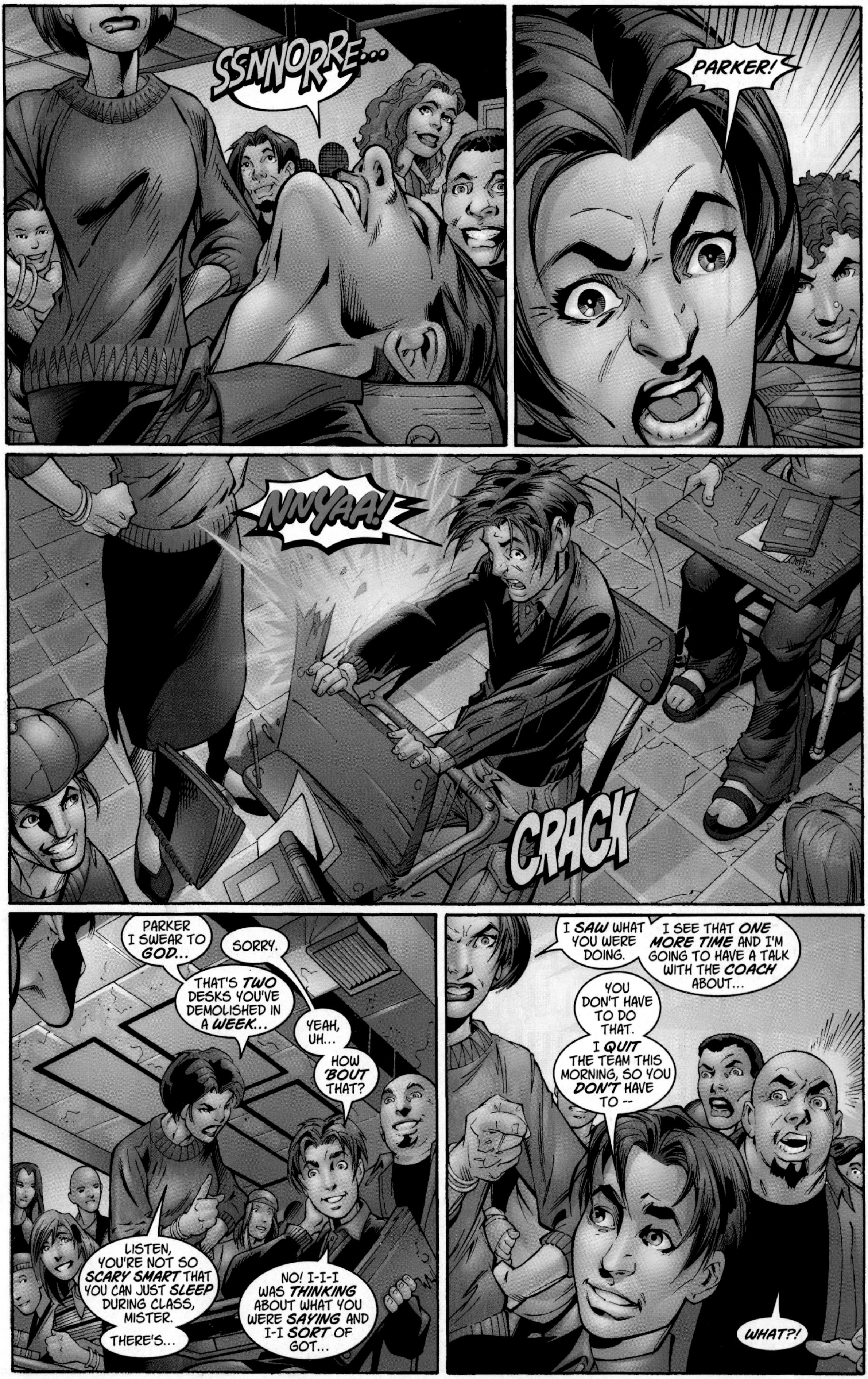
SSNNORRE...
PARKER!
NNYAA!
CRACK
PARKER I SWEAR TO GOD...
SORRY.
THAT'S TWO DESKS YOU'VE DEMOLISHED IN A WEEK...
YEAH, UH...
HOW 'BOUT THAT?
LISTEN, YOU'RE NOT SO SCARY SMART THAT YOU CAN JUST SLEEP DURING CLASS, MISTER.
THERE'S...
NO! I-I-I WAS THINKING ABOUT WHAT YOU WERE SAYING AND I-I SORT OF GOT...
I SAW WHAT YOU WERE DOING.
I SEE THAT ONE MORE TIME AND I'M GOING TO HAVE A TALK WITH THE COACH ABOUT...
YOU DON'T HAVE TO DO THAT.
I QUIT THE TEAM THIS MORNING, SO YOU DON'T HAVE TO --
WHAT?!

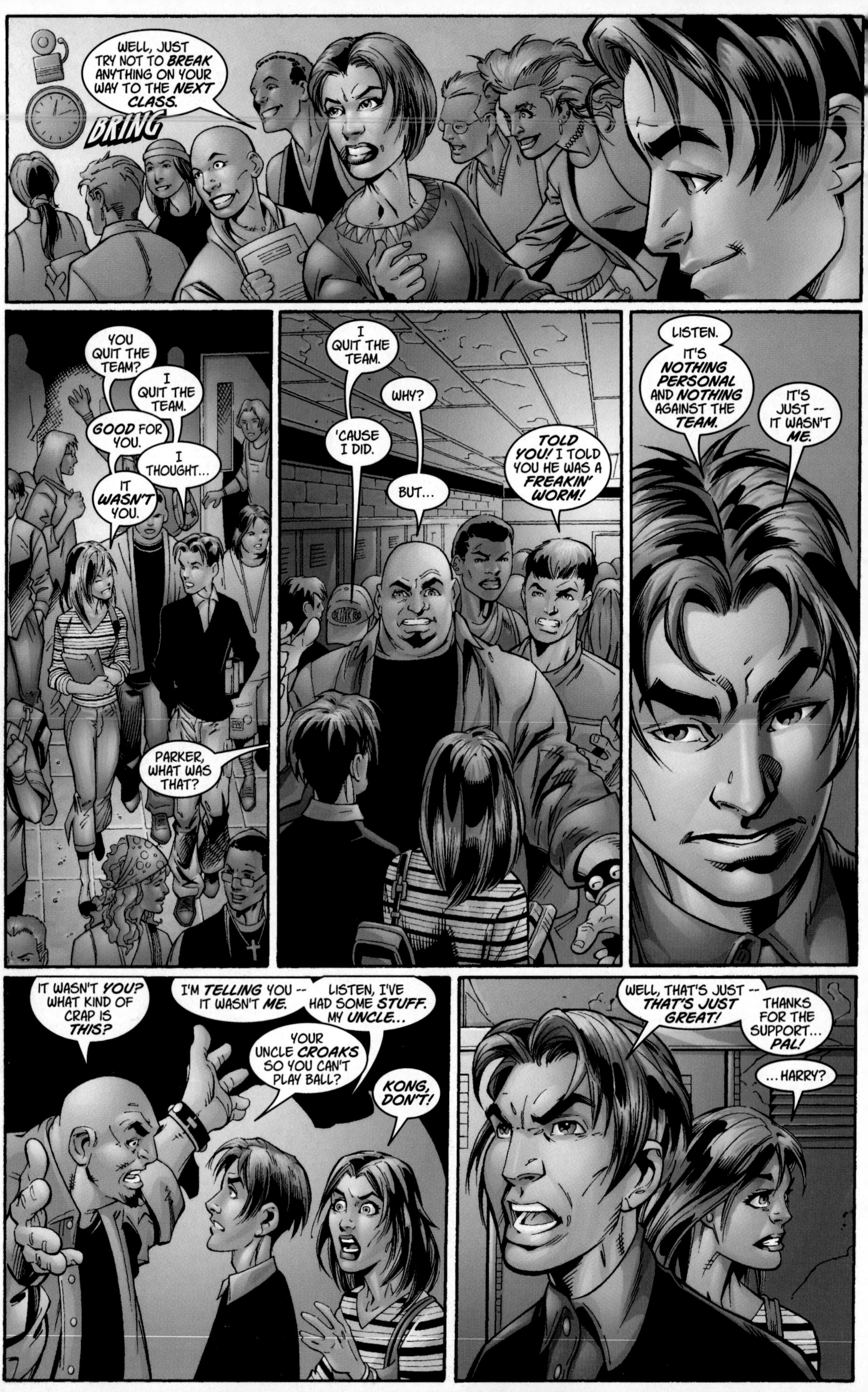
WELL, JUST TRY NOT TO BREAK ANYTHING ON YOUR WAY TO THE NEXT CLASS.
BRING
YOU QUIT THE TEAM?
I QUIT THE TEAM.
GOOD FOR YOU.
I THOUGHT...
IT WASN'T YOU.
PARKER, WHAT WAS THAT?
I QUIT THE TEAM.
WHY?
'CAUSE I DID.
BUT...
TOLD YOU! I TOLD YOU HE WAS A FREAKIN' WORM!
LISTEN.
IT'S NOTHING PERSONAL AND NOTHING AGAINST THE TEAM.
IT'S JUST -- IT WASN'T ME.
IT WASN'T YOU? WHAT KIND OF CRAP IS THIS?
I'M TELLING YOU -- IT WASN'T ME.
LISTEN, I'VE HAD SOME STUFF. MY UNCLE...
YOUR UNCLE CROAKS SO YOU CAN'T PLAY BALL?
KONG, DON'T!
WELL, THAT'S JUST -- THAT'S JUST GREAT!
THANKS FOR THE SUPPORT... PAL!
...HARRY?

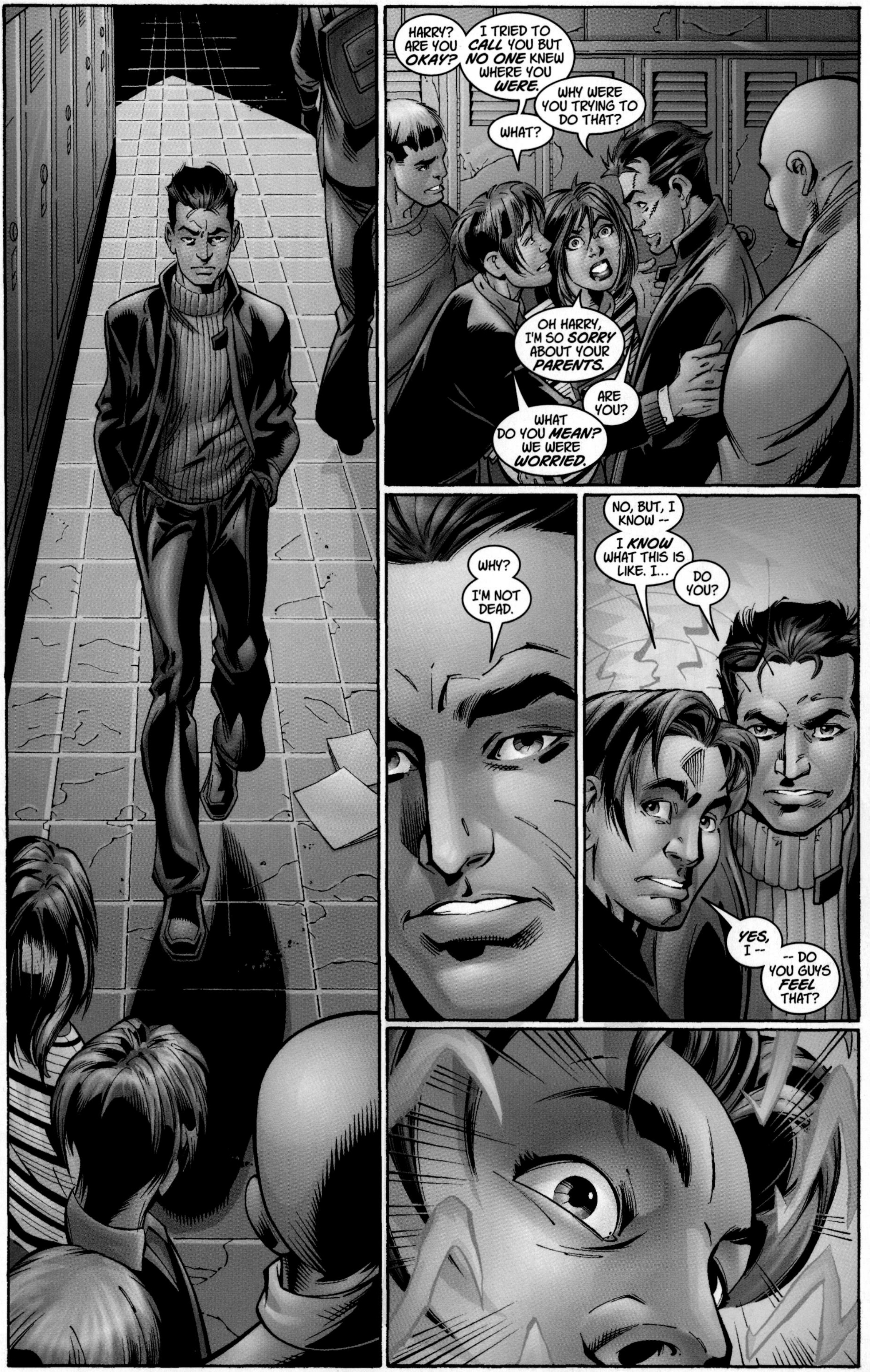
HARRY? ARE YOU OKAY?
I TRIED TO CALL YOU BUT NO ONE KNEW WHERE YOU WERE.
WHAT?
WHY WERE YOU TRYING TO DO THAT?
OH HARRY, I'M SO SORRY ABOUT YOUR PARENTS.
ARE YOU?
WHAT DO YOU MEAN? WE WERE WORRIED.
WHY?
I'M NOT DEAD.
NO, BUT, I KNOW --
I KNOW WHAT THIS IS LIKE. I...
DO YOU?
YES, I --
-- DO YOU GUYS FEEL THAT?

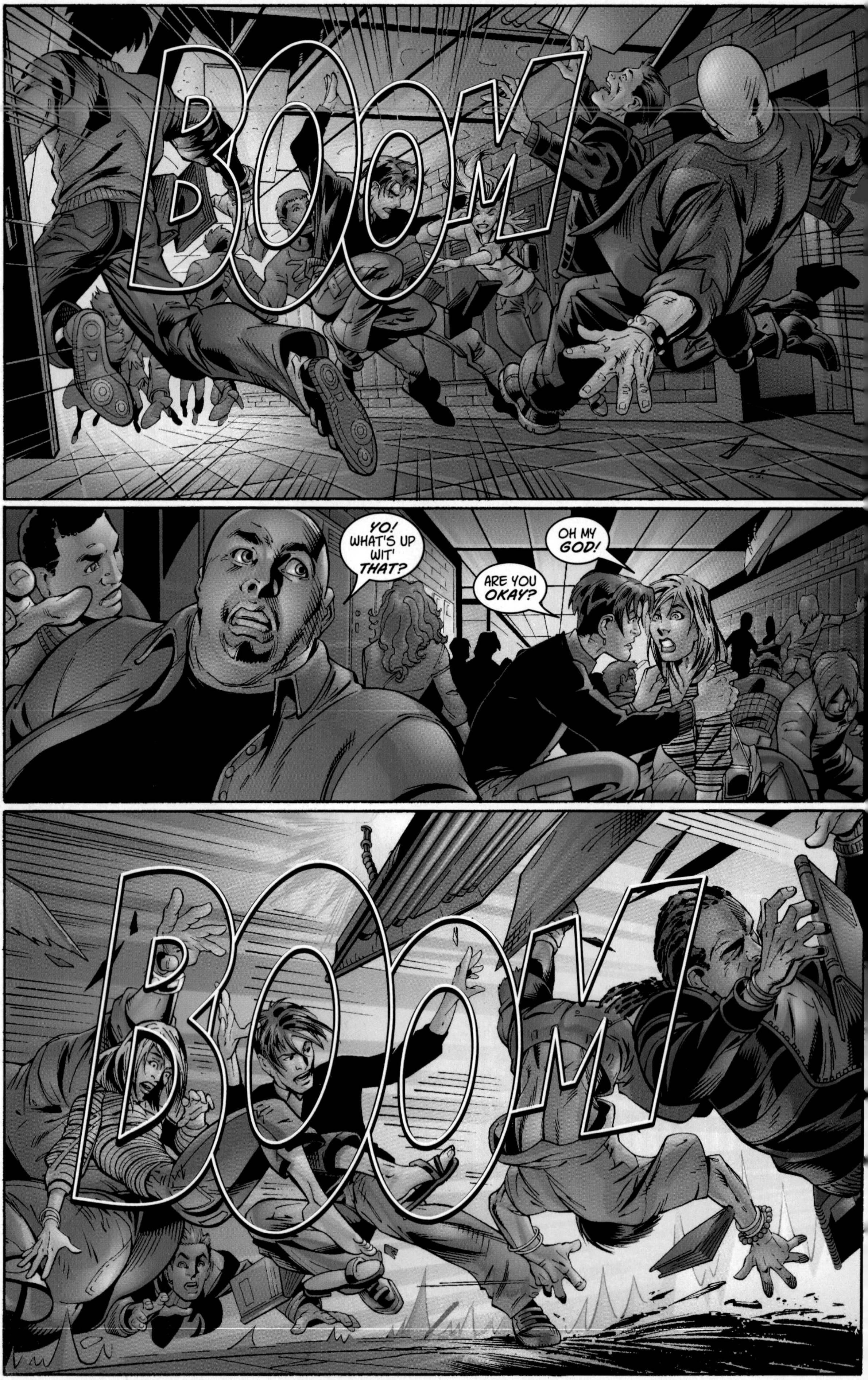
BOOM
YO! WHAT'S UP WIT' THAT?
OH MY GOD!
ARE YOU OKAY?
BOOM

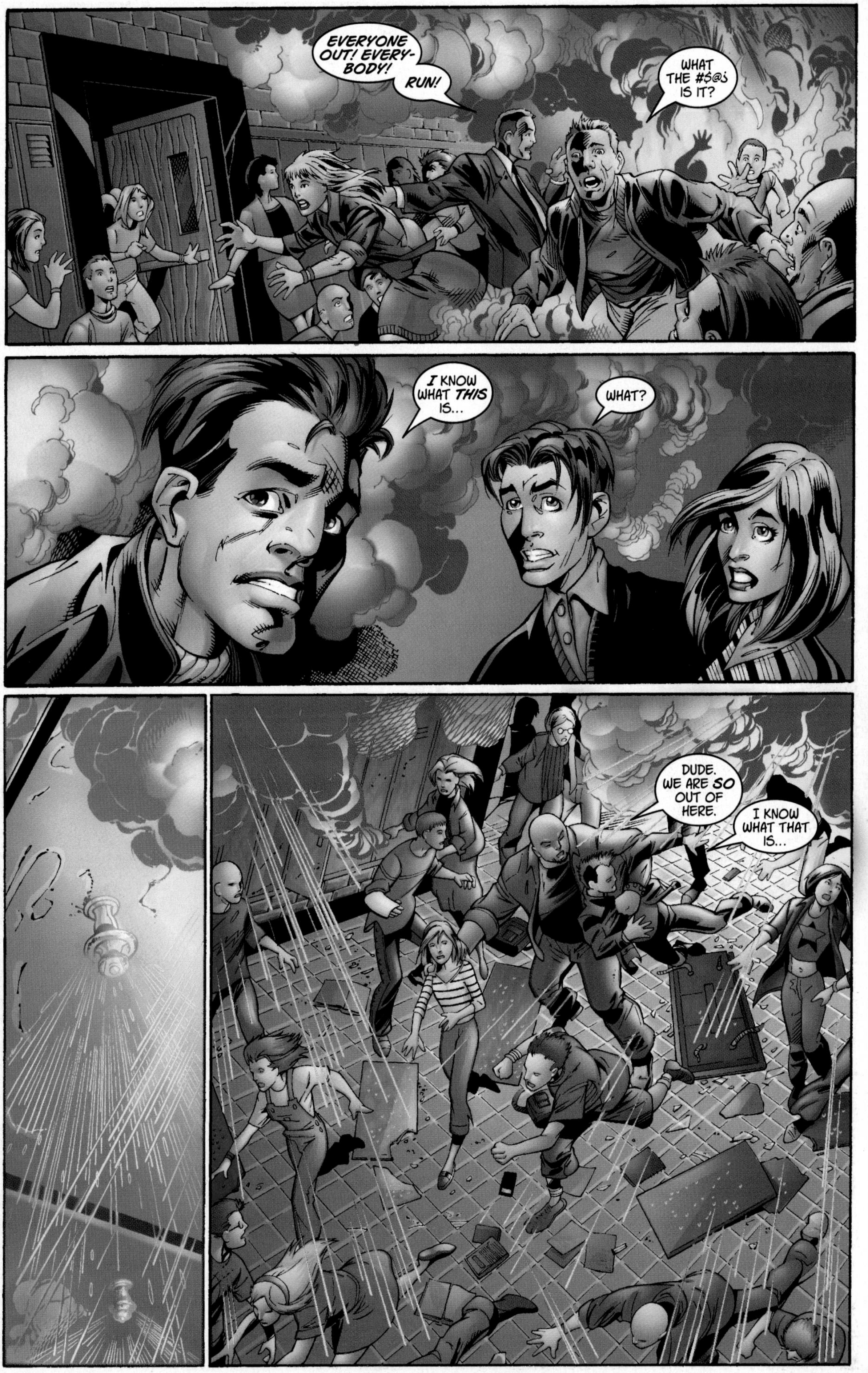
EVERYONE OUT! EVERY-BODY!
RUN!
WHAT THE #$@¿ IS IT?
I KNOW WHAT THIS IS...
WHAT?
DUDE. WE ARE SO OUT OF HERE.
I KNOW WHAT THAT IS...

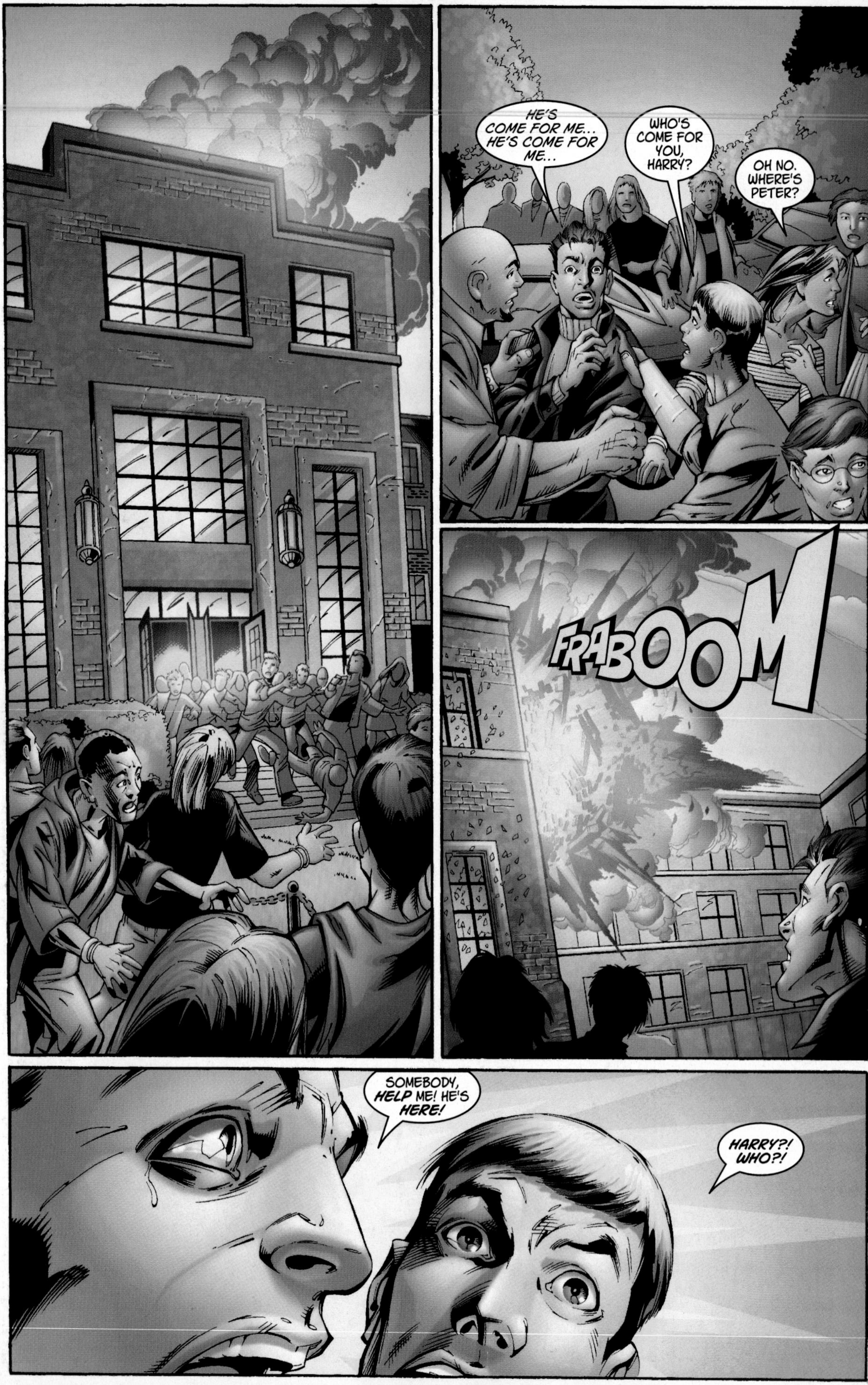
HE'S COME FOR ME... HE'S COME FOR ME...
WHO'S COME FOR YOU, HARRY?
OH NO. WHERE'S PETER?
FRABOOM
SOMEBODY, HELP ME! HE'S HERE!
HARRY?! WHO?!

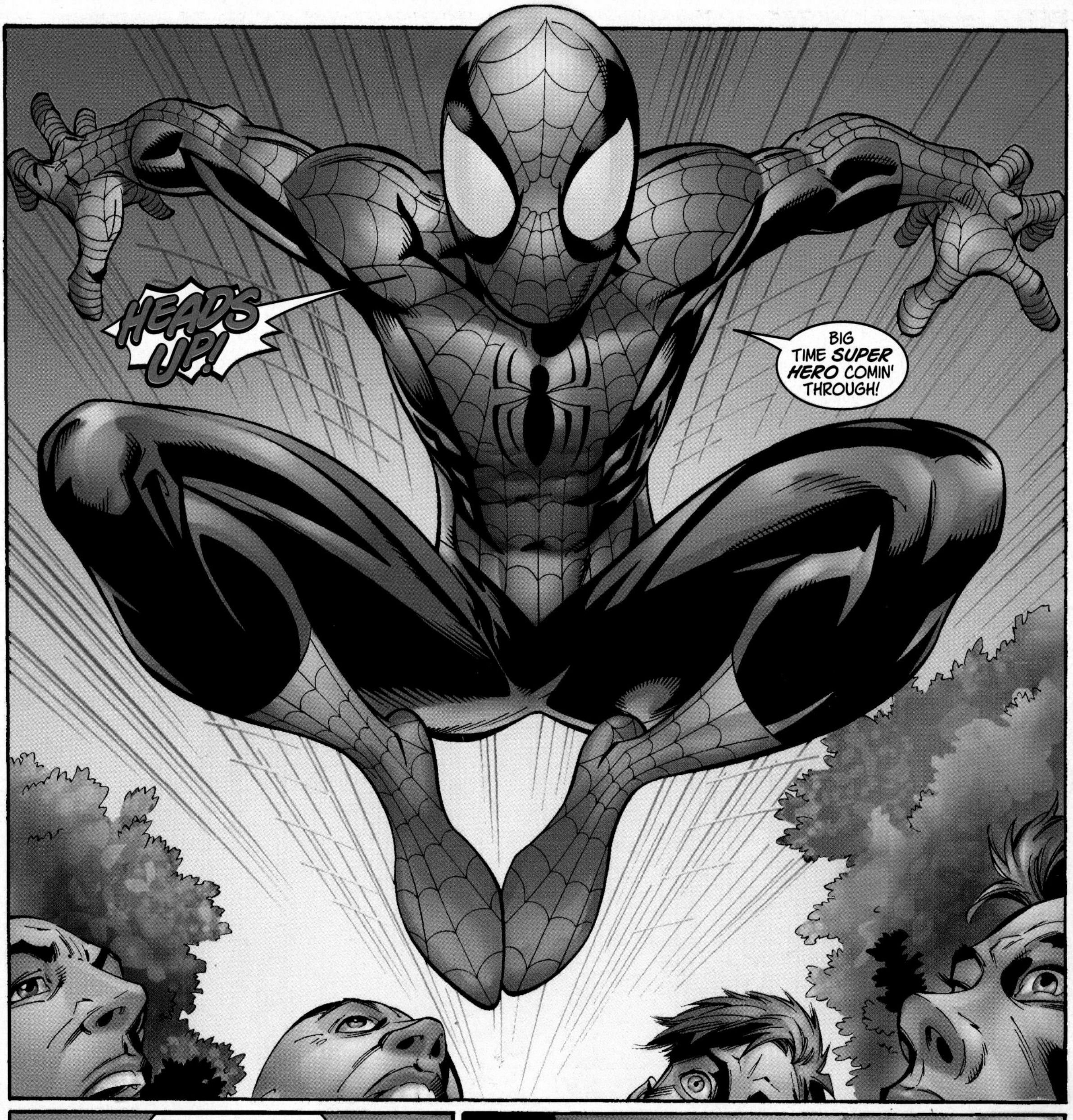
HEADS UP!
BIG TIME SUPER HERO COMIN' THROUGH!

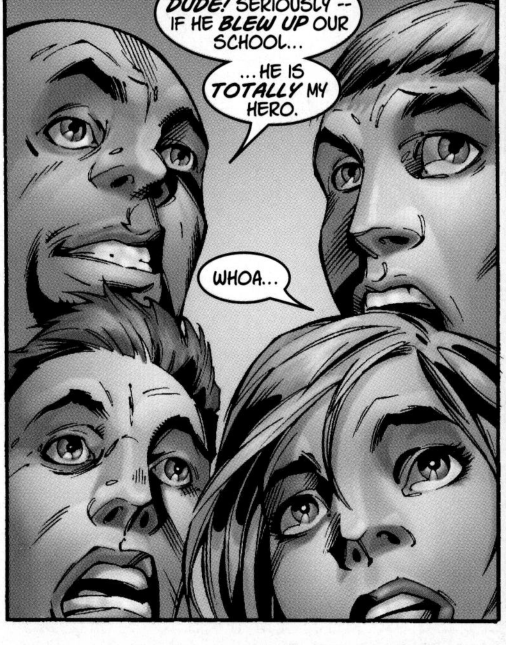
DUDE! SERIOUSLY -- IF HE BLEW UP OUR SCHOOL...
...HE IS TOTALLY MY HERO.
WHOA...

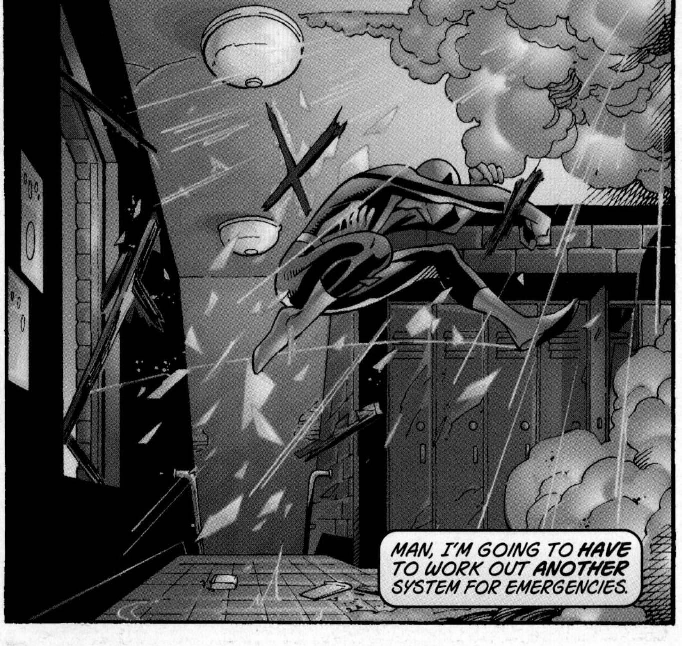
MAN, I'M GOING TO HAVE TO WORK OUT ANOTHER SYSTEM FOR EMERGENCIES.

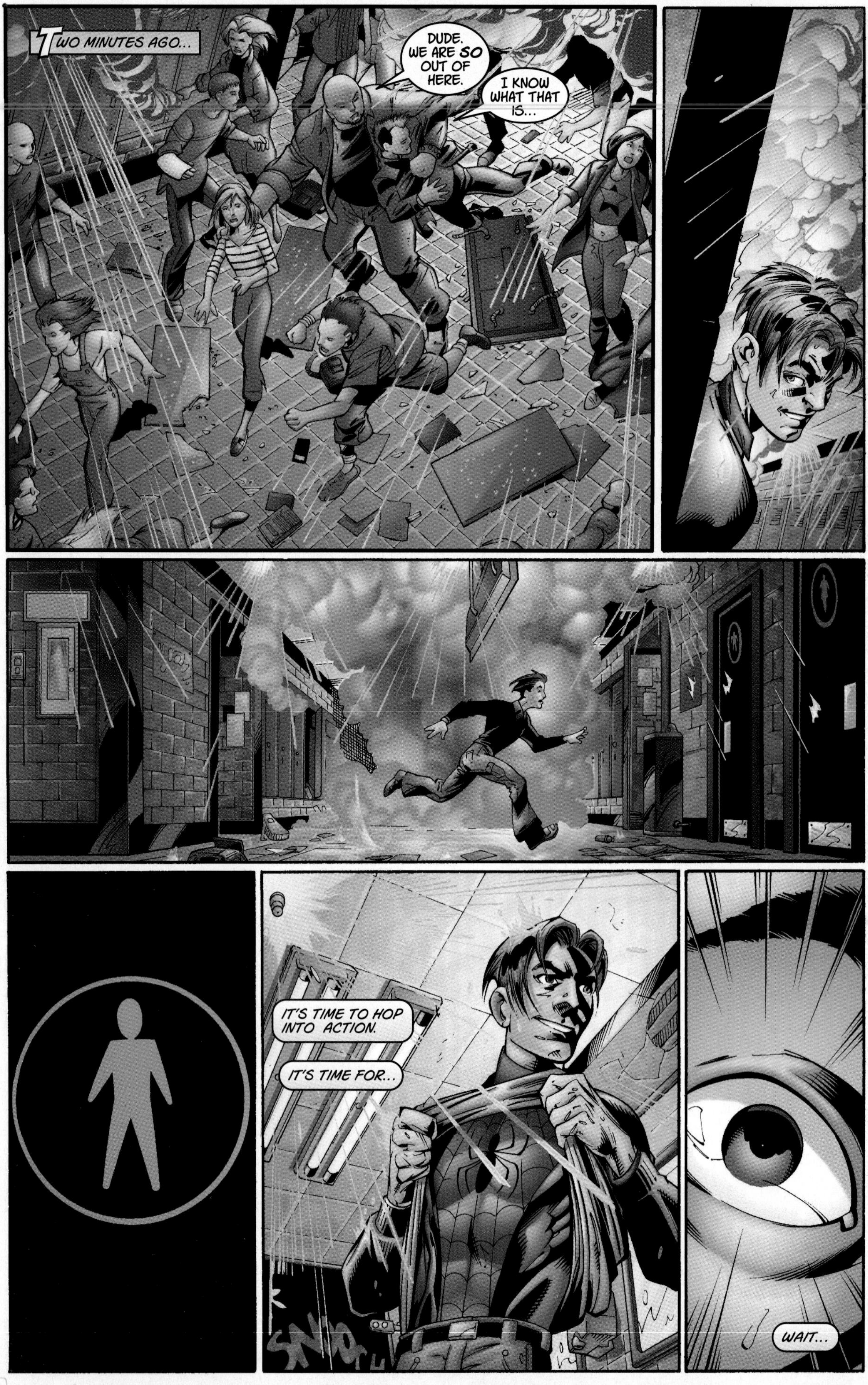
TWO MINUTES AGO...
DUDE. WE ARE SO OUT OF HERE.
I KNOW WHAT THAT IS...
IT'S TIME TO HOP INTO ACTION.
IT'S TIME FOR...
WAIT...

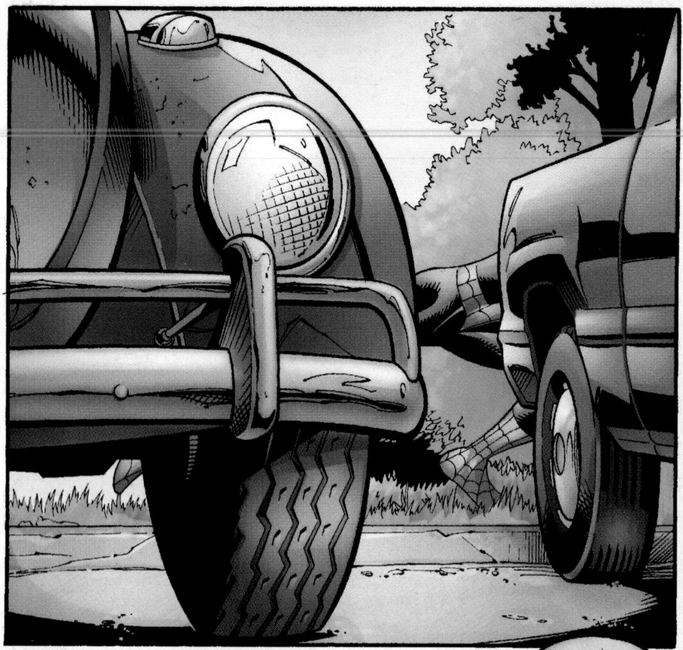

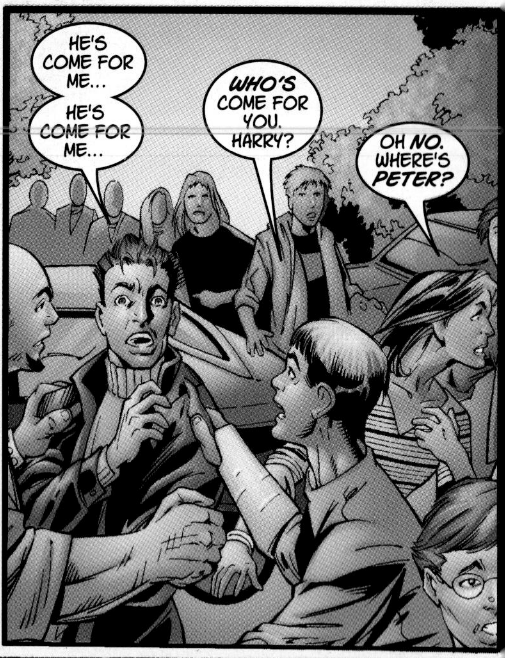
HE'S COME FOR ME...
HE'S COME FOR ME...
WHO'S COME FOR YOU. HARRY?
OH NO. WHERE'S PETER?

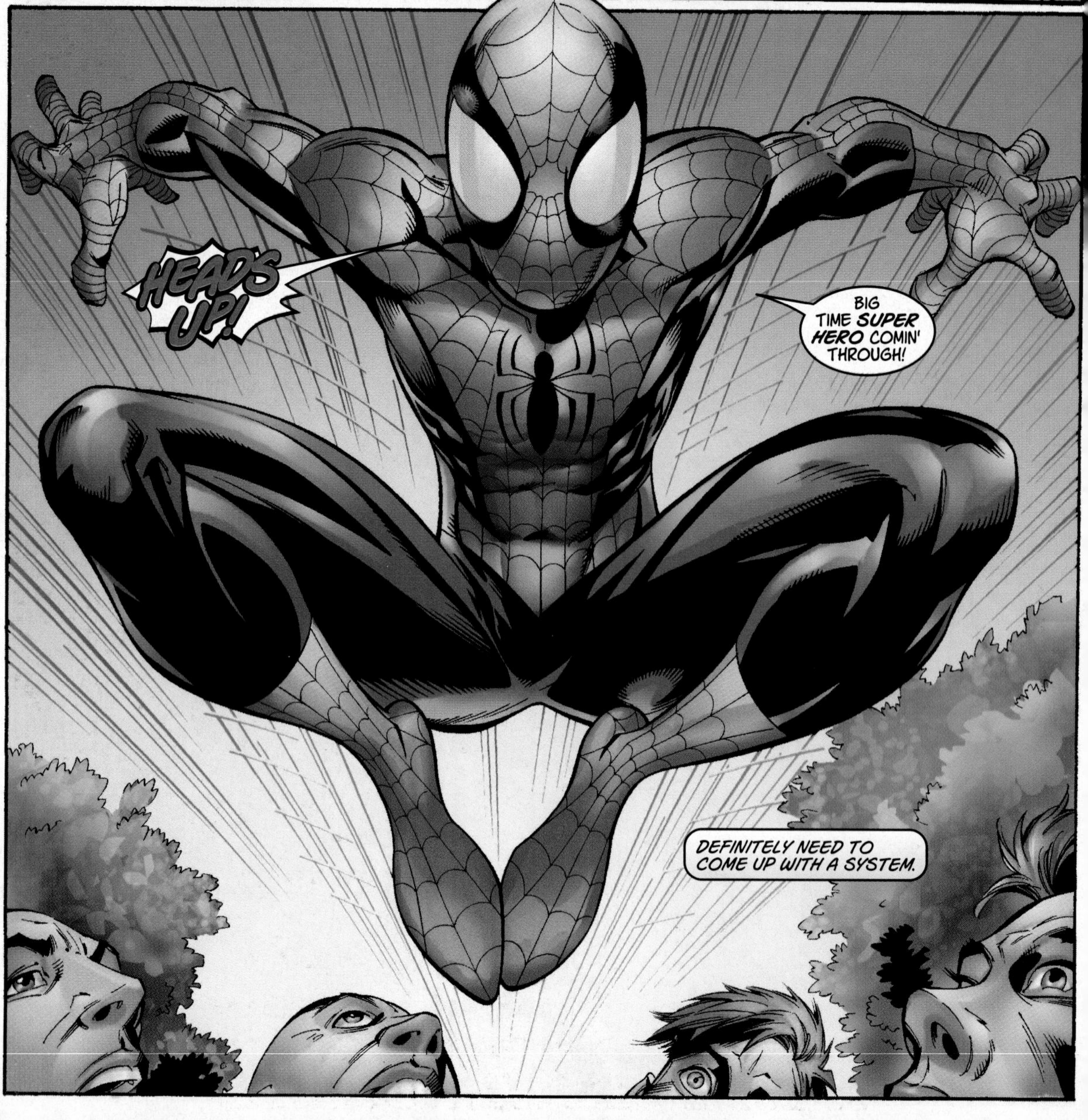
HEADS UP!
BIG TIME SUPER HERO COMIN' THROUGH!
DEFINITELY NEED TO COME UP WITH A SYSTEM.

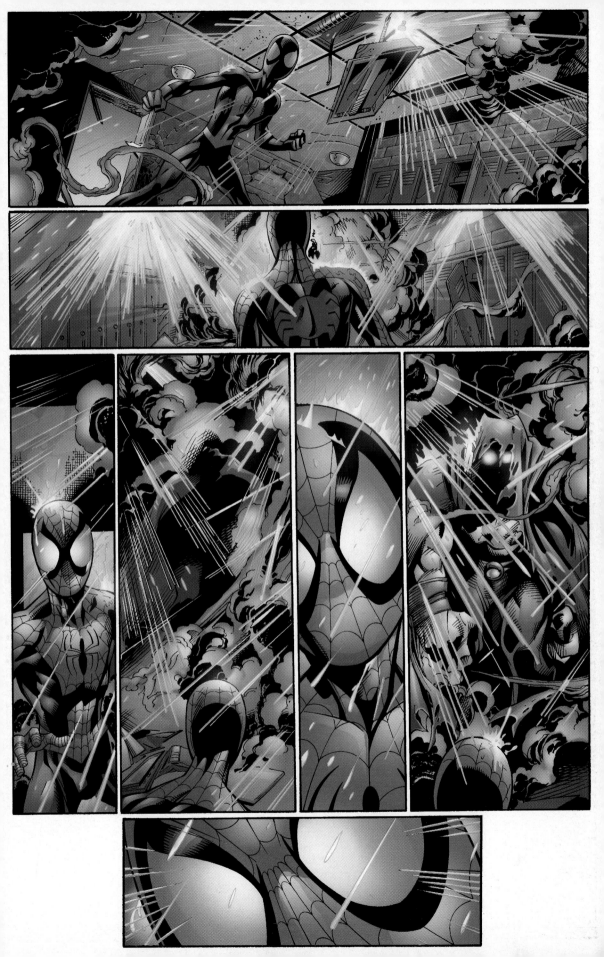

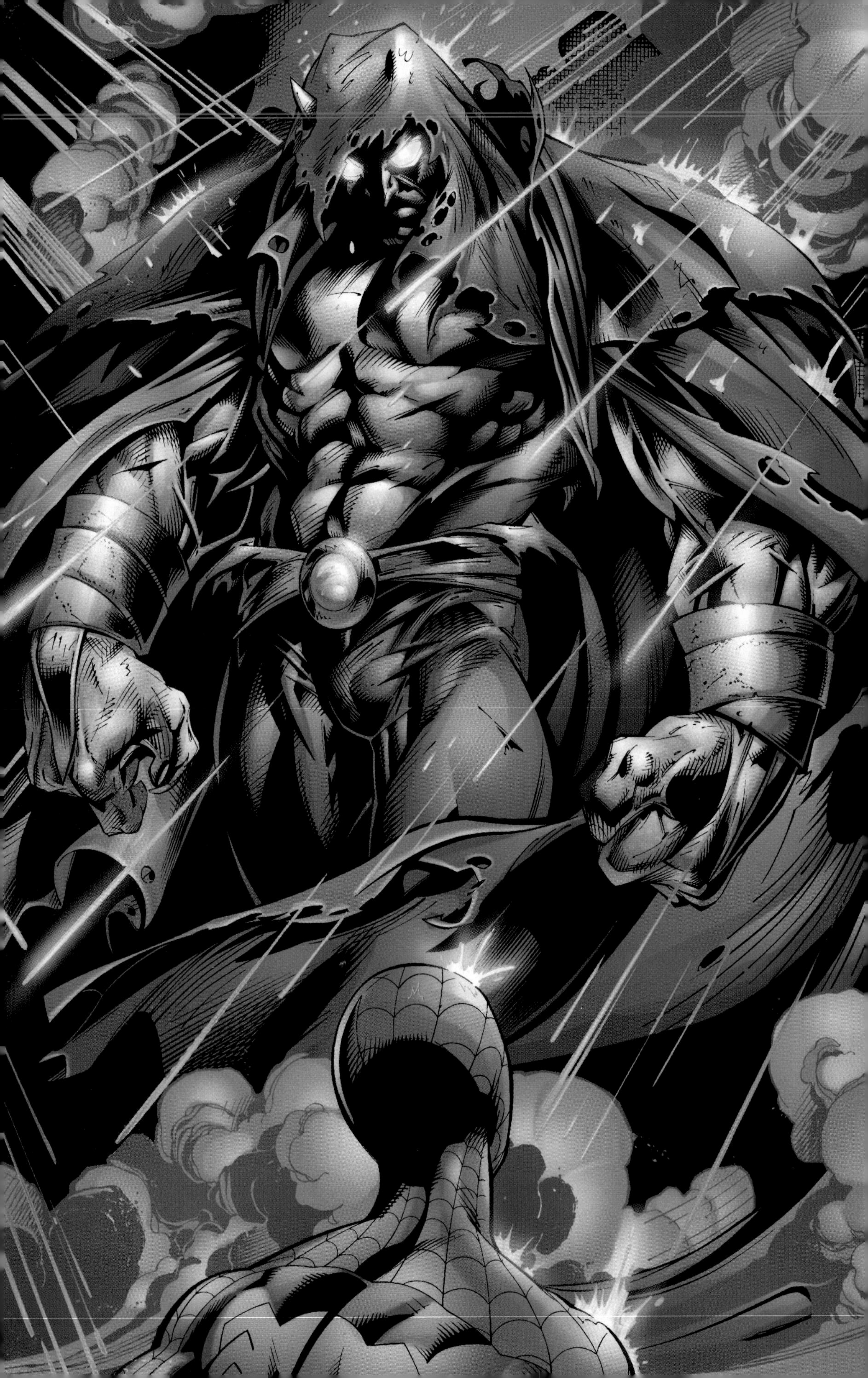

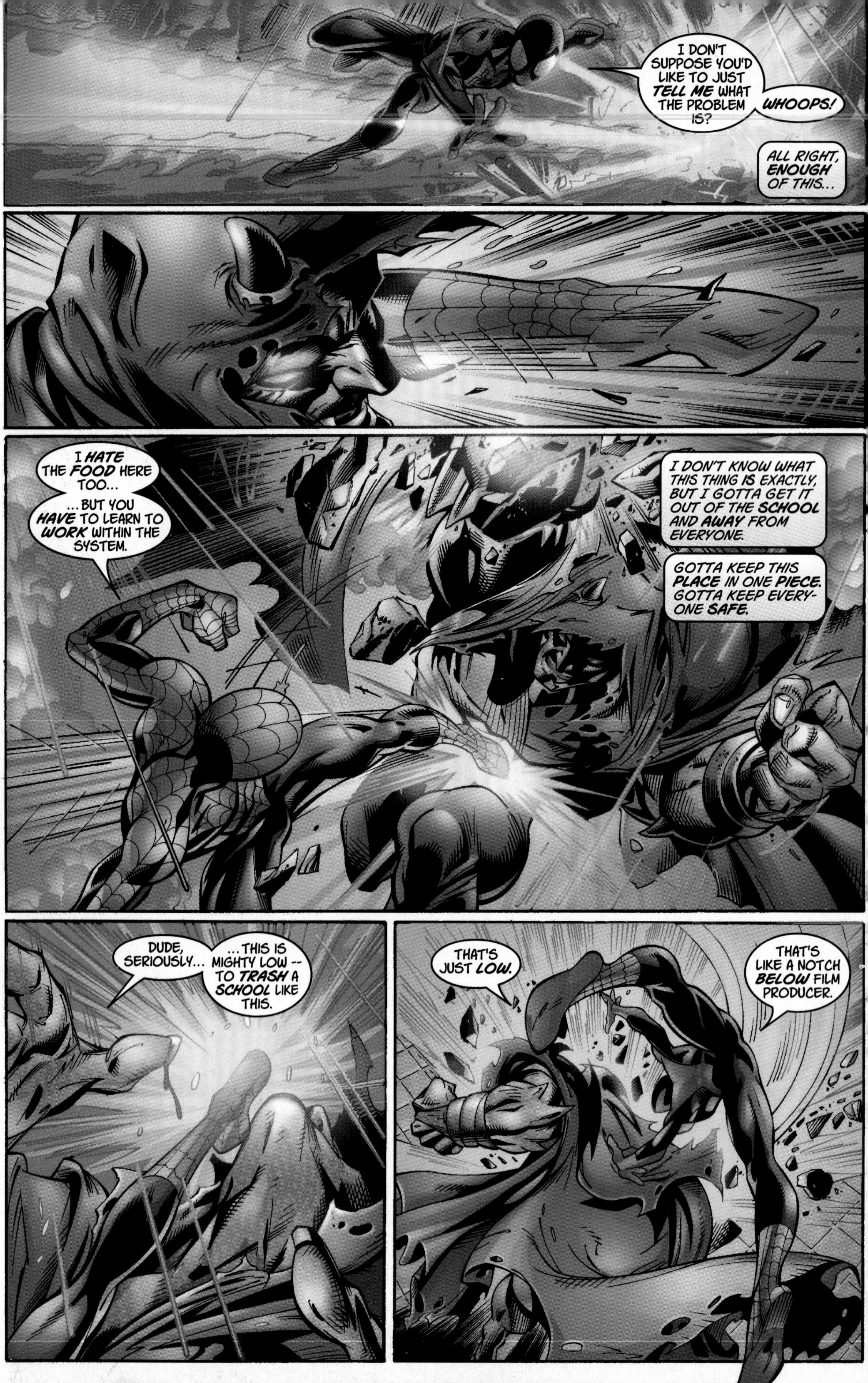
I DON'T SUPPOSE YOU'D LIKE TO JUST TELL ME WHAT THE PROBLEM IS?
WHOOPS!
ALL RIGHT, ENOUGH OF THIS...
I HATE THE FOOD HERE TOO...
...BUT YOU HAVE TO LEARN TO WORK WITHIN THE SYSTEM.
I DON'T KNOW WHAT THIS THING IS EXACTLY, BUT I GOTTA GET IT OUT OF THE SCHOOL AND AWAY FROM EVERYONE.
GOTTA KEEP THIS PLACE IN ONE PIECE. GOTTA KEEP EVERY-ONE SAFE.
DUDE, SERIOUSLY...
...THIS IS MIGHTY LOW -- TO TRASH A SCHOOL LIKE THIS.
THAT'S JUST LOW.
THAT'S LIKE A NOTCH BELOW FILM PRODUCER.

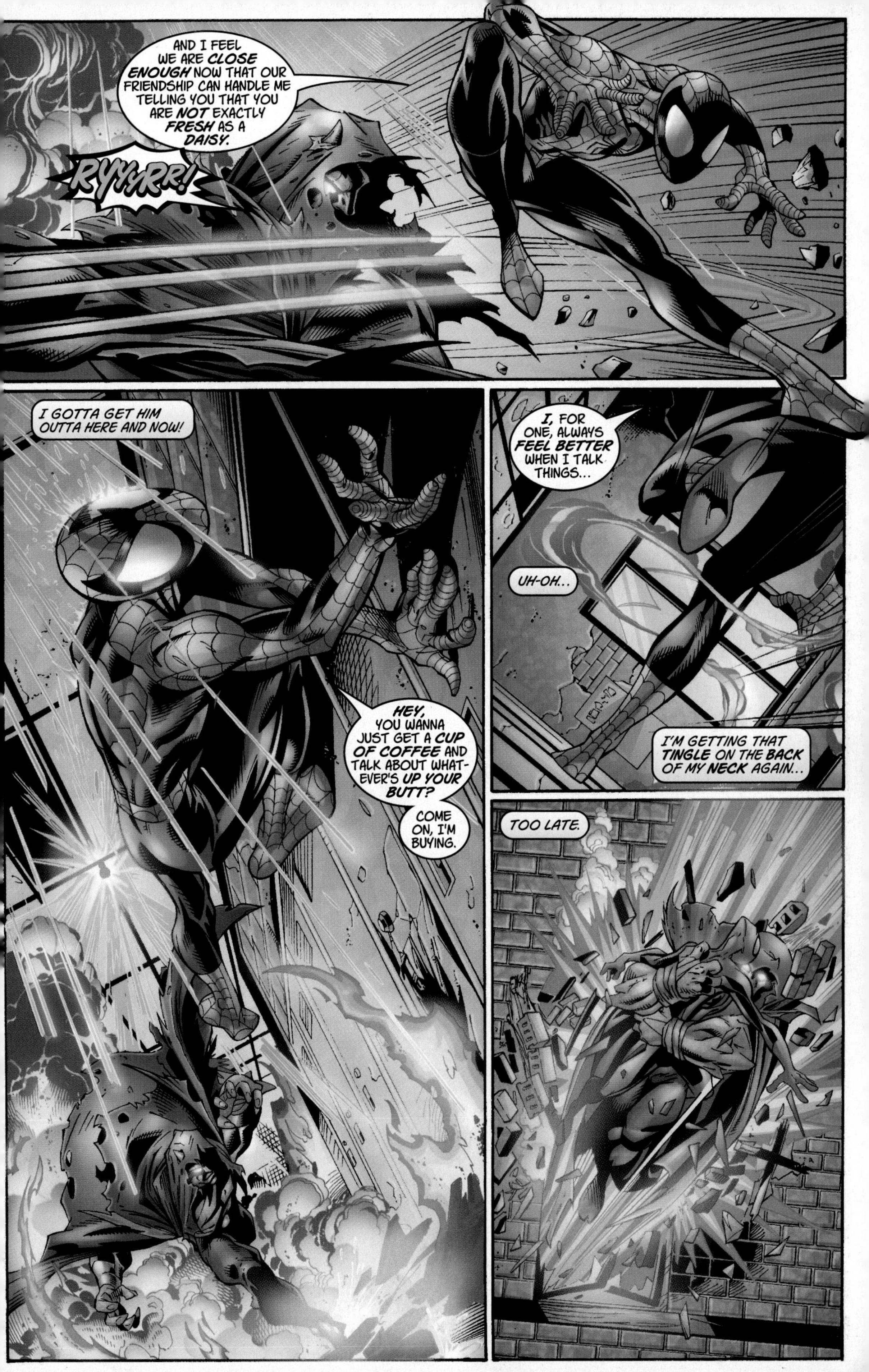

AND I FEEL WE ARE CLOSE ENOUGH NOW THAT OUR FRIENDSHIP CAN HANDLE ME TELLING YOU THAT YOU ARE NOT EXACTLY FRESH AS A DAISY.
RYYYRR!
I GOTTA GET HIM OUTTA HERE AND NOW!
HEY, YOU WANNA JUST GET A CUP OF COFFEE AND TALK ABOUT WHATEVER'S UP YOUR BUTT?
COME ON, I'M BUYING.
I, FOR ONE, ALWAYS FEEL BETTER WHEN I TALK THINGS...
UH-OH...
I'M GETTING THAT TINGLE ON THE BACK OF MY NECK AGAIN...
TOO LATE.

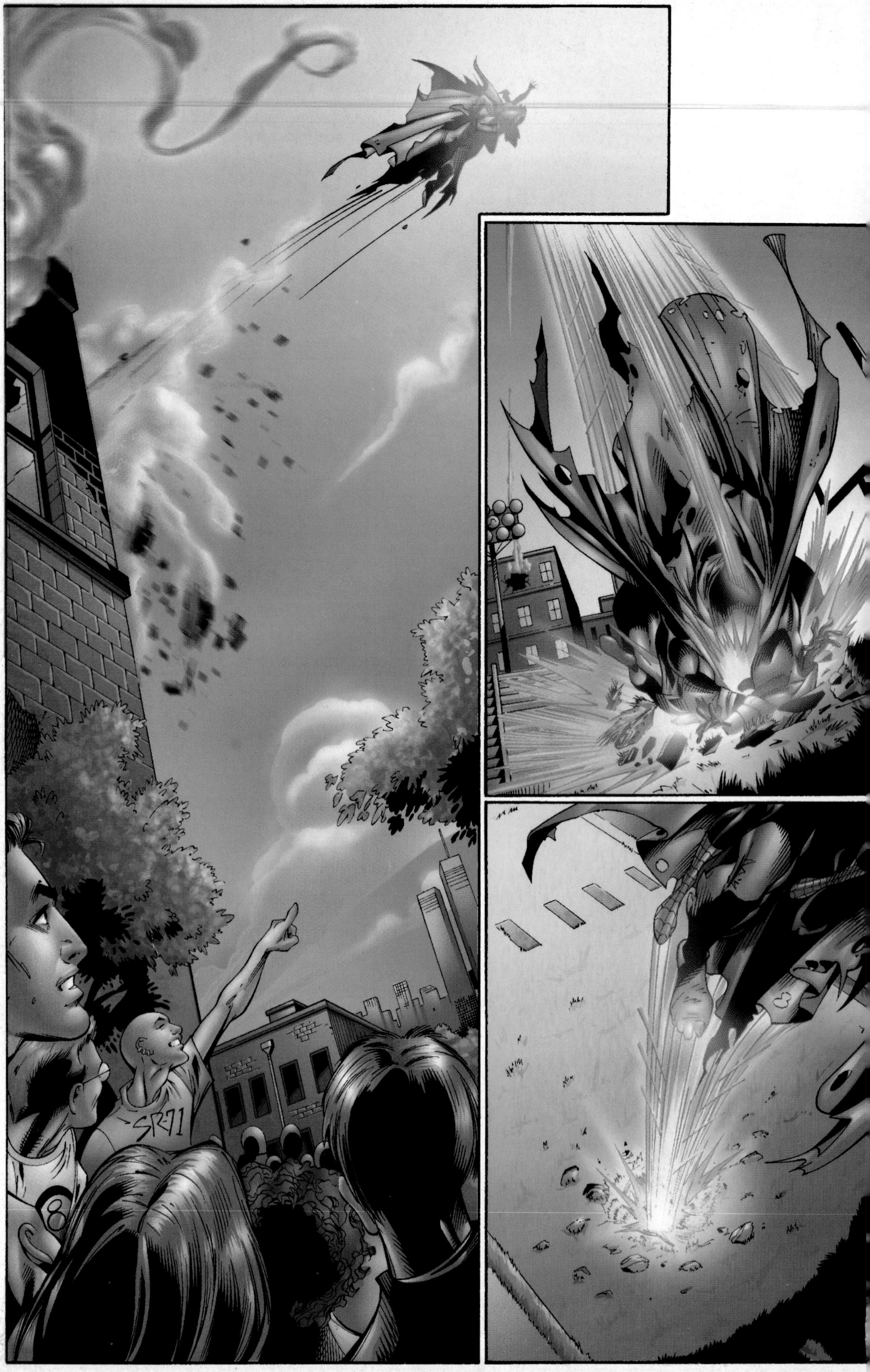
SR-71

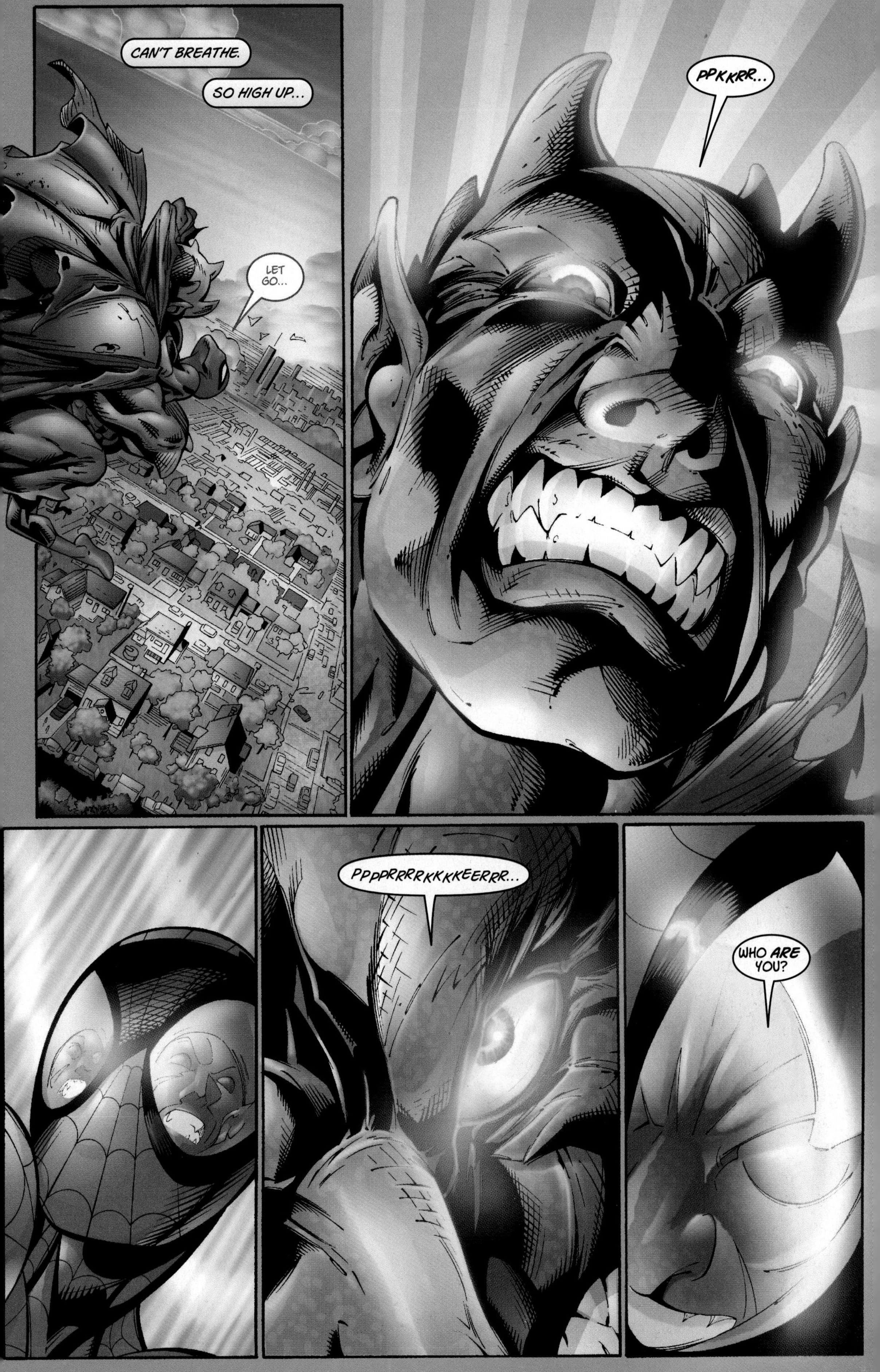
CAN'T BREATHE.
SO HIGH UP...
LET GO...
PPKKRR...
PPPPRRRRKKKKEERRR...
WHO ARE YOU?

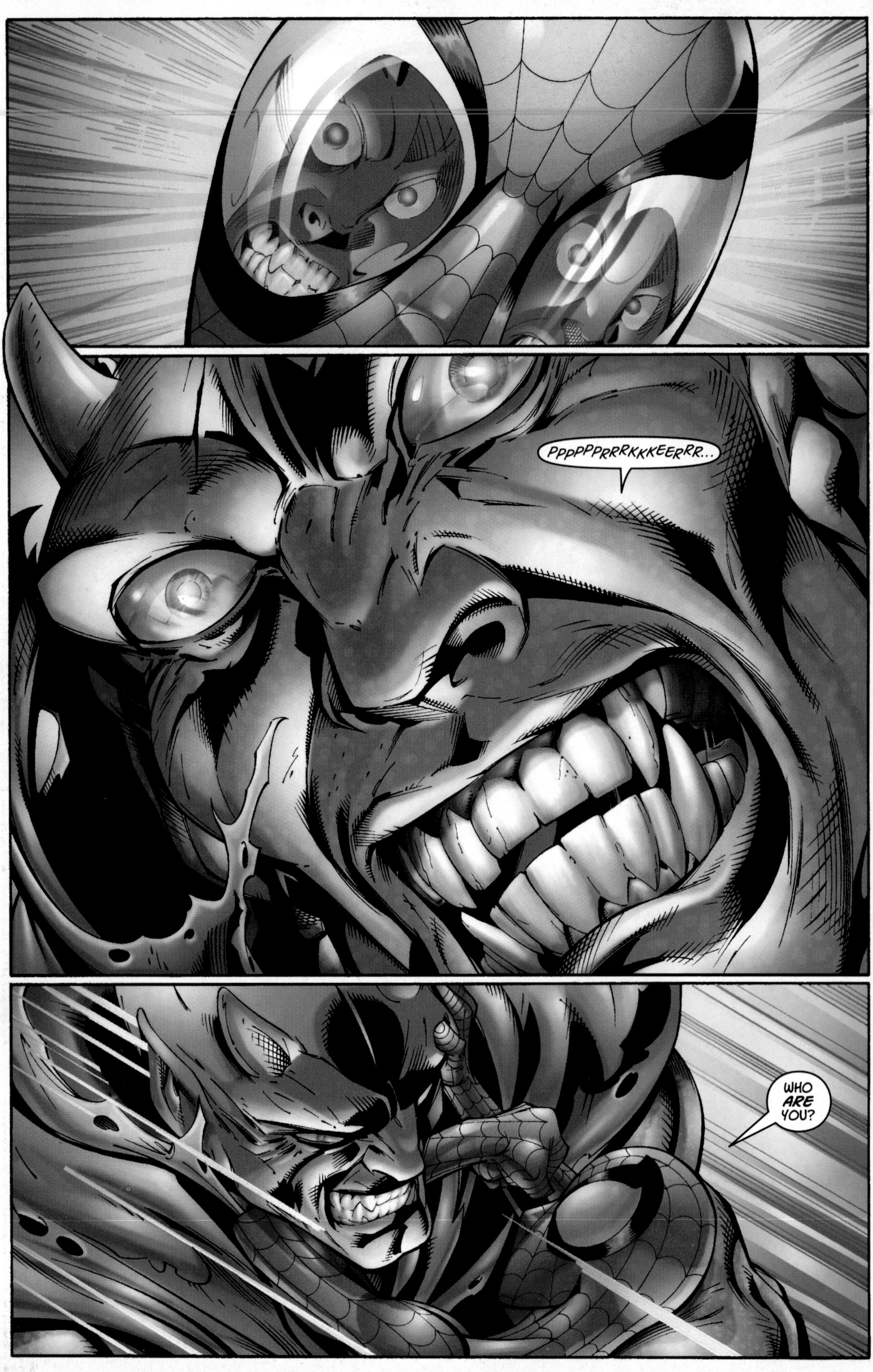
PPPPPPRRRKKKEERRR...
WHO ARE YOU?

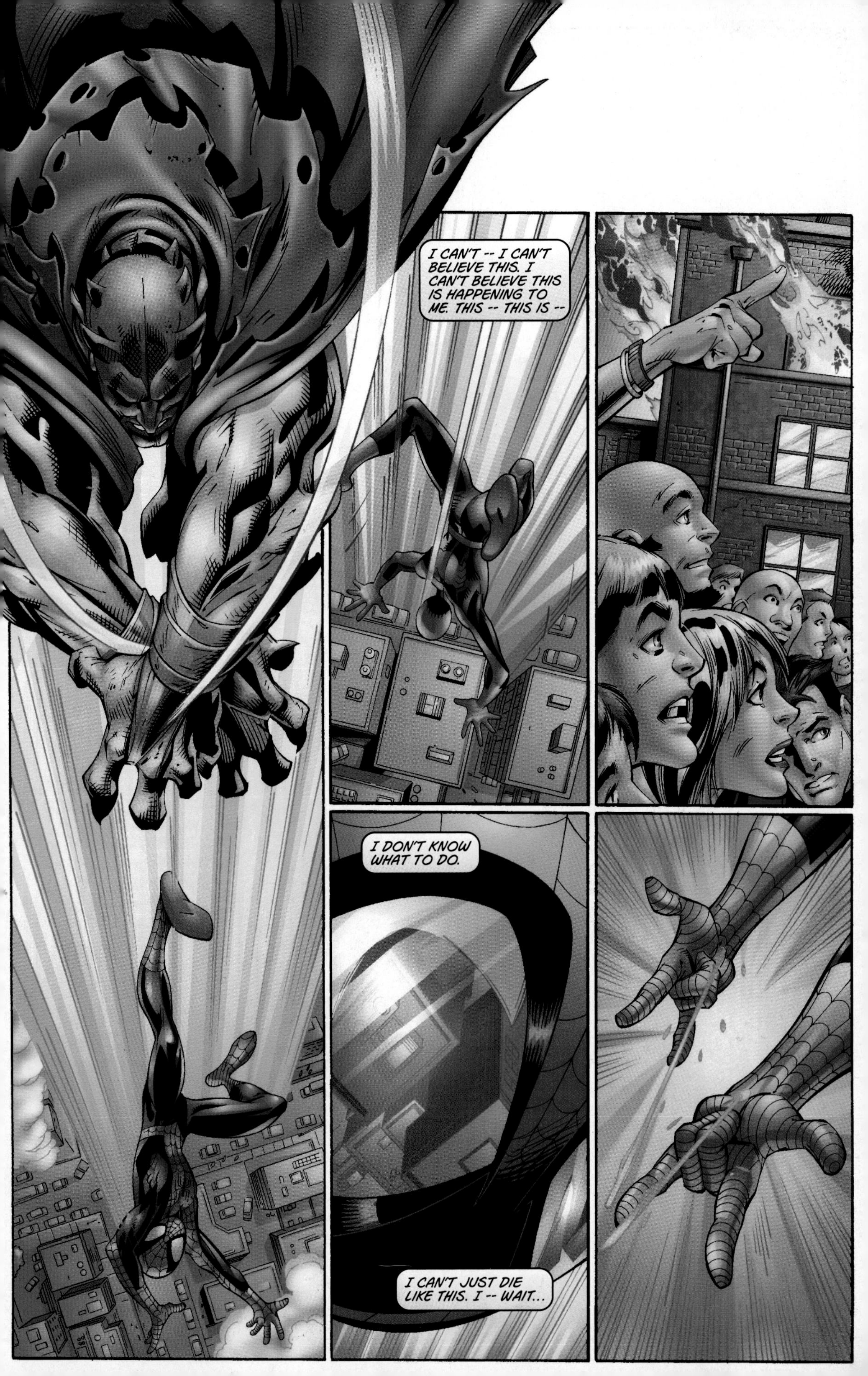
I CAN'T -- I CAN'T BELIEVE THIS. I CAN'T BELIEVE THIS IS HAPPENING TO ME. THIS -- THIS IS --
I DON'T KNOW WHAT TO DO.
I CAN'T JUST DIE LIKE THIS. I -- WAIT...

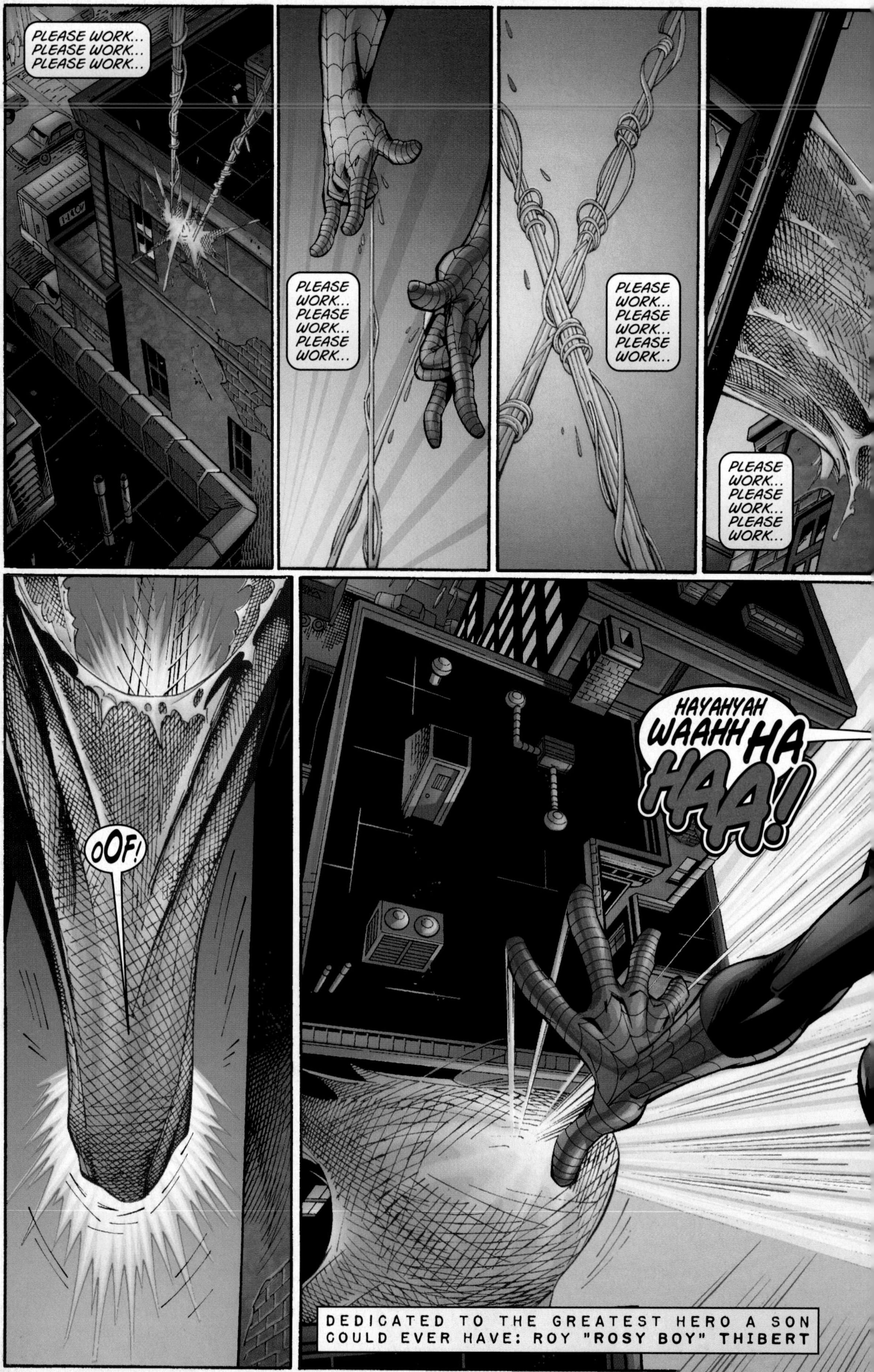
PLEASE WORK... PLEASE WORK... PLEASE WORK...
PLEASE WORK... PLEASE WORK... PLEASE WORK...
PLEASE WORK... PLEASE WORK... PLEASE WORK...
PLEASE WORK... PLEASE WORK... PLEASE WORK...
OOF!
HAYAHYAH WAAHH HA HAA!
DEDICATED TO THE GREATEST HERO A SON COULD EVER HAVE: ROY "ROSY BOY" THIBERT

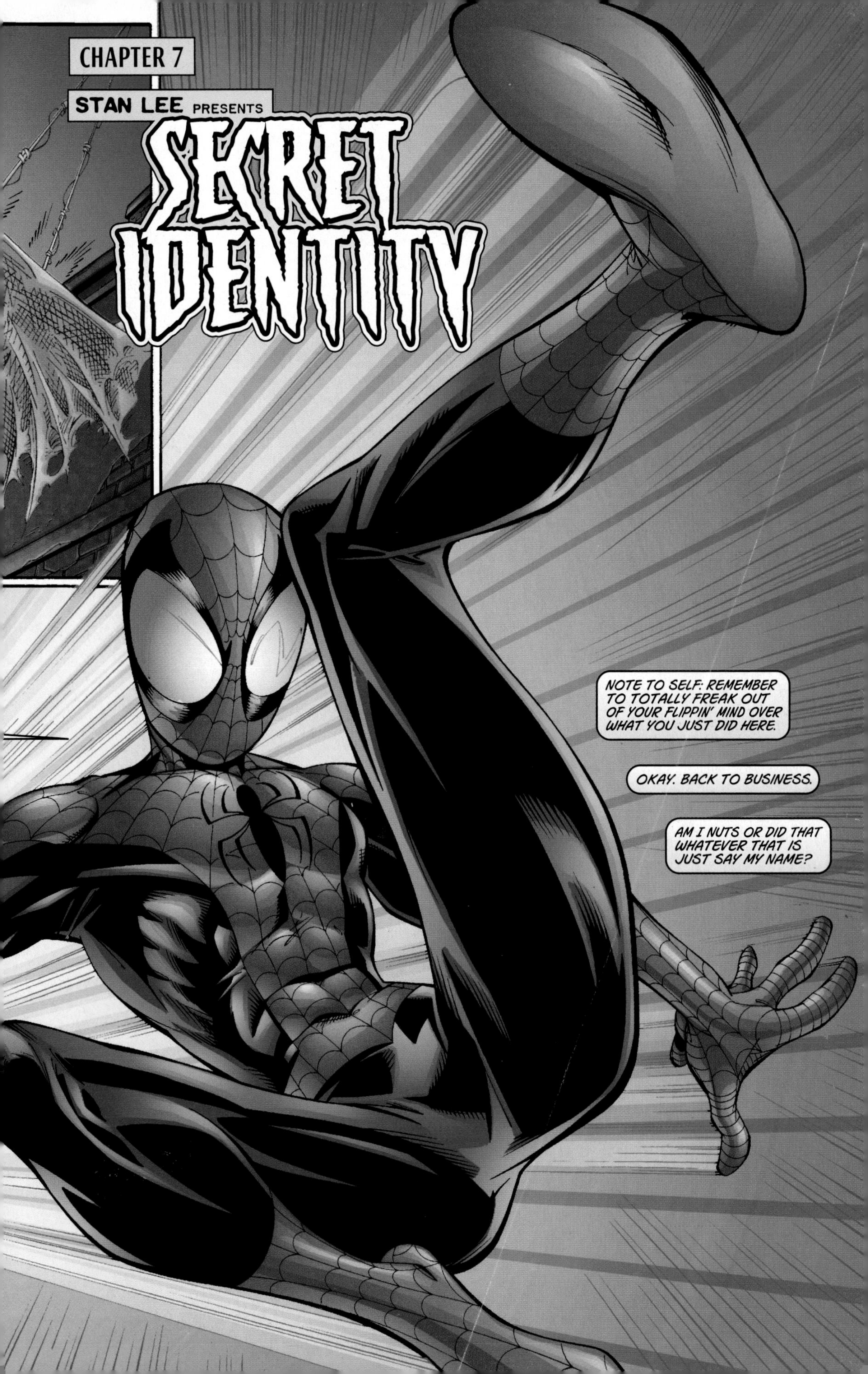
CHAPTER 7
STAN LEE PRESENTS
SECRET IDENTITY
NOTE TO SELF: REMEMBER TO TOTALLY FREAK OUT OF YOUR FLIPPIN' MIND OVER WHAT YOU JUST DID HERE.
OKAY. BACK TO BUSINESS.
AM I NUTS OR DID THAT WHATEVER THAT IS JUST SAY MY NAME?

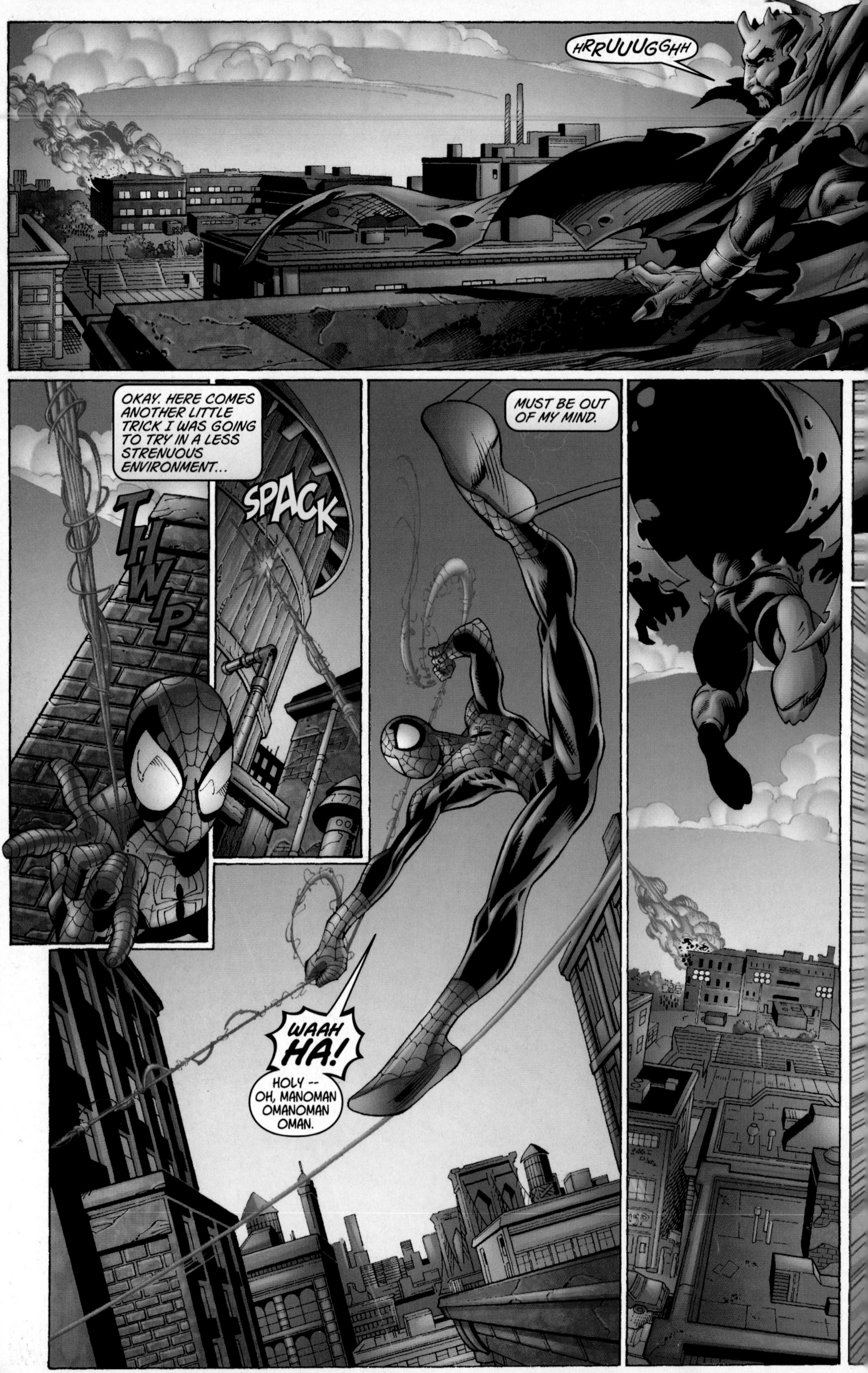
HRRUUUGGHH
OKAY. HERE COMES ANOTHER LITTLE TRICK I WAS GOING TO TRY IN A LESS STRENUOUS ENVIRONMENT...
THWIP
SPACK
MUST BE OUT OF MY MIND.
WAAH HA!
HOLY -- OH, MANOMAN OMANOMAN OMAN.

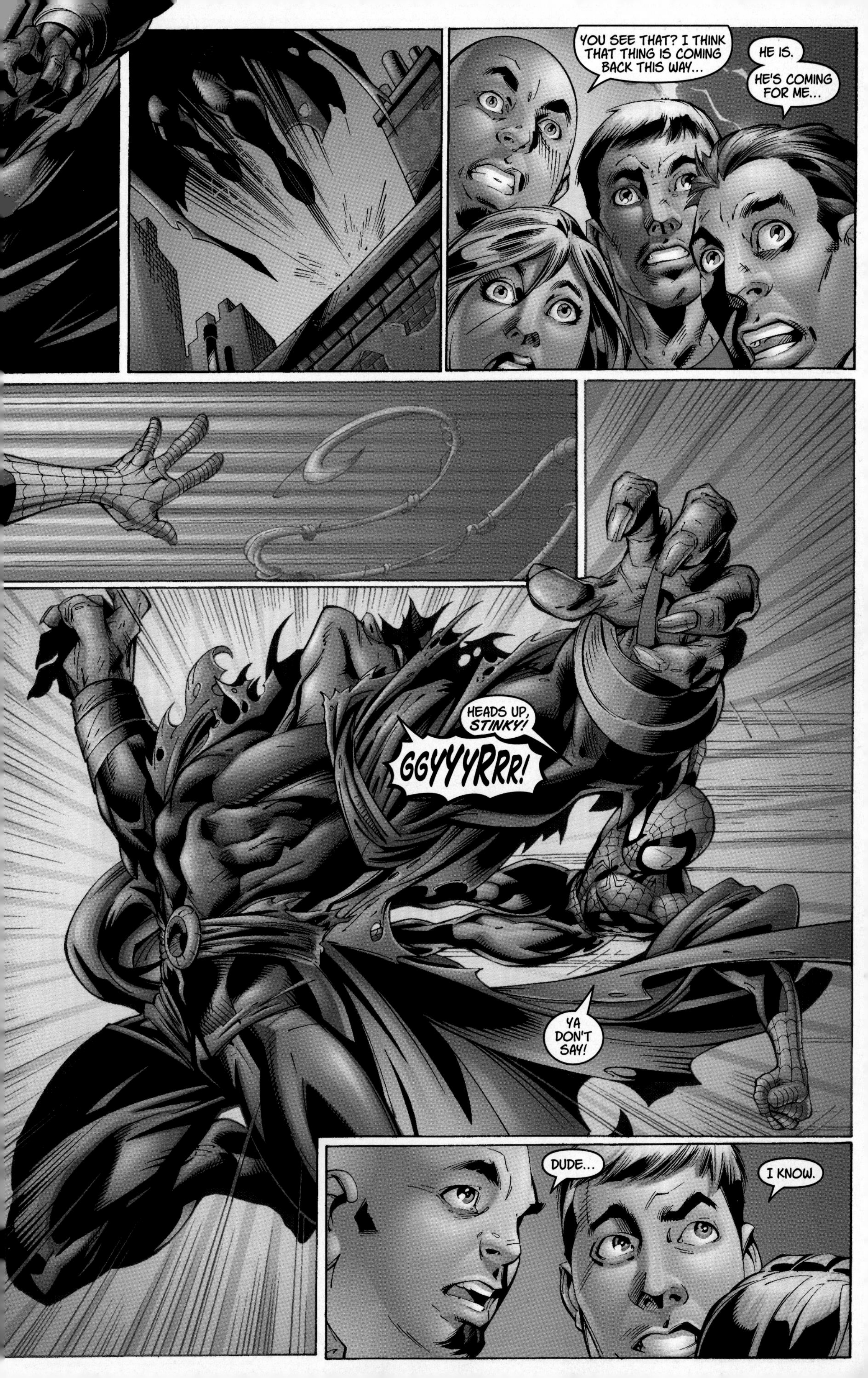
YOU SEE THAT? I THINK THAT THING IS COMING BACK THIS WAY...
HE IS.
HE'S COMING FOR ME...
HEADS UP, STINKY!
GGYYYRRR!
YA DON'T SAY!
DUDE...
I KNOW.

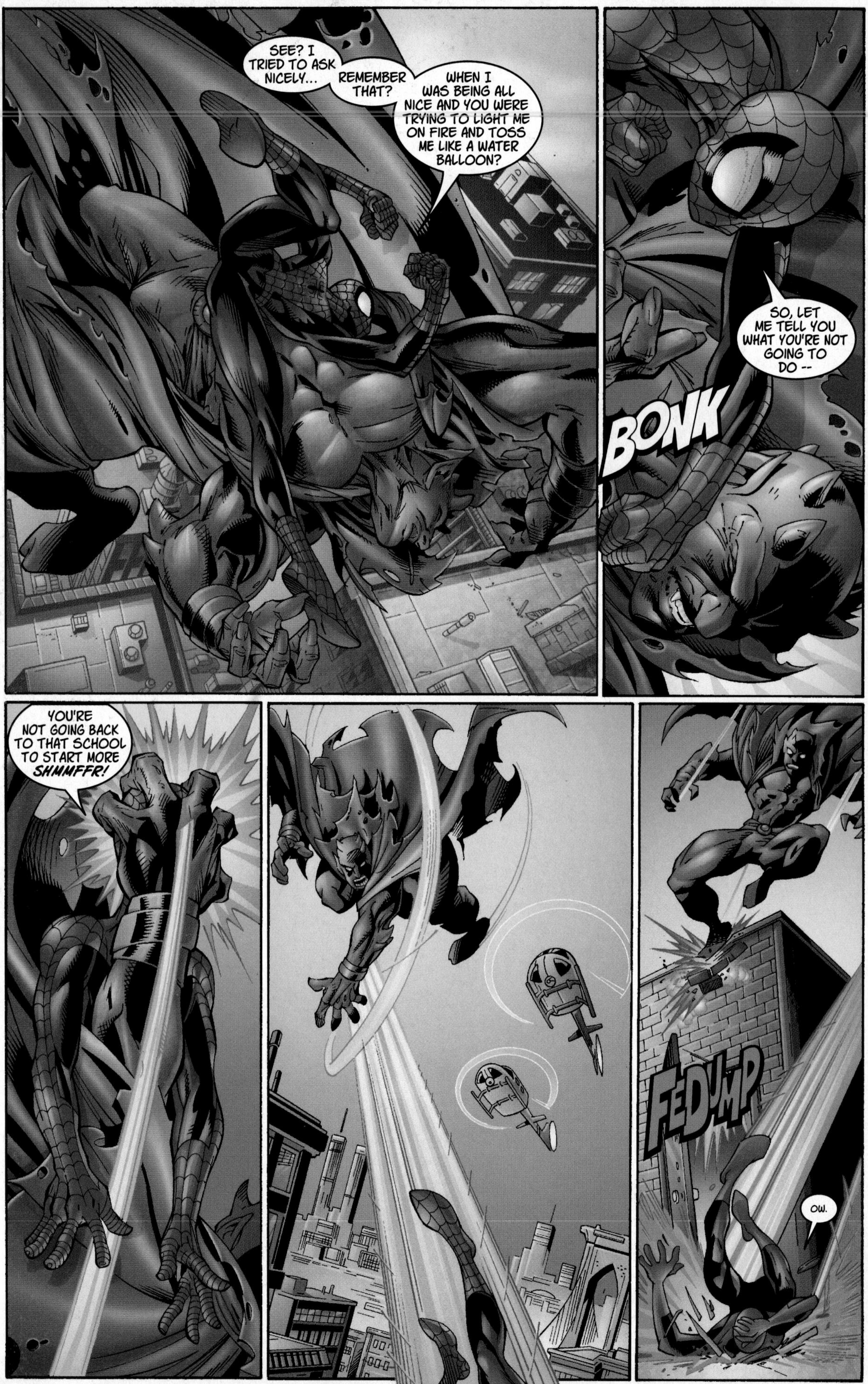
SEE? I TRIED TO ASK NICELY...
REMEMBER THAT?
WHEN I WAS BEING ALL NICE AND YOU WERE TRYING TO LIGHT ME ON FIRE AND TOSS ME LIKE A WATER BALLOON?
SO, LET ME TELL YOU WHAT YOU'RE NOT GOING TO DO --
BONK
YOU'RE NOT GOING BACK TO THAT SCHOOL TO START MORE SHMMFFR!
FEDUMP
OW.

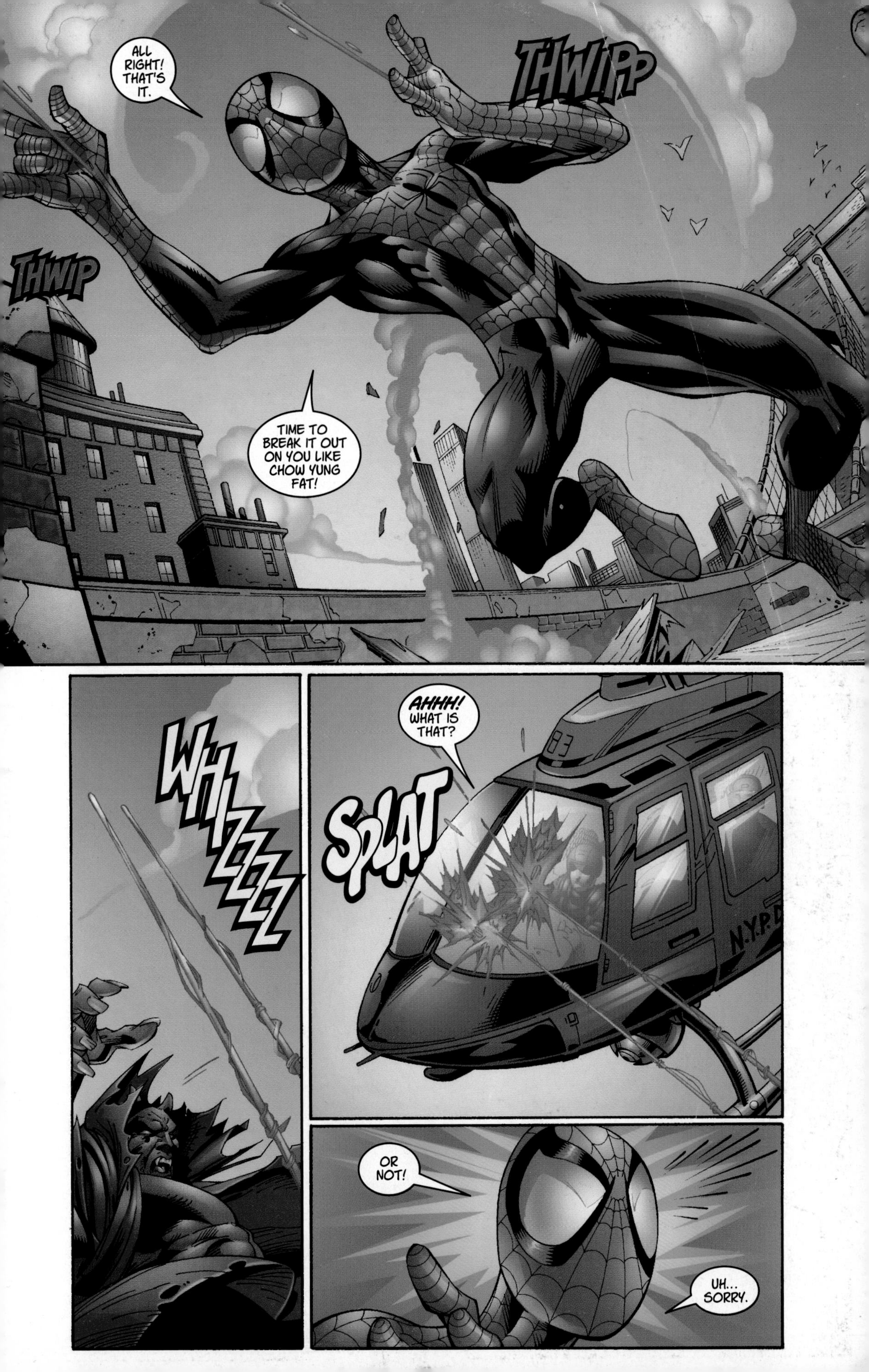
ALL RIGHT! THAT'S IT.
THWIPP
THWIP
TIME TO BREAK IT OUT ON YOU LIKE CHOW YUNG FAT!
WHIZZZZ
AHHH! WHAT IS THAT?
SPLAT
N.Y.P.D
OR NOT!
UH... SORRY.

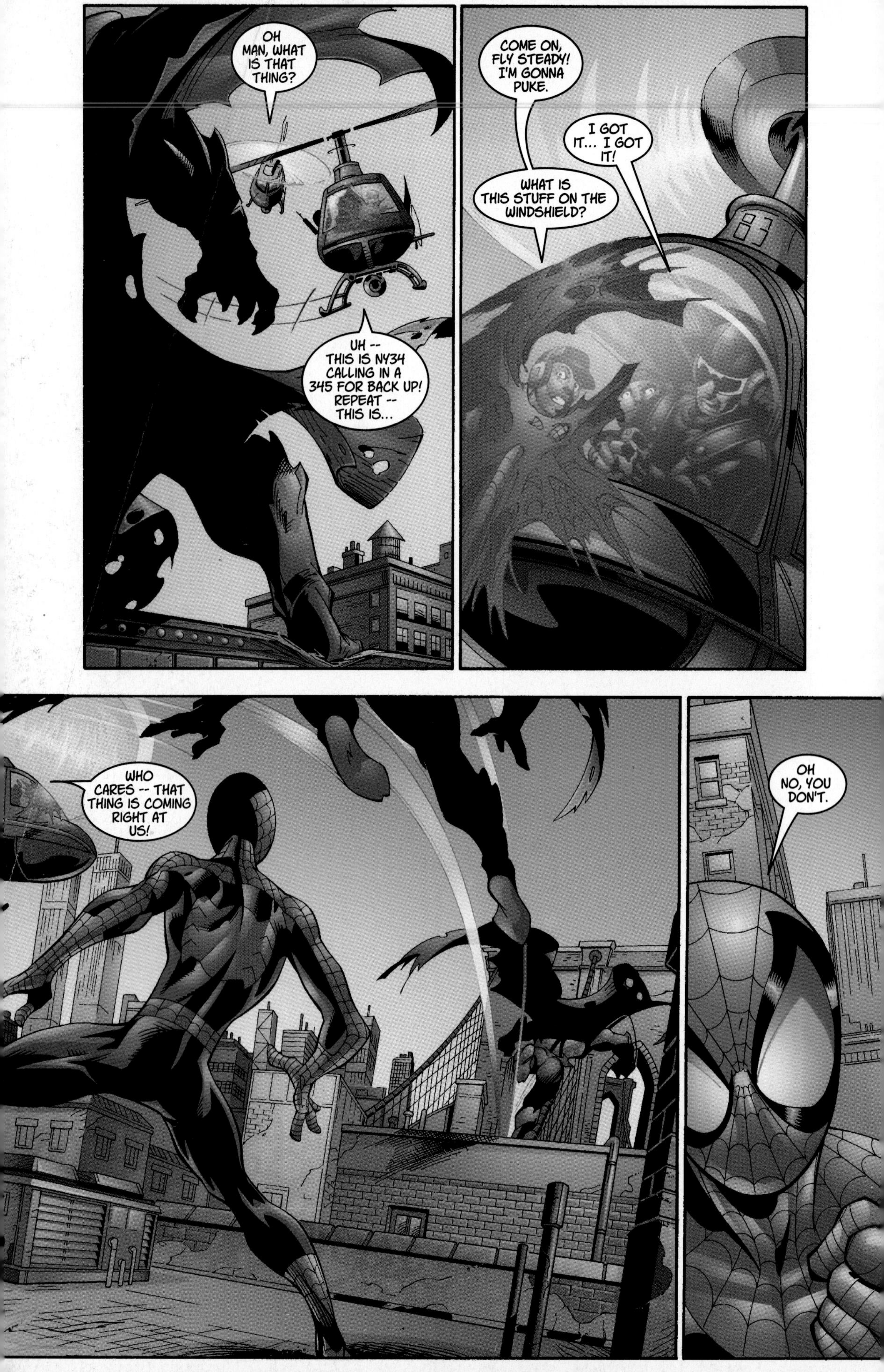
OH MAN, WHAT IS THAT THING?
UH -- THIS IS NY34 CALLING IN A 345 FOR BACK UP! REPEAT -- THIS IS...
COME ON, FLY STEADY! I'M GONNA PUKE.
WHAT IS THIS STUFF ON THE WINDSHIELD?
I GOT IT... I GOT IT!
WHO CARES -- THAT THING IS COMING RIGHT AT US!
OH NO, YOU DON'T.

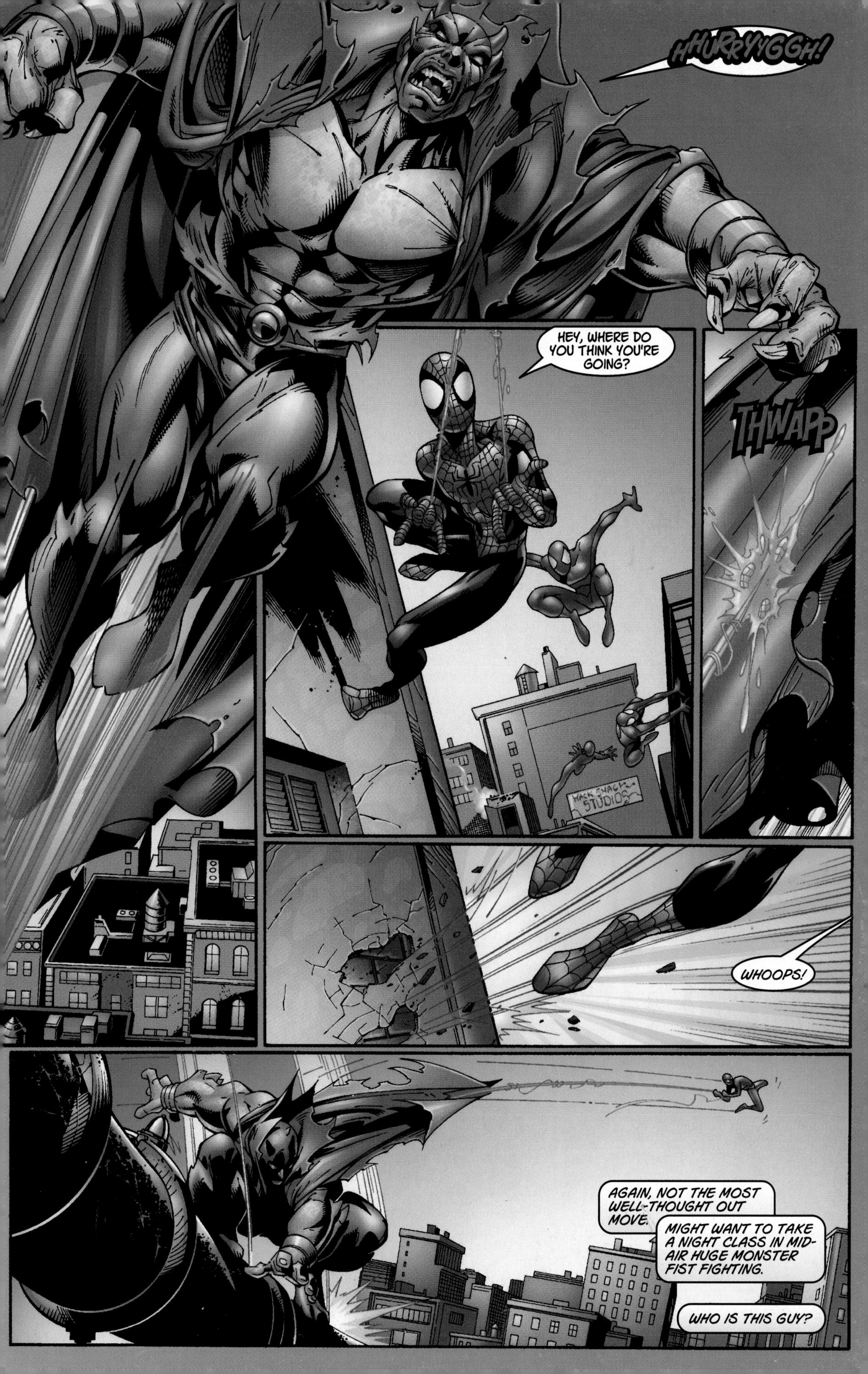

HHURRYYGGH!
HEY, WHERE DO YOU THINK YOU'RE GOING?
THWAPP
HACK SHACK STUDIOS
WHOOPS!
AGAIN, NOT THE MOST WELL-THOUGHT OUT MOVE.
MIGHT WANT TO TAKE A NIGHT CLASS IN MID-AIR HUGE MONSTER FIST FIGHTING.
WHO IS THIS GUY?

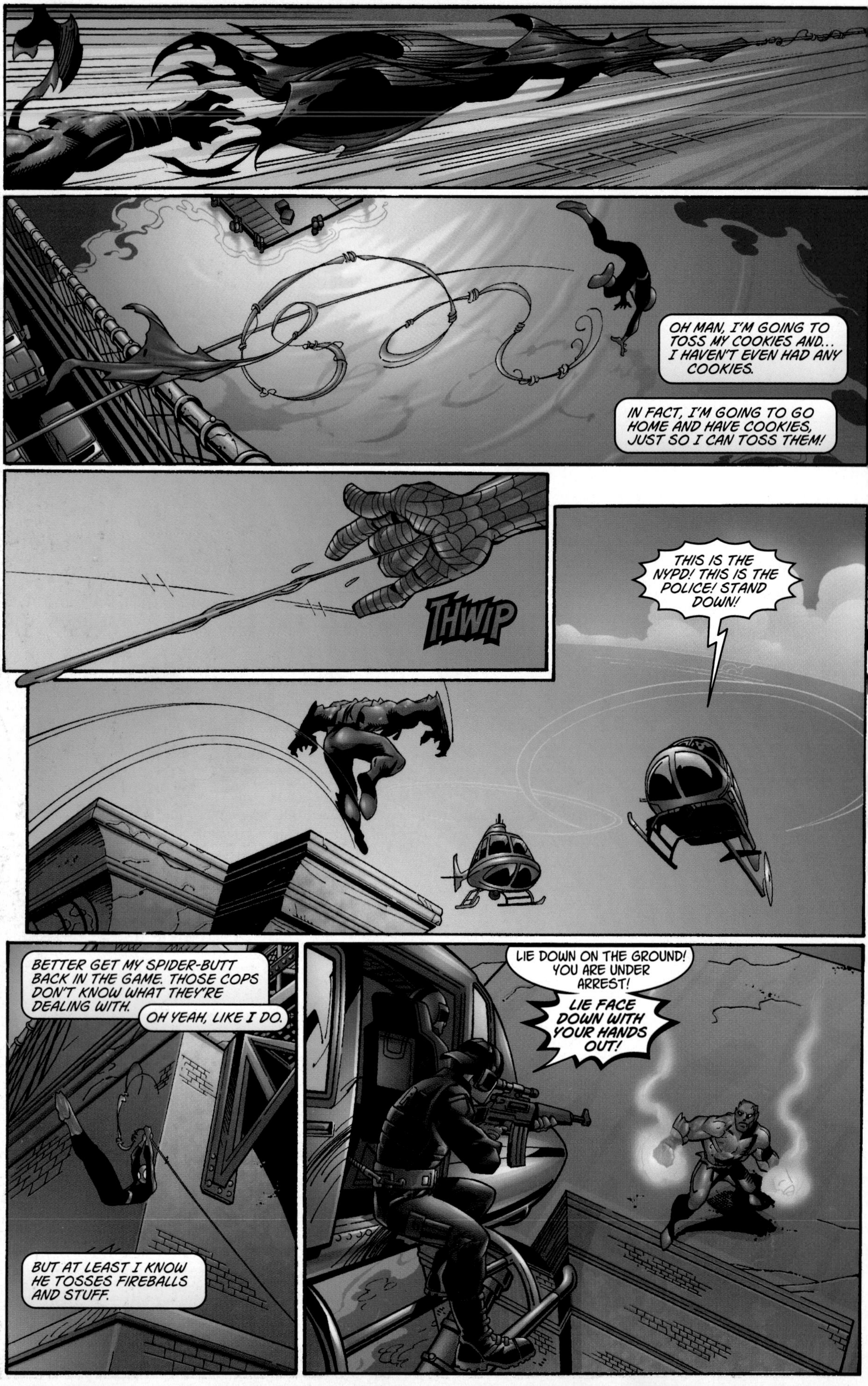
OH MAN, I'M GOING TO TOSS MY COOKIES AND... I HAVEN'T EVEN HAD ANY COOKIES.
IN FACT, I'M GOING TO GO HOME AND HAVE COOKIES, JUST SO I CAN TOSS THEM!
THWIP
THIS IS THE NYPD! THIS IS THE POLICE! STAND DOWN!
BETTER GET MY SPIDER-BUTT BACK IN THE GAME. THOSE COPS DON'T KNOW WHAT THEY'RE DEALING WITH.
OH YEAH, LIKE I DO.
BUT AT LEAST I KNOW HE TOSSES FIREBALLS AND STUFF.
LIE DOWN ON THE GROUND! YOU ARE UNDER ARREST!
LIE FACE DOWN WITH YOUR HANDS OUT!

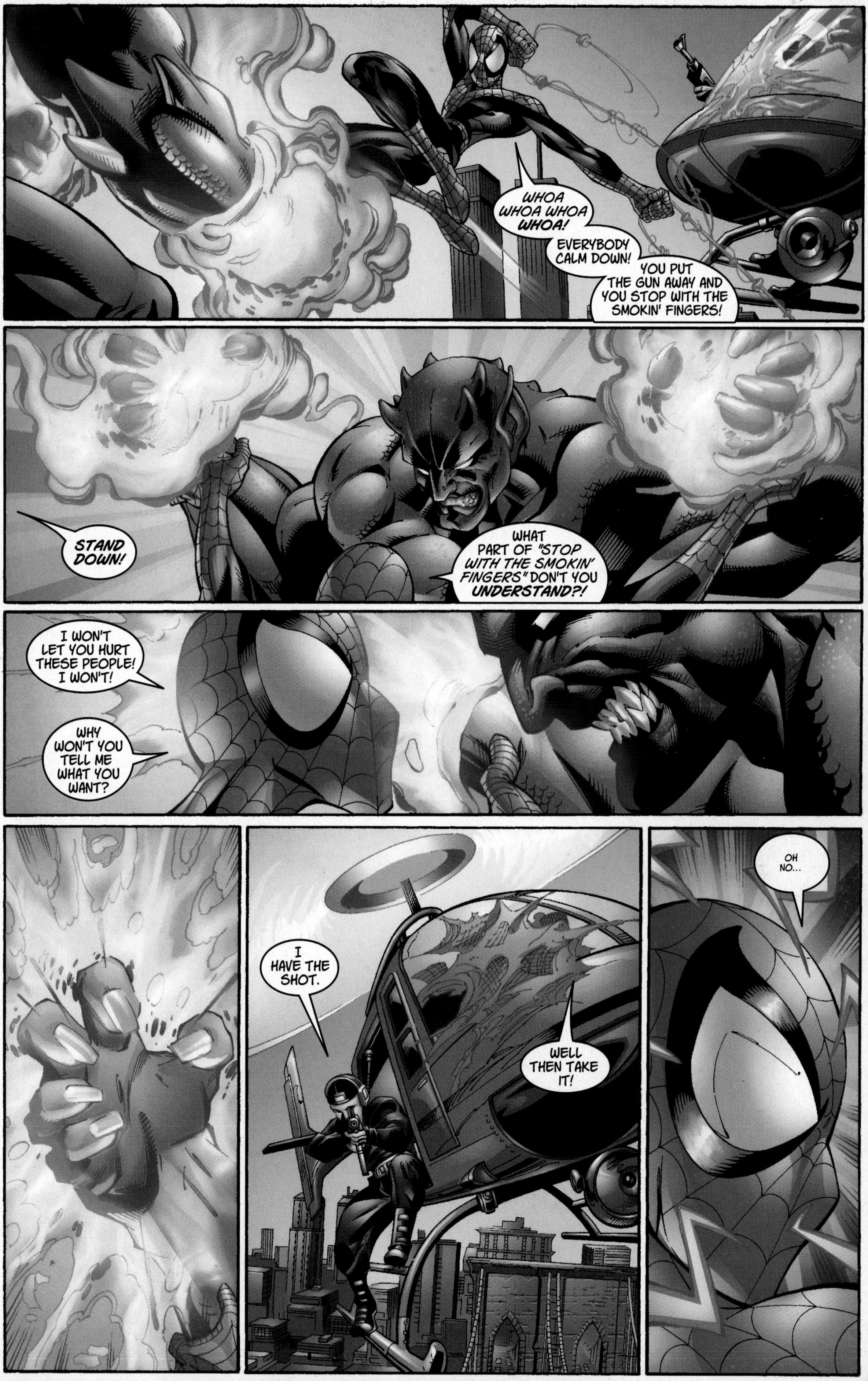
WHOA WHOA WHOA WHOA!
EVERYBODY CALM DOWN!
YOU PUT THE GUN AWAY AND YOU STOP WITH THE SMOKIN' FINGERS!
STAND DOWN!
WHAT PART OF "STOP WITH THE SMOKIN' FINGERS" DON'T YOU UNDERSTAND?!
I WON'T LET YOU HURT THESE PEOPLE! I WON'T!
WHY WON'T YOU TELL ME WHAT YOU WANT?
I HAVE THE SHOT.
WELL THEN TAKE IT!
OH NO...

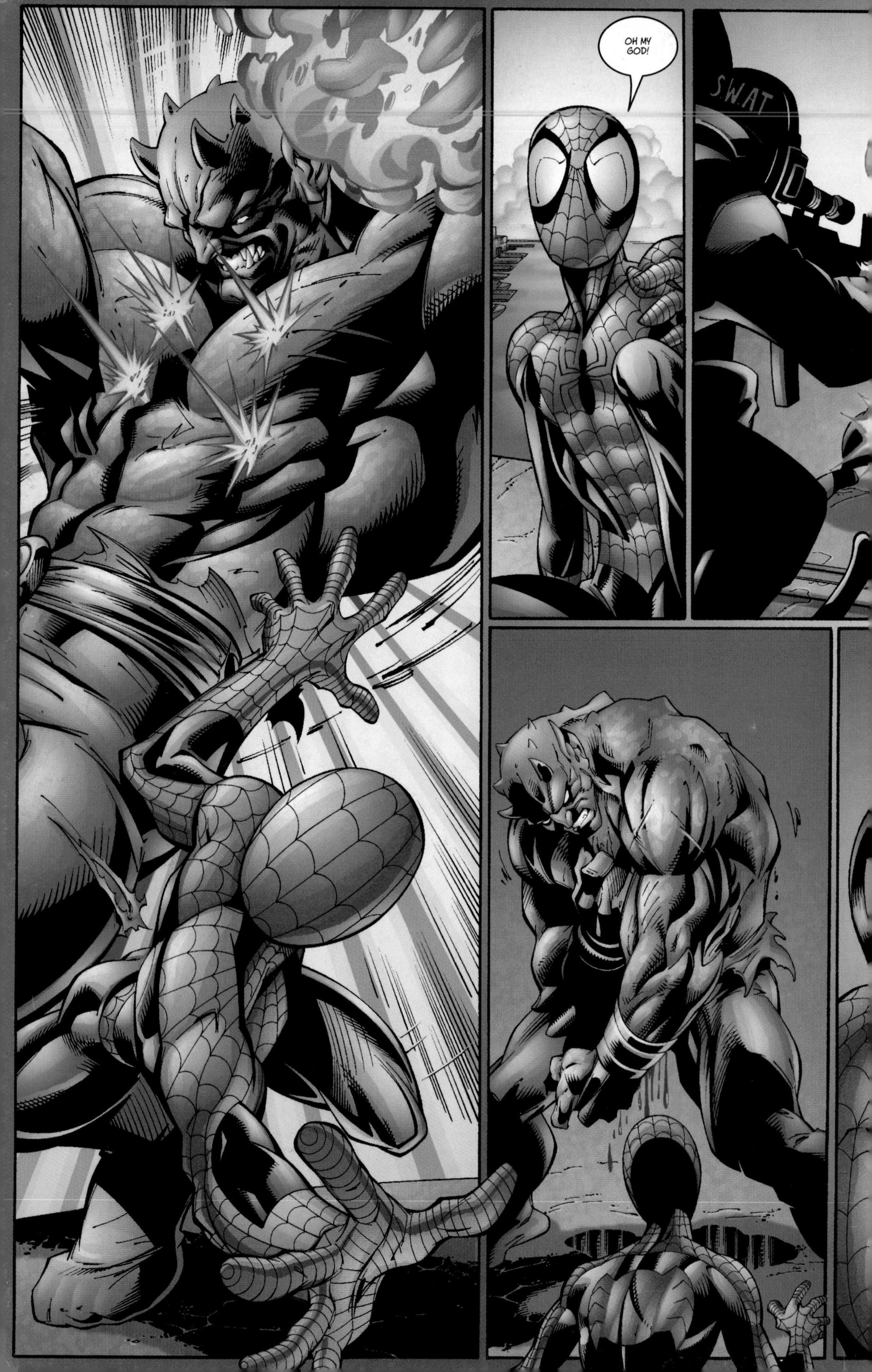
OH MY GOD!
S.W.A.T.

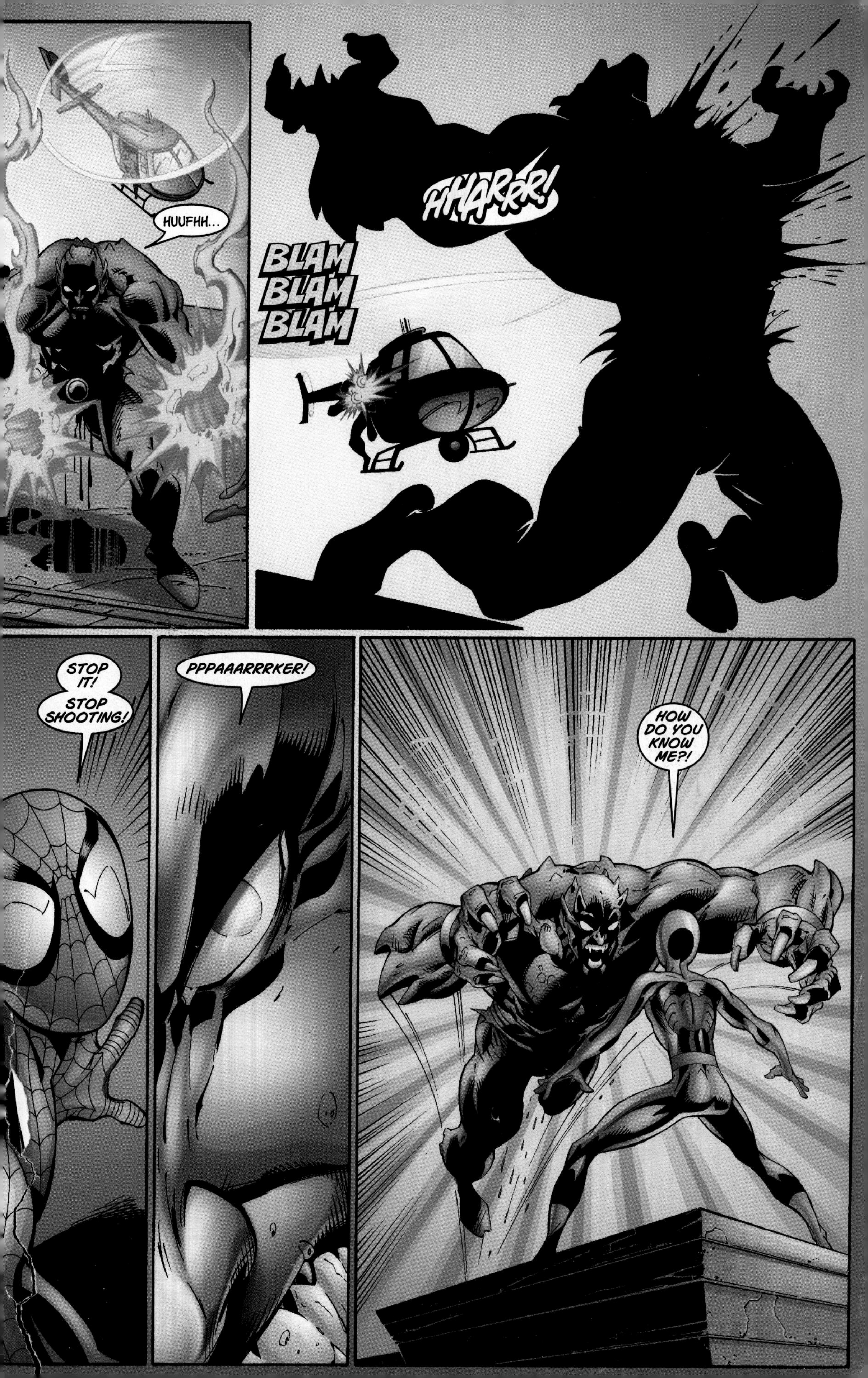
HUUFHH...
BLAM
BLAM
BLAM
HHARRR!
STOP IT! STOP SHOOTING!
PPPAAARRRKER!
HOW DO YOU KNOW ME?!

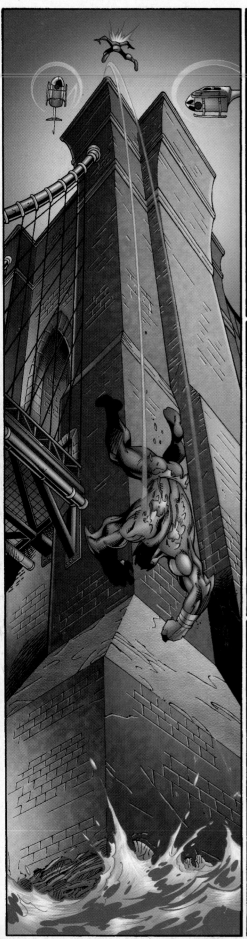

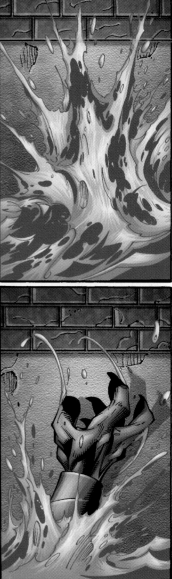

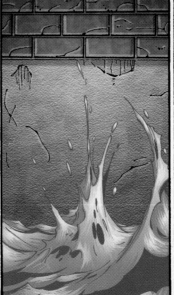

JEEZ...

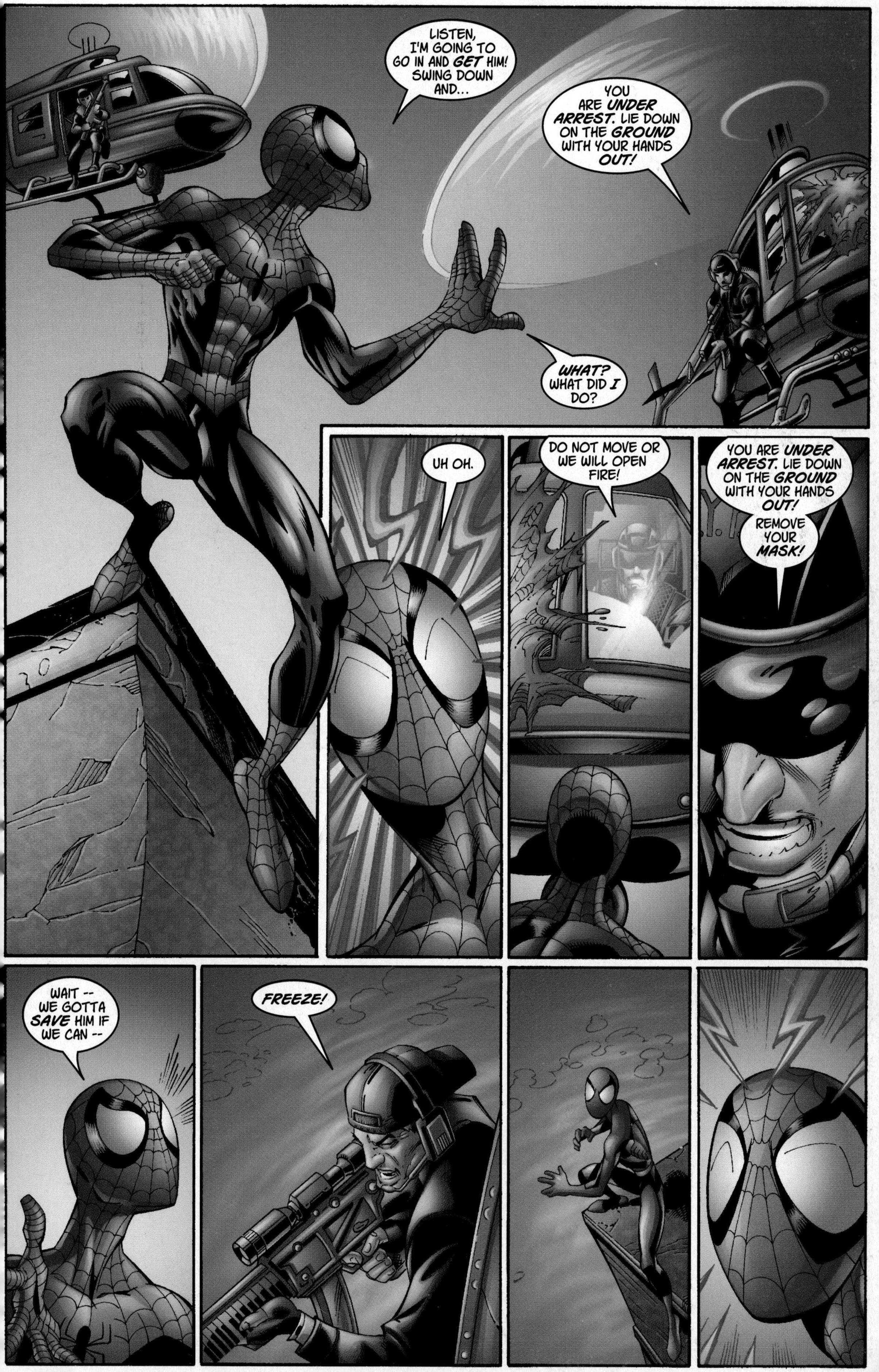
LISTEN, I'M GOING TO GO IN AND GET HIM! SWING DOWN AND...
YOU ARE UNDER ARREST. LIE DOWN ON THE GROUND WITH YOUR HANDS OUT!
WHAT? WHAT DID I DO?
UH OH.
DO NOT MOVE OR WE WILL OPEN FIRE!
YOU ARE UNDER ARREST. LIE DOWN ON THE GROUND WITH YOUR HANDS OUT!
REMOVE YOUR MASK!
WAIT -- WE GOTTA SAVE HIM IF WE CAN --
FREEZE!

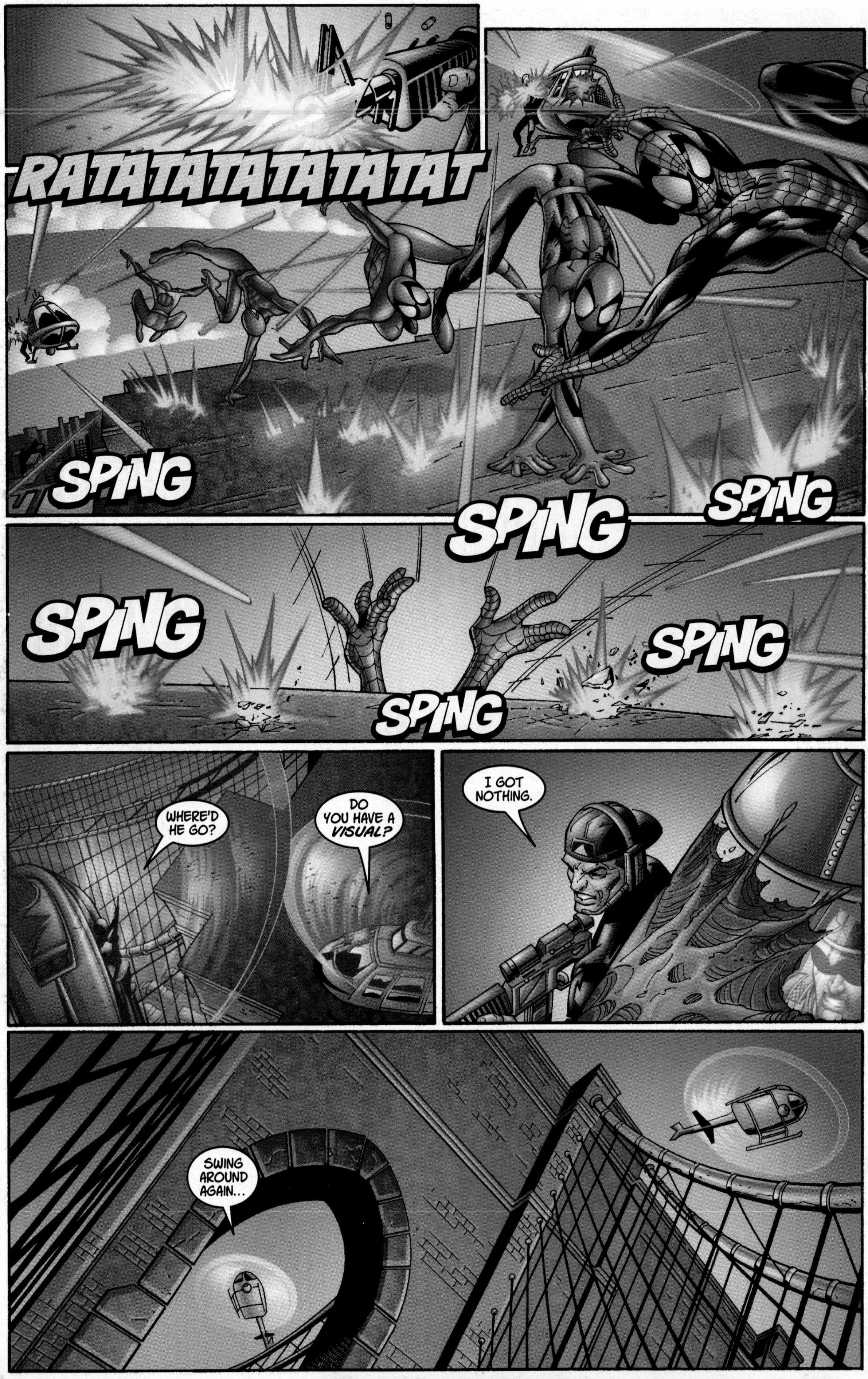
RATATATATATATAT
SPING
SPING
SPING
SPING
SPING
SPING
WHERE'D HE GO?
DO YOU HAVE A *VISUAL?*
I GOT NOTHING.
SWING AROUND AGAIN...

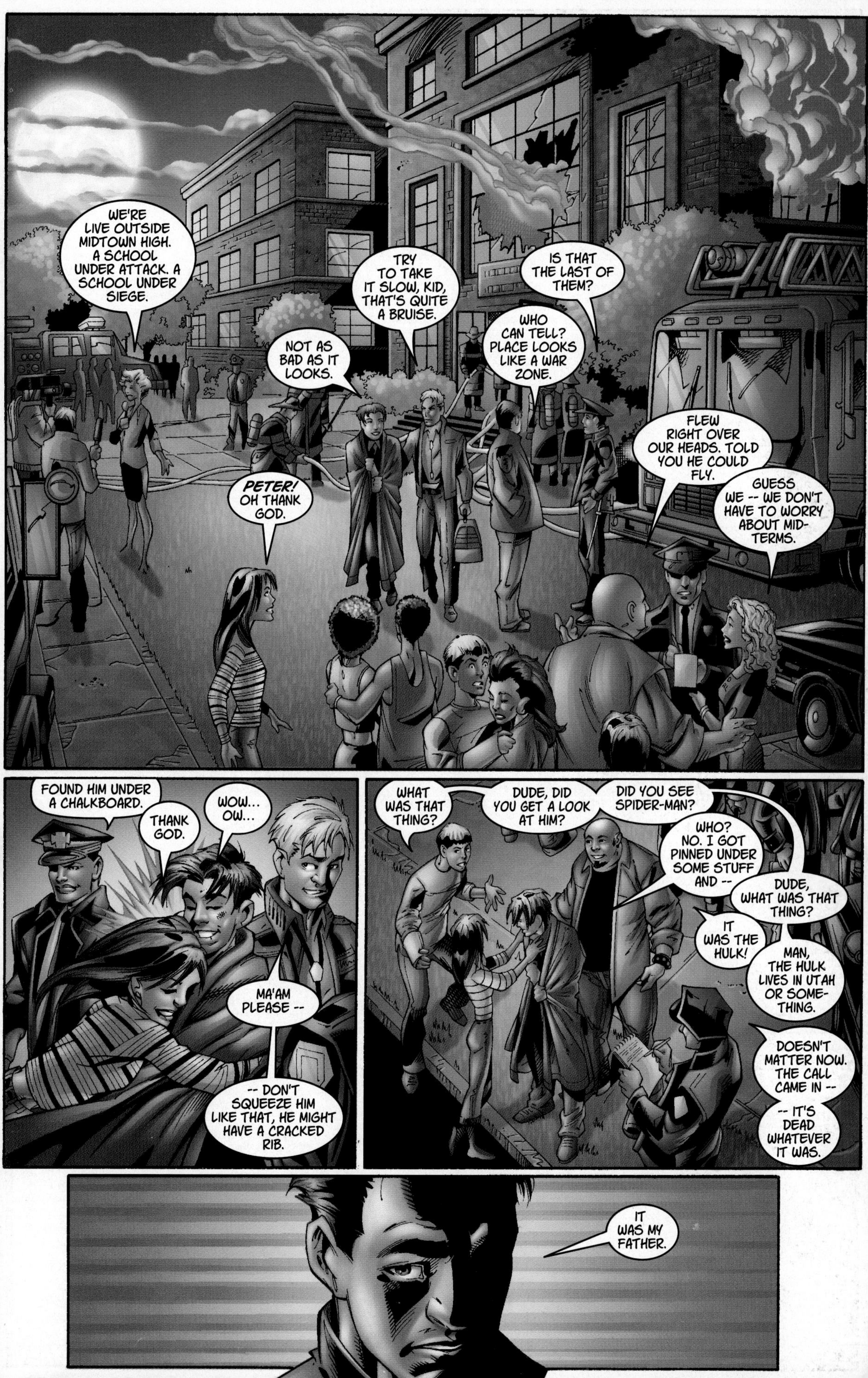
WE'RE LIVE OUTSIDE MIDTOWN HIGH. A SCHOOL UNDER ATTACK. A SCHOOL UNDER SIEGE.
TRY TO TAKE IT SLOW, KID, THAT'S QUITE A BRUISE.
NOT AS BAD AS IT LOOKS.
IS THAT THE LAST OF THEM?
WHO CAN TELL? PLACE LOOKS LIKE A WAR ZONE.
PETER! OH THANK GOD.
FLEW RIGHT OVER OUR HEADS. TOLD YOU HE COULD FLY.
GUESS WE -- WE DON'T HAVE TO WORRY ABOUT MID-TERMS.
FOUND HIM UNDER A CHALKBOARD.
THANK GOD.
WOW... OW...
MA'AM PLEASE --
-- DON'T SQUEEZE HIM LIKE THAT, HE MIGHT HAVE A CRACKED RIB.
WHAT WAS THAT THING?
DUDE, DID YOU GET A LOOK AT HIM?
DID YOU SEE SPIDER-MAN?
WHO? NO. I GOT PINNED UNDER SOME STUFF AND --
DUDE, WHAT WAS THAT THING?
IT WAS THE HULK!
MAN, THE HULK LIVES IN UTAH OR SOME-THING.
DOESN'T MATTER NOW. THE CALL CAME IN --
-- IT'S DEAD WHATEVER IT WAS.
IT WAS MY FATHER.

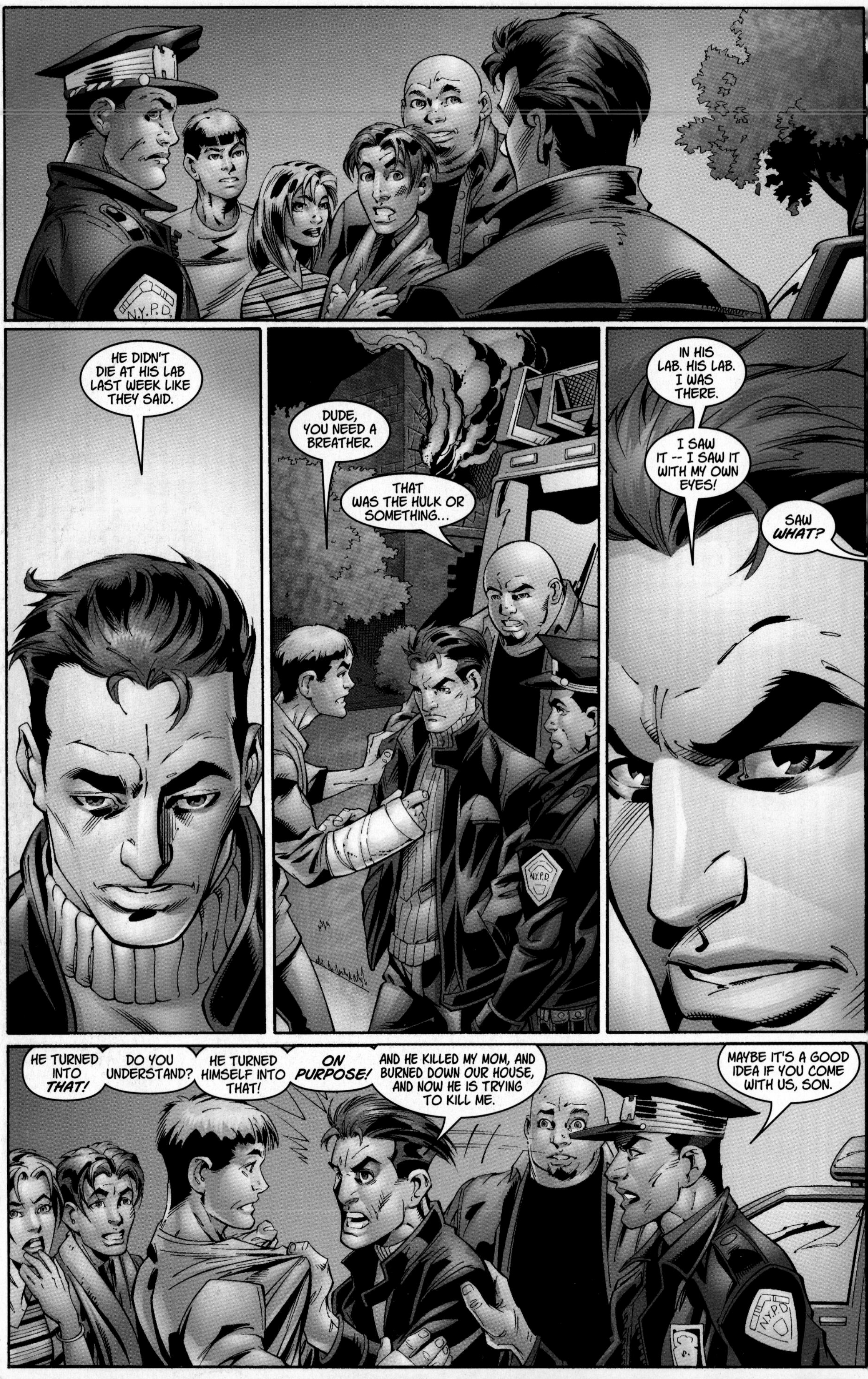

HE DIDN'T DIE AT HIS LAB LAST WEEK LIKE THEY SAID.
DUDE, YOU NEED A BREATHER.
THAT WAS THE HULK OR SOMETHING...
IN HIS LAB. HIS LAB. I WAS THERE.
I SAW IT -- I SAW IT WITH MY OWN EYES!
SAW *WHAT?*
HE TURNED INTO *THAT!*
DO YOU UNDERSTAND?
HE TURNED HIMSELF INTO THAT!
ON PURPOSE!
AND HE KILLED MY MOM, AND BURNED DOWN OUR HOUSE, AND NOW HE IS TRYING TO KILL ME.
MAYBE IT'S A GOOD IDEA IF YOU COME WITH US, SON.

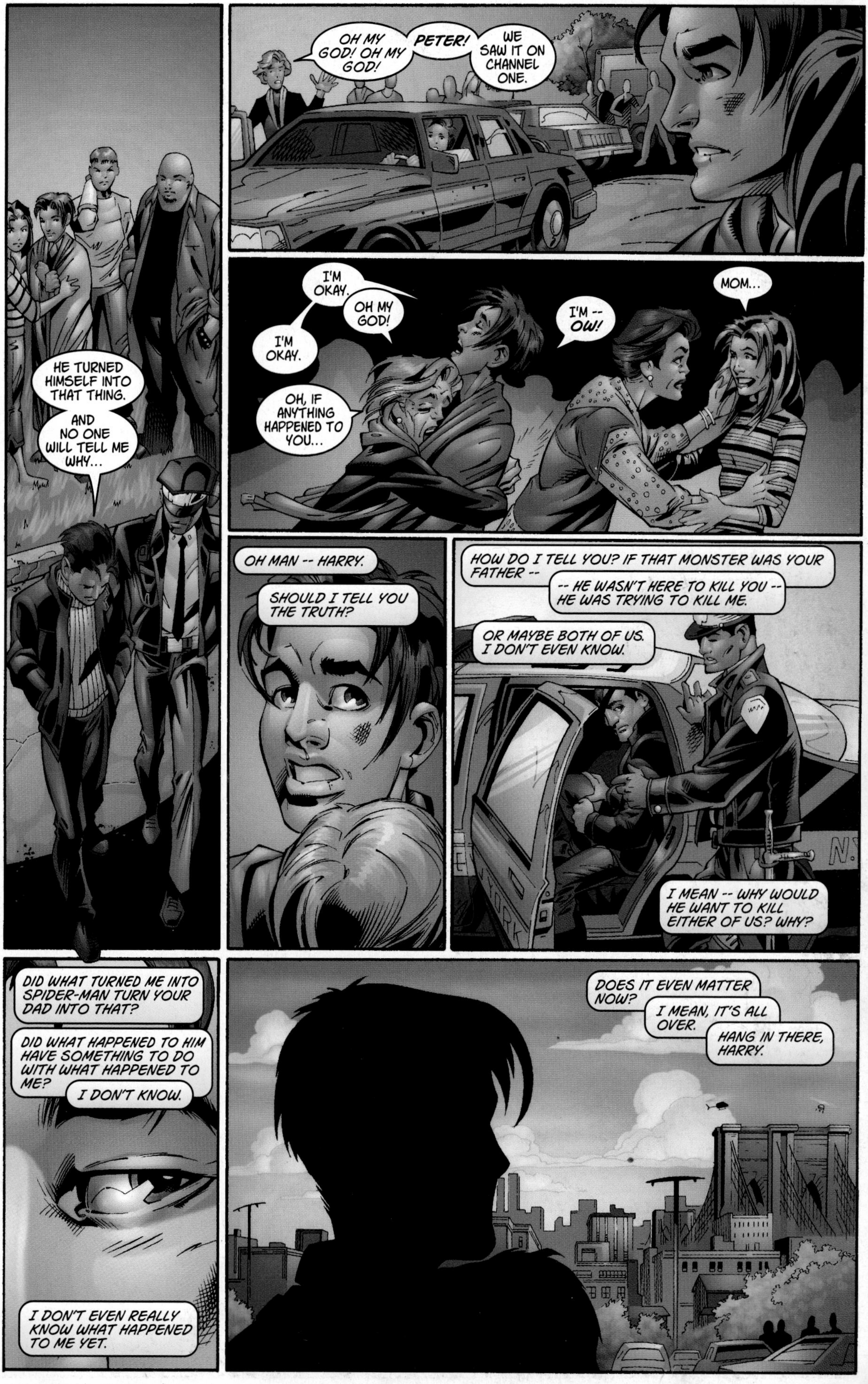
HE TURNED HIMSELF INTO THAT THING.
AND NO ONE WILL TELL ME WHY...
OH MY GOD! OH MY GOD!
PETER!
WE SAW IT ON CHANNEL ONE.
I'M OKAY.
OH MY GOD!
I'M OKAY.
OH, IF ANYTHING HAPPENED TO YOU...
I'M -- OW!
MOM...
OH MAN -- HARRY.
SHOULD I TELL YOU THE TRUTH?
HOW DO I TELL YOU? IF THAT MONSTER WAS YOUR FATHER --
-- HE WASN'T HERE TO KILL YOU -- HE WAS TRYING TO KILL ME.
OR MAYBE BOTH OF US. I DON'T EVEN KNOW.
I MEAN -- WHY WOULD HE WANT TO KILL EITHER OF US? WHY?
DID WHAT TURNED ME INTO SPIDER-MAN TURN YOUR DAD INTO THAT?
DID WHAT HAPPENED TO HIM HAVE SOMETHING TO DO WITH WHAT HAPPENED TO ME?
I DON'T KNOW.
I DON'T EVEN REALLY KNOW WHAT HAPPENED TO ME YET.
DOES IT EVEN MATTER NOW?
I MEAN, IT'S ALL OVER.
HANG IN THERE, HARRY.

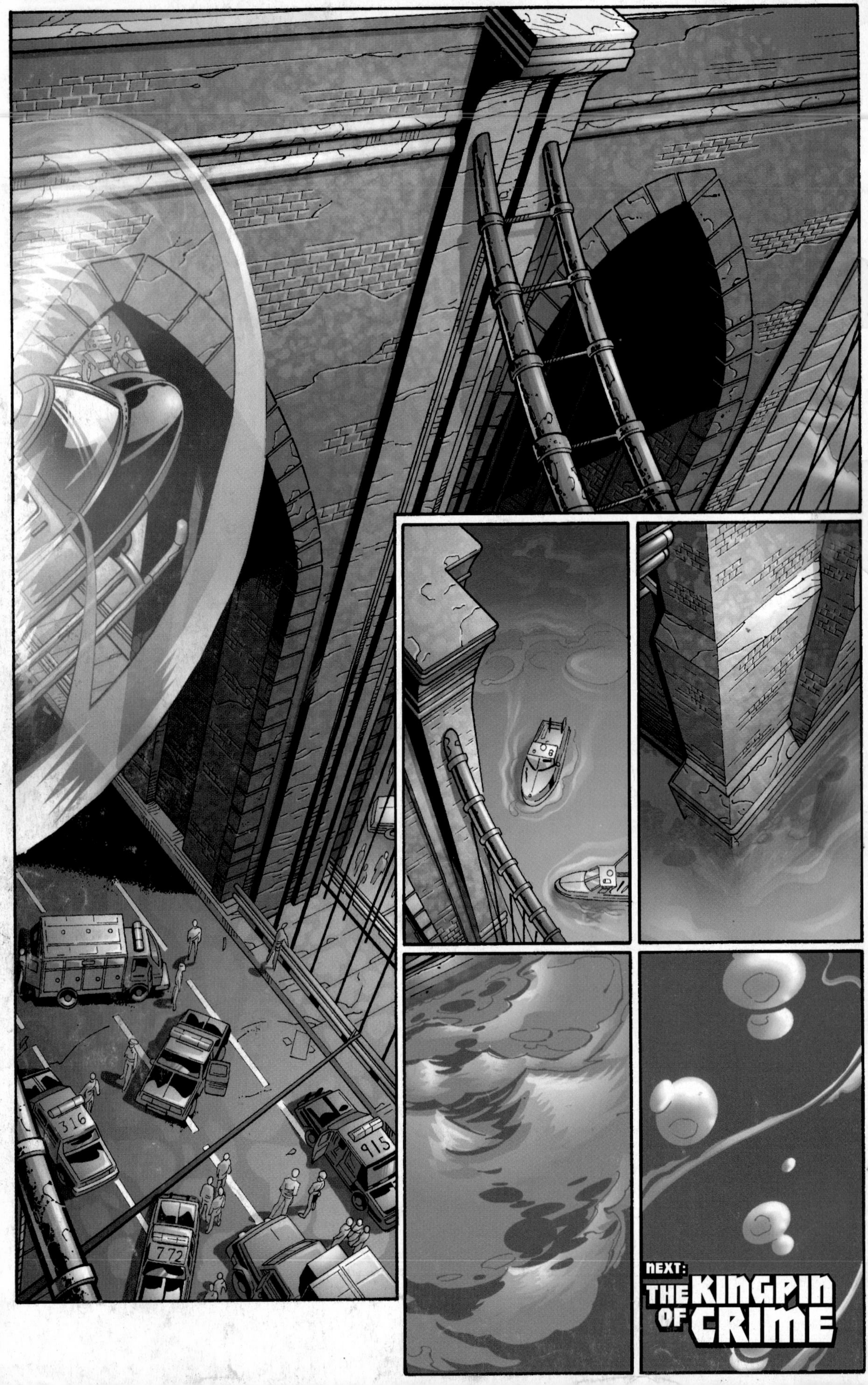
NEXT:
THE KINGPIN OF CRIME

SUBSCRIBE TODAY!

SUBSCRIBE AND SAVE!

1 Title For $23.97- A savings of $3!
2 Titles For $22.97- A savings of $8!
3 Or More Titles For $21.97 each-
A savings of $15 or more!

SPIDER-MAN
- ☐ AMZ — Amazing Spider-Man
- ☐ SPI — Peter Parker, Spider-Man
- ☐ TAW — Spider-Man: Tangled Web

MARVEL HEROES
- ☐ AVE — Avengers
- ☐ BPR — Black Panther
- ☐ CAM — Captain America
- ☐ CMV — Captain Marvel
- ☐ FAN — Fantastic Four
- ☐ INC — Hulk
- ☐ IRM — Iron Man
- ☐ THO — Thor
- ☐ BLT — Thunderbolts

X-MEN
- ☐ CAB — Cable
- ☐ DDP — Deadpool
- ☐ EXL — Exiles
- ☐ XME — Uncanny X-Men
- ☐ WOL — Wolverine
- ☐ XFO — X-Force
- ☐ MEN — New X-Men
- ☐ XTR — X-Treme X-Men

MARVEL ULTIMATES
- ☐ ULA — The Ultimates
- ☐ USP — Ultimate Spider-Man
- ☐ UXM — Ultimate X-Men

MARVEL KNIGHTS
- ☐ DDV — Daredevil
- ☐ ELK — Elektra (Mature Readers)
- ☐ PUN — Punisher (Mature Readers)

LIMITED TIME SPIDER-MAN OFFER

☐ **Yes!** I want both
Amazing Spider-Man and
Peter Parker, Spider-Man for just **$37.94**
A Savings of $16.00!

Exclusive Subscriber Savings and Services
Your satisfaction guaranteed or your money back on all remaining issues!
IMPROVED PACKAGING!
All issues are mailed with cardboard backing in
new weather resistant cellophane bags!

Ordering is fast and easy!
☐ **Yes!** Sign me up for home delivery
of the comics I've checked. I deserve the
most in savings, convenience, service,
and selection!
My satisfaction is guaranteed!
Check off the subscriptions you want delivered to your home
(12 issues each) and return this page or a copy to:
MARVEL ENTERTAINMENT GROUP, INC.
P.O. BOX 32 NEWBURGH, NY 12551.
Please provide credit card information or make your check or money
order payable to "Marvel Entertainment Group, Inc."
Or order Toll Free at 800-217-9158.
**OFFER GOOD UNTIL 12/31/2002.
YES, YOU CAN PHOTOCOPY THIS AD!**

Please print:

NAME OF READER _____ DATE OF BIRTH (M/D/Y) _____

STREET ADDRESS _____ E-MAIL _____

CITY _____ STATE ___ ZIP ____

# of subscriptions _____ Amount enclosed: $ _____

Charge my: ☐ VISA   ☐ MasterCard

CREDIT CARD # _____ EXPIRATION DATE _____

NAME OF CREDIT CARD HOLDER (IF DIFFERENT FROM NAME ABOVE) _____

SIGNATURE FOR CREDIT CARD ORDERS

Canada, add $10.00 per title (in U.S. funds only, includes GST#R127032852). Foreign, add $12 per title in U.S. funds
only. Allow 6 to 10 weeks for delivery of your first issue. TM & © 2002 Marvel Enterprises Inc. All rights reserved.

H1CMD2

"DADDY, DON'T LET UNCLE BEN DIE. IT'S OK IF HE GETS HURT AND GOES TO THE HOSPITAL, BUT PLEASE DO NOT LET HIM DIE."

That's what my son says to me after he reads issue #4. Unfortunately, by that time, issue #5 has been scripted, penciled, inked, half-colored, and poor old Ben is pushing up the daisies. Now he's a smart kid, but he's nine, and I can still outsmart him. So I thank him for the input and take him out for ice cream with his little brother.

But then, every day for the next week, I come home to the same thing: "don't kill Ben" (like it's me with the gun). And, to make it worse, the younger guy – who's six and has the reading thing just about nailed – has made his way through issue #4. Now he joins in with the big guy. They both say Ben ain't dying on their watch. These kids really like Uncle Ben, and they mean business, and a Dad has to know when he's beat. I'm not giving up on Santa till they're 20, but I have no choice other than to turn state's evidence on this one.

"Guys," I say, "Uncle Ben didn't die, because he never lived. We made him up with the rest of this story. We want kids to see what Peter learns the hard way. He is given a wonderful gift – spectacular spider powers beyond his wildest dreams. He could have used those abilities responsibly to do wonderful things for the world, but instead he used them selfishly. And because of that, he lost his best friend, Uncle Ben. See, with great power comes great responsibility."

So the big guy says, "OK about Ben, Dad, but comics are not supposed to be educational." And the little guy pipes up that a spider should bite Flash so he can become Venom.

I am honored to have played a part in the creation of this magical tale. There are so many people that deserve so much credit and so many thanks. Brian is a spectacular writer and has become a real friend. Mark Bagley and Jung Choi, who worked with me on some beautiful Marvel card sets in the early 1990s, have been nothing short of amazing on Ultimate Spider-Man. Joe Quesada, Ralph Macchio, and Brian Smith provided wise and wonderful insights. Key contributions in early development came from Bob Harras, Mark Powers and Lou Aronica. And, as always, we Marvel web-heads tip our hats to Stan Lee and Steve Ditko.

During the past year, our master-inker Art Thibert's father has fallen ill and we dedicated issue #7 to him.

And now, I'd like a word with my dad.

The tragedy of Spider-Man is not the death of Uncle Ben – or the unwitting role that poor powerful Peter played in his loss. The ultimate tragedy is that Ben up and died before Peter had the chance to tell him everything that every son should tell his dad. Pop, I want to dedicate this book – or at least my share of it – to you, for all you have brought to me, Jane, the boys and our whole family.

BILL JEMAS,
PRESIDENT, MARVEL ENTERPRISES
P.S. Hi, Mom!